T0261936

Image and Video Processing: Methods, Functionalities and Services

Image and Video Processing: Methods, Functionalities and Services

Edited by **Anna Sanders**

New York

Published by Willford Press,
118-35 Queens Blvd., Suite 400,
Forest Hills, NY 11375, USA
www.willfordpress.com

Image and Video Processing: Methods, Functionalities and Services
Edited by Anna Sanders

© 2016 Willford Press

International Standard Book Number: 978-1-68285-052-7 (Hardback)

This book contains information obtained from authentic and highly regarded sources. Copyright for all individual chapters remain with the respective authors as indicated. All chapters are published with permission under the Creative Commons Attribution License or equivalent. A wide variety of references are listed. Permission and sources are indicated; for detailed attributions, please refer to the permissions page and list of contributors. Reasonable efforts have been made to publish reliable data and information, but the authors, editors and publisher cannot assume any responsibility for the validity of all materials or the consequences of their use.

The publisher's policy is to use permanent paper from mills that operate a sustainable forestry policy. Furthermore, the publisher ensures that the text paper and cover boards used have met acceptable environmental accreditation standards.

Trademark Notice: Registered trademark of products or corporate names are used only for explanation and identification without intent to infringe.

Printed in the United States of America.

Contents

Permissions

List of Contributors

Preface

Image processing is a vast field of science that has undergone rapid developments in the recent times. This book unfolds the innovative aspects of image processing which will be crucial for the progress of this field in the future. This book presents a coherent overview of the field through latest researches on innovative image processing techniques such as wavelets, classification, identification, protection, restoration of images, etc. Those in search of information to further their knowledge about image and video processing will be greatly assisted by this book. It is an excellent resource guide for experts as well as students.

This book unites the global concepts and researches in an organized manner for a comprehensive understanding of the subject. It is a ripe text for all researchers, students, scientists or anyone else who is interested in acquiring a better knowledge of this dynamic field.

I extend my sincere thanks to the contributors for such eloquent research chapters. Finally, I thank my family for being a source of support and help.

Editor

Quantifying the importance of cyclopean view and binocular rivalry-related features for objective quality assessment of mobile 3D video

Lina Jin[*], Atanas Boev, Karen Egiazarian and Atanas Gotchev

Abstract

3D video is expected to provide an enhanced user experience by using the impression of depth to bring greater realism to the user. Quality assessment plays an important role in the design and optimization of 3D video processing systems. In this paper, a new 3D image quality model that is specifically tailored for mobile 3D video is proposed. The model adopts three quality components, called the cyclopean view, binocular rivalry, and the scene geometry, in which the quality must be quantified. The cyclopean view formation process is simulated and its quality is evaluated using the three proposed approaches. Binocular rivalry is quantified over the distorted stereo pairs, and the scene quality is quantified over the disparity map. Based on the model, the 3D image quality can then be assessed using state-of-the-art 2D quality measures selected appropriately through a machine learning approach. To make the metric simple, fast, and efficient, final selection of the quality features is accomplished by also considering the computational complexity and the CPU running time. The metric is compared with several currently available 2D and 3D metrics. Experimental results show that the compound metric gives a significantly high correlation with the mean opinion scores that were collected through large-scale subjective tests run on mobile 3D video content.

Keywords: 3D quality assessment; Cyclopean view; Binocular rivalry; Linear regression

1 Introduction

Recently, with the rapid advances being made in 3D video technologies, mobile 3D video has become a subject of interest for both the entertainment and consumer electronics industries. Mobile 3D video offers a number of challenges, because it is expected to deliver a high-quality experience to the mobile users while using limited resources, including lower bandwidths and error-prone wireless channels. One of the greatest challenges is the evaluation of 3D video quality in a perceptual manner. Normally, a 3D video system includes several signal processing stages, e.g., scene capture and content creation, video format conversion, encoding, transmission, possible post-processing at the receiver side, and rendering and display of the image. Each stage may contribute to the degradation of the 3D visual quality, and the errors that occur at certain steps may propagate through the chain.

Therefore, quality assessment (QA) plays an important role in the design and optimization of the system in relation to the prospective users, systems, and services.

QA of any multimedia content is best performed subjectively, i.e., by asking test participants to give their opinions on different aspects of the quality of the content that they experienced. While it is highly informative in that it directly reflects human perception, subjective evaluation has many limitations. It is a time-consuming and expensive process and is not suitable for real-time quality monitoring and adjustment of the systems. Therefore, research on objective QA usually follows the subjective studies to design algorithms that can automatically assess multimedia quality in a perceptually consistent manner. Consider, for example, a wireless multimedia network system: a server can be dedicated to the evaluation of the delivered content quality using objective QA measures, and the results can be used to control and allocate the streaming resources. At the encoding and decoding stages, objective QA can also be used to optimize the

* Correspondence: lina.jin@tut.fi
Department of Signal Processing, Tampere University of Technology, Korkeakoulunkatu 10, Tampere 33720, Finland

encoding and rendering algorithms. Objective QA of conventional (i.e., 2D) images and video have been an active research topic for several decades, but the research work on QA for 3D images and video is relatively young and less mature.

A 3D video can be defined as time-varying imagery that supports the binocular visual cue, which, in combination with other 3D visual cues, delivers a realistic perception of depth. In its simplest form, 3D video is formed using two separate video channels (i.e., left and right) in which the time-synchronized frames form stereo pairs. Early attempts to objectively quantify 3D video images have applied 2D metrics to each frame of the stereo pair. Each frame is viewed as a single image for which the quality is measured separately, and then the overall 3D quality is calculated by averaging over time and space (i.e., the mean of the left and right channel quality values). This approach, however, hardly corresponds to the actual binocular mechanisms of the human visual system (HVS) and, thus, hardly correlates with the subjective quality scores. Recently, the inclusion of some 3D factors as part of the quality evaluation process has been attempted [1]. In [2], a 3D discrete cosine transform (DCT)-based stereo QA method was proposed for mobile 3D video. The method attempts to model the mechanisms of binocular correspondence formation, using the information in the neighboring blocks and contrast masking by grouping similarly sized 4×4 blocks of pixels in the left and right channels for joint analysis in the 3D DCT domain. In [3], the local depth variance for each reference block is used to weigh the quality metric proposed in [2] appropriately. In [4], a monoscopic quality component and a stereoscopic quality component for measurement of stereoscopic image quality have been combined. The former component assesses the monoscopically perceived distortions caused by phenomena such as blurring, noise, and contrast change, while the latter assesses the perceived degradation of the binocular depth cues only. In [5], an overall stereo quality metric was proposed through the combination of image quality with disparity quality using a nonlinear function. In [6], the 3D video quality was analyzed on the basis of being composed of two parts: the stereoscopic 2D video quality and the depth map quality. In [7], a quality metric for color stereo images was proposed based on the use of the binocular energy contained in the left and right retinal images, which was calculated using the complex wavelet transform (CWT) and the bandelet transform. The authors of [8] proposed two approaches based on depth of image-based rendering to compare synthesized views and occlusions. Authors in [9] proposed an objective model for evaluation of the depth quality using subjective results. In [10], the performances of several state-of-the-art 2D quality metrics were compared for quantification of the

quality of stereo pairs formed from two synthesized views. In [11] the authors studied the perception of stereoscopic crosstalk and performed a set of subjective tests to obtain mean opinion scores (MOS) of stereoscopic videos. They attempted to predict the MOS by combination of a structural similarity index (SSIM) map and pre-filtered dense disparity map. The quality metric proposed in [12] attempts to predict the perceived quality of color stereo video by a combination of contrast sensitivity function (CSF) filters with rational thresholds.

In [1], an analysis of the factors that influence the 3D quality of experience has been conducted. According to that analysis, the following HVS properties should be taken into account in the design of 3D quality metrics [13]. First, the HVS perceives '2D' types of degradation after they are combined in the cyclopean view and not individually in the left and right channels. Therefore, it is meaningful to measure 2D artifacts on the cyclopean view. The forms of degradation related to the 3D geometry and perceived through disparity are characterized as '3D' artifacts. Thus, the cyclopean image of both the degraded and the reference video streams should be extracted and compared, along with the binocular disparity that is presented in the degraded stream. Second, while the 2D and 3D artifacts can be assessed separately, the content in one visual path may influence the other. The binocular perception of depth is influenced by pictorial depth cues. It is possible that there may be masking or facilitation between the depth cues that come from the two visual paths. Consequently, the 3D quality is influenced by the 2D content. The perception of the asymmetric quality depends on the scene depth. Artifacts in the cyclopean view may be masked by the convergence process. Consequently, the 2D quality is then influenced by the 3D content. The overall quality of a 3D scene is therefore a combination of the 'cyclopean' and 'binocular' perceptual qualities.

Based on the above analysis, a new model for the assessment of 3D image quality is investigated in this paper. The model considers three components: the cyclopean view, binocular rivalry, and the depth presence. This general model aims to reflect the peculiarities of 3D scene perception. These peculiarities include the fusion of the left and right (stereo) images into a single (cyclopean) image and its 2D quality, the possible influence of binocular rivalry on visual comfort, and the influence of the depth presence on correct perception of the 3D scene geometry. The investigation aims to find suitable features to quantify the qualities of these three components in a 3D image to enable their combination, leading to an objective metric that is in accordance with the objective opinion. An abundant set of features that are used in the state-of-the-art 2D QA metrics is adopted, and a machine learning approach is applied to find the best combinations of these features. With regard to the formation of the cyclopean view, three different quality models are investigated that depend on whether the image fusion process is simulated at pixel level or at block level. The binocular disparity, i.e., the differences between the images seen in each eye, is an important cue that the HVS uses to perceive 3D scenes. However, artifacts in a stereoscopic pair may introduce unnatural stereoscopic correspondences that cannot be interpreted by the binocular HVS. These effects are perceived as a binocular rivalry, and this binocular rivalry must be quantified. The binocular suppression theory states that masking and facilitation effects exist between the images that are perceived by each eye [14]. It is anticipated that the masking between the eyes works in a similar manner to the masking effects between the different spatial orientations. In this paper, a local method for binocular rivalry evaluation is proposed that quantifies the quality of the binocular rivalry between the viewed left channel and right channel. Also, the depth presence is quantified using the disparity map, which gives the apparent motion between corresponding pixels in the left and right images.

To fuse the three proposed components in a perceptually driven manner, two mobile 3D video databases and related subjective tests are used [15,16]. Earlier subjective studies aimed to set more precise limits for acceptance of the quality experienced when both the compression artifacts using different 3D video coding methods and varying amounts of depth are presented. They have also taken a more systematic approach to the examination of depth versus compression artifacts by varying a dense set of parameters that influence quality. In the first mobile 3D video database, the number of compression artifacts has been varied by selecting five quantization parameters (QPs) and the strength of the depth effect was varied by selecting two camera baseline ranges. The video sequences in the second 3D video database have been encoded using four different coding methods, including H.264/AVC Simulcast, H.264/AVC multiview video coding (MVC), mixed resolution stereo coding (MRSC), and video plus depth (V + D). The encoding parameters have been chosen in accordance with the settings of the prospective system for

mobile 3D video delivery [15] to evaluate the perceived quality provided by each type of content. The combinations of the quality features according to our model, leading to the quality metric, are tested on both databases. The results show that this metric outperforms the current popular metrics over different 3D video formats and compression methods.

2 Image processing channel in stereo vision

A simplified model of the stereoscopic HVS is presented in Figure 1. The model follows the main functional stages of binocular vision, as discussed in [1]. In the first stage, the light captured by the eyes is processed separately in each eye. A set of perceptual HVS properties are produced by this processing, including light adaptation, contrast sensitivity, and low chromatic resolution. These properties can be modeled by luminance masking, conversion to a perceptual color space, and CSF-based masking, as shown in Figure 2. In the next stage, the visual information passes through the lateral geniculate nucleus (LGN), where the inputs from both eyes are processed together. It is assumed that the LGN decorrelates the stereoscopic signal and then forms the so-called cyclopean view [17]. The visual information is then fed to the V1 brain center, which is sensitive to patches with different spatial frequencies and orientations. The processes in the LGN and the V1 center can be modeled as multichannel decomposition, followed by binocular, spatial and temporal masking, as shown in Figure 2 [17].

The perceptual properties of the binocular vision suggest that the visual information is simultaneously processed in two different pathways, as shown in Figure 3. One pathway performs a fusion process using the binocular information to form a cyclopean view, which is a 2D representation of the scene as if it was observed from a virtual point that appears between the eyes [1]. During fusion, the HVS attempts to reconstruct details that are available to one eye only, which allows the observer to reconstruct any partially occluded details of the scene. The other pathway compares the images that have been projected onto each retina and extracts the distance information (also known as binocular depth cues [17]). Larger

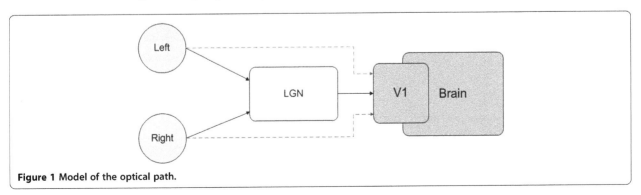

Figure 1 Model of the optical path.

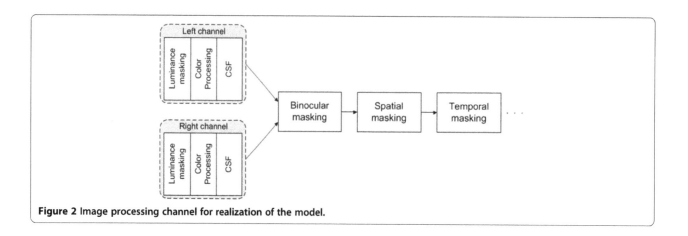

Figure 2 Image processing channel for realization of the model.

differences between the retinal images result in a more pronounced binocular depth. However, if these differences are too large, the images from the two eyes cannot be fused, and instead of the cyclopean view, the HVS perceives binocular rivalry [18]. Binocular rivalry is one of the major sources of visual discomfort in 3D video. This phenomenon can be caused by several factors, including physical misalignments, luminance, color, reflection, hyperconvergence, hyperdivergence, and ghosting [19].

Based on this model, we assume that the quality of a 3D image is perceived as a combination of two components: the quality of the cyclopean view, and the quality of the binocular image. The subjective experiments in [15] show that the presence of depth influences the perceived quality, and this influence can be either positive or negative, depending on the content. As described in [1], the same amount of blockiness is graded differently in scenes with differently pronounced depths. The presence of stereoscopic depth also affects the perceived overall quality. Larger binocular differences will increase the perceived binocular depth but may also reduce the quality of the cyclopean view. This effect is not monotonic, which indicates that there might be an 'optimal' global depth for a 3D scene on portable autostereoscopic displays, at which the HVS has the lowest sensitivity to any cyclopean image degradation.

3 Feature-based quality estimation

In this section, we propose a new 3D QA model composed of three components: the quality of the cyclopean view, the prominence of the binocular depth, and the presence of binocular rivalry. The block diagram of our model is shown in Figure 4. We select a set of features that (potentially) quantify each quality component. Combinations of these features are then matched against the MOS that were obtained from subjective quality tests.

3.1 Cyclopean view assessment

The quality of the cyclopean view can be measured in a full-reference setting. The first step is to create the cyclopean views of the reference and the distorted stereo pairs. When both cyclopean views are available, we can compare the structural differences between the two cyclopean views using an ordinary full-reference 2D quality metric.

One way to create the cyclopean view is to generate a dense disparity map of the stereo pair and reconstruct the view from an intermediate observation position. In case the corresponding pixels in the two observations have different colors or intensities, the mean values of both properties are taken. This roughly corresponds to the way that the cyclopean view is fused by the HVS in the absence of stereoscopic rivalry [1]. However,

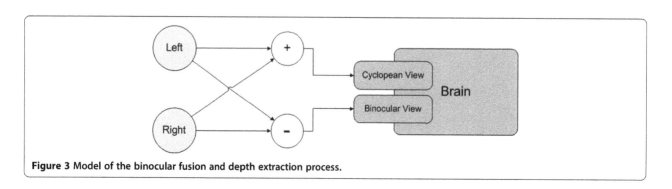

Figure 3 Model of the binocular fusion and depth extraction process.

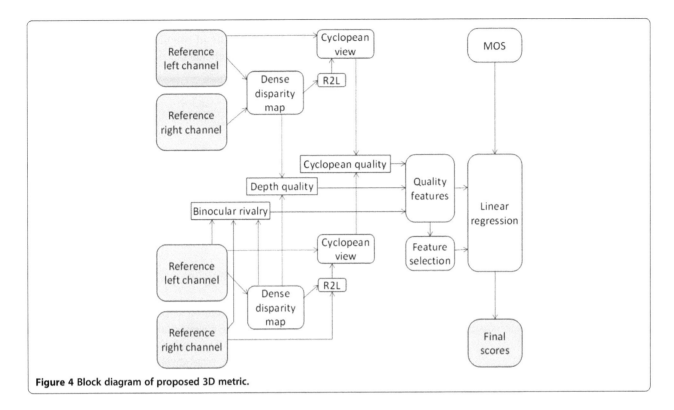

Figure 4 Block diagram of proposed 3D metric.

rendering of the intermediate camera involves the interpolation of pixels from both views. To reduce the influence of any interpolation errors, we can fuse the two views and reconstruct an observation that matches one of the views. This can be done by warping one of the views onto the other - for example, by rendering the right view using the left view pixels and the disparity map - and then fusing the two views. Because we aim to assess the structural differences between the two cyclopean views, we assume that this transformation would still allow any distortions in either view to be quantified. Wherever occlusions occur, the available pixels from the opposite view are used. In our approach, we calculate a dense disparity map and an occlusion map between the left and right images using a color-weighted local search method [20].

Using the disparity map, the pixels in the right channel are then mapped to their positions in the left channel, which is denoted here as a 'right to left' mapping, i.e., R2L:

$$R2L(x, y) = I^R(x + \Delta(x, y), y), x = 1 \dots N, y = 1 \dots M, \tag{1}$$

where (x, y) indicates the pixel location, M, N indicates the image size of one channel, I^R is the image from the right channel, and $\Delta(x, y)$ is the pixel shift for the pixel at position (x, y). Occluded pixels are handled by

replacing them with corresponding pixels from the left image:

$$\tilde{R2L}(x, y) = \begin{cases} I^L(x, y), & \text{if } \Omega(x, y) = 1 \\ R2L(x, y), & \text{otherwise,} \end{cases} \tag{2}$$

where I^L is the left image, Ω is the binary occlusion map, and $\Omega(x, y) = 1$ marks the occluded pixels. The final cyclopean view, I^{cyc}, is generated as the mean of the left image and the mapped image from the right image:

$$I^{\text{cyc}} = \frac{I^L + \tilde{R2L}}{2}. \tag{3}$$

The cyclopean view formation process is shown in Figure 5, and an example of the cyclopean view obtained is given in Figure 6.

When the cyclopean view is obtained, we then apply three quality evaluation models. Hereafter, we use the notation QA to denote *any* quality assessment measure, which compare the similarity (dissimilarity) between images or image blocks. Specific QAs are discussed in Section 3.4 where they are indexed (e.g., QA_1, QA_2...) to denote the particular assessment measure.

The first model assumes QA on a global basis:

$$Q_1^{CV} = QA(I_{\text{ref}}^{\text{cyc}}, I_{\text{dis}}^{\text{cyc}}), \tag{4}$$

where $I_{\text{ref}}^{\text{cyc}}$ and $I_{\text{dis}}^{\text{cyc}}$ are the cyclopean images that were obtained from the reference and distorted stereo pairs, respectively.

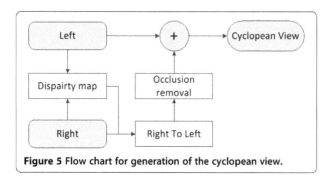

Figure 5 Flow chart for generation of the cyclopean view.

The second model evaluates the cyclopean view in a block-by-block fashion, as shown in Figure 7. In the left channel, an 8×8-sized reference block A starting at coordinates (i,j) is selected. The corresponding block in the disparity map is denoted by Δ_{ij}. In the right channel, the block with the same coordinates (i,j) is marked B'. Using the disparity map, the corresponding block B is then found by taking the median of the disparity values in the disparity patch Δ_{ij}:

$$\hat{d} = \left\lceil \text{median}\{\Delta_{ij}\}_{8 \times 8} \right\rceil, \tag{5}$$

where Δ_{ij} is the disparity mapping with coordinates (i,j), $\{\cdot\}_{8 \times 8}$ indicates an 8×8 block, and $\hat{d}$ can be a

positive value, zero, or a negative value. The model assumes that the quality of the block is represented by the quality of the better channel of the two,

$$Q_2^{CV} = \frac{\sum_{i=1}^{N_{\text{blk}}} \max\left(q_i^{L}, q_i^{R}\right)}{N_{\text{blk}}}, \tag{6}$$

where N_{blk} is the number of blocks, and q_i^{L} and q_i^{R} are the quality scores of the left and right channels, respectively,

$$q_i^{L} = \text{QA}(A_{\text{ref}}, A_{\text{dis}}) \tag{7}$$

$$q_i^{R} = \text{QA}(B_{\text{ref}}, B_{\text{dis}}), \tag{8}$$

where A_{ref} is the reference block in the original left image I_{ref}^{L}, I_{dis} is the corresponding block in the distorted left image I_{dis}^{L}, and B_{ref} and B_{dis} are the corresponding blocks in I_{ref}^{R} and I_{dis}^{R}, respectively.

The third model closely follows the second model but assumes that the block quality is represented by the average of the quality values measured in the left and right channels:

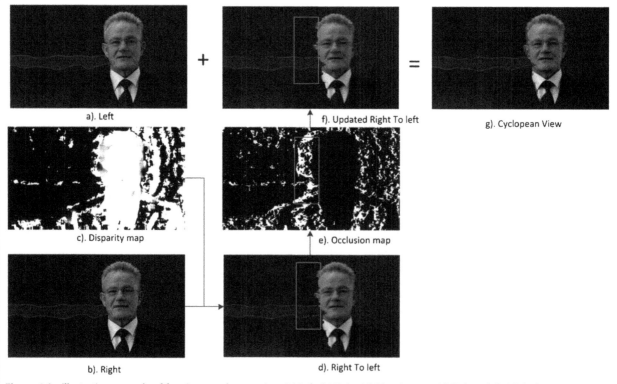

Figure 6 An illustration example of forming a cyclopean view. (a) Left. **(b)** Right. **(c)** Disparity map. **(d)** Right to left. **(e)** Occlusion map. **(f)** Updated right to left. **(g)** Cyclopean view.

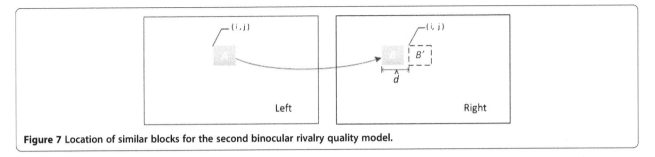

Figure 7 Location of similar blocks for the second binocular rivalry quality model.

$$Q_3^{CV} = \frac{\sum_{i=1}^{N_{blk}} \left(q_i^L + q_i^R\right)/2}{N_{blk}}. \tag{9}$$

3.2 Binocular rivalry assessment

Binocular rivalry occurs when the eyes attempt to converge on a single point in a scene, but the images seen by the two eyes are not sufficiently similar. Binocular rivalry can occur naturally in a complex 3D scene with numerous occlusions. However, the presence of severe artifacts in only one of the channels can cause unnatural binocular rivalry, which is perceived as a severe stereoscopic artifact. Binocular rivalry can be measured in a non-reference setting, i.e., by analyzing the distorted pair only. We assume that regardless of whether or not the rivalry is present in the original pair, its presence in the distorted pair would be equally disturbing. In our approach, we use the dense depth map to find the corresponding blocks in the two channels and measure the cumulative difference between the corresponding blocks, as follows:

$$Q^{BR} = \frac{\sum_{i=1}^{N_{blk}} QA(A_{dis}, B_{dis})}{N_{blk}}. \tag{10}$$

3.3 Binocular depth assessment

In this paper, we evaluate the presence of the binocular depth by estimation of the dense depth map for the stereo pair. We calculate a dense disparity map using the color-weighted local-window method described in [20]. The quality of depth Q^{DQ} is then studied as follows:

$$Q_1^{DQ} = QA(\Delta_{ref}, \Delta_{dis}), \tag{11}$$

where Δ_{ref} is the disparity map from the original stereoscopic image, and Δ_{dis} is the disparity map from the distorted stereoscopic image. Here, QA denotes a QA function that uses one of the candidate features, as described in the Section 3.4.

3.4 Candidate features

Each of the three quality components described above relies on a comparison function denoted by QA. However,

the data that are compared are not in the same modality in each case; in one case, we measure the similarity between the images, while in another we compare disparity maps. These cases are interpreted in different ways by the HVS, and the optimum similarity measure would be different for each case. To determine the most suitable measure in each case, we have selected and tested ten state-of-the-art QA methods.

We denote the original input image (block) by u and the distorted image (block) by v. The first quality feature is calculated based on the mean squared error (MSE), which is the most popular difference metric used in image and video processing:

$$QA_1(u, v) = \frac{1}{MN} \sum_i \sum_j \left(u_{ij} - v_{ij}\right)^2. \tag{12}$$

The MSE is chosen because it is simple to calculate, has clear physical meaning, and is mathematically convenient in the context of optimization.

The second quality feature is the gradient-normalized sum-of-squared-difference (SSD) [21]. The result is normalized with reference to the gradient map and is calculated as the mean of the SSD. Any local intensity variations in the textured areas between u and v are thus penalized:

$$QA_2(u, v) = \frac{1}{MN} \sum_i \sum_j \frac{\left(u_{ij} - v_{ij}\right)^2}{\left\|\nabla u_{ij}\right\|^2 + 1} \tag{13}$$

where ∇u_{ij} is the gradient value of input signal u.

Many studies have confirmed that the HVS is more sensitive to low-frequency distortions rather than to those at high frequencies. It is also very sensitive to contrast changes and noise. Therefore, the third measure aims to remove the mean shifting and contrast stretching in the manner shown in [22]. The measure is calculated in 8×8 blocks and uses the decorrelation properties of the block DCT and the effects of the individual DCT coefficients on the overall perception:

$$QA_3 = \frac{1}{N_{blk}} \sum_{i=1}^{M-7} \sum_{j=1}^{N-7} E_w(u - v) \tag{14}$$

$$E_{\mathrm{w}}(u) = \frac{1}{64} \sum_{i=1}^{8} \sum_{j=1}^{8} \mathrm{DCT}(u)_{ij}^2 Tc_{ij}, \qquad (15)$$

where Tc is the matrix of correction factors for each of the 8×8 DCT coefficients, which was normalized based on the JPEG quantization table in [22].

The fourth quality measure is inspired by [23], which was designed based on [22] by taking the CSF and the between-coefficient contrast masking of the DCT basis functions into account. In the same manner shown in [22], the measure operates with the values of the DCT coefficients of the 8×8 pixel block. The model allows each DCT coefficient to calculate its own maximum distortion value that is not visible because of the between-coefficient masking. It is assumed that the masking degree of each coefficient $\mathrm{DCT}(u)_{ij}$ depends upon its square value (power) and on the human eye sensitivity to this DCT basis function as determined using the CSF. Several basis functions can jointly mask one or several other basis functions. Then their masking effect value depends upon the sum of their weighted powers [23]. The final formula is expressed as follows:

$$\mathrm{QA}_4 = \frac{1}{N_{\mathrm{blk}}} \sum_{i=1}^{M-7} \sum_{j=1}^{N-7} E_{\mathrm{w}}(u-v) \cdot \mathrm{MaskEff}, \qquad (16)$$

where MaskEff is the reduction of the masking and contrast operation given in [23].

The fifth measure is based on the feature similarity index (FSIM) method proposed in [24]. FSIM was designed to compare the low-level feature sets of the reference image and the distorted image. Phase congruency (PC) and the gradient magnitude (GM) are used in FSIM and play complementary roles in the characterization of the local image quality. The measure is defined as

$$\mathrm{QA}_5 = \frac{\sum_i \sum_j S_{\mathrm{L}}\left(u_{ij}, v_{ij}\right) \mathrm{PC}_m\left(u_{ij}, v_{ij}\right)}{\sum_i \sum_j \mathrm{PC}_m\left(u_{ij}, v_{ij}\right)} \qquad (17)$$

$$\mathrm{PC}_m(x, y) = \mathrm{MAX}\{\mathrm{PC}(x), \mathrm{PC}(y)\}, \qquad (18)$$

where PC is the phase congruency operation of [25], and $S_{\mathrm{L}}(u, v)$ is the similarity map formed by combination of the similarities of PC and GM as $S_{\mathrm{L}} = S_{\mathrm{PC}} \times S_{\mathrm{GM}}$. S_{PC} and S_{GM} are calculated as

$$S_{\mathrm{PC}}(u, v) = \frac{2\mathrm{PC}(u) \cdot \mathrm{PC}(v) + T_1}{\mathrm{PC}^2(u) + \mathrm{PC}^2(v) + T_1} \qquad (19)$$

$$S_{\mathrm{GM}}(u, v) = \frac{2\mathrm{GM}(u) \cdot \mathrm{GM}(v) + T_2}{\mathrm{GM}^2(u) + \mathrm{GM}^2(v) + T_2}, \qquad (20)$$

where T_1 and T_2 are positive constants. In our work, in addition to the compound measure QA_5, we also consider the individual components, i.e., the PC and the

GM, separately, and thus form the sixth and seventh measures, respectively:

$$\mathrm{QA}_6 = \frac{\sum_i \sum_j S_{\mathrm{PC}}\left(u_{ij}, v_{ij}\right) \cdot \mathrm{PC}_m\left(u_{ij}, v_{ij}\right)}{\sum_i \sum_j \mathrm{PC}_m\left(u_{ij}, v_{ij}\right)} \qquad (21)$$

$$\mathrm{QA}_7 = S_{\mathrm{GM}}(u, v). \qquad (22)$$

The SSIM metric proposed in [26] is considered in the formation of the eighth candidate quality measure. The measure is composed using the luminance comparison $l(u,v)$, the contrast comparison $c(u, v)$ and the structure comparison $s(u,v)$, as follows:

$$\mathrm{QA}_8 = l(u, v) \cdot c(u, v) \cdot s(u, v), \qquad (23)$$

$$l(u, v) = \frac{2\mu_u \mu_v + c_1}{\mu_u^2 + \mu_v^2 + c_1}, \qquad (24)$$

$$c(u, v) = \frac{2\,\mathrm{cov}_{uv} + c_2}{\sigma_u^2 + \sigma_v^2 + c_2}, \qquad (25)$$

$$s(u, v) = \frac{\sigma_{uv} + C_3}{\sigma_u \sigma_v + C_3}, \qquad (26)$$

where μ_u and μ_v are the means of u and v, respectively, σ_u^2 and σ_v^2 are the variances of u and v, respectively, cov_{uv} is the covariance of v, c_1 and c_2 are the two variables used to stabilize the division with a weak denominator, and $c_3 = c_2 / 2$. In this paper, QA_9 is defined as the luminance comparison and $\mathrm{QA}_{10} = \frac{2\sigma_{uv} + c_2}{\sigma_u^2 + \sigma_v^2 + c_2}$, which is a simplified formula for $c(u, v) \times s(u, v)$, as shown in [26].

3.5 Machine learning methods for feature fusion

As described in the previous sections, the proposed quality approach aims to combine three different measures, by separately measuring the quality of the cyclopean view, the binocular rivalry, and the presence of depth. The limited knowledge of the subjective quality perception of 3D images means that it is not possible to predict which of the QA models will produce the best correlation with the subjective scores. Therefore, to find the best combination of quality measures and image features, we adopt a machine learning approach.

We assume that the best combination of features can be found by linear regression. Given a set of quality measures $\varphi_{(k,l)}$, the MOS over a set of test videos Θ_k are predicted using linear combinations where

$$\Theta_k = \hat{\theta}_0 + \sum_{l=1}^{\mathrm{L}} \varphi_{(k,l)} \hat{\theta}_l, \qquad (27)$$

or

$$\Theta = \begin{bmatrix} \Theta_1 \\ \Theta_2 \\ \vdots \\ \Theta_K \end{bmatrix} = \begin{bmatrix} 1, \varphi_{(1,1)}, \varphi_{(1,2)}, \cdots, \varphi_{(1,L)} \\ 1, \varphi_{(2,1)}, \varphi_{(2,2)}, \cdots, \varphi_{(2,L)} \\ \vdots \\ 1, \varphi_{(K,1)}, \varphi_{(K,2)}, \cdots, \varphi_{(K,L)} \end{bmatrix} \begin{bmatrix} \hat{\theta}_0 \\ \hat{\theta}_1 \\ \vdots \\ \hat{\theta}_L \end{bmatrix},$$

$$(28)$$

where the vector Θ represents the subjective scores, L is the number of quality measures, K is the number of test stimuli (videos), and $\hat{\theta}_{0,1,2,\ldots,L}$ are the parameters of the model. The above linear model in vector form can also be rewritten as an inner product:

$$\Theta = \varphi^T \hat{\theta}. \qquad (29)$$

To fit the linear model to a set of training data, $\hat{\theta}$ is normally determined using the least squares method [27]:

$$f(\theta) = \sum_{i=1}^{K} \left(\vec{\Theta}_i - \varphi_i^T \theta \right)^2 = \left(\vec{\Theta} - \varphi^T \theta \right)^T \left(\vec{\Theta} - \varphi^T \theta \right),$$

$$(30)$$

where $f(\theta)$ is the cost function, and θ can be chosen to minimize $f(\theta)$ using its derivatives, where

$$\nabla_\theta f(\theta) = \nabla_\theta \left(\vec{\Theta} - \varphi^T \theta \right)^T \left(\vec{\Theta} - \varphi^T \theta \right)$$
$$= \varphi^T \vec{\Theta} - \varphi^T \varphi \theta = 0. \qquad (31)$$

Then,

$$\theta = \left(\varphi^T \varphi \right)^{-1} \varphi^T \vec{\Theta}, \qquad (32)$$

where the array of quality measures φ is formed by the proposed 3D quality models, where $\varphi = [Q^{CV}, Q^{BR}, Q^{DQ}]$.

Efficient solution of Equation 28. Using Equation 32 requires a simple, reasonable, and efficient quality measure array and the use of subjective scores from properly conducted subjective experiments. The subjective experiments are described in the Section 4.

4 Mobile 3D video test content and related subjective tests

Two mobile 3D video databases and their corresponding subjective tests have been used for this study. The first database, denoted by '3D database I', contains four stereoscopic videos, called Akko&Kayo, Champagne Tower, Pantomime, and LoveBirds1, with varying levels of compression artifacts and depth presence [16]. Thumbnails of the videos in this database are shown in Figure 8. The database has 60 videos and consists of four scenes; each scene is captured in stereo using three different baselines, and each captured video is compressed by an H.264 encoder using five different values for the QP.

The original videos are high-resolution multiview videos. They have been converted into stereo videos with lower resolution by suitable rescaling. To maintain the variable depth levels, each video sequence has been retargeted by selecting different camera pairs from the available multiview video sequences. For all sequences, the left camera has been retained, while the right camera was selected at two different depth levels called the *short* baseline and the *wide* baseline. In addition, a monoscopic video sequence was generated by repeating the left channel sequence in the place of the right channel sequence. This would effectively present a 2D view with no depth effects on the 3D display. The short baseline produces a 3D scene within a limited disparity range but with visible 3D effects. The wide baseline provides an optimal

Figure 8 Contents of 3D video database I.

disparity range for the mobile stereoscopic display by setting the right camera position. All sequences were then downscaled to lower resolutions for the target display device. After that, each video was encoded using the H.264/AVC Simulcast method in intra-frame mode. The QP was selected in the [25, 30, 35, 40, 45] range and compression was independently applied to the left and right channels.

Thirty-two observers were involved in the subjective tests and were equally distributed in terms of gender with an age range between 18 and 37. The test materials were presented one by one in a pseudo-random order. The display device used was an autostereoscopic screen with a resolution of 428 × 240 pixels per view. After each clip, the test participants were asked to provide overall quality scores on a scale from 0 to 10 and indicate the acceptability of the quality for viewing the mobile 3D video on a yes/no scale. At the beginning of each session, a training set of seven clips was shown. Each test stimulus was shown twice during the test. A set of dummy videos was also shown at the beginning and in the middle of each test session. A total of 164 video clips were shown to each observer [15]. The overall ratings of the stereoscopic videos were finally ranked in terms of their MOS.

The second database contains six different videos spanning different genres of mobile 3DTV and video: these videos are Bullinger, Butterfly, Car, Horse, Mountain, and Soccer2, as shown in Figure 9. This set of videos is intended to represent a range of stereoscopic videos with different content properties, including varying spatial details, temporal changes, and depth complexity. Each video sequence lasts 10 s.

The sequences were encoded using four different methods: H.264/AVC Simulcast, H.264/AVC MVC, MRSC, and V + D. The encoding parameters were chosen as shown in Table 1 [15]. Coding was carried out using two codec profiles: the baseline profile and the high profile. The simple baseline profile uses an IPPP prediction structure and context-adaptive variable-length code (CAVLC) [28] prediction. The group of picture (GOP) size was set at 1. This refers to the low-complexity encoder for mobile devices. The more complex high profile enables hierarchical B-frames with GOP sizes of 8 and context-based adaptive binary arithmetic coding (CABAC) quantization. Because of the variable compressibilities of the different sequences, individual bit rate points were determined for each sequence [15]. The QP of the codec was set at 30 for high quality and 37 for low quality. In total, the database has six reference sequences and 96 distorted 3D video sequences.

Subjective tests were carried out with 87 test participants that were evenly divided in terms of gender and with ages ranging between 16 and 37 years. The visualization process was performed by following the same test procedure and using the same autostereoscopic display as that used in the tests with 3D database I. The MOS for both tests are of the same scale.

5 Feature selection

Both subjective experiments were performed while following the same protocol and using the same device and the same quality evaluation scale. Therefore, we were able to combine the entries from the two databases into a single group of opinion scores within the same scale. We picked 70% of the entries by random selection for forming a training set. The rest of the entries were included in a test set. We measured the prediction performances of the different feature groups using the Spearman rank-order correlation coefficient (SROCC). The SROCC output is in the [−1, 1] range, where a higher absolute value

Figure 9 Contents of 3D video database II.

Table 1 Codec settings of the two profiles

Profile	Baseline	High
GOP size	1 (IPPP)	8 (hierarchical B-frames)
Symbol mode	CAVLC	CABAC
Search range	48	48
Intra-period	16	16
Quality level	QP (30, 37)	QP (30, 37)

or SROCC indicates a stronger monotonic relationship between the MOS and the values that were predicted using the metric.

The set of feature candidates consists of 50 items, numbered between $\mathscr{F}_1$ and $\mathscr{F}_{50}$. There are three quality components: the cyclopean view (denoted by Q^{CV}), the binocular rivalry (Q^{BR}), and the depth quality (Q^{DQ}). The quality of the cyclopean view is assessed using three alternative approaches: global comparison $\left(Q_1^{CV}\right)$, block-wise selection of the better channel $\left(Q_2^{CV}0029\right)$, and the block-wise average $\left(Q_2^{CV}\right)$. A set of ten measures was applied to each quality component. The feature candidates are listed in the first row of Table 2. The measures are listed in the first column of the same table. For example, $\mathscr{F}_1$ indicates the quality assessment QA_1 under cyclopean view model 1, i.e., $\left\{Q_1^{CV}, QA_1\right\}$; $\mathscr{F}_{33}$ indicates the quality assessment QA_3 under the binocular rivalry model, i.e., $\{Q^{BR}, QA_3\}$. The quality measures that are not relevant to the comparison of the depth maps are excluded from the experiments. These combinations are marked with a dash in Table 2.

We use a regression fitting to measure the performances of the individual features. First, the output of each candidate feature listed in Section 3.4 was

normalized to the range $[-10, 10]$, using logistic fitting as follows:

$$f(x) = \beta_1 \left(1 + \frac{\beta_2 - \beta_3}{\beta_3 + e^{-\frac{x}{\beta_4}}}\right). \tag{33}$$

The parameters β_1, β_2, β_3, and β_4 have been selected in each individual case so that the output of each feature fits into the desired range. Then we evaluate the performance of each i feature in terms of Spearman correlation. The results of this evaluation are given in Table 2 in columns 2 to 6. The combined performances of all quality measurements applied to a given component are shown on the bottom row of the table, and this measure is denoted by $SROCC_1$. The results in this row indicate the applicability of a single component for use in subjective quality prediction. The combined performance values for the single quality measure when applied to all components are given in the last column of the table, which is labeled $SROCC_2$. These results indicate the applicability of a given quality measure.

From these results, we can see that the use of a single quality component is insufficient because the quality values predicted by a single component do not correlate well with the subjective scores. The best correlation is achieved when using feature $\mathscr{F}_{15}$, i.e., $\left\{Q_2^{CV}, QA_5\right\}$. Using the cyclopean view components (e.g., $\left\{Q_{i\in[1,2,3]}^{CR}, QA_{i\in[1,...,10]}\right\}$), we can achieve SROCC values of more than 0.9. This result can be interpreted as evidence that the 2D quality of the cyclopean view is a major component of the overall perceived quality.

In the next experiment, we attempted to find a combination of features and quality measures that produced a good trade-off between prediction accuracy and

Table 2 Spearman correlations of each quality feature and each quality component

Metrics	Q_1^{CV}	Q_2^{CV}	Q_3^{C}	Q^{BR}	Q^{DQ}	$SROCC_2$
	$\mathscr{F}_1 \sim \mathscr{F}_{10}$	$\mathscr{F}_{11} \sim \mathscr{F}_{20}$	$\mathscr{F}_{21} \sim \mathscr{F}_{30}$	$\mathscr{F}_{31} \sim \mathscr{F}_{40}$	$\mathscr{F}_{41} \sim \mathscr{F}_{50}$	
QA_1	0.5591	0.6022	0.4784	−0.0109	0.4660	0.8240
QA_2	0.6703	0.7058	0.5849	0.2204	0.5124	0.7830
QA_3	0.5816	0.6511	0.5379	0.0345	-	0.6739
QA_4	0.5850	0.6839	0.5529	0.0656	-	0.7029
QA_5	0.7664	*0.8101*	0.7964	0.1085	0.4769	0.8598
QA_6	0.5588	0.5840	0.5240	−0.0675	0.4199	0.7543
QA_7	0.7493	0.7347	0.7389	0.3531	0.5870	0.7969
QA_8	0.5218	0.5234	0.4452	−0.0119	0.5146	0.7433
QA_9	0.4210	0.4680	0.3919	0.1617	0.4881	0.5375
QA_{10}	0.5247	0.5192	0.4460	−0.0327	0.3914	0.7407
$SROCC_1$	0.9025	0.9144	0.9164	0.6357	0.6806	0.9711

The highest correlation value is marked in italic.

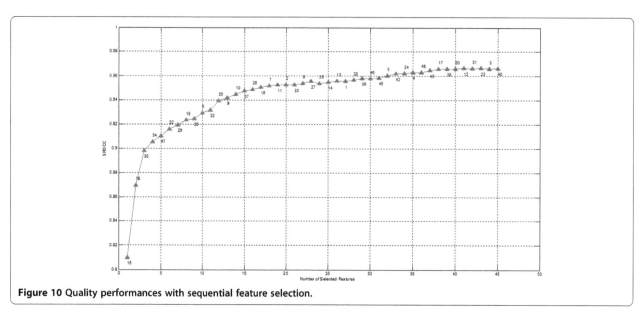

Figure 10 Quality performances with sequential feature selection.

computational complexity. We performed a sequential feature search, looking for the best combination of $n + 1$ features using the best combination of n features and adding one feature at a time. In this manner, we were able to extract 45 features until we reached the SROCC value of 0.97, as shown in Figure 10. By studying the performance improvements introduced by each feature selection (as shown in Figure 11), we see that a combination of four or five features will result in a good accuracy vs. complexity trade-off. The difference in performance for each two consecutive number of features is given in Figure 11, and the difference between the performance for four and five features is marked with a red circle. The first five features in the sequential search are $\{\mathscr{F}_{\{15,18,30,34,47\}}\}$, where $\mathscr{F}_{\{15,18,30\}}$ evaluates the cyclopean view, $\mathscr{F}_{34}$ evaluates the binocular rivalry, and $\mathscr{F}_{47}$ evaluates the depth quality.

The computational complexities of the best performing combinations of four or five features are shown in Table 3 and in Figure 12. The Big O complexity, the McCabe complexity, and the CPU running time for each combination are shown in Table 3. The Big O notation specifically describes the worst-case scenario. The McCabe complexity was proposed in [29] and was also called the cyclomatic complexity or the conditional complexity. McCabe describes the independent paths through the source code as a directed graph. The McCabe complexity is calculated from the cyclomatic number of its graph [29]. The CPU time listed in Table 3 is the time taken to run ten images in each QA$_i$ using MATLAB 2012b on the Win64 OS with the Intel Core Duo E8400 CPU. For comparison, the last row of Table 3 contains the complexity of dense depth estimation and the time it needs to calculate the disparity map of the ten images using search window of 50 pixels on the same computer.

Disparity estimation is a step which is required for the calculation of all considered features (see Figure 4), and its computational complexity is in the same range as the complexity of the features. The McCabe complexity and the CPU time of all candidates are compared with the complexity of disparity estimation in Figure 12.

To find an optimal group of features, we estimated the performances of all combinations of five and six features. Since the computational overhead for deriving dense disparity map is the same in each case, we did not take it into account in the feature selection process. We found that 5 groups of five features and 18 groups of six features had SROCC scores that were higher than 0.93. The best performing groups of five features are listed in Table 4, and the best performing groups of six features are listed in Table 5. The complexity levels of each group were calculated based on the McCabe complexities, and

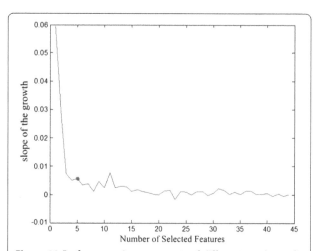

Figure 11 Performance improvements of different numbers of selected features.

Table 3 QA computational complexity

Metrics	Corresponding $\mathscr{F}_i$	Big O	McCabe	Time (s)
QA$_1$	$\mathscr{F}_1, \mathscr{F}_{11}, \mathscr{F}_{21}, \mathscr{F}_{31}, \mathscr{F}_{41}$	$O(N)$	2	0.156
QA$_2$	$\mathscr{F}_2, \mathscr{F}_{12}, \mathscr{F}_{22}, \mathscr{F}_{32}, \mathscr{F}_{42}$	$O(\delta N)$	9	0.328
QA$_3$	$\mathscr{F}_3, \mathscr{F}_{13}, \mathscr{F}_{23}, \mathscr{F}_{33}, -$	$O(N^2)$	15	7.535
QA$_4$	$\mathscr{F}_4, \mathscr{F}_{14}, \mathscr{F}_{24}, \mathscr{F}_{34}, -$	$O(N^2)$	22	22.32
QA$_5$	$\mathscr{F}_5, \mathscr{F}_{15}, \mathscr{F}_{25}, \mathscr{F}_{35}, \mathscr{F}_{45}$	$O(N^2)$	25	36.93
QA$_6$	$\mathscr{F}_6, \mathscr{F}_{16}, \mathscr{F}_{26}, \mathscr{F}_{36}, \mathscr{F}_{46}$	$O(N^2)$	22	37.02
QA$_7$	$\mathscr{F}_7, \mathscr{F}_{17}, \mathscr{F}_{27}, \mathscr{F}_{37}, \mathscr{F}_{47}$	$O(\delta N)$	3	0.484
QA$_8$	$\mathscr{F}_8, \mathscr{F}_{18}, \mathscr{F}_{28}, \mathscr{F}_{38}, \mathscr{F}_{48}$	$O(N^2)$	9	0.827
QA$_9$	$\mathscr{F}_9, \mathscr{F}_{19}, \mathscr{F}_{29}, \mathscr{F}_{39}, \mathscr{F}_{49}$	$O(N^2)$	9	0.343
QA$_{10}$	$\mathscr{F}_{10}, \mathscr{F}_{20}, \mathscr{F}_{30}, \mathscr{F}_{40}, \mathscr{F}_{50}$	$O(N^2)$	9	0.718
Dense disparity estimate	-	$O(\delta N)$	10	11.30

the CPU times are shown in Table 3 and Figure 12. From Table 4, we see that the previously found feature group, $\mathscr{F}_{\{15,18,30,34,47\}}$, is not the group with the lowest complexity, with a McCabe complexity of 108 and a running time for a single image set of 6.11 s. The fastest quality measure, $\mathscr{F}_{\{25,28,30,41,48\}}$, does not contain a component that is sensitive to binocular rivalry. Therefore, by considering the complexity, the correlation performance, and the sensitivity of the metric to different artifacts, we selected the second-fastest feature group $\mathscr{F}_{\{25,28,33,41,48\}}$ for the final quality metric. The output of each feature was normalized according to formula (33). The weighting and normalization coefficients used for each feature are given in Table 6.

This selection is also confirmed by the results of the full searches over six features. These combinations reach correlation performances of 0.93, but at considerably higher computational costs. However, we can see that the feature evaluation components from the first two groups (CV and BR) tend to dominate the best performing combinations. It should be noted that the performance is

calculated based only on the training subset of test videos, and by selecting a three-component combination, we aim to provide a balanced combination for a wider, and possibly more diverse, set of videos.

6 Comparative results

The prediction performance of an objective quality metric can be evaluated in terms of accuracy, monotonicity, and association. We use the normalized root mean squared error (RMSE), the SROCC, and the Pearson linear correlation coefficient (PLCC) to quantify the corresponding performance properties of our metric. Before calculation of the correlation performance, we apply a logistic fitting function to all quality metrics under comparison.

The subjective experiments performed on the two sets of test sequences have been analyzed in [15,16]. Some findings relevant to our current work are summarized here. The results of subjective experiments, involving 3D database I were interpreted in [15] as both the artifact level and the presence of stereoscopic depth affect the user acceptance of and satisfaction with the 3D video sequences. Also, according to the subjective test results for database II [16], MVC and the V + D approach provide the best subjective quality for all compression levels. We believe that a well-performing 3D quality metric should be able to predict these subjective preferences.

We compared the feature group proposed in Section 5 (i.e., $\mathscr{F}_{\{25,28,33,41,48\}}$) with several state-of-the-art quality metrics. The results are as shown in Tables 7 and 8. The metrics that were intended for 2D image quality [i.e., peak signal-to-noise ratio (PSNR), SSIM, normalized root mean squared error (NRMSE), and PSNR-HVS] have been applied separately to the left and right channels and the final results have been averaged. In the PSNR case, the MSE derived in each channel was averaged in advance. Four metrics that predict the quality of the stereoscopic content have been included in the comparison: PHVS3D [2], PHSD [3], 3DBE [7], and the stereo metric, described

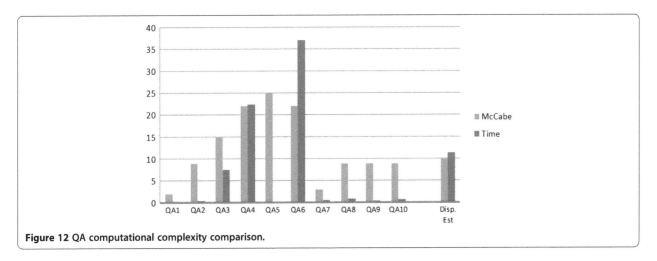

Figure 12 QA computational complexity comparison.

Table 4 Computational comparisons for five quality features (full search)

	Feature selection	Q^{CR}	Q^{BR}	Q^{DQ}	McCabe	Time (s)	SROCC
1	$\mathscr{F}_{\{25,28,30,41,48\}}$	+		+	54	3.95	0.9260
2	$\mathscr{F}_{\{15,16,17,25,29\}}$	+			84	11.16	0.9255
3	$\mathscr{F}_{\{9,15,16,32,35\}}$	+	+		90	11.15	0.9243
4	$\mathscr{F}_{\{25,28,34,41,48\}}$	+	+	+	67	6.11	0.9242
5	$\mathscr{F}_{\{25,28,33,41,48\}}$	+	+	+	*60*	*4.63*	*0.9236*
Sequential	$\mathscr{F}_{\{15,18,30,34,47\}}$	+	+	+	68	6.13	0.9106

The values for the selected set of features are marked in italic.

Table 6 Linearization and weighting coefficients used in the final quality metric

	$\mathscr{F}_{25}$	$\mathscr{F}_{28}$	$\mathscr{F}_{33}$	$\mathscr{F}_{41}$	$\mathscr{F}_{48}$
Weighting coefficient	1.8627	−1.0692	0.1202	0.4880	−0.4443
β_1	39.08	9.896	0.309	0.088	9.896
β_2	−166.6	370.8	3.281	9.749	370.8
β_3	4,483	3,577	−0.809	−0.866	3,577
β_4	0.139	0.114	803.6	454.2	0.1142

in [5]. The quality values for 3DBE were kindly provided by the authors of the metric in [7]. All metrics work on the luminance components of the images.

The SROCC, PLCC, and normalized RMSE values for each compared QA on 3D databases I and II can be seen in Tables 7 and 8, respectively. For visual comparison, prediction results for databases I and II are shown in Figures 13 and 14, respectively. To quantify the performance in terms of their different aspects, the videos from both databases are grouped into several subsets. Test sequences in 3D database I are classified into three subsets based on the depth levels in Table 7: 'mono' is used for monoscopic sequences, and short and wide are used for stereoscopic sequences. 3D database II is grouped into four subsets based on the encoding methods used, i.e., MRSC, MVC, SIM, and V + D. The two algorithms with the best performance levels are marked in bold.

The predominant distortions in this database are caused by DCT-based compression and are manifested as blocking and smearing artifact characteristic for harsh quantization levels. These distortions affect the cyclopean view quality and can be detected by quality metrics, sensitive to texture degradation. PSNR-HVS produces the third best performance on the mono set, where the SROCC, PLCC, and RMSE values are 0.921, 0.917, and 0.716, respectively. PHSD and PHVS3D also correlate well with the MOS in that database. PHSD is an improved version of PHVS3D, in which the disparity errors are considered. The SSIM metric, if used separately in each channel, does not correlate well with the subjective scores of 3D database I. The proposed combination of five quality features has the best correlation with the MOS, which were compared using either SROCC or PLCC. The overall correlations of SROCC, PLCC, and RMSE reach 0.935, 0.924, and 0.684 correspondingly. Most QA metrics fail on the wide baseline sets. The proposed metric shows higher correlations on *all* subsets,

Table 5 Computational comparisons for six quality features (full search)

Combination number	Feature selection	Q^{CR}	Q^{BR}	Q^{DQ}	McCabe	Time (s)	SROCC
1	$\mathscr{F}_{\{9,15,16,22,32,35\}}$	+	+		99	11.1868	0.9358
2	$\mathscr{F}_{\{15,16,22,29,32,35\}}$	+	+		99	11.1868	0.9352
3	$\mathscr{F}_{\{15,16,19,22,32,35\}}$	+	+		99	11.1868	0.9331
4	$\mathscr{F}_{\{9,12,15,16,32,35\}}$	+	+		99	11.1868	0.9329
5	$\mathscr{F}_{\{15,16,24,29,32,35\}}$	+	+		112	13.3864	0.9325
6	$\mathscr{F}_{\{9,15,16,24,32,35\}}$	+	+		112	13.3864	0.9321
7	$\mathscr{F}_{\{12,15,16,29,32,35\}}$	+	+		99	11.1868	0.9317
8	$\mathscr{F}_{\{15,16,23,29,32,35\}}$	+	+		105	11.9075	0.9317
9	$\mathscr{F}_{\{9,15,16,23,32,35\}}$	+	+		105	11.9075	0.9315
10	$\mathscr{F}_{\{9,15,16,21,32,35\}}$	+	+		92	11.1696	0.9313
11	$\mathscr{F}_{\{15,16,21,29,32,35\}}$	+	+		92	11.1696	0.931
12	$\mathscr{F}_{\{5,9,15,16,17,35\}}$	+	+		109	14.8621	0.9309
13	$\mathscr{F}_{\{9,15,16,17,32,35\}}$	+	+		93	11.2024	0.9309
14	$\mathscr{F}_{\{5,15,16,17,29,35\}}$	+	+		109	14.8621	0.9309
15	$\mathscr{F}_{\{12,25,28,30,41,48\}}$	+		+	63	3.9781	0.9306
16	$\mathscr{F}_{\{12,15,16,19,32,35\}}$	+	+		99	11.1868	0.9305
17	$\mathscr{F}_{\{9,12,25,28,41,48\}}$	+		+	63	3.9406	0.9304
Sequential	$\mathscr{F}_{\{15,18,30,34,47,22\}}$	+	+	+	77	6.1606	0.9162

Table 7 Spearman and Pearson correlations of compared metrics on 3D video database I

		PSNR	SSIM	PSNR-HVS	NRMSE	3DBE	Ref [5]	PHVS3D	PHSD	Proposed
SROCC	Mono	0.875	0.704	0.921	0.857	0.782	0.703	*0.929*	0.918	**0.939**
	Short	0.883	0.683	0.907	0.874	0.602	0.702	0.910	*0.935*	**0.956**
	Wide	0.850	0.599	0.877	0.833	0.549	0.609	0.896	*0.934*	**0.952**
	All	0.864	0.623	0.886	0.841	0.649	0.631	*0.917*	0.865	**0.935**
PLCC	Mono	0.874	0.768	0.917	0.903	0.801	0.755	*0.927*	0.915	**0.949**
	Short	0.877	0.756	0.915	0.920	0.577	0.739	0.914	*0.928*	**0.942**
	Wide	0.820	0.681	0.865	0.857	0.530	0.671	0.887	*0.920*	**0.941**
	All	0.843	0.707	0.885	0.879	0.613	0.694	*0.906*	0.844	**0.924**
RMSE	Mono	0.864	1.237	*0.716*	0.747	1.201	1.307	**0.695**	1.026	0.858
	Short	0.823	1.206	0.698	0.707	1.497	1.312	*0.693*	0.750	**0.556**
	Wide	0.921	1.346	0.781	0.830	1.587	1.449	*0.774*	0.821	**0.635**
	All	0.874	1.293	0.737	0.783	1.438	1.362	*0.715*	0.873	**0.684**

Values in bold indicate the best score; values in italic indicate the second best.

and the SROCC values of the short and wide baseline subsets are quite consistent at 0.956 and 0.952, respectively.

3D database II contains a wider range of video distortions, most notably some cases of severe binocular rivalry. Such distortions do not affect large areas of the image but are immediately visible to the observer. As a result, quality metrics assessing texture quality tend to grade such cases as being of high quality, while observers grade them as having annoying artifacts. Most of the metrics included in our comparison fail on the 'V + D' set, particularly PSNR, PSNR-HVS, PHVS3D, and SSIM, for which the PLCC values are less than 0.1. This can be attributed to the presence of binocular rivalry artifacts which are caused by view rendering based on the estimated depths. For most videos exhibiting stereoscopic distortions, 2D metrics fail to predict the subjective scores. The overall SROCC values of PSNR and PSNR-HVS are only 0.254 and 0.227, respectively. Although the results for SSIM and NRMSE are slightly improved, their overall SROCC values are still very low. Among the 3D quality metrics, the PHVS3D metric does not perform well, but the improved PHSD version has the second best correlation with all the MOS in the database. Finally, in Table 8, we see that the metric proposed in this paper shows better performance because it is sensitive to a wider range of stereoscopic distortions.

Table 8 Spearman and Pearson correlations of compared metrics on 3D video database II

		PSNR	SSIM	PSNR-HVS	NRMSE	Ref [5]	PHVS3D	PHSD	Proposed
SROCC	MRSC	0.076	0.398	0.399	0.452	0.562	0.306	*0.649*	**0.910**
	MVC	0.328	0.587	0.423	0.608	0.803	0.264	*0.810*	**0.973**
	SIM	0.368	0.543	0.418	0.561	0.699	0.292	*0.778*	**0.932**
	V + D	0.050	0.205	0.094	0.316	0.522	0.221	*0.737*	**0.877**
	All	0.254	0.443	0.227	0.413	0.646	0.323	*0.799*	**0.942**
PLCC	MRSC	0.196	0.361	0.369	0.487	0.519	0.271	*0.536*	**0.906**
	MVC	0.293	0.432	0.380	0.617	0.649	0.202	*0.726*	**0.963**
	SIM	0.301	0.420	0.411	0.561	0.564	0.317	*0.778*	**0.940**
	V + D	−0.170	0.099	−0.057	0.211	0.308	0.002	*0.653*	**0.907**
	All	0.236	0.379	0.223	0.425	0.541	0.294	*0.730*	**0.942**
RMSE	MRSC	1.581	1.475	1.588	1.488	1.315	1.468	*1.242*	**0.667**
	MVC	1.785	1.529	1.685	1.437	1.404	1.812	*1.258*	**0.544**
	SIM	1.883	1.699	1.854	1.691	1.579	1.769	*1.240*	**0.664**
	V + D	1.674	1.771	1.869	1.877	1.641	1.611	*1.143*	**0.754**
	All	1.735	1.623	1.753	1.633	1.491	1.671	*1.222*	**0.661**

Values in bold indicate the best score; values in italic indicate the second best.

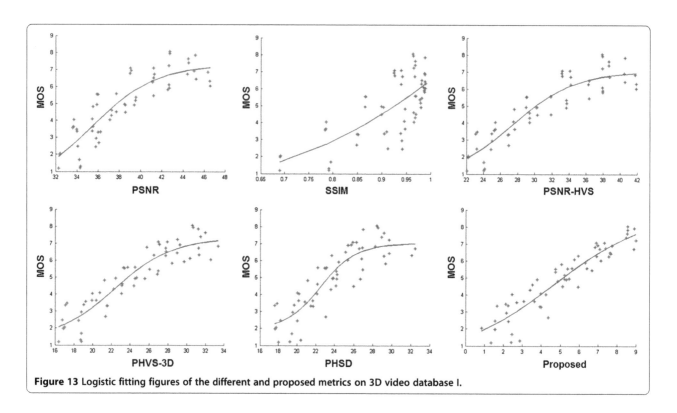

Figure 13 Logistic fitting figures of the different and proposed metrics on 3D video database I.

7 Conclusions

One of the biggest challenges in 3D QA is the calculation of the QA metric in a perceptual manner. In this paper, a novel full-reference stereoscopic quality metric that is applicable to mobile 3D video has been proposed.

First, we built two 3D quality databases that were annotated with subjective test results in terms of their MOS. The databases include not only compression distortions but also differently pronounced depth and 3D format conversion distortions. According to the results of subjective

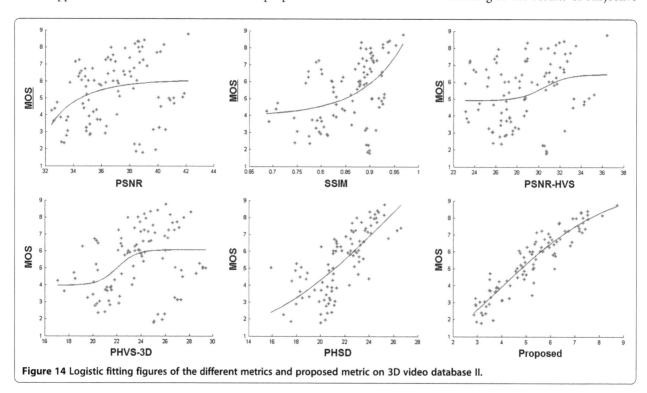

Figure 14 Logistic fitting figures of the different metrics and proposed metric on 3D video database II.

tests and interviews with the test participants [15], the number of compression artifacts is dominant in the evaluation of the content quality, whereas the presence of depth enhances the user experience. The viewers were very critical of the spatial quality and accepted only low numbers of artifacts in the content. The 3D effect enhances the user satisfaction and acceptance of the content; however, if the content is not presented with high spatial quality, then the content was declared to be less acceptable or completely unacceptable, regardless of the 3D effect. Motivated by these results, we modeled the 3D quality using three components: the cyclopean view, binocular rivalry, and the depth quality. The cyclopean view is simulated using three models. The first model generates a single cyclopean image by globally fusing the left and right views of a scene based on the properties of human stereo vision. The second and third models are based on local fusion methods, which calculate the quality on the block level between the left and right channels using a disparity map. Dissimilar visual stimuli between the two eyes bring binocular rivalry. In our approach, the amount of binocular rivalry is quantified by comparison of only the corresponding blocks in the distorted stereoscopic pair, using the disparity map that is provided by the reference pair. The differences between the images of a scene as seen by each eye are also used to form the perceived depth. The geometrical distortions are measured directly on the disparity map (and are called the depth quality).

Several QA methods are used to assess each quality component, with tests conducted using a training set that was extracted from the two available databases. To make the quality metric simple, fast, and efficient, the feature selection for all considered QAs is processed by studying their computational complexity and the CPU run times. Finally, six features are selected for the three components. The cyclopean view is measured by two quality assessment methods, i.e., QA_5 and QA_8, which are both under the third (local) cyclopean view model; binocular rivalry is evaluated using QA_3; and the depth quality is measured using the disparity map with QA_1 and QA_8. The experimental results have shown that the proposed metric significantly outperforms the current state-of-the-art quality metrics. We must note that our implementation does not take masking effects created by motion into account. This is will be studied in our future investigations. However, our experiments to date have shown that this masking plays a minor role in estimation of the quality. This observation has been confirmed by subjective tests on still images and videos with the same content, which resulted in very similar MOS.

Abbreviations
CSF: contrast sensitivity function; CWT: complex wavelet transform; DCT: discrete cosine transform; FSIM: feature similarity index; GM: gradient magnitude; HVS: human visual system; IQA: image quality assessment; LGN: lateral geniculate nucleus; MOS: mean opinion scores; MRSC: mixed resolution stereo coding; MSE: mean squared error; MVC: multiview video coding; PC: phase congruency; PLCC: Pearson rank-order correlation QA, quality assessment; QP: quantization parameters; SSD: sum-of-squared-difference; SSIM: structural similarity index; SROCC: Spearman rank-order correlation; V + D: video plus depth.

Competing interests
The authors declare that they have no competing interests.

References
1. A Boev, M Poikela, A Gotchev, A Aksay, Modeling of the stereoscopic HVS, Mobile3DTV. Technical Report D5.3. (2010). Available at http://sp.cs.tut.fi/mobile3dtv/results/tech/D5.3_Mobile3DTV_v2.0.pdf. Accessed on 13 January 2014
2. L Jin, A Boev, A Gotchev, K Egiazarian, 3D-DCT base perceptual quality assessment of stereo video, in *IEEE 18th International Conference on Image Processing (IEEE ICIP2011)*. Brussels, 11–14 September 2011
3. L Jin, A Boev, A Gotchev, K Egiazarian, Validation of a new full reference metric for quality assessment of mobile 3DTV content, in *The 19th European Signal Processing Conference (EUSIPCO-2011)*. Barcelona, 29 August to 2 September 2011
4. A Boev, A Gotchev, K Egiazarian, A Aksay, GB Akar, Towards compound stereo-video quality metric: a specific encoder-based framework, in *IEEE Southwest Symposium on Image Analysis and Interpretation*, pp. 218–222. Denver, June 2006
5. J You, L Xing, A Perkis, X Wang, Perceptual quality assessment for stereoscopic images based on 2D image quality metrics and disparity analysis, in *International Workshop on Video Processing and Quality Metrics for Consumer Electronics - VPQM*. Scottsdale, 13–15 January 2010
6. K Wang, K Brunnström, M Barkowsky, M Urvoy, M Sjöström, P Le Callet, S Tourancheau, B Andrén, Stereoscopic 3D video coding quality evaluation with 2D objective metrics. Proc. SPIE Electronic Imaging , 8648 (2013). Stereoscopic Displays and Applications XXIV, 86481L, San Francisco, March 12, 2013. doi: 10.1117/12.2003664
7. R Bensalma, MC Larabi, Towards a perceptual quality metric for color stereo images, in *IEEE 17th International Conferences on Image Processing*. Hong Kong, 26–29 September 2010
8. E Bosc, R Pepion, P Le Callet, M Koppel, P Ndjiki-Nya, M Pressigout, L Morin, Towards a new quality metric for 3-D synthesized view assessment. IEEE J. Sel. Top. Sign. Proces. **5**(7), 1332–1343 (2011)
9. PR Lebreton, A Raake, M Barkowsky, P Le Callet, Evaluating depth perception of 3D stereoscopic videos. IEEE Sel. Top. Sign. Proces. **6**(6), 710–720 (2012)
10. P Hanhart, T Ebrahimi, Quality assessment of a stereo pair formed from two synthesized views using objective metrics, in *Proceedings of Seventh International Workshop on Video Processing and Quality Metrics for Consumer Electronics (VPQM 2013)*. Scottsdale, 30 January to 1 February 2013
11. L Xing, J You, T Ebrahimi, A Perkis, Assessment of stereoscopic crosstalk perception. Multimedia, IEEE Trans. **14**(2), 326–337 (2012)
12. A Maalouf, MC Larabi, CYCLOP: a stereo color image quality assessment metric, in *2011 IEEE International Conference on Acoustics, Speech and Signal Processing (ICASSP)*, pp. 1161–1164. Prague, 22–27 May 2011
13. P Seuntiëns, Visual Experience of 3D TV, Thesis. (2006)
14. MTM Lambooij, WA Ijsselsteijn, I Heynderickx, Visual discomfort in stereoscopic displays: a review, in *Proceedings of SPIE, Stereoscopic Displays and Virtual Reality Systems XIV*. San Jose, 1–13 January 2007
15. D Strohmeier, S Jumisko-Pyykkö, K Kunze, G Tech, D Bugdayci, M Oguz Bici, Results of quality attributes of coding, transmission and their combinations, Mobile 3DTV Technical Report D4.3. , (2010). Available at http://sp.cs.tut.fi/mobile3dtv/results/tech/D4.3_Mobile3DTV_v1.0.pdf. Accessed on 13 January 2014
16. L Jin, A Boev, S Jumisko-Pyykkö, T Haustola, A Gotchev, Novel stereo quality metrics, MOBILIE 3DTV Technical Report D5.5, (2011). Available at http://sp.cs.tut.fi/mobile3dtv/results/tech/D5.5_Mobile3DTV_v1.0.pdf. Accessed on 14 January 2014
17. A Wandell Brian, *Foundations of Vision* (Sinauer Associates, Sunderland, 1995)

18. R Blake, A primer on binocular rivalry, including current controversies. Brain Mind **2**(1), 5–38 (2011)

19. S Knorr, K Ide, M Kunter, T Sikora, Basic rules for good 3D and avoidance of visual discomfort, in *International Broadcasting Convention (IBC)*. Amsterdam, 8–13 September 2011

20. S Smirnov, A Gotchev, M Hannuksela, Comparative analysis of local binocular and trinocular depth estimation approaches. Proc. of SPIE **7724**(2010) doi:10.1117/12.854765

21. S Baker, D Scharstein, J Lewis, S Roth, M Black, R Szeliski, A database and evaluation methodology for optical flow, in *Proceedings of the IEEE International Conference on Computer Vision*, pp. 243–246. Crete, Greece, 14–21 October 2007

22. K Egiazarian, J Astola, N Ponomarenko, V Lukin, F Battisti, M Carli, New full-reference quality metrics based on HVS, in *International Workshop on Video Processing and Quality Metrics*, p. 4. Scottsdale, January 2006

23. N Ponomarenko, F Silvestri, K Egiazarian, M Carli, J Astola, V Lukin, On between-coefficient contrast masking of DCT basis functions, in *International Workshop on Video Processing and Quality Metrics for Consumer Electronics*, pp. 25–26. Scottsdale, January 2007

24. L Zhang, L Zhang, X Mou, D Zhang, FSIM: a feature similarity index for image quality assessment. IEEE Trans. Image Process. **20**(8), 2378–2386 (2011)

25. P Kovesi, Image features from phase congruency. Videre: J Comput Vision Res (1999). MIT Press. Volume 1, Number 3

26. Z Wang, A Bovik, H Sheikh, E Simoncelli, Image quality assessment: from error visibility to structural similarity. IEEE Trans. Image Process. **13**(4), 600–612 (2004)

27. T Hastie, R Tibshirani, J Friedman, *The Elements of Statistical Learning: Data Mining, Inference, and Prediction*, 2nd edn. (Springer, Heidelberg, 2009)

28. T Wiegand, GJ Sullivan, G Bjøntegaard, A Luthra, Overview of the H.264/AVC video coding standard. IEEE Trans. Circ. Syst. Video Tech. **13**, 560 (2003)

29. TJ McCabe, A complexity measure. IEEE Trans. Soft. Eng. **SE-2**(4), 308 (1976)

2

Micro-crack detection of multicrystalline solar cells featuring an improved anisotropic diffusion filter and image segmentation technique

Said Amirul Anwar and Mohd Zaid Abdullah[*]

Abstract

This paper presents an algorithm for the detection of micro-crack defects in the multicrystalline solar cells. This detection goal is very challenging due to the presence of various types of image anomalies like dislocation clusters, grain boundaries, and other artifacts due to the spurious discontinuities in the gray levels. In this work, an algorithm featuring an improved anisotropic diffusion filter and advanced image segmentation technique is proposed. The methods and procedures are assessed using 600 electroluminescence images, comprising 313 intact and 287 defected samples. Results indicate that the methods and procedures can accurately detect micro-crack in solar cells with sensitivity, specificity, and accuracy averaging at 97%, 80%, and 88%, respectively.

Keywords: Micro-crack detection; Multicrystalline solar cell; Image segmentation; Anisotropic diffusion; Angular radial transform; Support vector machine

1. Introduction

The increasing demand for solar electrical energy has multiplied the need for photovoltaic (PV) arrays. As the major component of the PV array, the demand for solar cells has also increased. This demand has translated into an increased production of solar cells in recent years. Depending on the materials used in manufacturing, solar cells can be divided into two major types. They are (i) monocrystalline and (ii) multicrystalline silicones. Due to low manufacturing and processing cost of the multicrystalline silicon, this material is generally more preferred in the production of the solar wafer or PV module. There is great potential for the automation in solar cell industry because millions of solar cells are manufactured daily worldwide. According to recent statistics, the growth rate of the solar PV module reached a record high in 2011, generating more than US$93 billion in revenue with multicrystalline cells constituting more than 50% of the world production [1]. Although many operations in the PV industry have been automated, the inspection and grading processes continue to be based on manual or semi-manual efforts.

Finished solar cells are occasionally found to be defective or faulty. The defects fall into two groups: (i) intrinsic and (ii) extrinsic. Grain boundaries are an example of intrinsic defect, while micro-cracks belong to the second category. The former type of defects diminish the short-circuit current of the cell, and this leads to loss in the efficiency. The latter defects form a class of cracks that are entirely invisible to the naked eye. With dimensions smaller than 30 μm [2], this type of defect can only be visualized electronically like using the electroluminescence (EL) technique and high-resolution cameras.

In practice, there are various shapes and sizes of micro-cracks in a solar cell depending on how they are formed. For example a line-shaped micro-crack is caused by scratches, and it generally occurs during cell fabrication [3]. This type of defect can also be due to wafer sawing or laser cutting, which propagates and causes the detachment or internal breakage of the grainy materials within the solar cells [4]. In contrast, star-shaped micro-crack is formed due to a sharp point impact which induces several line cracks with a tendency to cross each other [5]. There are other types of micro-crack defects, but these two are the most commonly found in solar cell production. Köntges et al. [6] reported that there may be a risk of failure for PV modules containing cells that have micro-cracks or other types of

* Correspondence: mza@usm.my
School of Electrical and Electronic Engineering, Universiti Sains Malaysia, Engineering Campus, Penang 14300, Malaysia

defects. Hence, it is important to have high-quality, defect-free cells in the production of PV modules.

To date, few studies have highlighted the benefit of computer inspection for defect detection in EL images of solar cells. For example, multicrystalline solar cell images have been categorized into three distinct classes based on the features extracted from texture analysis [7]. An evaluation of crack formation in the PV module before and after mechanical load testing using EL images has been presented by Kajari-Schröder et al. [8]. Recently, a defect detection scheme based on Fourier image reconstruction has also been reported [9]. These authors presented a successful detection of a micro-crack which is geometrically simple like straight lines. A micro-crack detection scheme for a solar wafer based on an anisotropic diffusion filter has also been documented [10]. As reported by these authors, this filter is very efficient in preserving important edges in the image while smoothing other less important and connected regions. However, correct implementation of this technique depends crucially on the choice of an edge stopping threshold. In most cases, this value has to be determined interactively, frequently through trail-and-error method. Only under very unusual circumstances can anisotropic diffusion filtering be successful using a single threshold since images are likely to be gray level variations in objects and background due to non-uniform lighting and other factors. Clearly, a more robust approach is needed in order to increase the efficiency of this filtering strategy. In this paper, an enhanced version of the anisotropic diffusion filter featuring an adaptive thresholding via a sigmoid transformation function is presented. Meanwhile, pattern classification is established using support vector machines (SVMs) with supervised learning [11]. The methods and procedures are tested using intact and defected solar cells, and results are compared with other filters and artificial classifiers.

2. Methodology

2.1 Electroluminescence image

Micro-crack detection in the monocrystalline cell is relatively straightforward because this type of cell is characterized by a uniform background. However, this is not the case for the multicrystalline cell, which contains crystal grains as well as dark areas formed from intrinsic structures like dislocation clusters and grain boundaries. Distinguishing micro-crack pixels from the background (i.e., the multicrystalline grains) is a very challenging procedure because the gray scale values of these two areas are not significantly different. The presence of other defects, such as the dark area, darker grains, and broken fingers, complicates the problem. In spite of these difficulties, the identification is still possible because the micro-cracks tend to appear in the form of strong lines with a low intensity and a high gradient. Figure 1a (i) shows an example EL image

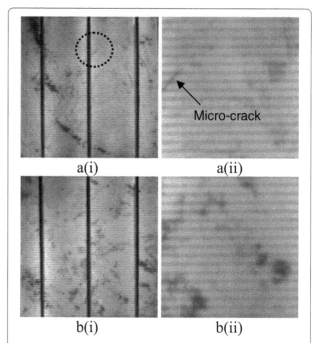

Figure 1 Examples of multicrystalline solar cell images. (a) Defected sample and **(b)** good sample. (i) Original image showing the formation of other image components like fingers, dark areas, and dislocation clusters. (ii) Close-up view of (i). The dashed circle in Figure 1a (i) shows the location of the micro-crack.

of a defected solar cell, and its close-up view of the region containing the micro-crack is displayed in Figure 1a (ii). For comparison, the EL image of a good solar cell is presented in Figure 1b (i), and its close-up view is shown in Figure 1b (ii). Meanwhile, the scan-line profile of gray level and gradient of the solar cell defected with a micro-crack is shown in Figure 2b,c, respectively. These figures highlight the unique textural characteristics of the micro-crack pixels.

All EL images used in this study including those shown in Figure 1 are 8-bit gray scale measuring 1,178 × 1,178 pixels in size. Other examples of defected solar cells containing various types and shapes of micro-cracks are shown in Figure 3. The micro-crack pixels appear in the form of a line or an intersection of lines forming a star-like artifact as depicted in Figure 3a. For comparison, Figure 3b shows examples of good solar cells highlighting the presence of dark regions having arbitrary shapes and sizes. They are formed by an aggregate of dislocation clusters or grainy materials, resembling dark shaped areas when visualized under the EL illumination. As seen from this figure, the presence of many dark areas or regions in both good and defected samples makes a micro-crack inspection an extremely difficult process. However, a close examination of Figure 3a reveals that micro-crack pixels exhibit unique shapes or patterns compared to dark regions even though

Micro-crack detection of multicrystalline solar cells featuring an improved anisotropic diffusion filter...

21

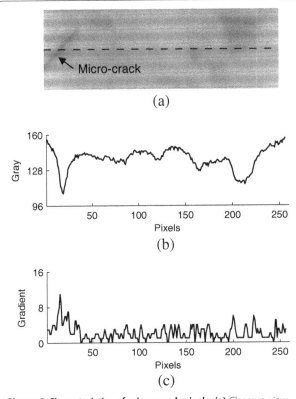

Figure 2 Characteristics of micro-crack pixels. (a) Close-up view of the region containing the micro-crack. **(b)** Gray level profile. **(c)** Gradient profile. The dashed line in **(a)** marks the location of the scan line.

they have the same gray scale values. Thus, some form of image analysis is needed in order to facilitate accurate detection and efficient classification.

In this study, a series of image processing procedures are performed, capitalizing the unique textural properties and multicrystalline grain inhomogeneity of the solar cell. The details are described in the next section.

2.2 Image pre-processing

As seen in Figures 1 and 3, the EL images of the solar cell contain various features, such as fingers (horizontal lines) that are periodic in nature and perpendicular to the bus-bar (thicker vertical lines in Figure 1a (i) and Figure 1b (i)). A close inspection of these figures revealed that the intensity distribution is not uniform both within the cell and among the cells. The presence of the broken fingers and non-uniform background luminescence directly affects the micro-crack analysis, especially if a simple image segmentation technique is used. The solutions to these problems are to remove the periodic interruption of fingers and minimize the effect on background inhomogeneity on image processing. This can be done by filtering in the frequency domain.

Let I_O be the original EL image of size $m \times n$, and $\hat{I}_O(u, v)$ is its Fourier transform representation. Due to the orthogonal properties, the fingers in the spatial domain appear as a straight vertical line located at the center of a spectrum. This line is dominated by high-frequency components because the contrast between fingers and background is relatively higher compared to other inhomogeneities. Meanwhile, the low-frequency regions contain other important components such as the grain boundaries, dislocation clusters, and micro-cracks. Hence, only the high-frequency components located around the vertical line needs to be removed while retaining the low-frequency components. Therefore, a custom-made filter is constructed to remove these artifacts. The filter function is given below:

$$\hat{V}(u, v) = \begin{cases} 0, & \hat{D}(u, v) \geq d \text{ and } \frac{n}{2} - w \leq \hat{D}(u, v) \leq \frac{n}{2} + w \\ 1 - \left[\exp\left(\frac{-\hat{D}^2(u, v)}{2\sigma^2} \right) \right], & \text{otherwise} \end{cases}$$

where

$$\hat{D}(u, v) = \sqrt{\left(u - \frac{m}{2} \right)^2 + \left(v - \frac{n}{2} \right)^2} \qquad (2)$$

(1)

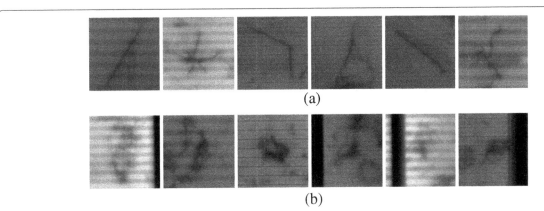

Figure 3 Examples of micro-cracks and dark regions. (a) Solar cells with various types and shapes of micro-cracks. **(b)** Good samples showing the formation of dark regions.

Parameters w, d, and σ in Equation 1 are chosen experimentally. The filtering is performed by pixel-to-pixel multiplication between $\hat{I}_O(u, v)$ and $\hat{V}(u, v)$ to produce $\hat{I}_e(u, v)$ as shown in Figure 4a. The resulting image is inverse Fourier transform, yielding $I_e(x, y)$ in spatial space. To minimize the error resulting from the inconsistency of the gray level between cells, $I_e(x, y)$ is normalized to 128. This filtered image is shown in Figure 4c,d,e. It can be seen from these figures that the fingers have been successfully removed and the background inhomogeneity is reduced. Also, the micro-crack pixels are not affected by this filtering operation as evident from Figure 4d (ii). Therefore, this local processing approach preserves the details in the image while attenuating the slow varying components such as the background irregularities.

2.3 Anisotropic diffusion filtering

This subsection presents an implementation of anisotropic diffusion filtering for image enhancement. As can be seen

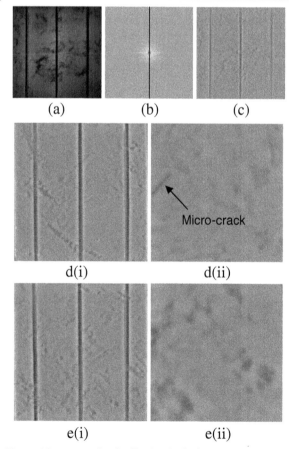

Figure 4 Pre-processing by filtering in the frequency domain.
(a) Original EL image. **(b)** Fourier spectrum after filtering with $w = 6$, $d = 10$, and $\sigma = 12$. **(c)** Filtered image after inverse Fourier transformation. **(d-e)** Results after pre-processing corresponding to images in Figure 1.

in Figure 4d (ii), the micro-crack pixels are characterized with low gray scale values but high gradients. The convolution of $I_e(x, y)$ with a simple edge detector (e.g., Sobel kernel) will yield high and low gradients at the edges and micro-crack pixels, respectively. Consequently, the result is that the produced image contains two lines, corresponding to regions with high and low intensity gradients. This will give rise to the difficulty in the detection leading to many false negatives. We solved this problem by means of the anisotropic diffusion filtering, which produces equal response to any pixels, including the micro-crack areas. In order to achieve this, the diffusion filter is programmed to take into account not only the intensity of the gradient but also the intensity of the gray level of each pixel. The details are explained below.

The anisotropic diffusion filtering can be defined in terms of the diffused image $I_d(x, y, t)$ at iteration t [12]. Mathematically,

$$I_d(x, y, t) = I_d(x, y, t-1) + \frac{1}{4} \sum_{i=1}^{4} c\left(\left|\nabla I_d^i\right|\right) \nabla I_d^i, \ t > 0$$

(3)

where ∇ is a gradient and c is a diffusion coefficient that is a non-negative function of the magnitude of the gradient of four Laplacian neighbors, $i = \{1, 2, ..., 4\}$. Letting $s = |\nabla I_d|$, then the diffusion coefficient in Equation 3 is given as

$$c(s) = \exp\left[-\left(\frac{s}{K}\right)^2\right]$$

(4)

or

$$c(s) = \left[1 + \left(\frac{s}{K}\right)^2\right]^{-1}$$

(5)

These diffusion coefficients exhibit a low value at high gradient purposely to preserve the corresponding edges. On the other hand, these coefficients produce high value at low gradient indicating a strong smoothing effect on the pixels involved. Thus, the anisotropic diffusion filtering will produce a smoothed image while the important edges are preserved. Parameter K appearing in Equations 4 and 5 is an edge stopping threshold, and it needs to be correctly specified in order to ensure a successful application of this filtering strategy. If K is too small, then the diffusion process will be terminated earlier, resulting in $I_d(x, y, t)$ which is approximately equal to $I_d(x, y, 0)$. In contrast, fixing K too large will significantly diffuse the image, resulting in image blurring. Therefore, the choice of the parameter K is important for producing a diffused image that retains the important edges while smoothing the other regions of the image.

In this study, a conventional anisotropic diffusion filtering technique is modified to produce the opposite effect. In doing so, the smoothing effect will now take place at the strong edges (high gradient) while the region with low gradient are preserved. This is achieved by inverting the original diffusion coefficient yielding

$$c(s) = 1 - \left[1 + \left(\frac{s}{K}\right)^2\right]^{-1} \qquad (6)$$

Theoretically, the function in Equation 5 privileges wide regions over smaller ones. Therefore, with modification in Equation 6, this trend is reversed to satisfy the characteristics of the micro-crack. Figure 5 shows a response of Equations 4, 5, and 6 with respect to gradient. As shown in this figure, the modified diffusion coefficient increases with the increasing gradient while the responses of the original coefficients are in the opposite sense.

Most of the approach reported in the literature used trial-and-error experiments in determining K. In contrast, this study used a diffusion coefficient function that eliminates the need to use this parameter. Referring to the micro-crack pixels defined in the previous section, we are interested in every pixel with a high gradient but a low intensity value. For this reason, the gradient threshold does not have to be rigidly fixed. In order to achieve this, parameter, K is replaced with the function that adaptively generates a unique threshold for each pixel using the input image gray values. The proposed diffusion coefficient is as follows:

$$c(s) = 1 - \left[1 + \frac{s^2}{g^2}\right]^{-1} \qquad (7)$$

where g is a mapping of the image intensity of $I_d(x, y, 0)$ through the sigmoid transfer function given by

$$g(x, y) = \frac{255}{1 + \exp[-b(I_d(x, y, 0) - \varepsilon)]} \qquad (8)$$

where b determines the gradient of ramp in the transfer function and ε is a threshold value where the intensity of $I_d(x, y, 0)$ is mapped to the center of the gray scale range. Equation 8 is defined as an edge stopping threshold matrix, and it has the same dimension as $I_e(x, y)$. Every element in $g(x, y)$ is the edge stopping threshold value for the corresponding pixel in $I_e(x, y)$. Equation 7 is plotted for different s and g values, and the result is graphically shown in Figure 6.

As seen in Figure 6, the response of the diffusion coefficient varies with the different threshold values. The response is more sensitive when the threshold value is low with respect to the same gradient s. High value of the coefficient yields a high diffusivity for the corresponding pixel in the image which leads to blurring effect. As mentioned earlier, existing techniques only used a single edge stopping threshold value for the whole image. In this study, an adaptive edge stopping threshold function given in Equation 8 is used. This resulted in different threshold values for different pixels depending on their gray scale values through a mapping process.

The proposed anisotropic diffusion method described above was tested using a synthetic image of size 256 × 256 pixels. As shown in Figure 7a, this image simulates a gradient profile comprising 16 discrete steps. Figure 7b shows the horizontal line scan of Figure 7a. The diffused image using the standard diffusion filter is shown in Figure 7c, while Figure 7d shows the result using the proposed algorithm. Clearly, image processing using standard diffusion filter produced a very blurred image, resulting

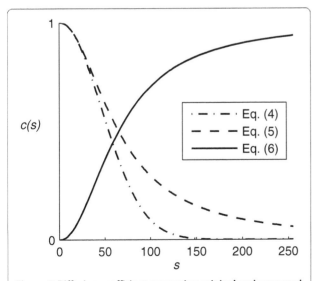

Figure 5 Diffusion coefficient comparing original and proposed equations. All responses are plotted with $K = 64$.

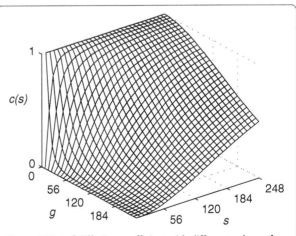

Figure 6 Plot of diffusion coefficient with different values of s and g.

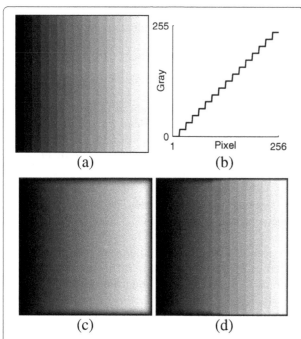

Figure 7 Image filtering comparing conventional and proposed anisotropic diffusion filters. (a) Synthetic image. **(b)** Horizontal scan line of **(a)**. **(c)** Diffused image using Equation 6 with $K = 2$ and $t = 100$; **(d)** Diffused image using Equation 7 with $b = 0.1$, $\varepsilon = 128$, and $t = 100$.

in incomplete or missing edges. In contrast, the proposed technique affects low gray scale edges only, while the high gray scale edges remain relatively intact. Processing the micro-crack using the proposed technique would result in blurred response in the diffused image since this type of defect is characterized by low gray scale and high gradient. Theoretically, subtracting this image from the original undiffused background would enhance the defect by removing some of the background components.

In this study, the proposed anisotropic diffusion filtering is performed in three steps. First, the filtered image, $I_e(x,y)$, is smoothed using a 2-D Gaussian filter of size 5×5 yielding $I_d(x,y,0)$. Second, the smoothed image is then processed using Equation 8 to produce the edge stopping threshold matrix, $g(x,y)$, which in turn is used to calculate the diffusion coefficient function given by Equation 7. Third, Equation 3 is invoked and the calculation is terminated after a few iterations. In this case, the iteration number is determined heuristically and is usually less than 10 in most cases.

The resulting diffused image has a blurred response due to the low-pass filtering effect of the diffusion process. The smoothing effect varies between pixels, and the extent of this depends on the edge stopping threshold value in $g(x,y)$. For a pixel with a low threshold value, the smoothing is significant and yields a very blurred response. In contrast, this image processing technique produces image

which is approximately equal to the original image if the smoothing effect is weak. As previously explained, the resulting image is obtained by subtracting $I_d(x,y,t)$ from $I_d(x,y,0)$ to produce the new, enhanced image denoted as $I_\Delta(x,y)$. Figure 8 illustrates the images produced by these enhancement procedures using Figure 4d (ii) and Figure 4e (ii) as input images. Referring to Figure 8a (iii), the micro-crack line is enhanced and clearly visible after subtraction.

2.4 Post-processing

This section presents a post-processing involved in the segmentation of the $I_\Delta(x,y)$. It consists of two thresholding stages: (i) binary image reconstruction using double thresholding and (ii) the intensity tracing and thresholding. All threshold values are calculated using an adaptive thresholding technique [13]. The general expression of adaptive thresholding is given by

$$\tau = \mu - \alpha\sigma \tag{9}$$

where μ and σ are the mean and the standard deviation of the gray level intensity of the input image, respectively, and α is a scaling factor.

In the first stage, we adopted a similar approach based on double thresholding technique described in Nashat et al. [14]. This method requires $I_\Delta(x,y)$ to be segmented twice, first using a high threshold value τ_S and second using a low threshold value τ_T. Equation 9 is used to compute τ_S and τ_T using scaling factors α_S and α_T, respectively. This segmentation technique produces two binary images referred herein as the seed image B_S and the target image B_T. In this case B_S consists of mainly incomplete but noise-free edges, whereas B_T contains complete edges and noise. The next step in the segmentation involves reconstructing the final binary image B_F from B_S and B_T followed by dilation and closing. In this case, B_F contains $\{S_1, S_2,..., S_N\}$ where S represents the shape in the form of binary connected components and N is the number of shapes following the first stage thresholding step. The resulting binary images are presented in Figure 9 using Figure 8a (iii) and Figure 8b (iii) as input images.

Next, the intensity tracing and thresholding are performed on B_F using $I_e(x,y)$ as the reference image. The purpose of this procedure is to further reduce the noise or the unwanted shapes, such as scratches, dislocation clusters, or grain boundaries. The gray values of these artifacts are relatively higher compared to those of the micro-crack pixels. This procedure helps to improve the feature extraction because it significantly reduces the number of shapes.

For each binary shape S in B_F, the value of the gray intensity composed of pixels at the same location and

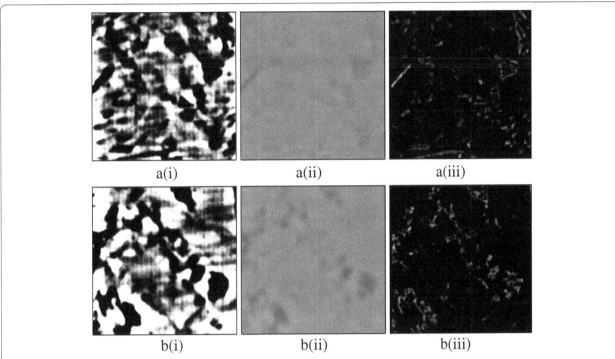

Figure 8 Image filtering using the proposed anisotropic diffusion technique. (a) Defected sample and **(b)** good sample: (i) image processing of $I_d(x, y, 0)$ using Equation 8 with $b = 1$ and $\varepsilon = \mu_{I_e}$, (ii) $I_d(x, y, t)$ for $t = 4$, and (iii) $I_\Delta(x, y)$.

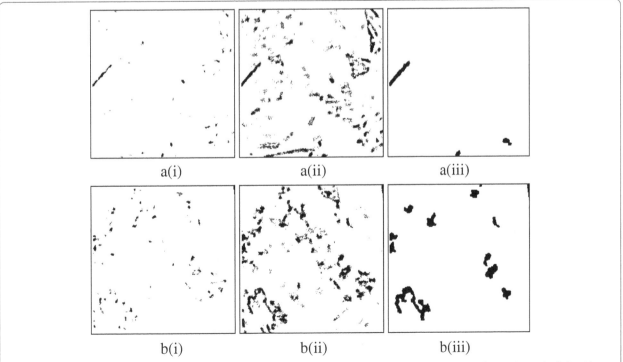

Figure 9 Results after image segmentation using double thresholding technique. (a) Defected sample and **(b)** good sample: (i) B_S with $a_S = 0$, (ii) B_T with $a_T = -4$, and (iii) B_F.

bounded by the same contour S is traced and extracted from the normalized image after pre-processing. The mean value of the gray intensity for each extracted pixels group is computed. Any shape that has a mean value which is less than the specific threshold is retained in B_F. Otherwise, it is treated as noise and hence eliminated. Again, the adaptive thresholding given in Equation 9 is used with α_{tr} fixed experimentally while μ and σ are obtained from $I_e(x, y)$. These procedures generate a new set of shapes $\{S_1, S_2, ..., S_{N_F}\}$ whose number is less than the ones contained in the original set (i.e., $N_F \leq N$). An example of the intensity tracing and thresholding is shown in Figure 10 using Figure 9a (iii) as an input image. In this example, the number of shapes is reduced from 3 to 1.

2.5 Shape analysis

The image processing procedures described in the above paragraph have successfully enhanced micro-cracks as well as other objects while suppressing most of the noise pixels. As seen from previous section, the resulted binary image contains several binary connected components that represent crack and other artifacts. Figure 11 displays some of the objects detected by the algorithm. From this figure, the pixels that represent micro-crack can be distinguished from other artifacts because the former is characterized by some unique shapes and sizes. Therefore, shape analysis is used in order to distinguish between micro-cracks and other objects. This analysis produced features from shape descriptors which are later used in machine learning and classification.

In performing shape analysis, the region-based descriptor known as angular radial transform (ART) [15,16] is investigated. The standard number of orders of ART is used to represent all binary shapes. The transform has 36 coefficients, and they are used as shape descriptors. Figure 12 shows examples of the ART spectrum for the micro-crack and arbitrary shapes. As seen in Figure 12,

a normalized ART spectrum for the micro-crack shape has more distinct fluctuation compared to the arbitrary shape. This translated into an increased average distance between the two spectrums and will result to a better discrimination of the shapes.

The features extracted are used to train the artificial classifier. In this study, support vector machines (SVMs) are used in machine learning and artificial intelligence. It is a supervised learning algorithm originally developed for two-class classification problems [11]. Therefore, this classifier is suitable for this type of application. Micro-crack shape features are assigned as positive class, while arbitrary shape features are assigned as negative class. Preliminary experiment suggested that the number of micro-crack shapes is far less than that of arbitrary shapes. Due to the unbalanced number of shapes between classes, the SVM classification may result in a bias toward the class having the most number of samples. This problem is addressed by utilizing a soft margin or penalty parameter which was set to different values for each class [17]. This approach is similar to the implementation of a fuzzy membership associated with the penalty parameter [18]. In this case, the optimal values of the penalty parameter for the positive and the negative classes are chosen experimentally. Also in this study, the SVM is trained using a kernel based on the Gaussian radial basis function (RBF). In summary, the methods and procedures implemented for micro-crack detection of solar cells are summarized in a block diagram shown in Figure 13.

3. Result and discussion

In this section, the experimental results from the methods and procedures described in the above sections are presented. This includes the image segmentation and classification. All experiments are performed on a desktop computer equipped with a dual core 2.80 GHz processor, 2 GB of RAM, and an installed MATLAB software package. The results obtained in this section are based on 600 samples of which 313 are good samples and the remaining are defected or cracked cells.

3.1 Image processing

Examples of the segmentation results for defected and good cells are shown in Figure 14. It can be seen from Figure 14a (i-iv) and the corresponding segmented images in Figure 14a (v-viii) that the integrity of the binary connected components (shapes) that represent the micro-crack pixels is well preserved. Referring to these figures, the micro-crack shapes can be easily distinguished from the arbitrary shapes visually. For comparison, the segmentation results of good or intact cells are shown in Figure 14b (v-viii).

For the thoroughness of analysis, the proposed segmentation technique is compared with standard methods such

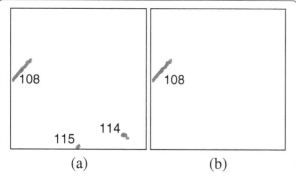

(a)   (b)

Figure 10 Results from intensity tracing and thresholding. (a) Before and **(b)** After with α_{tr} = 1.5. Each numeral in the image corresponds to the average gray intensity value of each shape.

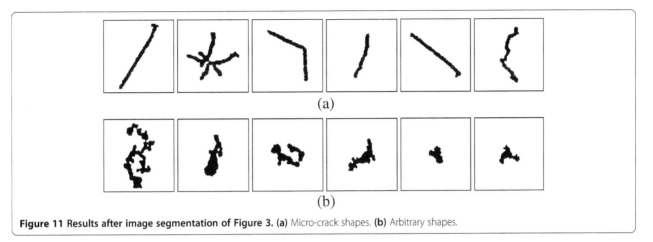

Figure 11 Results after image segmentation of Figure 3. (a) Micro-crack shapes. **(b)** Arbitrary shapes.

as Otsu's thresholding, the Canny hysteresis, the Sobel edge detector, and the Laplacian of Gaussian (LoG) filter. In addition, a recent method based on Fourier image reconstruction (FIR) [9] is also implemented. Figure 15 shows the close-up view of the results of these different segmentation techniques using images in Figure 14a (i-iv) as input images. In this case, the ground truth images are plotted manually by an expert human inspector. It can be seen from Figure 15b that the segmentation using Otsu's global thresholding technique is able to detect micro-crack as well as other pixels. Meanwhile, both the Sobel detector and Canny hysteresis thresholding resulted in incomplete or disjointed micro-crack pixels. On the other hand, the LoG is only effective in detecting a limited number of micro-crack pixels, particularly the large ones as evident

from Figure 15e. In contrast, the FIR method is accurate when detecting well-defined micro-crack pixels especially the ones appearing like straight lines. This method failed to completely detect star-shaped micro-crack pixels as evident from Figure 15f. In contrast, the results from the proposed segmentation technique are shown in Figure 15g. Clearly, the proposed method is able to detect all shapes and sizes of micro-crack pixels in the image. Close examination of this figures revealed that some unwanted pixels also appeared in the segmented images. They are mostly due to the presence of dark regions in the solar cell. Since their appearance are distinctly different from micro-crack pixels, the use of the ART shape descriptor helped reduce the error resulting from misdetection.

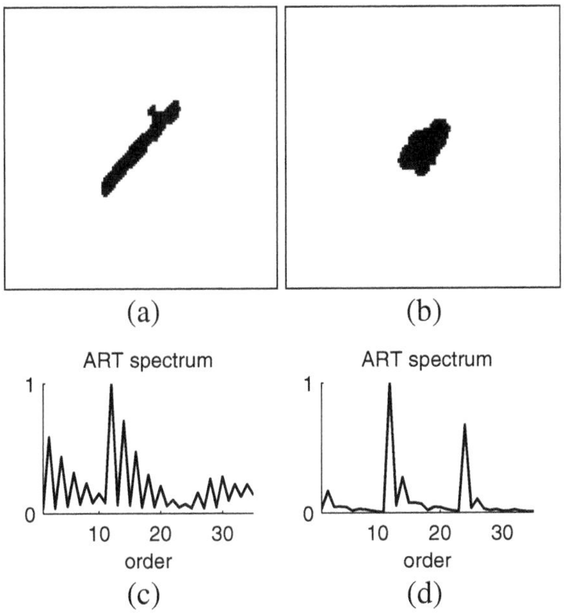

In order to quantitatively evaluate the accuracy of the proposed segmentation technique, the merit based on the F-measure is used [19]. Mathematically,

$$F = 2\frac{\text{cpt} \times \text{crt}}{\text{cpt} + \text{crt}} \qquad (10)$$

where cpt and crt are the completeness and correctness indices given by the following equations:

$$\text{cpt} = \frac{\ell_r}{\ell_{\text{GT}}} \qquad (11)$$

and

$$\text{crt} = \frac{\ell_r}{\ell_N} \qquad (12)$$

where ℓ_{GT} is the number of micro-crack pixels in the corresponding ground truth image, ℓ_r is the number of pixels in the segmented image which matches the ground truth micro-crack pixels, and ℓ_N is the total number of extracted pixels in the segmented image. Examples of ground truth images corresponding to defected cells in Figure 15a (i-iv) are shown in Figure 15h (i-iv), respectively. On the other hand, the cpt index indicates the completeness of the segmentation technique in detecting

Figure 12 Example of the ART spectrums for different types of shapes. (a) Micro-crack, **(b)** arbitrary, and **(c, d)** normalized ART spectrums corresponding to shapes in **(a)** and **(b)**, respectively.

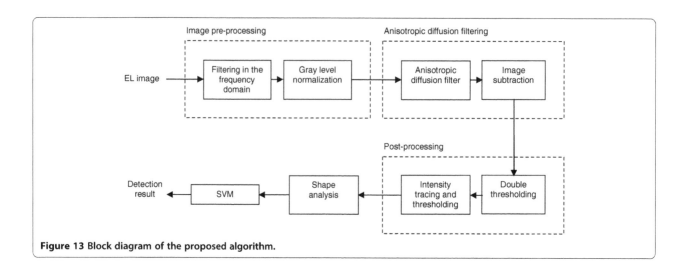

Figure 13 Block diagram of the proposed algorithm.

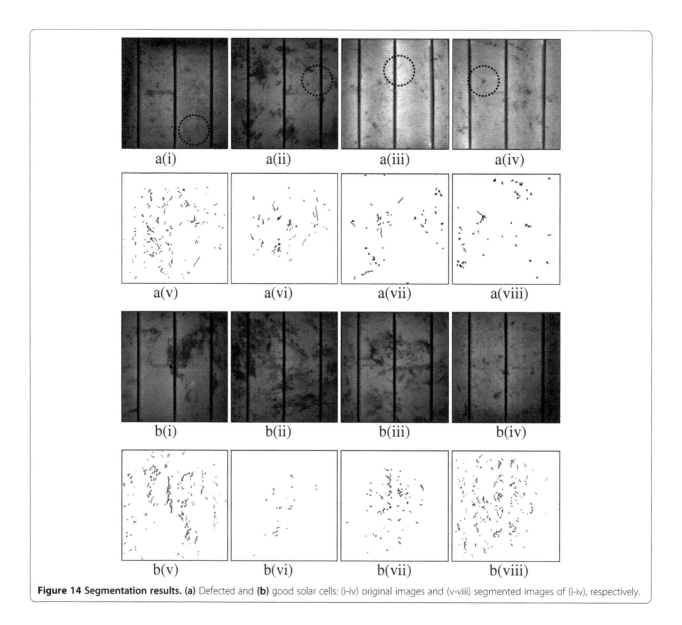

Figure 14 Segmentation results. (a) Defected and **(b)** good solar cells: (i-iv) original images and (v-viii) segmented images of (i-iv), respectively.

Micro-crack detection of multicrystalline solar cells featuring an improved anisotropic diffusion filter...

29

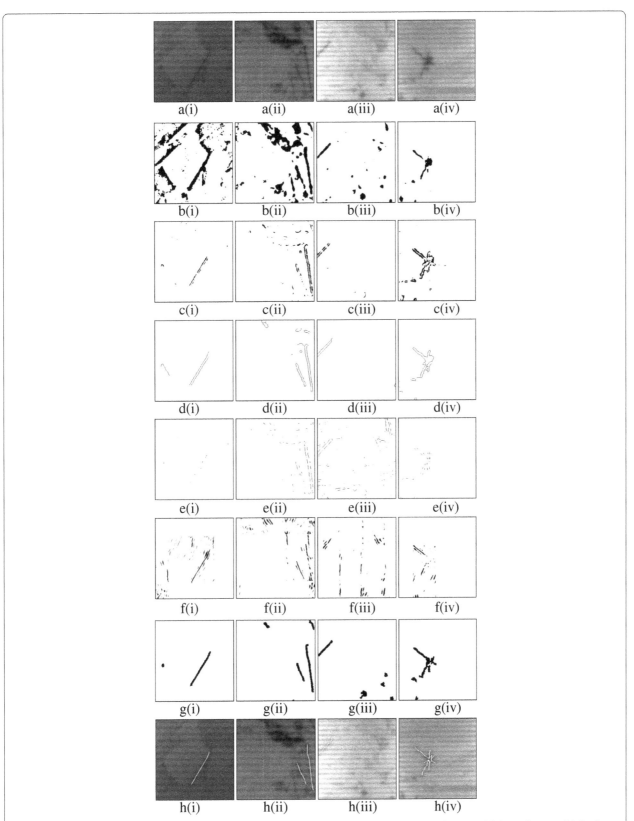

Figure 15 Image segmentation results comparing the proposed and standard segmentation techniques. (a) Original image, **(b)** Otsu's thresholding, **(c)** Sobel edge detector, **(d)** Canny's hysteresis, **(e)** LoG filter, **(f)** FIR, **(g)** the proposed method, and **(h)** ground truth images.

micro-crack pixels in the defected solar cells. Clearly, from Equation 11, cpt is equal to 1 if $\ell_r = \ell_{GT}$, indicating the perfect match between the number of micro-crack pixels detected by the algorithm and the ground truth image. In contrast, cpt is equal to 0 if there is no match. Meanwhile, the crt index measures the correctness of the segmented image produced. Similarly, this index is equal to 1 if the segmented image matches the ground truth. Practically, $\ell_r \leq \ell_N$ since micro-crack as well as noise pixels are also detected. Hence crt also ranges from 0 to 1. Calculating cpt and crt enables the F-measure to be computed using Equation 10. In this case, the higher the F-measure, the better the image segmentation.

The cpt and crt indices calculated from defected cell images in Figure 15 are tabulated in Table 1. These indices are also calculated for the remaining 110 defected cells which are not shown in this paper. The average values are listed in the last column of Table 1. Referring to this table, the completeness of Otsu's method is the highest compared to other algorithms. But this is not the case for correctness as the crt index for this algorithm is the second lowest. Consequently, Otsu's method reconstructs many micro-crack pixels as well as noise as evident visually in the examples in Figure 15. As expected, the Sobel edge detection and Canny hysteresis methods produce only average results for both completeness and correctness. The same trend is observed for the FIR method. In contrast, the LoG filter produces the lowest cpt and crt scores, suggesting that this method does not correctly or completely detect micro-crack pixels. Meanwhile, the proposed segmentation technique yields the highest crt and the second highest cpt scores. This result suggests that this method has the ability to completely and correctly characterize micro-crack with small amount of noise.

Meanwhile, the results of F-measure are shown graphically in Figure 16. It can be seen from this figure that the F-measure score produced by the proposed segmentation algorithm is consistently higher compared to other techniques. Overall, the proposed algorithm results in F-measure averaging at 0.0821 compared to 0.0216 FIR, 0.0028 LoG, 0.0258 Canny, 0.02288 Sobel, and 0.0153 Otsu. This again proves that the proposed method is more efficient in detecting micro-cracks in solar cells.

In the anisotropic diffusion filtering technique proposed in this study, there are few parameters that need to be tuned. These parameters are b and ε for the sigmoid mapping function and t which is the number of iterations for anisotropic diffusion. Meanwhile, ε corresponds to the average intensity of the input image μ_{I_e}. This simplified the computation of the mapping function as the target micro-crack pixels have the intensity below this average value. Meanwhile, parameter b represents the gradient of the sigmoid mapping function. Higher value of this parameter resulted in steeper gradient for the mapping function. Figure 17 demonstrates the effect of changes in the value of b on $I_\Delta(x, y)$ using Figure 15a as input images. Clearly from this figure, the best result is obtained for $b = 1$. Hence, this value was used to process all images reported in this paper.

Another important parameter in the anisotropic diffusion filtering is the number of iterations t in which the image needs to be diffused. This parameter must be properly chosen to ensure successful enhancement of the micro-crack pixels at a minimal computational cost. The higher the number of the iteration, the longer the computational time. Figure 18 shows the normalized values of cpt, crt, and F-measure for the different numbers of iteration. These indices are averaged from 114 defected cells. As can be seen from Figure 18, the highest value of F-measure occurred at $t = 1$. However, the cpt index corresponding to first iteration is significantly low, indicating the image that it produces is incomplete. Hence, the image needs

Table 1 Completeness and correctness measures of the segmentation results

Measure	Method	Figure 15a (i)	Figure 15a (ii)	Figure 15a (iii)	Figure 15a (iv)	Overall average
cpt	Otsu	0.9747	0.9706	0.8410	0.6304	0.8832
	Sobel	0.2686	0.4029	0.2538	0.4137	0.3703
	Canny	0.1248	0.1751	0.0275	0.1048	0.1248
	LoG	0.0316	0.0472	0	0.0520	0.0492
	FIR	0.4976	0.3668	0.3547	0.2057	0.2952
	Proposed	0.9368	0.8873	0.8899	0.7510	0.7185
crt	Otsu	0.0026	0.0089	0.0153	0.0586	0.0078
	Sobel	0.0064	0.0248	0.0061	0.0123	0.0122
	Canny	0.0086	0.0290	0.0015	0.0151	0.0157
	LoG	0.0004	0.0016	0	0.0034	0.0014
	FIR	0.0156	0.0302	0.0110	0.0286	0.0116
	Proposed	0.0195	0.0843	0.0258	0.0854	0.0462

Micro-crack detection of multicrystalline solar cells featuring an improved anisotropic diffusion filter...

31

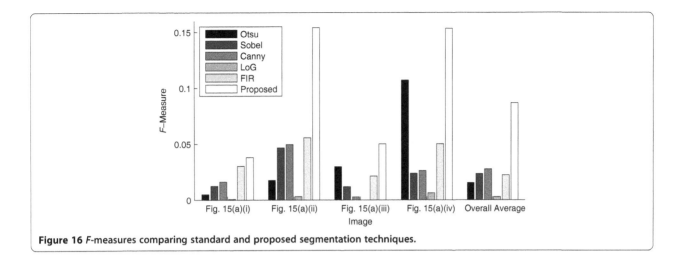

Figure 16 *F*-measures comparing standard and proposed segmentation techniques.

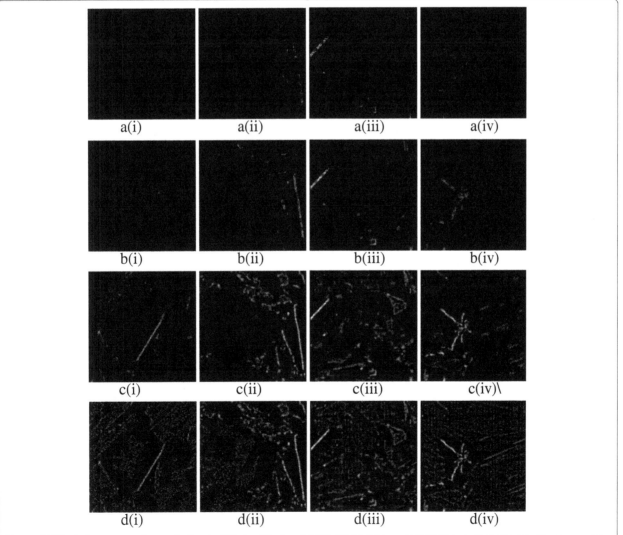

Figure 17 Effect of parameter *b* on anisotropic diffusion filtering. (a) 0.01, **(b)** 0.1, **(c)** 1, and **(d)** 10. All images are filtered using $\varepsilon = \mu_{l_e}$ and $t = 4$ for all images.

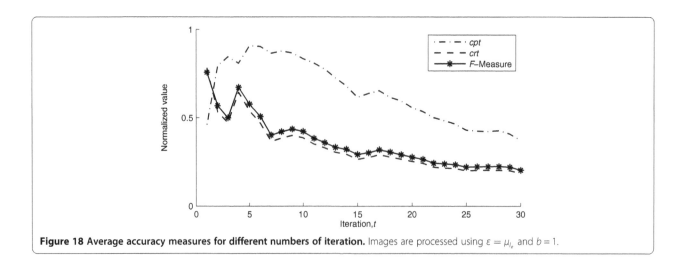

Figure 18 Average accuracy measures for different numbers of iteration. Images are processed using $\varepsilon = \mu_{I_e}$ and $b = 1$.

to be iterated further in order to improve the cpt index. Close examination of Figure 18 revealed that the second highest F-measure occurs at the fourth iteration. Even though the cpt decreases slightly at this iteration, the image is more complete and less noisy compared to the first iteration. A further increase in the number of iteration would result in the decrease of the F-measure as well as the cpt and crt indices. Therefore, the diffusion process of

all images shown in this paper is terminated after the fourth iteration ($t = 4$).

The performance of the proposed algorithm is also compared with the existing adaptive anisotropic diffusion techniques. Respectively, the images in Figure 19a,b are the results of improved diffusion filters [20,21], while Figure 19c is the image produced by the proposed algorithm. Clearly from this figure, the existing adaptive diffusion

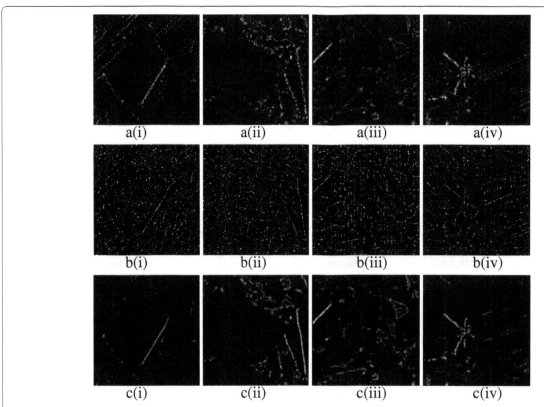

Figure 19 Image subtraction results comparing the proposed and existing adaptive anisotropic diffusion filters. (a) Filter proposed in [20] with $K_0 = 2$, **(b)** filter proposed in [21] with $K_0 = 80$, and **(c)** filter proposed in this study. All diffused images used in the subtraction are obtained after $t = 4$.

filters contain many spurious responses and noisy pixels. Visually, the defect, particularly in Figure 19b, appears to be completely buried in noise, causing the difficulty in extracting features from this image. In contrast, the image produced by the proposed algorithm is less noisy, and the defect can clearly be seen as evident from Figure 19c. Therefore, these results suggest that the existing adaptive anisotropic diffusion filters are not effective in processing micro-crack defects in solar cell images. Moreover, the algorithms can be very time-consuming since the diffusion coefficients are computed locally compared to the global technique employed in the proposed method.

3.2 Shape classification

Shape analysis is performed in order to primarily distinguish between micro-crack and other arbitrary pixels. This is due to the fact that the micro-crack pixels form shapes which are visually distinct like line or star patterns. On the other hand, shapes formed by the spurious intensity variation or gray level discontinuities produce arbitrarily patterns which are also detected by the proposed image processing algorithm. In doing so, the ART shape descriptor discussed earlier in Section 2.4 is implemented. The

algorithm is evaluated using 114 defected and 126 intact cells. Altogether, 5,598 shapes have been detected of which 218 belong to the micro-crack category and the remaining are arbitrary patterns. The ART is applied to these shapes, and the results are visualized in principal component plots in Figure 20a. In this case, only the first two dominant components, i.e., first and second components, are used in the visualization.

For comparison purpose, the scattered plots of shape features produced by the well-known methods like (i) the Fourier descriptor (FD) [22], (ii) the generic Fourier descriptor (GFD) [23], and (iii) the projection-based Radon composite features (RCF) [24] are also included in this figure. A close examination of Figure 20 shows that the overlap between micro-crack and other arbitrary shapes is more prominent in Figure 20b,c,d than in Figure 20a. All micro-crack shapes in Figure 20b,c,d occupy the regions that are enclosed within other arbitrary shapes. Clearly, there is no unique demarcation between these two groups in the PCA space. Hence, any attempt to use FD, GFD, or RCF as features in the classification scheme would result in many samples being misclassified. In contrast, the overlap between the groups is less prominent for ART features, as

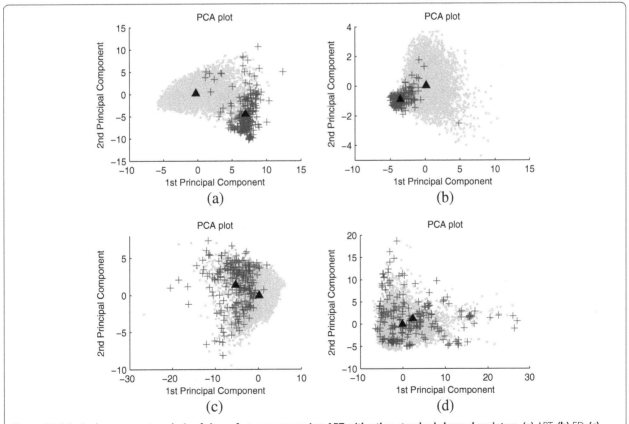

Figure 20 Principal component analysis of shape features comparing ART with other standard shape descriptors. (a) ART, **(b)** FD, **(c)** GFD, and **(d)** RCF. Here, the filled circle represents arbitrary shapes, the plus sign indicates micro-crack shapes, and the filled triangle symbolizes the centroid of each group.

shown in Figure 20a. It can be seen that the other arbitrary shapes are skewed to the right, whereas the micro-crack shapes are skewed to the left. Therefore, it is hypothesized that the features extracted using ART are more separable compared to those extracted using FD, GFD, and RCF.

This hypothesis is validated quantitatively using the separability measure. This measure reflects the discriminative capability in the features of each class; the higher the separability, the higher the discrimination between the groups. Figure 21 shows a comparison of the separability measure between ART, FD, GFD, and RCF. In this case, the separability measure for ART is the highest, registering a value of 12 compared to less than 9 for FD, GFD, and RCF. This result confirms that the features obtained using ART have more discriminative power compared to features obtained using FD, GFD, and RCF.

In this study, altogether 600 randomly selected solar cells have been evaluated from which 240 cells belong to the training set and the remaining 360 cells constitute the test set. Table 2 tabulates the distribution of cells in the training and testing sets. During testing, the classifier produced a positive output when the cell is defected with micro-crack and a negative output when it is intact.

For the training set, there are 5,598 shapes, of which 218 belong to micro-crack shapes and the remaining 5,380 are arbitrary patterns. These features are used to train the SVM. For the sake of completeness, the classifications are repeated using a linear discriminant analysis (LDA), quadratic discriminant analysis (QDA), and k-nearest neighbor algorithm (k-NN), from which the results are compared with SVM. Furthermore, the performance of each algorithm is quantitatively evaluated in terms of three measurable metrics: (i) sensitivity, (ii) specificity, and (iii) accuracy. These metrics are based on a simple measure of the true positive TP, the true

Table 2 Distribution of intact and defected cells in the dataset

Dataset	Defected	Intact	Total
Training	114	126	240
Testing	173	187	360

negative TN, the false positive FP, and the false negative FN. Mathematically, they are defined as follows:

$$\text{Sensitivity} = \frac{\text{TP}}{\text{TP} + \text{FN}} \qquad (13)$$

$$\text{Specificity} = \frac{\text{TN}}{\text{TN} + \text{FP}} \qquad (14)$$

$$\text{Accuracy} = \frac{\text{TP} + \text{TN}}{\text{TP} + \text{TN} + \text{FP} + \text{FN}} \qquad (15)$$

Additionally, the geometric mean is also used in the evaluation. The value of the geometric mean will be high when both the sensitivity and the specificity are high, and the difference between them is small [25]. The use of a geometric mean is an important measure when evaluating the classifier performance, especially for the unbalanced class sizes. The geometric mean is calculated as follows:

$$G\text{-Mean} = \sqrt{\text{Sensitivity} \times \text{Specificity}} \qquad (16)$$

The results using the testing set are shown in Table 3. In this table, the SVM is trained with the following parameters: $\sigma_{\text{RBF}} = 27$, $C^+ = 390$, and $C^- = 19$. Clearly, from Table 3, the SVM classifier outperformed LDA, QDA, and k-NN in term of sensitivity, accuracy, and G-Mean assessment metrics. Overall, less than 3% of defected cells are misclassified, and more than 80% of good cells are correctly classified. However, the k-NN classifier performed best in the classification of good cells with 88% specificity. Nevertheless, the SVM produces the highest G-Mean, indicating that the error in misclassification of this algorithm is consistently low. Therefore, SVM is overall the best classifier for this type of application.

For completeness, SVM experiments were repeated using FD, GFD, and RCF shape descriptors, and the results

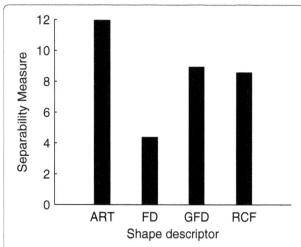

Figure 21 The separability measures comparing the ART, FD, GFD, and RCF shape descriptors.

Table 3 The classification results of the testing set

Classifier	Descriptor	Sensitivity	Specificity	Accuracy	G-Mean
LDA	ART	0.9306	0.7594	0.8417	0.8406
QDA	ART	0.9711	0.7166	0.8389	0.8342
k-NN	ART	0.8266	0.8824	0.8556	0.8540
SVM	ART	0.9769	0.8021	0.8861	0.8852
	FD	0.9711	0.4332	0.6917	0.6486
	GFD	0.9595	0.4973	0.7194	0.6908
	RCF	0.9653	0.5936	0.7722	0.7570

Micro-crack detection of multicrystalline solar cells featuring an improved anisotropic diffusion filter...

35

are also given in Table 3. Clearly, ART outperformed other shape descriptors in all assessment metrics. This again demonstrated that ART gives the best discriminating ability when dealing with this type of shape classification problem compared to other shape descriptors. In addition, the average processing time for each EL image is approximately 4.1 s which is comparable to the semi-manual inspection by a human expert. Meanwhile, the smallest micro-crack detected by the proposed algorithm is 47 pixels in size which physically corresponds to 6.22 mm in length.

4. Conclusions

The early detection of micro-cracks in solar cells is important in the production of PV modules. In this study, an image processing scheme composed of segmentation procedures based on anisotropic diffusion and shape classification is presented. The results show that the segmentation procedures can detect and identify micro-crack pixels efficiently in the presence of various forms of noise. The anisotropic diffusion filtering with gray level-based diffusion coefficient proposed in this study produced excellent enhancement and improved segmentation. The advantage of this filtering technique is its ability to enhance the pixels with low gray scale and high gradient such as the micro-crack defects in solar cell. Trained with SVM using 240 samples, this artificial classifier produced a correct classification rate of consistently higher than 88% with average sensitivity and specificity of 97.7% and 80.2%, respectively. These results are very promising as it demonstrates a first attempt of integrated image processing and machine learning platform toward its eventual application of micro-crack inspection of solar cells.

Competing interests
The authors declare that they have no competing interests.

Acknowledgements
This work is supported by the Malaysia Collaborative Research in Engineering, Science and Technology Centre (CREST) 304/PELECT/6050264/C121.

References
1. Solarbuzz, World solar photovoltaic market grew to 27.4 gigawatts in 2011, up 40% y/y. http://www.solarbuzz.com/news/recent-findings/world-solarphotovoltaic-market-grew-274-gigawatts-2011-40-yy-0 (2012). Accessed 27 of January 2013
2. YC Chiou, JZ Liu, YT Liang, Micro crack detection of multi-crystalline silicon solar wafer using machine vision techniques. Sens. Rev. **31**(2), 154–165 (2011)
3. TK Wen, CC Yin, Crack detection in photovoltaic cells by interferometric analysis of electronic speckle patterns. Sol. Energy. Mater. Sol. Cells. **98**, 216–223 (2012)
4. A Belyaev, O Polupan, W Dallas, S Ostapenko, D Hess, J Wohlgemuth, Crack detection and analyses using resonance ultrasonic vibrations in full-size crystalline silicon wafers. Appl. Phys. Lett. **88**(11), 111907 (2006)
5. M Demant, S Rein, J Krisch, S Schoenfelder, C Fischer, S Bartsch, R Preu, *Proceedings of the 2011 37th IEEE Photovoltaic Specialists Conference (PVSC)* (Seattle, Washington, USA, 2011), pp. 001641–001646
6. M Köntges, I Kunze, S Kajari-Schröder, X Breitenmoser, B Bjørneklett, The risk of power loss in crystalline silicon based photovoltaic modules due to micro-cracks. Sol. Energy. Mater. Sol. Cells. **95**(4), 1131–1137 (2011)
7. A Bastari, A Bruni, C Cristalli, Proceedings of the, IEEE International Symposium on Industrial Electronics (ISIE). Bari, Italy **2010**, 1722–1727 (2010)
8. S Kajari-Schröder, I Kunze, U Eitner, M Köntges, Spatial and orientational distribution of cracks in crystalline photovoltaic modules generated by mechanical load tests. Sol. Energy. Mater. Sol. Cells. **95**(11), 3054–3059 (2011)
9. DM Tsai, SC Wu, WC Li, Defect detection of solar cells in electroluminescence images using Fourier image reconstruction. Sol. Energy. Mater. Sol. Cells. **99**, 250–262 (2012)
10. DM Tsai, CC Chang, SM Chao, Micro-crack inspection in heterogeneously textured solar wafers using anisotropic diffusion. Image. Vis. Comput. **28**(3), 491–501 (2010)
11. C Cortes, V Vapnik, Support-vector networks. Mach. Learn. **20**(3), 273–297 (1995)
12. P Perona, J Malik, Scale-space and edge detection using anisotropic diffusion. IEEE. Trans. Pattern. Anal. Mach. Int. **12**(7), 629–639 (1990)
13. M Sezgin, S Bl, Survey over image thresholding techniques and quantitative performance evaluation. J. Electr. Imag. **13**(1), 146–168 (2004)
14. S Nashat, A Abdullah, MZ Abdullah, Unimodal thresholding for Laplacian-based Canny–Deriche filter. Pattern. Recogn. Lett. **33**(10), 1269–1286 (2012)
15. M Bober, MPEG-7 visual shape descriptors. IEEE. Trans. Circuits. Syst. Video. Technol. **11**(6), 716–719 (2001)
16. SK Hwang, WY Kim, Fast and efficient method for computing ART. IEEE. Trans. Image. Process. **15**(1), 112–117 (2006)
17. K Veropoulos, C Campbell, N Cristianini, *Proceedings of the International Joint Conference on AI* (Sweden, Stockholm, 1999). pp. 55–60
18. CF Lin, SD Wang, Fuzzy support vector machines. IEEE. Trans. Neural. Net. **13**(2), 464–471 (2002)
19. Q Li, Q Zou, D Zhang, Q Mao, SA Fo, F* seed-growing approach for crack-line detection from pavement images. Image. Vis. Comput. **29**(12), 861–872 (2011)
20. SM Chao, DM Tsai, Astronomical image restoration using an improved anisotropic diffusion. Pattern. Recogn. Lett. **27**(5), 335–344 (2006)
21. SM Chao, DM Tsai, An improved anisotropic diffusion model for detail- and edge-preserving smoothing. Pattern. Recogn. Lett. **31**(13), 2012–2023 (2010)
22. CT Zahn, RZ Roskies, Fourier descriptors for plane closed curves. IEEE. Trans. Comput. **C-21**(3), 269–281 (1972)
23. D Zhang, G Lu, Shape-based image retrieval using generic Fourier descriptor. Signal. Process. Image. Commun. **17**(10), 825–848 (2002)
24. YW Chen, YQ Chen, Invariant description and retrieval of planar shapes using radon composite features. IEEE. Trans. Signal. Process. **56**(10), 4762–4771 (2008)
25. M Kubat, RC Holte, S Matwin, Learning when negative examples abound, in *Machine Learning: ECML-97, vol. 1224. Lecture Notes in Computer Science*, ed. by M Someren, G Widmer, 1224th edn. (Springer, Berlin Heidelberg, 1997), pp. 146–153

3

Complementary feature sets for optimal face recognition

Chandan Singh[1], Neerja Mittal[2]* and Ekta Walia[3]

Abstract

In face recognition tasks, one kind of feature set is not adequate to generate superior results; thus, selection and combination of complementary features are crucial steps. In this paper, the fusion of two useful descriptors, i.e., the Zernike moments (ZMs) and the local binary pattern (LBP)/local ternary pattern (LTP), has been proposed. The ZM descriptor consists of good global image representation capabilities besides being invariant to image rotation and noise, while the LBP/LTP descriptors capture the innate details within some local parts of face image and are insensitive to illumination variations. The fusion of these two is observed to incorporate the traits of both of these individual descriptors. Subsequently, in this work, the performance of diverse feature sets of ZMs (i.e., magnitude features, magnitude plus phase features, and the real plus imaginary component features) combined with the LBP/LTP descriptor is analyzed on FERET, Yale, and ORL face databases. The recognition results achieved by the proposed method are approximately 10 to 30% higher than those obtained with these descriptors separately. Recognition rates of the proposed method are also found to be significantly better (i.e., by 8 to 24%) in case of single example image per person in the training.

Keywords: Face recognition; Zernike moments (ZMs); Local binary pattern (LBP); Local ternary pattern (LTP); Invariant image features

1 Introduction

In recent times, face recognition has become one of the widely used biometric techniques having a number of real-world applications like human-computer interaction, surveillance, authentication, computer vision applications, computer user interfaces, etc. An automatic face recognition system consists of some methods to ascertain a person's identity on the basis of his/her physiological characteristics. The sensitivity of available classifiers to different kinds of disparities such as illumination variation, facial expression, facial occlusion, pose variation, aging, etc. is among the most challenging problems that the researchers face [1].

In order to improve the existing face recognition techniques, discriminative competence of the invariant features selected to represent the face images should be high because, thereafter, classification is performed on the basis of these invariant features only. In literature,

the approaches used to represent the face images are classified broadly into two categories, namely, the global feature extraction approaches and the local feature extraction approaches [2]. The global feature extraction approaches are based on the statistical methods, wherein features are extracted from the whole face image. In this category, the subspace-based methods, namely, principal component analysis (PCA), Fisher linear discriminant (FLD), two-dimensional PCA (2DPCA), and two-directional two-dimensional PCA ($2D^2PCA$) [3-7], are some of the popular and most frequently employed techniques. Moment invariants, such as Hu's seven moment invariants and orthogonal rotation invariant moments such as Zernike moments (ZMs), pseudo-Zernike moments (PZMs), and orthogonal Fourier-Mellin moments (OFMMs), are observed to be very effective in global image description and recognition [8], and MPEG-7 uses some of them as region-based shape descriptors for image retrieval [9]. The magnitude of these moments is invariant to image rotation, and after applying some geometric transformations, it becomes invariant to translation and scale [10,11].

---

* Correspondence: neerjamittal_2k1@yahoo.com
[2]Central Scientific Instruments Organisation, Sector 30-C, Chandigarh 160030, India
Full list of author information is available at the end of the article

Local feature extraction approaches deal with fine information within the specific parts of face images such as eyes, nose, mouth, etc. Recently, a lot of work has been done on these methods because the local features are known to be robust against illumination, occlusion, expression, and noise variations. The local feature extraction approaches have been classified into two categories, i.e., the sparse descriptors and the dense descriptors. The sparse descriptors initially divide a face image into patches and then determine its invariant features. A prominent descriptor in this category is the scale-invariant feature transform (SIFT) introduced by Lowe [12], which possesses useful characteristics of being invariant to scale and rotation. Soyel et al. used the discriminative SIFT (D-SIFT) approach for optimal facial expression recognition, but this method is somewhat susceptible to the illumination variation [13]. In face recognition technology, Gabor wavelet is one of the most frequently used and successful local image descriptors. It incorporates the characteristics of space and frequency domains. The local features extracted by Gabor filters are invariant to scale and orientation and are able to detect edges and lines in the face images [14]. The main difficulty with Gabor filters is their high computational complexity. In case of the dense descriptors, local binary pattern (LBP) is one of the most widely used approaches due to its invariance to monotonic gray-level changes and ease in extraction of the local features. Apart from texture analysis, it has provided excellent results in many areas of image processing and computer vision including its wide use in face recognition [15,16]. Several variants of LBP are available in literature to represent face images with compact feature sets. Such variants also improve the classification performance of the basic LBP approach [17,18].

In complex applications like face recognition, it is observed that one kind of feature set is not rich enough to capture the entire face information. Thus, finding and combining the complementary feature sets have become an active research topic in recent years. Specifically, global features are related to the holistic characteristics of face, whereas local features describe the finer details within face images, so it seems logical to combine both of these feature sets since the information conveyed by them belongs to different attributes of the face images. In recent times, many researchers are developing the face recognition algorithms by combining the multiple feature sets. Kim et al. [19] have proposed a combined subspace-based approach using both global and local features obtained by applying linear discriminant analysis (LDA)-based method for face recognition. Zhou and Yang [20] have proposed fusing feature Fisher classifier (F^{3}C) approach where the face image is first divided into smaller subimages and then the discrete cosine transform (DCT)

technique is applied to the whole image and some subimages to extract the holistic and local facial features. After concatenating these DCT-based holistic and local facial features, the enhanced Fisher linear discriminant model (EFM) has been employed to generate a low-dimensional feature vector. Similarly, local and global information extracted by using DCT coefficients along with the Fisher classifier developed for high-dimensional multiclass problem have been proposed in [21]. Singh et al. proposed a robust two-stage face recognition approach by the fusion of global ZMs and Weber law descriptor (WLD)-based local features [22]. The usefulness of combining the global and local facial features is presented in [23] where a hierarchical ensemble of global and local features is performed. In this technique, 2D Fourier transform is used to extract the global features and the Gabor wavelet is opted to extract local features. Subsequently, equal weights are assigned to both the global and local features for combining the outputs of two classifiers (although it is established by the authors that the contribution of both global and local features is different). Wong et al. have proposed dual optimal multiband feature (DOMF) method for face recognition in which wavelet packet transform (WPT) decomposes the image into frequency subbands and the multiband feature fusion technique is incorporated to select optimal multiband feature sets that are invariant to illumination and facial expression. In this method, parallel radial basis function (RBF) neural networks are used to classify the two sets of features. The decision scores are then combined and processed by an adaptive fusion mechanism [24]. The use of steerable pyramid decomposition (S-P transform) both in global and local appearance and feature/score fusion has been analyzed in [25]. In this work, each face image is described by a subset of band-filtered images containing steerable pyramid coefficient. These S-P subbands are divided into small subblocks to extract the compact and meaningful feature vectors that provide a better representation of the class information. Recently, Liu and Liu [26] have proposed an approach for face recognition that fuses color and local spatial and global frequency information. This method is composed of multiple features of face images derived from LBP, DCT, hybrid color space, and the Gabor image representation. The combination of Gabor and LBP enhances the power of spatial histogram that is impressively insensitive to appearance variations. This method has proven to be robust against illumination, pose, and expression variations [27,28]. However, the combination of Gabor and multiresolution LBP descriptors requires significantly greater computation time.

Although a lot of research is going on combining the multiple feature sets, still the selection of complementary feature sets for fusion and the techniques for combining these divergent feature sets are a challenge. In view of that, in this paper, a fusion of two complementary feature sets is proposed, where the global information of the face images is extracted by the ZM descriptor employing its rotation invariance characteristic, while the LBP/LTP descriptor captures the significant local information. Among various global shape descriptors, ZMs are observed to be one of the best shape descriptors because of their many attractive characteristics [8]. They possess minimum information redundancy, rotation invariance of their magnitude, robustness to noise, etc. The estimation of head movement by using the phase coefficients of ZMs of the original image and that of the rotated image has been employed to generate a set of features that is significantly tolerant to pose variation as well [29]. The magnitude features of ZMs obtained at some higher order of moments are observed to be invariant to expression variation [30]. On the other hand, the LBP descriptor is observed to be relatively more insensitive to illumination changes. It is computationally efficient as well as quite simple to implement. Recently, a useful extension to this approach is introduced, namely, the local ternary patterns (LTP), that is observed to be more discriminative and invariant to image noise in near-uniform regions as compared to LBP [18]. Particularly, combining the feature sets that are invariant to global variations as well as to local changes of face images would be an effective approach to achieve an optimal face recognition system. As discussed earlier, the information conveyed by the ZM and LBP/LTP descriptors are distinct and belong to different aspects of a facial image. Fusion of these descriptors is expected to be enriched with the useful characteristics of both of them. One of the critical issues involved in the fusion process is the time spent in the computation of the combined features. It is shown through time analysis of the proposed approach that the total time required for the recognition process is very small and can be afforded by PCs and other low computation devices.

The ZM descriptor provides three different sets of features, namely, magnitude features, combined magnitude and phase features [31,32], and the modified real and imaginary component features [29]. In this study, these diverse feature sets of ZMs are referred to as ZM_{mag}, $ZM_{magPhase}$, and $ZM_{component}$, respectively. The performance of the feature sets of ZMs combined with LBP descriptor, in comparison to that of the ZMs coupled with the LTP descriptor, is also analyzed. Consequently, the proposed fusion of the diverse feature sets of ZMs and the LBP/LTP descriptors provides various combined approaches such as $ZM_{mag}LBP$, $ZM_{magPhase}LBP$, $ZM_{component}LBP$, $ZM_{mag}LTP$, $ZM_{magPhase}LTP$, and $ZM_{component}LTP$. In order to compare the performance of these combined approaches to that of the individual ZM and LBP/LTP approaches, exhaustive experiments are performed on three prominent face databases, namely, FERET, Yale, and ORL,

against pose, illumination, expression, and noise variations. The results obtained show that the recognition rate of the combined approaches, in comparison to that of their individual counterparts, is significantly better varying between 10 and 30%. Experimental results also prove the efficacy of the proposed methods over other existing works. A significant improvement in recognition rate is achieved for the case of single training image per person.

The rest of the paper is organized as follows: Section 2 presents a brief overview of the ZM approach and the diverse feature sets obtained from it and includes a brief introduction to the LBP/LTP approaches, Section 3 describes the similarity measures used to evaluate the matching score of these methods, the procedure involved in the proposed fusion of the ZM and the LBP/LTP descriptors is described in Section 4, the experiments and results obtained are presented in Section 5, and the conclusions and future directions are presented in Section 6.

2 Baseline image descriptors
2.1 Global image descriptor
2.1.1 Zernike moments
The Zernike functions constitute a set of orthogonal basis functions mapped over the unit circle. Zernike moments of a function $f(x, y)$ are constructed by projecting it onto those functions. The ZMs of order n and repetition m are defined by

$$Z_{nm} = \frac{n+1}{\pi} \iint_{x^2+y^2 \leq 1} f(x, y) V_{nm}^*(x, y) dx dy \qquad (1)$$

where $n \geq 0$, $|m| \leq n$, and $V_{nm}^*(x, y)$ are the complex conjugates of the Zernike function $V_{nm}(x, y)$, where

$$V_{nm}(x, y) = R_{nm}(x, y)e^{jm\theta} \qquad (2)$$

with $= \sqrt{-1}$, $\theta = \tan^{-1}(y/x)$, $\theta \in [0, 2\pi]$, and

$$R_{nm}(x, y) = \sum_{s=0}^{(n-|m|)/2} \frac{(-1)^s (n-s)!(x^2+y^2)^{\frac{n-2s}{2}}}{s!\left(\frac{(n+|m|)}{2}-s\right)!\left(\frac{(n-|m|)}{2}-s\right)!} \qquad (3)$$

The ZMs are derived for a discrete image function using zeroth-order approximation of Equation 1 given by [10]

$$Z_{nm} = \frac{n+1}{\pi} \sum_{i=0}^{N-1}\sum_{k=0}^{N-1} f(i, k) V_{nm}^*(x_i, y_k)\Delta^2 \qquad (4)$$
$$x_i^2 + y_k^2 \leq 1$$

where

$$x_i = \frac{2i + 1 - N}{N\sqrt{2}}, y_k = \frac{2k + 1 - N}{N\sqrt{2}}, \qquad (5)$$

$$i, k = 0, 1, 2, ..., N-1, \text{ and } \Delta = \frac{2}{N\sqrt{2}}$$

2.1.2 Diverse feature sets of ZMs and related work

Since the magnitude of ZMs is invariant to rotation, usually it is used as invariant image descriptor in many image analysis and pattern recognition applications. The phase component of ZMs is, however, ignored. It is observed that the phase component also carries equally significant information as the magnitude component does [31]. Therefore, in recent years, significant research work has been carried out to incorporate ZM phase coefficients along with their magnitudes as invariant feature descriptors. At present, there are two approaches to realize this objective. In the first approach, developed by Revaud et al. [33], a similarity measure incorporating both the magnitude and phase coefficients of the query and database image is used. The method provides excellent pattern matching performance but at the cost of enhanced computation time. In the second approach, the rotation angle between a query image and the database image is estimated. It is assumed that the query image is the rotated version of the original database image. The estimated rotation angle is used to cancel the effect of rotation in order to compare the phases of the query and database images. Recently, we devised a novel way to correct phase coefficients without estimating rotation angle. The method was applied successfully in face recognition [29]. The method works as follows: Suppose Z_{nm} and Z'_{nm} are the ZMs of database and query images, respectively, and ϕ_{nm} and ϕ'_{nm} are their respective phase angles. We compute $m\theta = \phi_{nm} - \phi'_{nm}$ and correct the ZMs of the query image by evaluating $Z'^c_{nm} = Z'_{nm} e^{jm\theta}$. If the two images are same, then $Z'^c_{nm} = Z_{nm}$, otherwise $Z'^c_{nm} \neq Z_{nm}$; therefore, the real and imaginary components of ZMs of the query and database images can be compared separately, instead of comparing only their magnitude. An attractive advantage of this approach is that by using two-component feature vectors, the number of features is almost doubled as compared to the ZM magnitude only features for the same order of moments. This approach has additional advantages of having low computation cost, less susceptibility to image noise, and numerical stability, in addition to providing better recognition rate [29]. Throughout the paper, these features of ZMs based on magnitude, magnitude together with corrected phase [31], and the corrected real and imaginary parts of ZMs [29] are

referred to as ZM_{mag}, $ZM_{magPhase}$, and $ZM_{component}$, respectively.

2.2 Local image descriptor

2.2.1 Local binary pattern

Ojala et al. have introduced the local binary patterns (LBP) for effective texture description that has been used in many image processing and computer vision applications [15]. The most important property of this approach is its tolerance against illumination variation. Being computationally simple, it provides significant advantage over other approaches. The LBP operator takes some specific neighborhood around each pixel, and it then thresholds the values of these neighborhood pixels with respect to the central pixel's value. The resulting binary pattern is used as an element of the local image descriptor. Thus, it assigns a label to every pixel p_i of an image by thresholding its respective 3×3 neighborhood values with the value of the central pixel p_c and producing the result in the form of an 8-bit binary code. The LBP operator is computed as

$$LBP = \sum_{i=0}^{7} 2^i b(p_i - p_c) \qquad (6)$$

$$b(p_i - p_c) = \begin{cases} 1, & \text{if } p_i \geq p_c \\ 0, & \text{otherwise} \end{cases} \qquad (7)$$

where the values of i move along the eight neighbors of the central pixel. In case of 8-bit patterns, Ojala et al. [15] have observed that out of 2^8 patterns, only 58 uniform patterns provide approximately 90% information of the image neighborhoods while the remaining patterns consist of mostly noise. This attribute significantly reduces the number of LBP histogram bins from 256 to 59 where all the non-uniform patterns are stored in a single bin, the 59th bin.

2.2.2 Local ternary patterns

The local histogram features obtained from LBP have proven to be highly discriminative in face recognition [16,17]. However, they are found to be sensitive to noise because of the fact that they are thresholded exactly at the value of the central pixel especially in near-uniform and smooth regions of face images like cheeks or forehead. Recently, an important extension to the original LBP is provided by Tan et al. [18]. It generates three-valued codes corresponding to each image pixel. In their method, the binary LBP code is replaced with the ternary LTP code and the gray values in a zone of width $\pm w$ around the central pixel p_c are quantized to 0 and the values above this zone are quantized to +1 while those below it are quantized to −1. Specifically, the value of

$b(x)$ given in Equation 7 is replaced with the following three-valued function:

$$b'\left(p_i, p_c, w\right) = \begin{cases} 1, & p_i \geq (p_c + w) \\ 0, & |p_i - p_c| < w \\ -1, & p_i \leq (p_c - w) \end{cases} \qquad (8)$$

where w is a user-defined threshold. The LTP code is assumed to be invariant to image noise but may not be strictly invariant to gray-level transformations. The concept of uniform patterns to obtain histogram features is also applicable to LTP. For simplicity, the three-valued LTP codes are split into their positive and negative bisects which generate two sets of histogram features out of which one corresponds to the positive patterns and the other represents the negative patterns [18].

3 Similarity measures used

In this section, the similarity measures used for finding the matching scores of ZM and LBP/LTP descriptors are discussed briefly. In this work, it is observed that the fusion of matching scores obtained by applying $L_2 -$ Norm/$L_1 -$ Norm on the ZM descriptor and histogram intersection on the LBP/LTP descriptor generates superior performance. Hence, these different similarity measurement techniques are used on the feature sets generated by these descriptors. Since the matching scores obtained from these different approaches are heterogeneous, normalization is required to transform these matching scores to a common range before combining them.

3.1 Similarity measure for ZM descriptor

The magnitude features of ZMs, i.e., ZM_{mag}, of two images are compared by evaluating the normalized Euclidean distance ($L_2 -$ Norm) between them. The normalized $L_2 -$ Norm between the two sets of feature vectors of ZMs is given by

$$d_{mag} = \frac{1}{L} \sqrt{\frac{\left(|Z'_i| - |Z_i|\right)^2}{\max\left(|Z'_i|^2, |Z_i|^2\right)}} \qquad (9)$$

where Z'_i and Z_i are the feature vectors of the query and the database images, respectively, and L represents the size of the feature vector consisting of the magnitude of ZMs. The normalized Euclidean distance d_{Phase} defined by [31], between ZM phases of the query and the database images, is computed as

$$d_{Phase} = \frac{1}{L} \sqrt{\sum_{i=1}^{L} \frac{1}{2\pi}\left(|\varphi'_i| - |\varphi_i|\right)^2} \qquad (10)$$

where φ is the phase angle of the database image and φ' is the phase angle after estimating the rotation angle between the query and database images and correcting the

phase [31]. The total distance $d_{magPhase}$ between the feature vectors consisting of $ZM_{magPhase}$ coefficients has been evaluated by using the distances d_{mag} and d_{Phase}, computed as per Equations 9 and 10, respectively. The formula used to compute the $d_{magPhase}$ is given as

$$d_{magPhase} = \left(w_1 d_{mag} + w_2 d_{Phase}\right)/(w_1 + w_2) \qquad (11)$$

Normally, equal weights are assigned to simplify this process, i.e., $w_1 = w_2 = 0.5$.

The $ZM_{component}$ descriptor includes the modified real and imaginary parts of ZMs to formulate a two-component feature vector for each ZM. The normalized $L_1 -$ Norm-based distance measure for the evaluation of similarity between component features of the database and the query images is given as under

$$d_{comp} = \frac{1}{L}\sum_{i=1}^{L} \frac{\left(|Re(Z_i) - Re(Z'^c_i)|\right)}{\max\left(|Re(Z_i)|, |Re(Z'^c_i)|\right)} + \frac{\left(|Im(Z_i) - Im(Z'^c_i)|\right)}{\max\left(|Im(Z_i)|, |Im(Z'^c_i)|\right)} \qquad (12)$$

The above mentioned distance metric d_{comp} has proven to be a better similarity measure between two sets of component feature vectors [29].

3.2 Similarity measure for LBP/LTP descriptor

The histogram intersection distance has been used to compare the feature vectors of query and database images for both the LBP and the LTP descriptors. The histogram intersection distance evaluated for every bin n between the database image and the query image is given as

$$D_h(Hd, Hq) = \frac{\sum_{n=1}^{B} \min(Hd_n, Hq_n)}{\min\left(\sum_{n=1}^{B} Hd_n, \sum_{n=1}^{B} Hq_n\right)}, \quad D_h(Hd, Hq) \in [0, 1] \qquad (13)$$

where Hd and Hq are the histograms consisting of LBP/LTP features of the database and the query images, respectively. B is the total number of bins in the histograms. If either of the two images, i.e., the database and the query images is identical, then the value of $D_h(Hd, Hq)$ is 1.

4 Fusion of ZM and LBP/LTP descriptors

The ZM descriptor and the LBP/LTP descriptors are observed to be complementary to each other, and their fusion is expected to be able to discriminate the face images even in the presence of diverse variations. The ZM descriptor is observed to extract the global information of the images more effectively as compared to that of any other global descriptor [9]. On the other hand, the LBP and the LTP descriptors have been established to be successful methods for representing the finer interior details within the face images. The feature set established by the fusion of these autonomous approaches, i.e., ZMs and the LBP/LTP, is supposed to be enriched with the invariant characteristics of both of them. Exhaustive experiments performed against pose, illumination, expression, and noise variations on the suitable databases prove that the said hypothesis is correct.

The procedure followed to recognize the face images by the proposed combined approaches, i.e., $ZM_{mag}LBP$, $ZM_{magPhase}LBP$, $ZM_{component}LBP$, $ZM_{mag}LTP$, $ZM_{magPhase}$ LTP, and $ZM_{component}LTP$, is briefly described in Figure 1. The recognition of face images through the proposed fusion of feature sets includes three stages - feature extraction, fusion of similarity score, and classification. The first stage of this procedure creates the invariant feature sets extracted by using ZM and LBP/LTP descriptors. The second stage involves fusion of the matching scores obtained from these feature sets after applying the similarity measures as described in the previous section. A number of feasible techniques such as fusion at the feature extraction level, matching score level, or decision level exist for combining the multiple feature sets. It is not easy to combine the information at the feature level when the feature sets obtained by different techniques are either inaccessible or incompatible. Fusion at the decision level is too rigid as only a limited amount of information is available at this level. Therefore, integration at the matching score level is generally preferred due to the

ease of accessing and combining matching scores [34]. In the proposed work, feature vectors are obtained by applying ZM and LBP/LTP descriptors which provide complementary information. Further, we observed that for the LBP/LTP descriptor, the matching score evaluated by the histogram intersection measure gives better results than using $L_2 - $Norm. Hence, in this work, the fusion at the matching score level is employed wherein the histogram intersection (using Equation 13) and $L_2 - $Norm (using Equations 9 and 11 for ZM_{mag} and $ZM_{mag-Phase}$)/$L_1 - $Norm (using Equation 12 for $ZM_{component}$) is used for evaluating the matching scores of the feature vectors obtained from the LBP/LTP and ZM descriptors, respectively. Thereafter, these individual matching scores are combined by using the sum rule to generate a single scalar score which is then used to make the final decision. The sum rule to compute the fusion of individual matching scores is given as below

$$\text{sum rule } (F_{sr}) = \frac{\{S_Z + (1-S_L)\}}{2} \qquad (14)$$

where S_Z and S_L represent the matching scores of the ZM descriptor and the LBP/LTP descriptors, respectively. The matching scores of these approaches are normalized before fusion. Normalization is required to map the matching scores obtained from multiple frameworks to a common range so that they can be easily combined. In order to combine these matching scores, S_L is subtracted

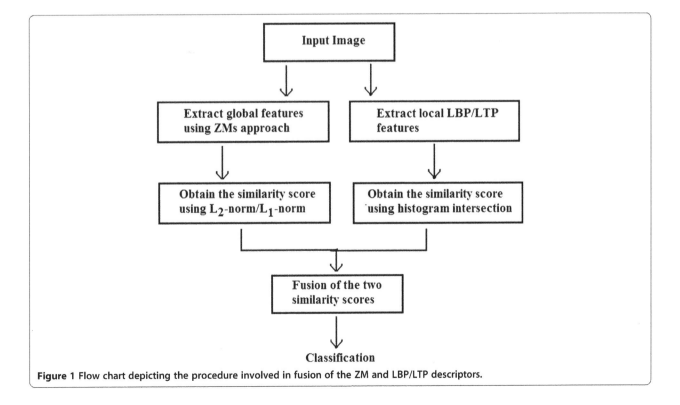

Figure 1 Flow chart depicting the procedure involved in fusion of the ZM and LBP/LTP descriptors.

from 1, so that the histogram intersection would now signify higher similarity with lower values. Finally, in the third stage, we use the nearest neighbor rule to perform classification. This method always gives us only one recognized image which is labeled as either correct or incorrect in order to evaluate the recognition performance. The recognition rate (in percentage) is measured by using the following formula:

$$\text{RecRate} = \frac{(N\text{test}-Nf)}{N\text{test}} \times 100 \qquad (15)$$

where $N\text{test}$ is the total number of images in the test set and Nf is the number of images recognized incorrectly.

5 Experiments and results

In order to evaluate the performance of the considered autonomous approaches in comparison to that of the proposed combined approaches, experiments are performed on three well-known and calibrated face databases, namely, FERET face database [35] consisting of images in diverse variations, Yale face database [36] consisting of illumination and expression variations, and ORL face database [37] having small pose (tilt/yaw) changes. It is well known that the accuracy of the face recognition system is significantly affected by the kind of variations present in images of the face database as well as by the number of images of each subject (i.e., person) in the training set. Thus, exhaustive experiments in a comprehensive and deterministic manner are performed with respect to different types of variations present in these databases. The number of training images per person is also varied to observe its effect on recognition accuracy. The best results are highlighted in italics. All the experiments are performed in Visual C++6.0 under Microsoft Windows environment on a PC with a 3.0-GHz CPU and a 3-GB RAM.

5.1 Performance on FERET database

FERET grayscale face database has become the most popular and standard database in the field of face recognition. We have performed experiments on two subsets of this database, consisting of the frontal to profile pose variation. The first subset is formed by randomly selecting 100 persons with seven different poses (yaw) 0°, ±22.5°, ±67.5°, and ±90°. The second subset consisted of FERET 'b' category images of 200 persons in different illumination, expression, and pose angles of 0°, ±15°, ±25°, ±40°, and ±60°. In this work, the first subset is called FERET_A. It consists of 700 images. The second subset is named as FERET_B and contains 2,200 images. FERET evaluation protocol partitions the database into gallery (1,196 images of 1,196 persons) and four probe sets, namely, *fafb, fc, dup I*, and *dup II*. The images in the *fafb* set are with facial expression

variation, the *fc* set contains images with illumination variations, and the images in the *dupI* and *dupII* sets represent aging effects. For detailed experimentation against pose, expression, and illumination variations, various data partitions are generated for these subsets which are described in Table 1. The original images of this database are of size 256 × 384 pixels. We transformed these images into 128 × 128-pixel size in order to reduce the time taken for conducting the experiments, while the face images from FERET_Gallery/Probe subset are cropped and resized to 64 × 64 pixels. Some sample images, for one person, from this database are shown in Figure 2. The face images of FERET_A, FERET_B, and FERET_Gallery/Probe subsets are partitioned into 64 patches of 16 × 16 and 8 × 8 pixels, respectively, to extract the local LBP/LTP features, while the global ZM features are extracted from whole face images.

In order to analyze the performance of the proposed combined approaches, the first set of comprehensive experiments is performed on FERET_A1 category as described in Table 1. The different possible trials for this setup, containing various combinations of the training and the test sets, are shown in Table 2. The average recognition performance of the individual and the combined approaches over these different trials (seven) is presented in Figure 3 for different values of maximum order of ZMs, denoted by n_{max}. Further, it is pertinent to mention here that the values of n_{max} have no effect on the performance of the LBP and LTP descriptors. So, the results presented for the LBP/LTP descriptors remain the same for each value of n_{max}. From the results presented, it is observed that among the autonomous approaches, the performance of the $ZM_{component}$ approach is better than that of others. However, the proposed combined approaches exhibit significantly high recognition rates compared to their individual counterparts. In this experiment, the $ZM_{magPhase}LBP$ approach provides the highest recognition rate at 71.24%.

Next, experiments are performed on FERET_A2 category, and the recognition results are presented in Figure 4 for both the individual and the combined approaches over different order of moments n_{max} used for the ZM descriptors. The basic LBP/LTP descriptors are not invariant to rotation; however, in this category, they perform better than the ZM descriptor. This is due to the fact that the higher pose angles occlude a significant portion of the face and on this kind of distortion, the local feature sets are observed to be more successful than the global features. On the other hand, the proposed fusion of the ZM descriptors and the LBP/LTP descriptors achieves approximately 20% improvement in the recognition results in comparison to that of these independent approaches. It is also noticed that the ZM descriptors coupled with the LBP descriptor generate superior results and the highest recognition rate

Table 1 Data partition on FERET database for performing various experiments

Set of experiment	Category	Training	Testing	Remarks
1	FERET_A1	One image of each person resulting in a total of 100 images	Remaining six images of each person in different pose variations, i.e., a total of 600 images	Seven different trials of this setup (as shown in Table 2) have been taken, and the recognition result given in Figure 3 is the average of all these trials
2	FERET_A2	One image of each person in frontal, i.e., 0° pose	Six remaining images having pose variations of ±22.5°, ±67.5°, and ±90°	Against the frontal pose image, all the images in different poses (≤ ±90°) are taken for testing
3	FERET_A3	One image in frontal pose	Four images having pose variations of ±22.5° and ±67.5°	Testing the performance for small and large pose variation up to ±67.5°
4	FERET_A4	One image in frontal pose	Two images in ±67.5° pose angle	Testing the performance for large pose variation in the left and right directions
5	FERET_A5	One image in frontal pose	Two images in ±22.5° pose angle	Testing the performance for small pose variation in the left and right directions
6	FERET_B1	One image in frontal pose, i.e., the image labeled 'ba', is in the training set	Ten remaining images having illumination, expression, and pose (up to ±60°) variations, i.e., the images labeled bk, bj, bb, bc, bd, be, bf, bg, bh, and bi, are kept in the test set	Images consisting of all the three variations, i.e., illumination, expression, and pose (up to ±60°), are taken for testing against the frontal pose image. A total of 200 images are in the training set, and 2,000 images are in the test set
7	FERET_B2	Three random images of each person resulting in a total of 600 images	Remaining seven images of each person in different variations, i.e., 1,600 images	Ten different trials of this setup have been taken, and the recognition result (Table 3) is the average of all these trials
8	FERET_B3	One image of each person in frontal pose, i.e., the image labeled 'ba,' is in the training set and contains a maximum of 200 face images in it	Eight images of each person having pose variations (up to ±60°), i.e., the images labeled bb, bc, bd, be, bf, bg, bh, and bi, are kept in the test set resulting in a maximum of 1,600 images in it	This category consists of the images of 200 persons in 9 pose variations, from frontal to profile pose, resulting in a total of 1,800 images in it. In this category, the different experiments are carried out by varying the number of subjects (persons) in the database
9	FERET_Gallery/ Probe	Standard gallery set fa contains 1,196 images of 1,196 subjects in frontal view	fafb, fc, dupl, and dupll	The images in the fafb (1,195 images) set are with facial expression variation, the fc (194 images) set contains images with illumination variation, and the images in the dupl (722 images) and dupll (234 images) sets represent aging effects

of 77.33% is accomplished by the $ZM_{magPhase}LBP$ approach. In case of the LTP descriptor, the LTP combined with the $ZM_{component}$ descriptor, i.e., $ZM_{component}LTP$, provides better results than those of other combinations.

Further experiments are performed on FERET_A3, FERET_A4, and FERET_A5 categories. The recognition results for these setups are shown in Table 3. On this database, fusion of the ZM features obtained for $n_{max} = 9$ provides better results. Accordingly, here, all other experiments have been conducted only for this order of moments. It is observed from Table 3 that there is an improvement in recognition rates by approximately 10 to 20% due to the fusion of the ZM and LBP/LTP descriptors. Further, it is observed that the recognition rates decline significantly with increase in the pose angle of test images (e.g., the highest recognition rate of only 74.5% is noticed for FERET_A4 which contains pose variations of ±67.5° in test images). This outcome is

obvious because of the fact that the presence of the higher pose angle will occlude a significant part of the face image. The highest recognition rate of 86.5% is achieved by the $ZM_{magPhase}LBP$ approach on FERET_A3 category. On FERET_A5 category, a superior recognition

Table 2 Different trials for one image in training and remaining six in test set for FERET_A1 category

Trial	Image in training set in pose angle	Images in test set in pose angle
1	0°	±22.5°, ±67.5°, ±90°
2	+22.5°	0°, −22.5°, ±67.5°, ±90°
3	−22.5°	0°, +22.5°, ±67.5°, ±90°
4	+67.5°	0°, ±22.5°, −67.5°, ±90°
5	−67.5°	0°, ±22.5°, +67.5°, ±90°
6	+90°	0°, ±22.5°, ±67.5°, −90°
7	−90°	0°, ±22.5°, ±67.5°, +90°

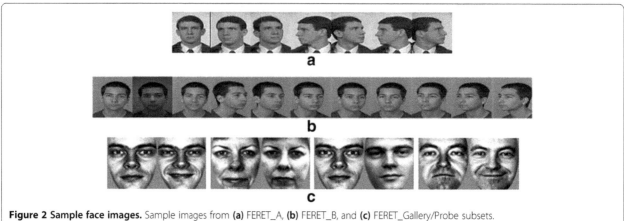

Figure 2 Sample face images. Sample images from **(a)** FERET_A, **(b)** FERET_B, and **(c)** FERET_Gallery/Probe subsets.

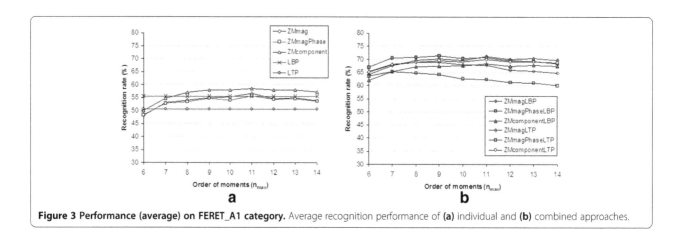

Figure 3 Performance (average) on FERET_A1 category. Average recognition performance of **(a)** individual and **(b)** combined approaches.

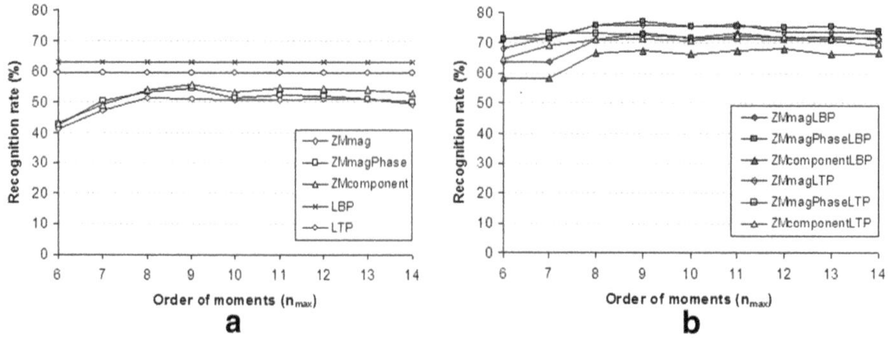

Figure 4 Performance on FERET_A2 category. Recognition results of **(a)** individual and **(b)** combined approaches.

Table 3 Performance of the considered approaches on FERET database

Descriptor	FERET_A3	FERET_A4	FERET_A5	FERET_B1	FERET_B2	FERET_Gallery/Probe			
						fb	fc	dupI	dupII
ZM_{mag}	63.75	34.0	93.5	62.0	76.3	67.53	31.8	35.0	38.0
$ZM_{magPhase}$	67.25	40.0	94.5	60.5	75.87	68.02	32.96	35.8	39.0
$ZM_{component}$	68.75	41.5	96.0	63.45	76.93	65.0	30.36	33.0	37.0
LBP	74.75	56.0	93.5	66.7	80.71	96.87	79.0	66.0	63.7
LTP	70.5	50.0	91.0	64.75	80.08	94.87	72.74	62.0	56.0
$ZM_{mag}LBP$	83.0	67.0	99.0	77.5	86.43	97.58	89.18	69.25	66.0
$ZM_{magPhase}LBP$	*86.5*	*74.5*	98.5	*78.5*	*88.2*	*98.04*	*91.5*	*69.39*	*66.5*
$ZM_{component}LBP$	79.5	59.5	*99.5*	74.05	84.69	96.0	88.0	68.5	64.0
$ZM_{mag}LTP$	84.5	70.0	99.0	76.3	85.48	93.0	85.0	65.0	59.5
$ZM_{magPhase}LTP$	81.75	65.5	98.0	75.55	85.97	93.5	85.8	65.7	58.5
$ZM_{component}LTP$	82.25	65.0	*99.5*	74.6	84.74	91.2	84.0	64.0	58.0

rate of 99.5% is achieved by both the $ZM_{component}LBP$ and the $ZM_{component}LTP$ approaches. Similarly, the $ZM_{magPhase}LBP$ approach provides the highest recognition rate on FERET_A4 category which reveals the contribution of ZM phase coefficients towards the improvement in recognition results.

For FERET_B, the recognition results obtained by performing the experiments on FERET_B1 and FERET_B2 categories are also shown in Table 3. It is clear from the experimental results that the combined approaches exhibit approximately 15 to 20% hike in the recognition rate than that obtained by the individual approaches. The highest recognition rate of 78.5 and 88.2% is achieved by the $ZM_{magPhase}LBP$ descriptor for FERET_B1 and FERET_B2 categories, respectively. The result obtained on FERET_Gallery/Probe set ascertains the robustness of the proposed system against changes in expression and lighting; however, further research in aging is required. In general, on FERET_B and FERET_Gallery/Probe subsets, the combination of $ZM_{magPhase}$ with LBP descriptor generates higher results than others.

5.2 Performance on Yale database

The Yale face database contains 11 images per person for 15 individuals resulting in a total of 165 images. The images in this database have major variations in illumination and facial expressions. They also have images demonstrating occlusion of eyes with eyeglasses. The original size of the images in this database is 243×320 pixels with 256 gray levels. For the experiments, these are cropped down to 64×64 pixels. Sample cropped images from this database, for one person, are shown in Figure 5. Here also, the face images are partitioned into 64 patches of 8×8 pixels to extract the local LBP/LTP features.

In order to examine the improvement in performance by the proposed combined approaches across the expression and illumination variations, exhaustive experiments are performed on this database by taking different number of images in training and test sets. Accordingly, for this purpose, various data partitions have been generated which are presented in Table 4. The first set of comprehensive experiments is performed on YALE 1 category where out of total 11 images of each person, one image is taken in the training set and all the remaining are placed in the test set. This process is repeated 11 times by taking different face images of each person in the training set. Average recognition results over 11 different runs of training and test sets are presented in Figure 6 for different n_{max} of ZMs.

From the results obtained, it is observed that an average improvement of approximately 12% is achieved by the proposed combined descriptors as compared to the individual approaches. In case of individual approaches, the performance of both the LBP and LTP approaches is better than that of the three descriptors of ZMs. The result obtained depicts that the local approaches are able to capture the interior details of a face image more efficiently than the global ones. This certainly enhances the

Figure 5 Sample cropped face images (a-k) for one person from Yale database.

Table 4 Data partition on Yale database for performing various experiments

Set of experiment	Category	Training	Testing	Remarks
1	YALE 1	Random one	All remaining (i.e., remaining ten images except the one selected for the training)	Eleven different trials of this setup have been taken, and the recognition result (Figure 6) is the average of all these trials
2	YALE 2.1	Random two	Remaining nine	The recognition result (Table 5) is the average of ten random trials on each setup, i.e., YALE 2.1, YALE 2.2, YALE 2.3, YALE 2.4, and YALE 2.5
	YALE 2.2	Random three	Remaining eight	
	YALE 2.3	Random four	Remaining seven	
	YALE 2.4	Random five	Remaining six	
	YALE 2.5	Random six	Remaining five	
3	YALE 3.1	a	f, g, h, i	Testing consists of experiments against illumination variation
	YALE 3.2	b, c, d, e, j, k	a, f, g, h, i	
	YALE 4.1	a	b, c, d, e, j, k	Testing consists of experiments against expression variation
	YALE 4.2	f, g, h, i	a, b, c, d, e, j, k	

suitability of these methods to outperform even in the presence of only a single exemplar image per person. From the results depicted in Figure 6, it is observed that among all the combined approaches, the highest recognition results are achieved by the $ZM_{magPhase}LBP$ descriptor. It is also observed that for the proposed combined methods, fusion of ZM features obtained for $n_{max} = 11$ provides better results. Hence, on this database, all other experiments have been carried out for this order of moments.

Next, the experiments are performed on YALE 2.1, YALE 2.2, YALE 2.3, YALE 2.4, and YALE 2.5 categories. The average recognition results over ten trials of each group of the training and the test sets are presented in Table 5. It is well known that the LBP and LTP descriptors are invariant to changes in intensities of the images, so the results obtained by these two approaches are quite higher than those obtained by the ZM descriptors. Hence, on this database, it has been realized that the LBP/LTP feature sets contribute much more towards the improvement in the recognition rate of the proposed

combined approaches which are significantly higher than the individual approaches. In most of the cases, the LBP and LTP descriptors combined with ZM_{mag} features generate superior results. For example, on YALE 2.4 category, the highest recognition rate of 97.56% is achieved by the $ZM_{mag}LBP$ approach. However, on YALE 2.3 category, the average highest recognition rate is 97.14% with the $ZM_{mag}LBP$ approach. Thus, in general, the proposed $ZM_{mag}LBP$ approach outperforms the others.

Thereafter, experiments are performed on YALE 3.1 and YALE 3.2 categories against illumination variation. Similarly, in order to examine the performance of the proposed approaches particularly over expression variation, experiments are carried out on YALE 4.1 and YALE 4.2 categories. The results obtained from these experiments are presented in Table 6. From the results shown, it is clearly noticed that the proposed combined approaches show an improvement in performance by approximately 30% over the ZM descriptors alone, whereas in comparison to the performance of individual LBP/LTP descriptors, an improvement of approximately 10% is achieved. As

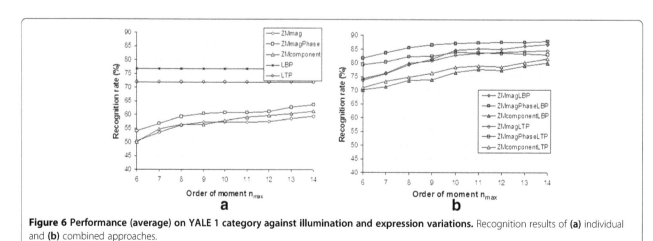

Figure 6 Performance (average) on YALE 1 category against illumination and expression variations. Recognition results of **(a)** individual and **(b)** combined approaches.

Table 5 Performance (average) of the individual/combined approaches on Yale database

Descriptor	YALE 2.1	YALE 2.2	YALE 2.3	YALE 2.4	YALE 2.5
ZM_{mag}	70.96	74.42	79.43	80.56	84.27
$ZM_{magPhase}$	74.37	79.08	81.62	81.33	84.53
$ZM_{component}$	74.29	77.75	81.05	81.22	83.6
LBP	89.11	89.67	93.14	92.89	93.33
LTP	85.85	89.75	92.57	94.22	93.73
$ZM_{mag}LBP$	93.19	94.83	*97.14*	*97.56*	*98.27*
$ZM_{magPhase}LBP$	*94.59*	94.83	96.67	96.78	96.67
$ZM_{component}LBP$	90.15	92.67	93.91	95.22	96.67
$ZM_{mag}LTP$	92.96	94.75	96.38	97.44	98.13
$ZM_{magPhase}LTP$	93.11	*95.5*	96.38	97.0	97.6
$ZM_{component}LTP$	91.04	93.92	94.57	95.89	96.53

described earlier, among the individual approaches, the performance of the LBP/LTP descriptors is better than that of the ZM descriptor. Between these two descriptors, the LBP descriptor generates higher recognition rate against the illumination and expression variations on YALE 3.1, YALE 3.2, and YALE 4.2 categories while the LTP descriptor gives higher results on only YALE 4.1 category for expression variation.

For illumination variation, i.e., on YALE 3.1 category, the highest recognition rate of 91.67% is achieved by the proposed $ZM_{mag}LBP$ approach, whereas against expression variation, the $ZM_{magPhase}LBP$ descriptor gives the highest recognition rate at 85.56% on YALE 4.1 category. Experiments are also conducted on YALE 3.2 category wherein all of the face images consisting of expression variation are taken in the training set and the remaining ones, i.e., one neutral and four images with illumination changes, are placed in the test set. The results for this setup are also shown in Table 6, from which it is observed that the performance of the $ZM_{mag}LBP$ as well as that of $ZM_{component}LBP$ is better. Particularly, on YALE 3.2

category, a superior recognition rate of 97.33% is achieved by both approaches. Similarly, in case of YALE 4.2 category, four images of each person consisting of illumination variation are used to create the training set while all of the remaining ones (i.e., one neutral and six images in varying expressions) are placed in the test set. As shown in Table 6, $ZM_{magPhase}LBP$ achieves a high recognition rate of 98.89% for this category. Thus, from the results shown in Table 6, it can be concluded that $ZM_{mag}LBP$ is illumination invariant and $ZM_{magPhase}LBP$ is expression invariant. If we look at the overall performance of the proposed approaches on Yale database, $ZM_{mag}LBP$ and $ZM_{magPhase}LBP$ outperform the other combinations.

5.3 Performance on ORL database

The ORL face database consists of a total of 400 images of size 112×92 pixels of 40 persons with ten images per person in different states of variation. All the face images in this database are taken against a dark homogenous background. These images contain slight pose variation (tilt and yaw) up to $\pm 20°$ with some basic facial

Table 6 Performance of the individual/combined approaches over illumination and expression variation on Yale database

Descriptor	YALE 3.1	YALE 3.2	YALE 4.1	YALE 4.2
ZM_{mag}	46.67	80.0	47.78	82.22
$ZM_{magPhase}$	61.67	84.0	54.44	81.11
$ZM_{component}$	53.33	81.33	50.0	81.11
LBP	83.33	85.33	66.67	96.67
LTP	76.67	76.0	72.22	96.67
$ZM_{mag}LBP$	*91.67*	*97.33*	84.44	97.78
$ZM_{magPhase}LBP$	88.33	96.0	*85.56*	*98.89*
$ZM_{component}LBP$	88.33	*97.33*	77.78	94.44
$ZM_{mag}LTP$	90.0	96.0	77.78	97.78
$ZM_{magPhase}LTP$	90.0	96.0	82.22	97.78
$ZM_{component}LTP$	88.33	94.67	72.22	96.67

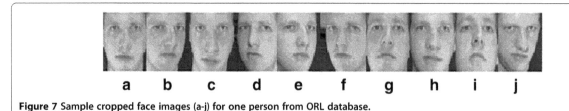

a   b   c   d   e   f   g   h   i   j

Figure 7 Sample cropped face images (a-j) for one person from ORL database.

expressions (smiling/not smiling, open/closed eyes). For performing experiments, the images of this database are cropped to 64×64 pixels. Sample cropped images for one person are shown in Figure 7. The face images of these databases are partitioned into 64 patches of 8×8 pixels to extract the local LBP/LTP features. Detailed experiments are performed on this database in order to analyze robustness of the proposed combined approaches against the pose variation. Various data partitions generated for this purpose are presented in Table 7.

Firstly, experiments are performed on ORL 1 category by taking one image of each person in the training set, and all of the remaining ones are used to formulate the test set. Different trials are framed in this case. As there are nine different images in the test set, ten combinations of different training and test images are possible here. The average recognition results over these ten different trials are shown in Figure 8a,b. The results on different values of n_{max} are depicted in order to analyze the effect of maximum order of moments n_{max} of ZMs on the performance of the proposed combined approaches. As the basic LBP and the LTP descriptors used in this work are not invariant to image rotation whereas the ZM descriptor is an established rotation invariant scheme, it is observed from the results that the performance of the individual ZM descriptors is better than that of the LBP/LTP descriptors for this database. Among the ZM-based descriptors, $ZM_{component}$ and $ZM_{magPhase}$ descriptors give the highest recognition rates because of the inclusion of phase coefficients. However, an improvement of more

than 10% is achieved by fusion of the invariant feature sets of the ZM and LBP/LTP descriptors wherein the ZM descriptor plays a significant role in achieving rotation invariance. The highest recognition rate of 81.22% is achieved by the proposed $ZM_{mag}LTP$ approach. From the results presented in Figure 8a,b, it is observed that in the proposed combined methods, fusion of the ZM features obtained at $n_{max} = 9$ provides better results on this database. Accordingly, further experiments have been conducted only on this order of moments.

The average recognition results over ten different trials of each group (i.e., ORL 2.1, ORL 2.2, ORL 2.3, and ORL 2.4) of the training and the test sets are presented in Table 8. Excellent results are obtained by the proposed combined approaches, while $ZM_{component}LTP$ provides the best results. On taking five images in training and the remaining five in the test set (i.e., for ORL 2.4 over ten runs), the average recognition rate of 99.2% is achieved by both the $ZM_{mag}LBP$ and $ZM_{component}LTP$ approaches. Further, $ZM_{component}$ features have proven to be invariant to image rotation and tolerant to pose variations to some extent [29]. From this analysis, we can state that the $ZM_{component}$ combined with LTP as well as the ZM_{mag} coupled with LBP provides superior results against pose variations.

Next, experiments are performed on ORL 3 category by taking two neutral face images in the training set, while four images of each person consisting of scale and up/down head movement are taken in the test set. Similarly, in order to examine the performance of the

Table 7 Data partition on ORL database for performing various experiments

Set of experiment	Category	Training	Testing	Remarks
1	ORL 1	Random one	All remaining (i.e., remaining ten images except the one selected for the training)	Ten different trials of this setup have been taken, and the recognition result (Figure 8) is the average of all these trials
2	ORL 2.1	Random two	Remaining eight	The recognition result (shown in Table 8) is the average of ten random trials on each setup, i.e., ORL 2.1, ORL 2.2, ORL 2.3, and ORL 2.4
	ORL 2.2	Random three	Remaining seven	
	ORL 2.3	Random four	Remaining six	
	ORL 2.4	Random five	Remaining five	
3	ORL 3	a, b	c, g, i, j	Testing consists of experiments against scale and up/down (tilt) pose variation
4	ORL 4	a, b	b, d, e, f	Testing consists of experiments against left/right (yaw) pose variation

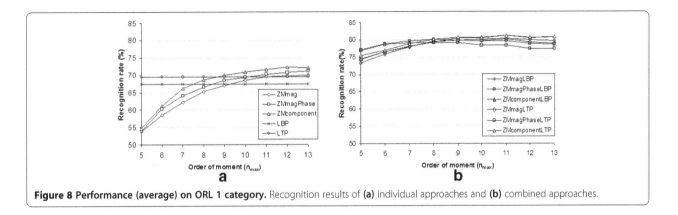

Figure 8 Performance (average) on ORL 1 category. Recognition results of **(a)** individual approaches and **(b)** combined approaches.

proposed approaches over yaw pose variation, two neutral images of each person are placed in the training set and four images with slight left/right head movement are placed in the test set, i.e., ORL 4 category. The results obtained from this experimental analysis are also presented in Table 8. On ORL 3 category, the performance of the $ZM_{component}$ coupled with that of the LBP/LTP descriptors is better, achieving a recognition rate of 90.0%. Similarly, on ORL 4 category, the highest recognition rate of 91.25% is achieved by both the $ZM_{mag}LBP$ and the $ZM_{magPhase}LBP$ approaches. Thus, in most of the cases of ORL database, the $ZM_{component}$ combined with LBP/LTP outperforms the other proposed combinations.

5.4 Performance analysis against noise variation

To examine the effect of noise on the recognition accuracy, we add impulsive noise, commonly named salt-and-pepper or spike noise, to the face images of the three databases. In the presence of impulsive noise, an image has dark pixels in bright regions and white pixels in dark regions [30]. In this analysis, a noise of 0.05 is added to the images of the test set whereas the training is done on original face images, i.e., on images with no noise.

The procedure of experimental setup to examine the performance of these approaches against additive noise is the same as before. That is, in order to analyze the performance on FERET database, experiments are performed on FERET_A3 data partition in which one frontal image (0° pose) is selected in the training set and the four images in different poses ($\pm22.5°$, $\pm67.5°$ and with additive noise) for each person are used in the test set. On YALE 2.4 data partition, robustness of the proposed approaches is analyzed against noise variation by selecting five images of each person in the training set and the remaining six images (with additive noise) in the test set. The results presented are the average recognition rates over ten different runs of training and test sets. In a similar manner, the experiments on the images of ORL 2.4 data partition are performed by taking random five images of each person in the training set and the remaining five images (with additive noise) in the test set, and the recognition results for the same are also the averaged recognition rates over ten different runs of training and test sets. The experimental results on the said databases are shown in Table 9.

From the results presented, it is observed that among the individual approaches, the LTP descriptor is more

Table 8 Performance of the considered approaches against different pose variations on ORL database

Descriptor	ORL 2.1	ORL 2.2	ORL 2.3	ORL 2.4	ORL 3	ORL 4
ZM_{mag}	81.87	88.71	93.08	94.55	81.88	80.63
$ZM_{magPhase}$	83.5	89.18	94.21	95.3	85.63	81.88
$ZM_{component}$	84.81	90.82	94.96	95.95	84.38	83.75
LBP	82.23	88.75	92.92	95.7	80.0	84.38
LTP	83.28	89.14	92.21	95.4	82.5	86.25
$ZM_{mag}LBP$	91.24	94.96	97.5	99.2	88.75	91.25
$ZM_{magPhase}LBP$	91.34	94.57	96.71	98.25	88.75	91.25
$ZM_{component}LBP$	92.47	95.07	97.5	98.9	90.0	88.75
$ZM_{mag}LTP$	90.69	94.39	97.08	98.85	88.13	88.13
$ZM_{magPhase}LTP$	90.0	93.64	96.5	98.35	86.88	90.0
$ZM_{component}LTP$	92.17	95.21	97.79	99.2	90.0	88.13

Table 9 Performance of the considered approaches against noise variation

Descriptor	Face datasets comprising additive noise in testing		
	FERET_A3	YALE 2.4	ORL 2.4
ZM_{mag}	62.75	80.22	94.65
$ZM_{magPhase}$	65.75	75.33	94.45
$ZM_{component}$	64.75	80.11	95.55
LBP	64.75	91.0	95.45
LTP	67.75	94.0	95.85
$ZM_{mag}LBP$	80.0	96.22	98.55
$ZM_{magPhase}LBP$	*81.5*	94.56	98.0
$ZM_{component}LBP$	77.0	93.33	98.85
$ZM_{mag}LTP$	*81.0*	*96.44*	98.85
$ZM_{magPhase}LTP$	79.25	96.11	98.45
$ZM_{component}LTP$	79.0	94.33	*99.0*

robust to noise variation than the LBP. On Yale and ORL databases (with noise variation), the performance of the proposed $ZM_{mag}LTP$ and $ZM_{component}LTP$ descriptors, respectively, is better as compared to all other combined approaches. On the other hand, if FERET images with noise variations are assessed, then the recognition rate of $ZM_{magPhase}LBP$ is 81.5%, whereas the recognition rate of $ZM_{mag}LTP$ is 81.0%. The percentage difference between the actual results obtained (without adding noise and with noise) for both approaches is 5 and 3.5%, respectively. Hence, from this observation, we can say that on FERET database, the performance of the proposed $ZM_{mag}LTP$ descriptor is better against noise variation. For the case of Yale and ORL databases, the degradation due to noise in recognition rates is very less.

5.5 Time complexity

One of the important issues involved in using combined approaches similar to the ones proposed here is the time complexity of these approaches. It is a common perception

Table 10 Dimensionality of the feature vectors of the ZM and LBP/LTP descriptors

Approach	Size of the feature vector	Remarks
ZM_{mag}	40	For moments up to order $n_{max} = 11$
$ZM_{magPhase}$	2×40	Size of the feature vector is double the size of magnitude features
$ZM_{component}$	2×40	Size of the feature vector is double the size of magnitude features
LBP	3,776	Taking image patch size of 8×8 pixels for uniform local binary patterns
LTP	$2 \times 3,776$	Number of features is double the number of LBP features because two feature vectors consisting of the positive and the negative uniform binary patterns are taken

that the moment-based descriptors are computation intensive which is true to some extent especially in case of the ZM calculation. The time complexity of the ZMs is of order $O(N^2 n_{max}^3)$ if all moments up to a maximum order n_{max} are computed for an image of $N \times N$ pixels. However, with the use of fast algorithms [10,11], the time complexity is reduced to $O(N^2 n_{max}^2)$. Further significant reduction in computation time is achieved by using symmetry/antisymmetry properties of kernel function of ZMs. The ZMs of the database images are computed offline and indexed with the images themselves. The ZMs of the test image are computed online. Although the time complexity of ZM calculation is still high, in this work, better recognition results have been obtained with $n_{max} = 9$ for FERET and ORL databases whereas Yale database exhibits good results by taking $n_{max} = 11$; therefore, we consider moments only up to these orders. As $Z_{0,0}$ and $Z_{1,1}$ have no discriminative capabilities, they do not affect the recognition rate. Hence, with $n_{max} = 11$, we have 40 features after discarding the coefficients $Z_{0,0}$ and $Z_{1,1}$. In contrast, although the number of features in the feature vector containing local histogram features of the LBP/LTP descriptors is high, the computation time of these descriptors is very low. Thus, the proposed fusion of the ZM and LBP/LTP descriptors maintains a good balance between speed and dimensionality. The size of feature vectors of the ZM and LBP/LTP descriptors is shown in Table 10.

We observe that for an image of 256×256 pixels, the CPU elapse time for calculating ZMs is only 0.032 s for $n_{max} = 12$ on a PC with a 3.0-GHz CPU and a 1-GB RAM under Microsoft Windows environment. The time

Table 11 Performance comparison (%) of some recent approaches with proposed methods on Yale and ORL databases

Method	ORL	Yale
PCA	55.0	55.0
2DPCA	54.0	56.0
$(PC)^2A$	57.0	55.0
$E(PC)^2A$	58.0	57.0
$2D(PC)^2A$	56.0	55.0
SVD perturbation	61.0	62.0
Hybrid Fourier-AFMT transform	76.0	52.0
RES [40]	0.77	0.78
$ZM_{mag}LBP$	*84.44*	*86.67*
$ZM_{magPhase}LBP$	84.17	*86.67*
$ZM_{component}LBP$	84.17	80.67
$ZM_{mag}LTP$	80.0	82.67
$ZM_{magPhase}LTP$	82.78	85.33
$ZM_{component}LTP$	81.22	81.52

Table 12 Performance comparison (%) of the proposed approaches with recent methods on Yale and ORL databases

Method	Yale database	ORL database
Two-dimensional LDA (2D-LDA) [42]	86.57	92.50
2D-WLDA [42]	88.00	93.50
2D-DWLDA [42]	89.33	94.00
Direct LDA (DLDA) [21]	93.20	92.50
Enhanced Fisher linear discriminant model (EFM) [21]	93.90	92.50
Intrinsicfaces [43]	74.00	97.00
Combined feature Fisher classifier (CF^{2}C) [21]	96.90	96.80
Feature Fisher classifier (F^{3}C) [20]	96.4	94.9
Block based S-P[a] [25]	100.0[a]	99.0
Algorithm A (WMs) [41]	–	93.5
Algorithm B (CWMs) [41]	–	96.0
ZM$_{mag}$LBP	*97.56*	*99.20*
ZM$_{magPhase}$LBP	96.78	98.25
ZM$_{component}$LBP	95.67	98.95
ZM$_{mag}$LTP	*97.56*	98.85
ZM$_{magPhase}$LTP	97.00	98.35
ZM$_{component}$LTP	97.00	*99.20*

Comparison of recognition performance for five random training images. [a]The results are presented on only one random set of five images in the training set and all the remaining in the test set.

taken for computing LBP and LTP features is 0.015 and 0.016 s, respectively. Thus, the total time elapsed for the extraction of the local and global features of a test image does not exceed 0.048 s. The time taken for classification is much less than the feature extraction time. Thus, in comparison to the gain in the recognition performance, the time taken by the combined features is much less and can be afforded by the low computation power devices in online mode. Since the time complexity does not depend on the contents of the image, these experiments are carried out for one image only.

5.6 Performance comparison

We have compared the performance of the proposed combined descriptors with other popular methods such as PCA, 2DPCA, (PC)^{2}A, E(PC)^{2}A, 2D(PC)^{2}A, SVD perturbation [38], and hybrid Fourier-AFMT transform [39] for face recognition with single (first) example image per person. As shown in Table 11, the proposed combined descriptors give the best recognition rate when compared with other well-established methods. On the other hand, the time complexity of PCA-based methods is very high as compared to the proposed approaches.

Comparison of performance of the proposed combined descriptors with other popular methods for face recognition with single (first) example image per person.

Dual optimal multiband features (DOMF) [24] give a recognition rate of 92.6 and 88.4% on Yale and ORL

databases, respectively, when two images of each person are taken in the training set and all the remaining are kept in the test set. On this similar setup for training and test images, the highest recognition rate achieved by the proposed ZM$_{magPhase}$LBP descriptor for YALE 2.1 is 94.59% while the ZM$_{component}$LBP descriptor achieves a recognition rate of 92.47% for ORL 2.1 category.

The performance of the proposed combined approaches is also compared with that of some recent face recognition methods when five images of each person are used for training. The recognition results of the proposed combined approaches and those of these recent methods on Yale and ORL databases for this case are shown in Table 12. The best results are highlighted in italics. All these methods use multidimensional features or combined approaches to represent the face images. As can be seen from the results presented, the recognition rate of the proposed approaches is higher as compared to that of the recent methods. In case of block-based S-P approach [25], one random set of five images per person is taken in the training set while all the remaining are kept in the test set for both the Yale and ORL databases, whereas the results presented for our proposed approaches are the average of ten random trials of training and test sets. It is worth mentioning here that on some of the random trials, our proposed descriptors also provide 100% recognition rate. Recently introduced wavelet moment (WM) and complex WM (CWM) approaches

[41] have achieved a recognition rate of 51.5 and 54.3%, respectively, on FERET_A2 subset, while the proposed $ZM_{magPhase}LBP$ descriptor has attained a recognition rate of 77.33%. On the *fafb* subset of FERET database, the recognition rate obtained by the RES [40], WM, and CWM [41] approaches is 95.0, 88.0, and 91.0% whereas the highest recognition rate achieved by the proposed $ZM_{magPhase}LBP$ approach is 98.04%. Thus, on the basis of superior results obtained by the proposed fusion technique, it can be concluded that combining the feature sets of the ZM and LBP/LTP descriptors is an efficient and practical approach for robust face recognition.

6 Conclusions

This paper proposes the fusion of two useful feature sets, i.e., the global ZMs and the local LBP/LTP descriptor. Face images capture extensive variation under varying pose and lighting conditions accompanied by the presence of expression and noise. Individually, the ZM and LBP/LTP descriptors are observed to be very effective in providing good recognition performance on the face images containing certain variations. In particular, the ZM descriptor extracts rotationally invariant shape features from the whole face images, whereas the LBP/LTP descriptors are able to capture the fine details and illumination-invariant characteristics within some local regions of the face images. However, the fusion of these two complementary approaches incorporates the benefits of both of these descriptors and as such proves to be invariant against various distortions present in the face images. Herein this work, diverse feature sets of ZMs are combined with LBP/LTP descriptors to generate various combined approaches, namely, $ZM_{mag}LBP$, $ZM_{magPhase}LBP$, $ZM_{component}LBP$, $ZM_{mag}LTP$, $ZM_{magPhase}LTP$, and $ZM_{component}LTP$. From the detailed experiments performed on FERET, Yale, and ORL face databases, it has been observed that the proposed combined approaches are highly robust against pose, expression, illumination, and noise variations, as the recognition rate achieved by the proposed approaches is approximately 10 to 30% higher than that obtained by applying these approaches individually. Fusion of ZM and LBP descriptor performs better over the pose, expression, and illumination variations, while in the presence of noise, ZMs combined with LTP descriptor generate superior results. Experimental results also prove the efficacy of the proposed methods over other existing techniques. Also, significant improvement in the recognition rate is achieved by the proposed scheme when only single training image per person is available.

Future work is suggested towards discovering the optimal ways to utilize the information acquired by the phase coefficients of ZM descriptor in addition to using different methods of classification to further improve the performance of the proposed fusion approach.

Competing interests
The authors declare that they have no competing interests.

Acknowledgements
The authors are thankful to the useful comments and suggestions of the anonymous reviewers for raising the standard of the paper. The authors are grateful to the All India Council for Technical Education (AICTE), Govt. of India, New Delhi, India, for supporting the research work vide their file number 8013/RID/BOR/RPS-77/2005-06. We are also grateful to the National Institute of Standards and Technology (colorferet@nist.gov) for providing FERET face database.

Author details
[1]Department of Computer Science, Punjabi University, Patiala 147002, India. [2]Central Scientific Instruments Organisation, Sector 30-C, Chandigarh 160030, India. [3]Department of Computer Science, South Asian University, Akbar Bhawan, Chanakyapuri, Delhi 110021, India.

References
1. W Zhao, R Chellappa, P Phillips, A Rosenfeld, Face recognition: a literature survey. ACM Comput. Surv. **35**(4), 399–458 (2003)
2. E Hjelmas, BK Low, Face detection: a survey. Comput. Vision. Image. Underst. **83**, 236–274 (2001)
3. M Turk, A random walk through Eigenspace. IEICE Trans. Inf. Syst. **E84-D**(12), 1586–1595 (2001)
4. N Mittal, E Walia, Face recognition using improved fast PCA algorithm, in *Proceedings of the IEEE International Congress on Image and Signal Processing (CISp '08)* (Sanya, Hainan, 2008), pp. 554–558
5. PN Belhumeur, JP Hespanha, DJ Kriegman, Eigenfaces vs. Fisherfaces: recognition using class specific linear projection. IEEE. IEEE Trans. Pattern Anal. Mach. Intell. **19**, 711–720 (1997)
6. Y Xu, D Zhang, J Yang, Y J–Y, An approach for directly extracting features from matrix data and its application in face recognition. Neurocomputing **71**, 1857–1865 (2008)
7. Z Daoqiang, Z Zhi-Hua, (2D)^{2}PCA: Two-directional two-dimensional PCA for efficient face representation and recognition. Neurocomputing **69**, 224–231 (2005)
8. D Zhang, G Lu, Review of shape representation and description techniques. Pattern Recognit. **37**(1), 1–19 (2004)
9. D Zhang, G Lu, Evaluation of MPEG-7 shape descriptors against other shape descriptors. Multimed. Syst. **9**, 15–30 (2003)
10. C Singh, E Walia, Fast and numerically stable methods for the computation of Zernike moments. Pattern Recognit. **43**(7), 2497–2506 (2010)
11. W C–Y, R Paramesran, On the computational aspects of Zernike moments. Image Vis. Comput. **25**, 967–980 (2007)
12. DG Lowe, Distinctive image features from scale-invariant keypoints. Int. J. Comput. Vis. **60**(2), 91–110 (2004)
13. H Soyel, H Demirel, Facial expression recognition based on discriminative scale invariant feature transform. IET Electron. Lett. **46**(5), 343–345 (2010)
14. L Huang, A Shimizu, H Kobatake, Robust face detection using Gabor filter features. Pattern Recognit. Lett. **26**(11), 1641–1649 (2005)
15. T Ojala, M Pietikäinen, Multiresolution gray-scale and rotation invariant texture classification with local binary patterns. IEEE Trans. Pattern Anal. Mach. Intell. **24**(7), 971–987 (2002)
16. T Ahonen, A Hadid, M Pietikäinen, Face description with local binary patterns: application to face recognition. IEEE Trans. Pattern Anal. Mach. Intell. **28**(12), 2037–2041 (2006)
17. B Jun, T Kim, D Kim, A compact local binary pattern using maximization of mutual information for face analysis. Pattern Recognit. **44**, 532–543 (2011)
18. X Tan, B Triggs, Enhanced local texture feature sets for face recognition under difficult lighting conditions. IEEE Trans. Image Process. **19**(6), 1635–1648 (2010)
19. C Kim, J Oh, C Choi, *Combined Subspace Method Using Global and Local features For Face Recognition*, 4th edn. (Proceedings of the IEEE International Joint Conference on Neural Networks (IJCNN '05), Montreal Canada, 2005), pp. 2030–2035

20. D Zhou, X Yang, Feature fusion based face recognition using EFM. Proceedings International Conference on Image Analysis and Recognition (ICIAR '04). Lect. Notes Comput. Sci. **3212**, 643–650 (2004)

21. D Zhou, X Yang, N Peng, Y Wang, Improved-LDA based face recognition using both facial global and local information. Pattern Recognit. Lett. **27**, 536–543 (2006)

22. C Singh, E Walia, N Mittal, Robust two-stage face recognition approach using global and local features. Vis. Comput. **28**(11), 1085–1098 (2012)

23. Y Su, S Shan, X Chen, W Gao, Hierarchical ensemble of global and local classifiers for face recognition. IEEE Trans. Image Process. **18**(8), 1885–1895 (2009)

24. Y-W Wong, KP Seng, A Li-M, Dual optimal multiband features for face recognition. Expert Syst, Appl **37**(4), 2957–2962 (2010)

25. ME Aroussi, ME Hassouni, S Ghouzali, M Rziza, D Aboutajdine, Local appearance based face recognition method using block based steerable pyramid transform. Signal Process **91**, 38–50 (2011)

26. Z Liu, C Liu, Fusion of color, local spatial and global frequency information for face recognition. Pattern Recognit. **43**, 2882–2890 (2010)

27. B Jun, J Lee, D Kim, A novel illumination-robust face recognition using statistical and non-statistical method. Pattern Recognit. Lett. **32**, 329–336 (2011)

28. S Moore, R Bowden, Local binary patterns for multi-view facial expression recognition. Comput. Vision Image Underst. **115**, 541–558 (2011)

29. C Singh, E Walia, N Mittal, Rotation invariant complex Zernike moments features and their application to human face and character recognition. IET Comput. Vision **5**(5), 255–265 (2011)

30. SM Lajevardi, ZM Hussain, Higher order orthogonal moments for invariant facial expression recognition. Digit Signal Process **20**, 1771–1779 (2010)

31. S Li, L M–C, P Chi-Man, Complex Zernike moments features for shape based image retrieval. IEEE Trans. Syst. Man. Cybern. C Appl. Rev. **39**, 227–237 (2009)

32. C Singh, N Mittal, E Walia, Face recognition using Zernike and complex Zernike moment features. Pattern Recognit. Image Anal. **21**(1), 71–81 (2011)

33. J Revaud, G Lavoue, A Baskurt, Improving Zernike moments comparison for optimal similarity and rotation angle retrieval. IEEE Trans. Pattern Anal. Mach. Intell. **31**(4), 627–636 (2009)

34. A Jain, K Nandakumar, A Ross, Score normalization in multimodal biometric systems. Pattern Recognit. **38**, 2270–2285 (2005)

35. The Facial Recognition Technology (FERET) face database. http://www.nist.gov/itl/iad/ig/colorferet.cfm

36. Yale face database. http://www.cl.cam.ac.uk/research/dtg/attarchive/facedatabase.html

37. Olivetti Research Laboratory (ORL) face database. http://www.cl.cam.ac.uk/research/dtg/attarchive/facedatabase.html

38. J Li, J-S Pan, A novel pose and illumination robust face recognition with a single training image per person algorithm. Chin. Optic. Lett. **6**(4), 255–257 (2008)

39. YM Chen, J-H Chiang, Fusing multiple features for Fourier Mellin-based face recognition with single example image per person. Neurocomputing **73**(16–18), 3089–3096 (2010)

40. C-H Kuo, JD Lee, Face recognition based on a two-view projective transformation using one sample per subject. IET Comput. Vision **6**(5), 489–498 (2012)

41. C Singh, AM Sahan, Face recognition using complex wavelet moments. Opt. Laser Technol. **47**, 256–267 (2013)

42. R Zhi, Q Ruan, Two-dimensional direct and weighted linear discriminant analysis for face recognition. Neurocomputing **71**, 3607–3611 (2008)

43. Y Wang, Y Wu, Face recognition using Intrinsicfaces. Pattern Recognit. **43**, 3580–3590 (2010)

4

A genetic optimized neural network for image retrieval in telemedicine

Mohandass Divya[1*], Jude Janet[2] and Ramadass Suguna[1]

Abstract

Telemedicine integrates information and communication technologies in providing clinical services to health professionals in different places. Medical images are required to be transmitted for diagnosis and opinion as part of the telemedicine process. Thus, telemedicine challenges include limited bandwidth and large amount of diagnostic data. Content-based image retrieval is used in retrieving relevant images from the database, and image compression addresses the problem of limited bandwidth. This paper proposes a novel method to enable telemedicine using soft computing approaches. In the present study, images are compressed to minimize bandwidth utilization, and compressed images similar to the query medical image are retrieved using a novel feature extraction and a genetic optimized classifier. The effectiveness of compressed image retrieval on magnetic resonance scan images of stroke patients is presented in this study.

Keywords: Telemedicine; Feature extraction; Image retrieval; Classification; Neural network

1. Introduction

Telemedicine integrates information and communication technologies in providing clinical services to health professionals in different places. It provides expert-based healthcare services to exchange information required for diagnosis, consultation, and referential purposes. Telemedicine not only includes diagnostic, remote monitoring, and interactive services but also drug evaluation, medical research, and training. People living in remote areas and isolated regions find telemedicine very helpful. It is also useful in critical care and emergency situations. The main challenges faced by telemedicine are limited bandwidth, large volume of data, and availability of expert opinion [1,2]. With the progress of medical technologies, obtaining digital images of human anatomy through X-rays, magnetic resonance imaging (MRI), electrocardiography (ECG), and computed tomography (CT) has become a norm. The digital images are stored in databases and can be easily accessed through internet for training and diagnostic purposes. The difficulty of getting an expert either online or offline to advice on diagnosis based on the medical image is addressed by

the use of content-based image retrieval (CBIR). CBIR can be used to retrieve diagnostic cases similar to the query medical image from the medical database [3,4]. CBIR is of significance in medical image retrieval as the medical databases contain a huge amount of data in visual form, conventional method of retrieval based on semantics is not feasible, and image content is more versatile than the text. CBIR is increasingly applied in medical image applications; many CBIR algorithms, architectures, and systems are reviewed in the literature [5,6].

Though medical image retrieval has been successfully implemented in nontelemedicine applications, the limited bandwidth and large amount of diagnostic data required to be transmitted are two of the major issues that need to be addressed in using CBIR in telemedicine. Transmitting compressed medical images can be an option for physical diagnosis by an expert; however, automated retrieval of compressed medical images has not been extensively studied. Image compression reduces data required to represent an image; it reduces the storage and transmission requirements. Redundancies in the image are removed during the compression process to yield a compact representation of the image. Lossless

* Correspondence: divya.skrec@gmail.com
[1]Department of CSE, SKR Engineering College, Chennai, India
Full list of author information is available at the end of the article

compression techniques are used when the original image is to be perfectly recovered, and lossy compression techniques are used when a high compression rate is required with minor loss in details. Limited techniques for compressed medical image retrieval have been proposed in [7-9]. Compression techniques using lossless methods have been studied in [10,11] where attempts have been made to propose encoding techniques that showed improvements over existing techniques including Huffman coding. As image transmission is part of telemedicine, wavelet-based coding has been found to be robust for compressed image transmission and has proved to be efficient at low bit rates [12].

This work focuses on compressed medical image retrieval. CBIR has been successfully applied in classifying MRI brain images. Studies in [13-15] show feature extraction techniques and classification algorithm for stroke identification and classification in uncompressed images. Cocosco et al. [16] proposed techniques for feature extraction which showed robustness against variability in MRI image quality. Lahmiri and Boukadoum [17] proposed a feature extraction technique using discrete wavelet transform (DWT) and obtained good classification accuracies using a probabilistic neural network (PNN) algorithm. El-dahshan et al. [18] presented techniques for feature reduction using principal component analysis (PCA) of the features extracted using DWT. Using k-nearest neighbor (k-NN) and feedforward back propagation-artificial neural network (FP-ANN) classifications, accuracies of 95.6% and 98.6% were obtained. Bagher-Ebadian et al. [19] proposed a method to study ischemic stroke using ANN. The method identifies the extent of ischemic lesion recovery. Experiments using new datasets showed that the prediction made by ANN had an excellent overall performance and was very well correlated to the 3-month ischemic lesion on the T2-weighted image. Stroke classification using various feature techniques and classifiers has been proposed in [20-22].

Though good classification accuracy has been demonstrated in the literature, a detailed study of compressed MRI stroke image retrieval which is crucial for telemedicine has not been studied extensively to the best of our knowledge. This work focuses on compressed image retrieval for the classification of stroke and nonstroke MRI images. The proposed method is subdivided to the following techniques comprising compression, feature extraction, and classification. Haar wavelet for decomposition and Huffman encoding have been used to compress the images. The main contributions of this study are listed as

- A novel feature extraction technique using the proposed image retrieval-specific fast Fourier transform (IRS-FFT)

- An improved neural network classifier, genetic optimized parallel neural network (GOP-parallel NN).

2. Proposed feature extraction

The proposed IRS-FFT for feature extraction can be derived as given in [23-25]. Feature extraction was performed on diffusion weighted imaging (DWI) scan images showing stroke.

Fast Fourier transform has the tendency to produce large values which may introduce an artifact. In order to overcome the issue of artifact, a normalization procedure is proposed and integrated with Fast Fourier transform. The proposed normalization model is shown in Equations 1 and 2.

Consider a matrix U of dimension $N \times N$ with its (m, n)th element defined as in Equations 1 and 2:

$$u[m,n]u_N^{mn} = \left(e^{-j2\Pi/N}\right)^{mn} \tag{1}$$

where (m, $n = 0, 1, 2,..., N-1$).

$$u_N \frac{1}{\sqrt{N}} e^{-j2\Pi/N}. \tag{2}$$

The IRS-FFT can be defined as in Equation 3:

$$X_{irs}[n] = \int_{-\alpha}^{n} \frac{1}{\sqrt{2\Pi\sigma^2}} e^{-\frac{(n-\mu)^2}{2\sigma^2}} X[n], \tag{3}$$

where $X[n]$ and μ is given as in Equations 4 and 5:

$$X[n] = \begin{bmatrix} u[0,0] & u[0,1] & ... & u[0,N-1] \\ u[1,0] & u[1,1] & ... & u[1,N-1] \\ ... & .... & ... & ... \\ u[N-1,0] & u[N-1,1] & ... & u[N-1,N-1] \end{bmatrix} \begin{bmatrix} x[0] \\ x[1] \\ ... \\ x[N-1] \end{bmatrix} \tag{4}$$

and

$$\mu = \frac{1}{N} \sum_{0}^{n-1} X(n). \tag{5}$$

Sample images after feature extraction is given in Figure 1.

The proposed feature extraction technique produces a large number of feature vectors. Information gain (IG) is used to reduce the feature vectors by selecting the top ranked features. The information gain that has to be

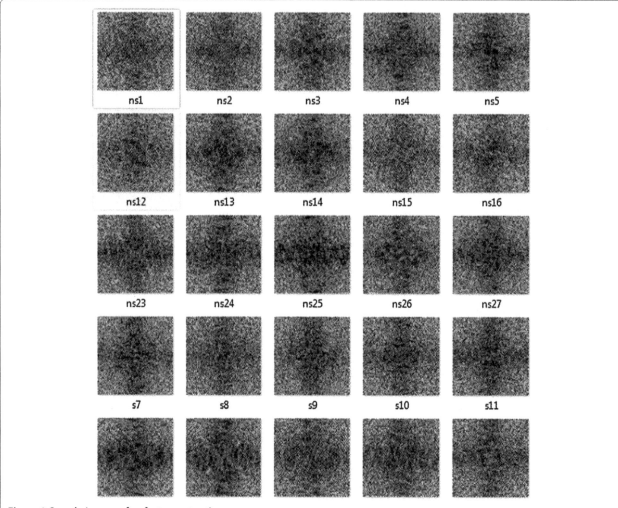

Figure 1 Sample Images after feature extraction.

computed for an attribute A whose class attribute B is given by the conditional entropy of B given A, $H(B|A)$ is

$$I(B;A) = H(B) - H(B|A).$$

The conditional entropy of B given A is

$$H(B|A) = -\sum_{i=1}^{j=1} P(A = a_j) H(B|A = a_j).$$

3. Proposed genetic optimized parallel MLP neural network

Neural network are modeled similar to the neurons in the brain. The proposed neural network genetic optimized parallel multilayer perceptron neural network (GOP-MLP NN) is an extension of the existing multilayer perceptron (MLP) model. Unlike the MLP, full interconnectivity between the layers is not achieved. The network processing the input signals uses several parallel

MLPs as it reduces the number of weights required, and hence, the training time for the network is reduced over the traditional MLP network. The block diagram of the proposed GOP MLP neural network is shown in Figure 2.

It could be observed from Figure 2 that the proposed neural network consists of two parallel MLPs with each performing different subtasks. Each MLP consists of two layers. The first submodule MLP uses the first 50% of the attributes, and the remaining are used by the second submodule. The number of weights is reduced by 50% using this process.

A genetic optimization function is introduced in the second hidden layer of the proposed network to find the best learning rule and momentum. The GOP-MLP NN proposed in this paper uses the criteria specified in Table 1.

The learning capability and the generalization capability of the proposed neural network model are calculated

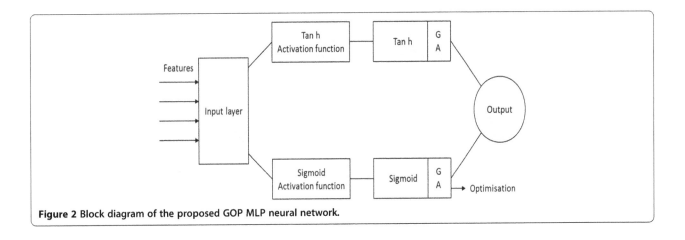

Figure 2 Block diagram of the proposed GOP MLP neural network.

using the performance measure of the mean square error (MSE). The MSE is given as

$$MSE = \frac{\sum_{j=0}^{E} \sum_{i=0}^{N} \left(o_{ij} - y_{ij} \right)^2}{EN}, \quad (6)$$

where E is the number of processing elements, N is the number of exemplars, o is the desired output for exemplar i at processing element j, y is the obtained output for exemplar i at processing element j; tan h will squash the range of each neuron to between −1 and 1, and its activation function is given as

$$\tan h(i) = \frac{e^i - e^{-i}}{e^i + e^{-i}}, \quad (7)$$

where i is the sum of the input patterns.

Table 1 Parameters for the proposed GOP-MLP NN

Parameter	Value/description
Output neuron	2
Number of hidden layer	2
Number of processing elements	
Upper	4
Lower	4
Transfer function of hidden layer	
Upper	tan h
Lower	Sigmoid
Learning rule of hidden layer	Momentum with genetic optimization
Step size	0.1
Momentum	0.7
Transfer function of output layer	tan h
Learning rule of output layer	Momentum
Step size	0.1
Momentum	0.7

Genetic optimization is used in the hidden layer of the network. Genetic algorithms (GA) are a class of optimization algorithms inspired by evolution. The steps in GA include reproduction, crossover, and mutation to evolve better solutions. Generally, the solutions available are evaluated using fitness function. Based on the fitness function, the evolutionary process is iterated till an ideal solution is reached or a specific number of generations has occurred. The proposed neural network architecture is optimized for ideal momentum value using GA with the following parameters specified in Table 2.

The flow diagram of the proposed GOP MLP neural network is presented in Figure 3.

The genetic algorithm iterates and evolves the population, forming a new population at each step. The genetic algorithm iteration consists of the following steps:

1. *Selection.* The first step consists of selecting individuals/chromosomes for reproduction. Fitness value plays an important role in this selection and is completed randomly. Individuals with better fitness

Table 2 Genetic optimization parameters

Parameter	Value/description
Number of iterations	500
Population size	10
Maximum generations	100
Momentum optimization lower bound value	0.05
Momentum optimization upper bound value	0.95
Encoder mechanism	Roulette
Crossover type	One point
Crossover probability	0.75
Mutation	Uniform
Mutation probability	0.02

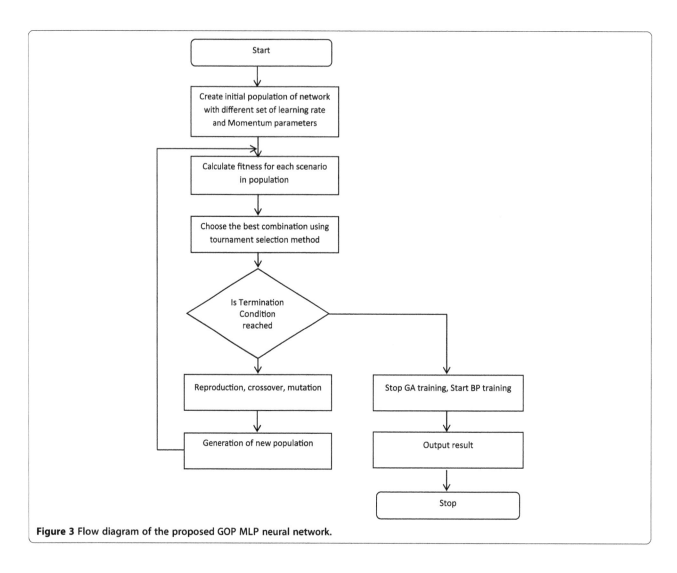

Figure 3 Flow diagram of the proposed GOP MLP neural network.

value are chosen more often for reproduction than poor ones.

2. *Reproduction.* Offspring are produced by the selected individuals. Both recombination and mutation techniques are used in generating new chromosomes.
3. *Evaluation.* The fitness of the new chromosomes is then evaluated.
4. *Replacement.* During the last step, individuals from the old population are removed and replaced by the new ones.

In the present design, the MSE is evaluated as the fitness function with a total of 100 generations. The MSE was found to decrease, and no significant change was observed as presented in Figure 4.

4. Experimental results and discussions

In order to test the effectiveness of our approach, a set of 52 DWI scan images consisting of 25 positive stroke

patients was used. These images were provided by the MRI Department of Vijaya Health Centre in India. The MRI images were reviewed by an expert in the radiology department for a precise classification of patients with positive stroke. Figure 5 shows some of the stroke images used in the present study. Experiments were performed on the uncompressed and the compressed images to show the effectiveness of compressed images for image retrieval.

4.1 Experiment 1 for uncompressed images

The following are the steps in experiment 1 for uncompressed images:

1. Preprocessing of the image using a median filter for noise removal
2. Extracting of features using IRS-FFT
3. Feature reduction using Information gain
4. Classification using the proposed genetic optimized parallel neural network for 20, 40, 60, 80, and 100 features

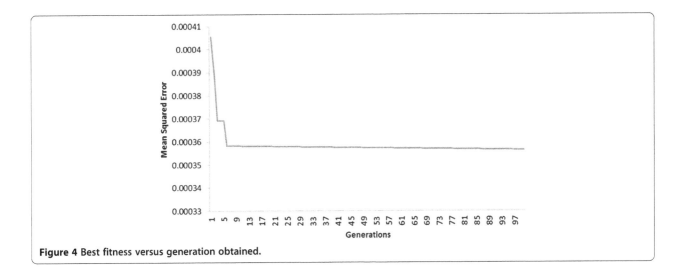

Figure 4 Best fitness versus generation obtained.

5. Performance evaluation of the proposed system with the MLP neural network.

4.2 Experiment 2 for compressed images

The following are the steps in experiment 2 for compressed images:

1. Preprocessing of the image using a median filter
2. Compression of images using Haar wavelet with Huffman encoding
3. Extracting of features using IRS-FFT

4. Feature reduction using information gain
5. Classification using the proposed genetic optimized parallel neural network for 20, 40, 60, 80, and 100 attributes
6. Performance evaluation of the proposed system with MLP neural network.

It is evident in Table 3 that the proposed GOP NN shows a higher degree of precision and classification accuracy compared to the MLP NN. It is observed that classification accuracy decreases when the number of features extracted is 60.

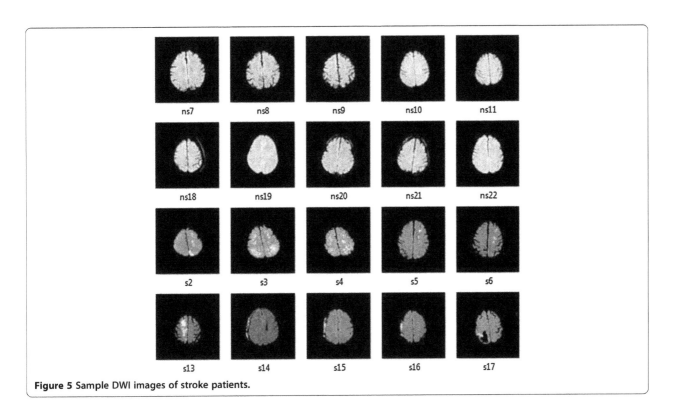

Figure 5 Sample DWI images of stroke patients.

Table 3 Classification parameters for uncompressed and compressed images

Number of features	Parameters	Classifiers	Uncompressed		Compressed	
			Feature extraction using FFT	Feature extraction using the proposed IRS-FFT	Feature extraction using FFT	Feature extraction using proposed IRS-FFT
20	Classification accuracy	MLP NN	88.46	92.31	90.38	92.31
		GOP NN	92.31	94.23	94.23	98.08
	Precision	MLP NN	0.92	0.96	0.86	1
		GOP NN	0.96	1	1	1
	Recall	MLP NN	0.85	0.89	1	0.86
		GOP NN	0.89	0.89	0.89	0.96
40	Classification accuracy	MLP NN	90.38	94.23	92.31	94.23
		GOP NN	94.23	96.15	94.23	98.08
	Precision	MLP NN	0.96	0.96	1	1
		GOP NN	1	1	1	1
	Recall	MLP NN	0.86	0.92	0.86	0.89
		GOP NN	0.89	0.93	0.89	0.96
60	Classification accuracy	MLP NN	88.46	90.38	92.31	94.23
		GOP NN	92.31	94.23	92.31	98.08
	Precision	MLP NN	0.92	0.96	1	1
		GOP NN	1	1	1	1
	Recall	MLP NN	0.85	0.86	0.86	0.89
		GOP NN	0.86	0.89	0.86	0.96
80	Classification accuracy	MLP NN	90.38	94.23	92.31	94.23
		GOP NN	94.23	96.15	98.08	98.08
	Precision	MLP NN	0.96	0.96	1	1
		GOP NN	1	1	1	1
	Recall	MLP NN	0.86	0.92	0.86	0.89
		GOP NN	0.89	0.93	0.96	0.96
100	Classification accuracy	MLP NN	90.38	94.23	92.31	94.23
		GOP NN	94.23	96.15	98.08	98.08
	Precision	MLP NN	0.96	0.96	1	1
		GOP NN	1	1	1	1
	Recall	MLP NN	0.86	0.92	0.86	0.89
		GOP NN	0.89	0.93	0.96	0.96

This seems to be a minor abnormality which could be associated with the data used as 40 and 80 features show linear approach. The classification accuracy, precision, and recall are computed as

Further, the accuracy of the proposed feature extraction technique is higher with a minimum of 40 feature vectors.

The graphs depicted in Figure 6 shows the classification accuracy of the proposed and existing MLP neural

$$\text{Classification accuracy} = \frac{\text{Number of correctly classified samples}}{\text{Total number of tested samples}} \times 100$$

$$\text{Precision} = \frac{\text{Number of relevent images retrived}}{\text{Total number of images retrieved}}$$

$$\text{Recall} = \frac{\text{Number of relevent images retrived}}{\text{Total number of relevent images in the database}}.$$

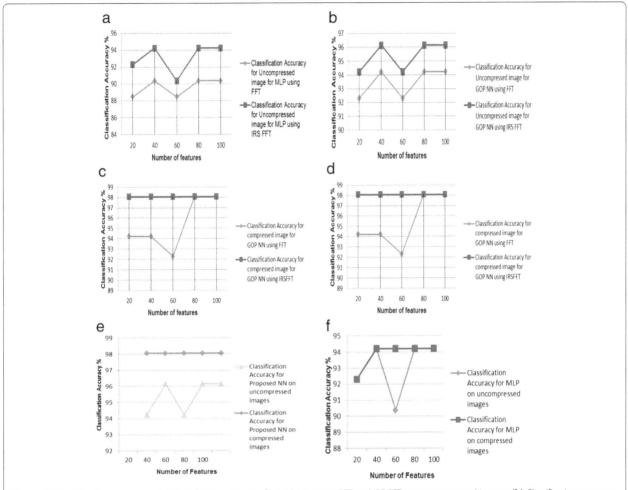

Figure 6 Classification accuracy. (a) Classification accuracy for MLP NN using FFT and IRS-FFT on uncompressed images. **(b)** Classification accuracy for GOP NN using FFT and IRS-FFT on uncompressed images. **(c)** Classification accuracy for MLP NN using FFT and IRS-FFT on compressed images. **(d)** Classification accuracy for GOP NN using FFT and IRS-FFT on compressed images. **(e)** Classification accuracy of the proposed GOP NN on uncompressed and compressed images. **(f)** Classification accuracy of the proposed MLP on uncompressed and compressed images.

network using conventional FFT and the proposed IRS-FFT for both compressed and uncompressed images. It is seen that the classification accuracy of the compressed images are better than that of the uncompressed images, thereby utilizing the bandwidth effectively and justifying its applicability in a telemedicine scenario.

5. Conclusions

In this paper, a modified IRS-FFT-based feature extraction technique was proposed. The basic idea of the proposed algorithm is to squash the values of FFT, thereby reducing noise and improving the classification accuracy. A novel neural network with parallel perceptrons to reduce the weights along with genetic optimization to find the ideal momentum was proposed. A two-class problem on MRI stroke images was used in evaluating the proposed feature extraction and classifier. Experiments were conducted using uncompressed and compressed images. IG was used

to rank the extracted features, and the experiments were conducted with varying numbers of features. Multilayer perceptron neural network and the proposed NN architecture with genetic optimization classified the images based on the selected features. Results show the improvement in precision for the compressed images using the proposed system.

The proposed CBIR system achieves satisfactory retrieval accuracy for compressed medical images. An average compression ratio of 35.84 was achieved which translates to proportional savings in bandwidth critical for a telemedicine application. Compressing images for transmission in limited bandwidth is a norm in telemedicine. The proposed method efficiently extracts features and retrieves relevant images from compressed images which will be a good support for telemedicine applications. The proposed method can further be investigated for various types of medical images and also validated for a multiclass problem.

Competing interests
The authors declare that they have no competing interests.

Acknowledgements
We would like to express our sincere gratitude to Dr. Ezhilarasu, Consultant Radiologist, Vijay Health Centre, India for providing us the database necessary to perform the experiments.

Author details
[1]Department of CSE, SKR Engineering College, Chennai, India. [2]Department of CSE, SVCE, Andhra Pradesh, India.

References
1. S Singh, V Kumar, HK Verma, Adaptive threshold block classification in medical image compression for teleradiology. Comput Biol Med **37**, 811–819 (2007)
2. A Bruckmann, A Uhl, Selective Medical Image Compression techniques for telemedical and archiving application. Comput Biol Med **30**(3), 153–169 (2000)
3. TM Lehmann, H Schubert, D Keysers, M Kohnen, BB Wein, The IRMA code for unique classification of medical image. Proceedings of the SPIE 5033 **5033**, 109–117 (2003)
4. SG Armato 3rd, G McLennan, MF McNitt-Gray, CR Meyer, D Yankelevitz, DR Aberle, CI Henschke, EA Hoffman, EA Kazerooni, H MacMahon, AP Reeves, BY Croft, LP Clarke, Lung Image Database Consortium Research Group, Lung image database consortium: developing a resource for the medical imaging research community. Radiology **232**, 739–748 (2004)
5. WM Smeulders, M Worring, S Santini, A Gupta, R Jain, Content-based image retrieval at the end of the early years. IEEE Trans Pattern Anal Mach Intell **22**(12), 1349–1380 (2000)
6. H Muller, N Michoux, D Bandon, A Geissbuhler, A review of content based image retrieval systems in medical applications—clinical benefits and future directions. Int J Med Inform **73**, 1–23 (2004)
7. VR Khapli, AS Bhalachandra, Performance evaluation of image retrieval using VQ for compressed and uncompressed images, in *Proceedings of 2nd International Conference on Emerging Trends in Engineering and Technology ICETET, Nagpur, 16–18 Dec 2009*, ed. by (IEEE, Piscataway, 2009), pp. 885–888
8. MG Liu, J Jiang, CH Hou, A combination of image retrieval and compression. Proceedings of IEEE International Conference on Acoustics, Speech and Signal Processing ICASSP **4**, 13–17 (2002)
9. D Cerra, M Datcu, *Image retrieval using compression based techniques, in Proceedings of the International Conference on Source and Channel Coding (SCC), Siegen, 18–21 Jan 2010* (Piscataway, IEEE, 2010), pp. 1–6
10. JH Pujar, LM Kadlaskar, A new lossless method of image compression and decompression using Huffman coding techniques. Journal of Theoretical and Applied Information Technology **15**, 18–23
11. H Yu Chen, C Chin-Chen, A new lossless compression scheme based on Huffman coding scheme for image compression. Signal Processing, Image Communication **16**(4), 367–372 (2000)
12. M Vetterli, J Kovacevic, *Wavelets and Subband Coding* (Prentice Hall, Englewood Cliffs NJ, 1995)
13. D Shanthi, G Sahoo, N Saravanan, Input feature selection using hybrid neuro-genetic approach in the diagnosis of stroke disease. IJCSNS **8**(12), 99–107 (2008)
14. MFB Othman, NB Abdullah, NFB Kamal, MRI brain classification using support vector machine, in *Proceedings of the 4th International Conference on Modeling, Simulation and Applied Optimization (ICMSAO), Kuala Lumpur, 19–21 April 2011*, ed. by (IEEE, Piscataway, 2011), pp. 1–4
15. TA Dinh, T Silander, CC Tchoyoson Lim, TY Leong, A generative model based approach to retrieving ischemic stroke images. AMIA Annu Symp Proc **2011**, 312–321 (2011)
16. CA Cocosco, AP Zijdenbos, AC Evans, A fully automatic and robust brain MRI tissue classification method. Med Image Anal **7**(4), 513–527 (2003)
17. S Lahmiri, M Boukadoum, Brain MRI classification using an ensemble system and LH and HL wavelet sub-bands features, in *2011 IEEE Third International Workshop on Computational Intelligence In Medical Imaging (CIMI), Paris, 11–15 April 2011*, ed. by (IEEE, Piscataway, 2011), pp. 1–7
18. E-SA El-dahshan, E-BM Salem, TH Younis, A hybrid technique for automatic MRI brain images classification. Studia Univ Babes Boloyai, Informatica **54**, 55–67 (2009)
19. H Bagher-Ebadian, K Jafari-Khouzani, PD Mitsias, H Soltanian-Zadeh, M Chopp, JR Ewing, *Predicting final extent of ischemic infarction using an artificial neural network analysis of multiparametric MRI in patients with stroke. International Joint Conference on Neural Networks, Atlanta, 14–19 June 2009* (IEEE, Piscataway, 2009), pp. 229–235
20. Y Kabir, M Dojat, B Scherrer, C Garbay, F Forbes, Multimodal MRI segmentation of ischemic stroke lesions. Conf Proc IEEE Eng Med Biol Soc **2007**, 1595–1598 (2007)
21. JA Gutierrez-Celaya, R Leder, R Carrillo, A Hawayek, J Hernandez, E Sucar, fMRI-based inverse analysis of stroke patients' motor functions, in *2011 Pan American Health Care Exchanges (PAHCE), Rio de Janiero, March 28 2011-April 1 2011*, ed. by (IEEE, Piscataway, 2011), pp. 1–6
22. Y Cherfa, A Cherfa, Y Kabir, S Kassous, A Jaillard, M Dojat, C Garbay, Segmentation of magnetic resonance brain images using edge and region cooperation characterization of stroke lesions. Int Arab J Inf Techn **4**(3), 281–288 (2007)
23. A Haar, Zur Theorie der orthogonalen Funktionen systeme. Mathematics Annua **69**(3), 331–371 (1910). doi:10.1007/BF01456326
24. KH Talukder, K Harada, Haar wavelet based approach for image compression and quality assessment of compressed image. IAENG Int J Appl Math **36**(1), IJAM_36_1_9
25. D Mohandass, J Janet, Performance evaluation of compressed medical image classification for telemedicine. Eur J Sci Res **57**, 286–292 (2011)

5

Magnitude-phase of the dual-tree quaternionic wavelet transform for multispectral satellite image denoising

Mohammed Kadiri[1,2*], Mohamed Djebbouri[3] and Philippe Carré[4]

Abstract

In this paper, we study the potential of the quaternionic wavelet transform for the analysis and processing of multispectral images with strong structural information. This new representation gives a very good division of the coefficients in terms of magnitude and three-phase angles and generalizes better the concept of analytic signal to image. Furthermore, it retains the property of shift invariant and directivity. We show an application of this transform in satellite image denoising. The proposed approach relies on the adaptation of thresholding procedures based on the dependency between magnitude quaternionic coefficients in local neighborhoods and phase regularization. In addition a non-marginal aspect of multispectral representation is introduced. Thanks to coherent analysis provided by the quaternionic wavelet transformation, the results obtained indicate the potential of this multispectral representation with magnitude thresholding and phase smoothing in noise reduction and edge preservation compared with classical wavelet thresholding methods that do not use phase or multiband information.

Keywords: Multispectral satellite image; Quaternionic wavelet analysis; Magnitude thresholding; Phase regularization; Structural similarity measure

1 Introduction

Wavelet transform have shown great success in diverse fields such as pattern recognition, image denoising, image compression, and computer graphics. The wavelet methods tend to give a good compromise for images containing such a mixture of discontinuities and texture. Previously, most researchers used the discrete wavelet transform (DWT) for image processing [1,2]. However, in many applications, it reaches its limitations, such as oscillations of coefficients at a singularity, lack of directional selectivity in higher dimensions, aliasing, and consequent shift variance. To overcome these problems, Bamberger and Smith [3] had proposed an effective filter bank for the directional decomposition of images. This filter has the important property that it can be critically sampled while achieving perfect reconstruction. Later, the undecimated

wavelet transform [4] was used in noise reduction and provides a shift invariant transformation, but at the cost of high redundancy.

More recently, the complex discrete wavelet transform (CDWT)[a] and the new quaternionic wavelet transform (QWT) employ analytic filters and propose magnitude-phase representations, shift invariance, and no aliasing. Several authors have studied the CDWT and its application to image denoising. Kingsbury [5-7] introduced a very elegant computational structure, the dual-tree complex wavelet transform (DT-CDWT), and incorporates it into the image restoration and enhancement. The DT-CDWT overcomes two drawbacks of the DWT. First is that the real and imaginary parts of CDWT associated with the pair of the Hilbert transforms are in quadrature; their magnitudes are almost shift invariant and redundancy is limited (factor 2 to compare with the undecimated wavelet transform ratio). Second, the complex phase encodes the signal location. However, in 2D, the complex representation by dual tree is not a satisfactory generalization of the analytic wavelet [8]. It has poor directional selectivity: its single phase can lead to ambiguity

* Correspondence: kadiri_univ_b@yahoo.fr
[1]Laboratory of Telecommunications and Digital Signal Processing, Department of Electronics, Faculty of Technology, Djillali Liabes University, Sidi Bel Abbes 22000, Algeria
[2]Department of Material Science, Faculty of Sciences and Technology, University of Mascara, Mascara 29000, Algeria
Full list of author information is available at the end of the article

when translating the image in two directions. Recently, the concept of generalizing complex wavelets to quaternion algebra has gained a lot of popularity [8-11]. The quaternionic wavelet transform has solved the problem of 2D localization. The phase of the QWT is represented by three angles: the first two encode horizontal and vertical orientations, while the third encodes texture information and edge. For the first application, QWT is used for multiscale image flow estimation [11]. Recently, Soulard studied the QWT [12] and its application in texture classification [13]. Gai et al. [14] used the dual-tree QWT (DT-QWT) in mono-spectral image denoising.

For denoising by classical DWT, Donoho and Johnstone have introduced the point-wise thresholding method [1,2]. In this scheme, all the wavelet coefficients below a certain value are set to zero, while the remaining ones were kept either unchanged (hardshrink) or reduced by the threshold value (softshrink). This approach offers the advantages of smoothness and adaptation. After that, several approaches which consider the influence of other wavelet coefficients on the current coefficient to be thresholded have been successively introduced. Cai and Silverman [15] proposed a thresholding algorithm by taking into account the neighboring coefficients. Their experimental results showed apparent advantages over the traditional term-by-term wavelet denoising. Chen and Bui [16] extended this idea to the multiwavelet case. They claimed that multiwavelet denoising outperforms the neighbor single-wavelet denoising for some standard test signals. Hailiang et al. [17] proved the efficacy of the multiwavelet coefficient dependency in the fault diagnosis of rolling bearings. Chinna Rao and Madhavi Latha [18] and Chen et al. [19] considered the relationship between the selective wavelet coefficients in a neighboring square window localized on the same scale. Experimental results show that these two methods produce better results in extended image denoising.

In addition to considering neighbor dependency in the same wavelet sub-band, Sendur and Selesnick [20] initiated the approach which takes into account the parent-child dependency. This idea was taken by Gai et al. [14]. For thresholding, they applied the bivariate shrinkage function to model the dependencies between current QWT coefficients and their corresponding parents. This method is based on a probabilistic estimator that seeks the relationship between the coefficients of two successive scales. They use a marginal approach applied on the real and imaginary parts of the wavelet coefficients, but the structural information (magnitude and phase) is not taken into account. In addition, only the real part is used in noise estimation.

In another work, the Bayes least squares-Gaussian scale mixture (BLS-GSM) method [21] is used for distributing visual artifacts in images during denoising. The intuition of this method is the following: the neighborhoods of coefficients at the adjacent positions and scales are modeled as the Gaussian scale mixture. The wavelet coefficients are updated by the Bayesian least squares estimation. The contributions of this method are twofold: the full optimal BLS solution is computed for estimating coefficients, and the covariance between signal and noise is defined by the vectorial form of the linear least square (LLS). The pyramidal representation in the local model for spatial neighbors makes this algorithm efficient. However, the BLS-GSM approach requires an accurate estimation of the original signal spectrum density which makes this algorithm not adaptive. Later, new denoising algorithms based on the transforms are introduced. Dabov et al. [22] proposed a block matching and 3D filtering (BM3D) method inspired by the BLS-GSM and the non-local filters. 2D noisy image patches are separated in 3D data groups. In each group, patches have similar local structures. The 3D transform includes the 2D transform (discrete cosine transform, discrete Fourier transform, or periodized wavelet) within a group, and the 1D Haar transform in spatial dimensions which is applied to the matched 2D transformed groups. Shrinkage is done in two separate steps. In the first, hard thresholding is employed, and in the second, Wiener filter. BM3D exploits similarity between overlapping patches and the correlation of wavelet coefficients and have had optimal performances. But, when there are a few similar patches in the image, the method produces suboptimal results.

The local pixel grouping-principal component analysis (LPG-PCA) denoising procedure [23] has a similar structure to the BM3D. The difference is in the basis transform. Each pixel and his neighborhood are grouped into vector variables (LPG). This vector is PCA transformed, and the noise is removed by two shrinkage stages. The input of the second stage is filtered coefficients of the first. LPG-PCA is based on the local adaptive basis function and preserves the fine edges, whereas the previous BM3D method uses the fixed basis function which is less adapted to the local geometry of the image.

Satellite imaging has an important role in gathering information about the earth's surface. However, thermal effects, sensor saturation, quantization errors, and transmission errors generate a noise that deteriorates the quality and creates a bad effect on image analysis [24]. In [24,25], the parameters of noise in remote sensing imagery are estimated. The characteristics of the noise depend on the type of the image to be processed and on the system of acquisition. The radar remote sensing systems, such as a Synthetic Aperture Radar (SAR), are affected by multiplicative noise in addition to additive noise. In optical remote sensing multispectral imagery (the images used in our work), the noise is typically independent of the data and it is generally additive in nature. This type of noise can be represented as a normal distribution (Gaussian), zero-mean random process. Ultimately, noise reduces the performances of important techniques of image processing such as detection, segmentation, and classification. These processes are performed by assuming that the noise is an integral part of the process. We can find some works where image denoising is made as a pretreatment. However, these approaches are not specified for satellite imaging. They are an extension of color image denoising. Luisier and Blu [26] proposed a new SURE-LET approach to image denoising. In [27], the authors extend this method to multichannel images. They used the parent-child coefficient relationship for thresholding. The efficiency of SURE-LET algorithm was demonstrated for color and satellite image processing. In [28], Saeedi et al. use the inter-channel relationship and dual-tree discrete wavelet shrinkage algorithm based on fuzzy logic. The authors have focused their work on the thresholding strategy, but they use a discrete wavelet transform which has a lack of shift variant. Chaux et al. [29] proposes a multichannel image denoising algorithm based on Stein's unbiased risk estimator [30] and on the discrete wavelet transform. A non-linear spatial estimator is proposed where this multivariate procedure operates by cleaning all components (spatial correlations are taken into account), but an inter-scale relationship is not considered. To conclude, it is interesting to note that for these three methods, the phase information is absent as in the case of the classical denoising approach. In our work, as we will see later, we propose to introduce this structural information into the denoising process.

The goal of this paper is not the comparison of different denoising method categories. More precisely, the comparison of new methods such as BM3D or LPG-PCA, which are based on bloc matching, distances us from the context of this work. We aim to show the contribution of analytic dimension and denoising based on regularization of coefficients depending on the local neighborhood and phase. At the same time, we introduce the concept of non-marginal processing in multiband case: due to the presence of potentially strong common information between the various bands, we developed a denoising method based on dual-tree quaternionic transform that supports all spectral bands simultaneously. Most of the existing algorithms apply the linear non-optimal processing separately or marginally in each band.

Another important point considered in our work is phase information. In most analytical wavelet denoising methods, only the magnitude of the wavelet is thresholded because the energy from the image is directed into a limited number of magnitude coefficients which 'stand out' from the noise. However, one quantity that appears to be very important in the human perception of images is phase as illustrated in [31]. The authors took the Fourier transforms of two images and used the magnitude information from one image and phase information from the other to construct a new synthetic Fourier transform which was then back-transformed to produce a new image. The features seen in such an image, while somewhat scrambled, clearly correspond to those in the image from which the phase data was obtained (see Figure 1). This idea is preserved in wavelet domain mainly for quaternionic wavelets where the phase is encoded in three angles. Regularization of this phase can greatly increase denoising results.

In this paper, we combine non-marginal DT-QWT, spatial and multiband neighboring thresholding, and phase regularization, adapted to satellite images, hence its originality.

The remainder of this article is organized as followed. The next section summarizes the theory of analytic signal and of the quaternionic wavelet transform. Section 3 explains how we can incorporate neighboring wavelet coefficients and phase regularization into image denoising. In Section 4, we propose a new algorithm by DT-QWT and neighborhood shrinkage/phase regularization function adapted to multiband or multichannel images. In Section 5, experimental results are provided, illustrating the potential of our approach for the class of real images. Finally, Section 6 is devoted to conclusions.

2 Summary of the quaternionic wavelet theory

In this section, we give the theoretical properties of the quaternionic wavelet transform which is based on the generalization of the analytic signal to image. Bulow [8] provided a strong 2D description of the analytic signal. He showed that complex algebra is only adapted to 1D signals, and 2D signal-like images are best described by quaternion algebra H.

The quaternion algebra is an extension of complex numbers to four-dimension (4D) algebra. Every element of H is a linear combination of a real scalar and three imaginary units i, j, k with real coefficients, as shown in [8]:

$$H = \{q = q_0 + i\,q_1 + j\,q_2 + k\,q_3 | q_0, q_1, q_2, q_3 \in R\},$$

(1)

with $i^2 = j^2 = k^2 = ijk = -1$, $ij = -ji = k$, $jk = -kj = i$, and $ki = -ik = j$.

In a polar form, a quaternion is defined by module and three angles which encode the phase, such as

$$q = |q|e^{i\theta}e^{j\psi}e^{k\varnothing}$$

(2)

$(\theta, \psi, \varnothing)$ are computed by the following formulas (for q normalized, i.e., $|q| = 1$) [10]:

$$\theta = \frac{1}{2}\arctan\left(\frac{2(q_0q_2 + q_1q_3)}{q_0^2 + q_1^2 - q_2^2 - q_3^2}\right)$$

(3)

Figure 1 Importance of phase in image processing. Sample images **(a, b)**. Second row: the phase of **(a)** appears in the left image and the phase of **(b)** appears in the right image.

$$\psi = \frac{1}{2}\arctan\left(\frac{2(q_0q_1 + q_2q_3)}{q_0^2 - q_1^2 + q_2^2 - q_3^2}\right) \qquad (4)$$

$$\varnothing = \frac{1}{2}\arcsin(2(q_0q_3 - q_1q_2)) \qquad (5)$$

Each quaternion phase angle is uniquely defined within the range $(\theta,\ \psi,\ \varnothing) \in [-\pi, \pi] \times \left[-\frac{\pi}{2}, \frac{\pi}{2}\right] \times \left[-\frac{\pi}{4}, \frac{\pi}{4}\right]$.

For the complex case, the analytic signal $f_A(t)$ is constructed by adding to its associate 1D real signal $f(t)$ its Hilbert transform $Hf(t)$ in imaginary part. f_A and its spectrum are given by

$$f_A(t) = f(t) + i\,Hf(t) \Leftrightarrow F_A(\omega) = \begin{cases} 0 & \text{if } \omega < 0 \\ F(\omega) & \text{if } \omega = 0 \\ 2F(\omega) & \text{if } \omega > 0. \end{cases} \qquad (6)$$

The modulus and the argument of f_A can be interpreted as the instantaneous magnitude and phase. Strong oscillation around one point of interest is a high magnitude, and phase indicates the relative location of this point. For generalization to 2D, Bulow introduced a definition of the quaternionic bidimensional analytic signal based on the quaternionic Fourier transform (QFT). The 2D quaternionic analytic signal for real signal f is defined as [8]

$$f_A^q(X) = f(X) + i f_{\mathrm{Hi}_1}(X) + j f_{\mathrm{Hi}_2}(X) + k f_{\mathrm{Hi}}(X), \qquad (7)$$

where $X = (x,y)$.

The functions $\left(f_{\mathrm{Hi}}, f_{\mathrm{Hi}_1}, f_{\mathrm{Hi}_2}\right)$ are, respectfully, the total Hilbert transformation and the partial Hilbert transformations, such as

$$f_{\mathrm{Hi}}(X) = f(X) ** \frac{1}{\pi^2 xy}, f_{\mathrm{Hi}_1}(X) = f(X) ** \frac{\delta(y)}{\pi x},$$
$$f_{\mathrm{Hi}_2}(X) = f(X) ** \frac{\delta(x)}{\pi y},$$

$\delta(x)$ and $\delta(y)$ are 2D Dirac distributions along the y-axis and x-axis, respectively; and ** denotes 2D convolution.

For each spatial position of the 2D analytical signal, the polar form of Equation 7 provides 2D local magnitude and phase that can be used to analyze 2D signals.

In order to obtain 2D analytical multiresolution representation, the construction of the quaternionic wavelet transform is based on the generalization of the DT scheme proposed by Kingsbury [5]. We obtain a 2D analytic wavelet and its associated quaternionic wavelet transform by organizing the four quadrature components of a 2D wavelet (real wavelet and its three Hilbert transformations: one total and two partial) as a quaternion [11].

To compute the QWT coefficients [12], we can use a separable 2D implementation of the dual-tree filter bank shown in Figure 2. During each stage of filtering, we

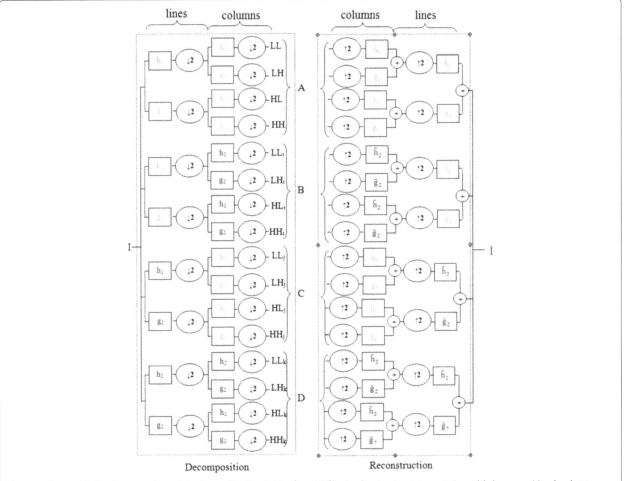

Figure 2 Separable implementation of dual-tree filterbank. The four 2D filterbanks give two interpretations: (1) decomposition by three quaternionic wavelets oriented in horizontal, vertical, and diagonal directions. The sub-bands are A + iB + jC + kD. (2) Decomposition by six complex Gabor-type wavelets oriented in $n\pi/6$ directions. The sub-bands are (A + D) + i (B − C) and (A − D) + i (C − B).

independently apply the two sets of h and g filters, two Hilbert pairs, to each dimension (x and y) of a 2D image. Therefore, the resulting 2D dual-tree implementation comprises four independent filter banks (hh, hg, gh, and gg) applied to each dimension and operating on the same 2D image. We combine the wavelet coefficients of the same sub-band from the output of each filter bank using quaternion algebra to obtain the QWT coefficients. These coefficients allow us to have a multiscale representation of analytic signal with module and phase information (see Equations 1 and 2).

3 Incorporating selective neighboring wavelet coefficients and phase regularization in image denoising

3.1 Thresholding by selective neighboring magnitude coefficients

From the 2D quaternionic wavelet transform, at every decomposition level, we get magnitude (module) of four frequency sub-bands, corresponding to an approximation

part and three detail parts. The principle is the same as that of the classical wavelets. Thresholding is applied to the coefficients of successive scales and the low-pass approximation is unchanged. Due to the linearity of the wavelet transform, the additive noise model in the image domain remains additive in the wavelet domain [18] as well as

$$w_{k,l}(x, y) = y_{k,l}(x, y) + n_{k,l}(x, y), \tag{8}$$

where $w_{k,l}(x,y)$, $y_{k,l}(x,y)$, and $n_{k,l}(x,y)$ denote noisy, noise-free wavelet coefficients, and noise components of scale k and orientation l, respectively.

As explained in Section 1, the noise is assumed Gaussian and additive. The probabilistic model adapted to the magnitude of noisy quaternionic wavelet coefficients is the *Rayleigh* distribution. The Rayleigh model is a function of the Gaussian estimation of the squared real part added to the Gaussian estimation of the squared imaginary part of noisy coefficients.

To define the denoising method, it is necessary to introduce a thresholding strategy adapted to the QWT. The basic motivation of neighbor thresholding is that if the current coefficient contains information, it is likely that the neighbor coefficients also do. (Wavelet coefficients are correlated in a small neighborhood.) We choose local windows around every coefficient of our interest, and we threshold it by using the coefficients in this neighborhood. The size of the window is predefined as a function of the image size. We shrink the magnitude of the noisy wavelet coefficients according to the following formula [18]:

$$\left| w_{k,l}(x,y) \right| = \left| w_{k,l}(x,y) \right| \times T(x,y) \qquad (9)$$

$T(x,y)$ is the shrinkage factor defined as

$$T(x,y) = 1 - \frac{\lambda^2}{S_j^2(x,y)} \qquad (10)$$

$$T(x,y) = \begin{cases} T(x,y) & \text{if } \lambda^2 < S_j^2 \\ 0 & \text{if } \lambda^2 > S_j^2, \end{cases}$$

λ is the universal threshold, with $\lambda^2 = 2\sigma^2 \log b^2$; σ is the standard deviation of corrupted coefficients; and b^2 is the size of local neighborhood window.

In Equation 10, S_j^2 is the summation of squared coefficients in the local window defined as in [19]:

$$S_j^2(x,y) = \sum_{(p,q) \in b^2} \left| w_j(p,q) \right|^2, \quad b = b_0 - j, \qquad (11)$$

where j is the level of decomposition and b_0 is a constant defined according to the size of noisy image and the support of the wavelet filter. (p,q) varies in the neighboring window centered on the coefficient $w\ (x,y)$. The window size b^2 varies depending on the level of decomposition because the correlation between coefficients varies in successive scales. Figure 3 illustrates a variable size neighborhood window centered at the wavelet coefficient to be thresholded. The choice of a larger size decreases the correlation between neighboring coefficients, while a smaller size brings us back to the term-by-term case (the neighbor dependency is neglected).

The shrinkage factor T of Equation 10 is a function of the adaptive sum S_j and universal threshold λ. S_j depends on the neighboring window size b^2. For each wavelet coefficient candidate to thresholding, T is calculated by comparing the sum of neighboring coefficients to λ. Then, the wavelet coefficient is either reduced or set to zero. Neighboring shrinkage is a generalization of the term-by-term thresholding.

A recent method proposed by Luisier and Blu [26], which is based on Stein's unbiased risk estimator [30], can be used to perform denoising in wavelet domain. Authors parameterize the denoising process as a sum of elementary non-linear processes with unknown weight. They minimize an estimate of the mean-squared error between the clean image and the denoised one based on the noisy data alone. However, the neighboring strategy adopted in our work is based on the direct thresholding of the coefficients. We want to place our approach among those using the same concept, but they differ in the adopted wavelet transform. We can see later that this strategy is more adapted to combination with the following phase regularization.

In some applications of image denoising, the value of the input noise variance σ^2 is known or can be measured based on the information other than the corrupted data. If this information is not available, one has to estimate it from the input data, eliminating the input of the actual signal. All frequency sub-bands of the decomposition are used in the noise estimation [1,2]. For estimating the *Gaussian* noise variance in real and in imaginary parts of noisy wavelet coefficients, we use the mean absolute deviation relation proposed by Donoho and Johnstone [2] that is denoted as

$$\sigma_g^2 = \left(\frac{\text{median}|W|}{0.6745} \right)^2, \qquad (12)$$

where median $|W|$ is the median of neighboring coefficients in the local window centered on the coefficient $w(x,y)$.

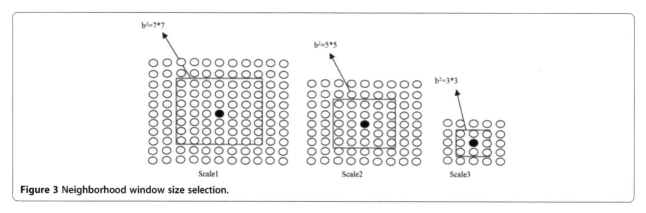

Figure 3 Neighborhood window size selection.

Then, the noise variance according to the *Rayleigh* distribution [24] is given by

$$\sigma^2 = \frac{4-\pi}{2}\sigma_g^2 \tag{13}$$

To conclude, the algorithm described in this section is the adaptation of the method called *NeighShrink* based on the squared sum of all the processed magnitude wavelet coefficients with variable neighborhood window sizes. These sizes are in function of decomposition levels. The adaptive threshold value selected according to neighborhood provides a powerful thresholding procedure greater than the term-by-term shrinkage approach (experimental proofs for real wavelet are proposed in [18,19]).

3.2 Phase regularization
In addition to the image denoising by thresholding the magnitude of the quaternionic wavelet transform, it is important that the phase of this transform is not excluded from the process. The three quaternion phase angles (θ, ψ, $\varnothing$) for Equations 3, 4, and 5 are separable. The first two encode the shift and the third encodes the textures. More precisely, Bulow [8] defined a shift theorem for the quaternionic Fourier transform such as a shift of the image is an equivalent an offsite of the two first terms θ and ψ of the phase.

The shift theorem for the QFT [8] approximately holds for the QWT that conducts a local QFT analysis. When a shift of image $f(X)$ to $f(X - d)$ occurs, the QFT phase undergoes the following changes:

$$(\theta(\mathbf{u}), \psi(\mathbf{u}), \varnothing(\mathbf{u})) \rightarrow (\theta(\mathbf{u}) - 2\pi u d_1, \psi(\mathbf{u}) - 2\pi v d_2, \varnothing(\mathbf{u})),$$

where $\mathbf{u} = (u,v)$ are the axes of the 2D QFT domain. $\boldsymbol{d} = (d_1, d_2)$.

Note that the 1D shift is equivalent to the structural information, but the 2D structure (e.g., corners, T-junctions) may be more complex than lines or edges and cannot be described by the shift of the first two angles. The author observed that when the third angle $\varnothing$ is around $\pm\frac{\pi}{4}$, the codec structure is a line or an edge oriented along a diagonal. The angle $\varnothing$ can be interpreted as the relative amplitude of signal energy along the 1D which manifolds in two orthogonal directions.

Chan et al. [11] demonstrated the importance of the quaternionic wavelet transform phase in image processing and analysis. Chan and his co-authors also developed a multiscale flow/motion estimation algorithm that computes a disparity flow map between two images with respect to local object motion [32]. Soulard and Carré have developed an efficient method for texture classification, thanks to coherent multiscale analysis brought by the magnitude and phase of the quaternionic wavelet

transform [13]. In their approach, the authors used a global measure of energy from the magnitude, and they combine it with the weighted standard deviation of the third-angle quaternionic phase. They observed that this last measure phase contains structural information that contributed to improving the classification.

From those analyses, we observed that the combination of QWT magnitude and phase is effective in several image processing tools. In our algorithm, by adjusting only $\varnothing$ of the quaternionic sub-band coefficients, a potential interesting change can be observed in image quality, and therefore, we can improve denoising performance. In our knowledge, there are very few methods that use phase in the process of denoising. With analytical decomposition, the only proposition is the Miller and Kingsbury approach [33]. They have modeled discontinuities in image by using wavelet coefficients derotated by twice the phase in local scale and the next coarser scale at the same spatial location. In our work, we propose a regularization of the phase information. This approach is sufficient if we want to reduce complexity. We use a typical first-order regularizer $R(\varnothing) = C\varnothing$ to enforce spatial smoothness [34]. From this concept, quaternionic wavelet coefficients become

$$w_{k,l}(x,y) = \left(\left| w_{k,l}(x,y) \right|_T \right) e^{i\theta} e^{j\psi} e^{kC\varnothing}, \tag{14}$$

where $|w_{k,l}(x, y)|_T$ is the thresholded magnitude coefficient from the NeighShrink method.

We want to extract unique value that defines the global direction in a sub-band and has structural information at the same time. For this, the finite matrix C is chosen as a simple median filter with variant size. The size of smoothing matrix C changes according to the scale. It should be noted that the regularization of the phase by median filter is applied to the thresholded magnitude coefficients; consequently, the phase regularization is controlled by the value of the magnitude.

To conclude, we note that the denoising method does not increase the computational cost dramatically. If a real wavelet transform spends N operations, the construction of QWT would need $4N$ operations. Moreover, denoising-based real wavelet requires the estimation of the threshold and the thresholding operation for each coefficient, with the quaternionic transform. This process is applied for two informations: magnitude and phase. Finally, the new operation is the polar conversion.

The process of denoising is illustrated in Figure 4. The experimental efficiency of phase regularization is shown in Section 5.

4 Multispectral image denoising by the DT-QWT and the NeighShrink/phase regularization algorithm
In the previous sections, we defined the quaternionic wavelet transform and the thresholding/regularization

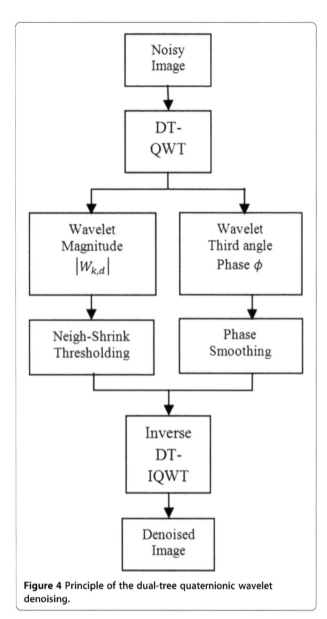

Figure 4 Principle of the dual-tree quaternionic wavelet denoising.

The 'clean' multichannel wavelet coefficients contain $M \in N^*$ components y^m with $m \in [1, ..., M]$. Typically, M is equal to three in RGB images. It might be larger for satellite images. Therefore, the multichannel noisy observation in the wavelet domain is as follows:

$$W_{k,l}(x,y) = Y_{k,l}(x,y) + N_{k,l}(x,y) , \qquad (15)$$

where $Y \triangleq (y^{(1)}, ..., y^{(M)})$ is the noise-free wavelet vector, $N \triangleq (n^{(1)}, ..., n^{(M)})$ is the noise vector, and $W \triangleq (w^{(1)}, ..., w^{(M)})$ is the noisy wavelet vector. (x,y) are the coordinates of the coefficient in the corresponding sub-band, and k and l are scale and orientation, respectively.

We see that each coefficient located in position (x, y) and scale k is taken in the vector W (vectors Y, N) with the coefficients of the remaining channels according to the same position and the same scale.

In color imaging, it is important to treat pixels as color components, not as three separate RGB colors. When only the separate channels are considered, more artifacts are introduced. For thresholding in the mth channel, the wavelet coefficient $w_{k,l}^m(x, y)$ must be modified according to its spatial neighboring but also depending on the corresponding coefficients of the same scale in the remaining channels. For this, we propose to combine multichannel information and spatial information. As in single channel thresholding, the intra-scale/inter-channel shrinkage factor T is a function of squared summation S_j^2 and universal threshold λ^2 (return to Equation 10). These parameters are defined in a multichannel case according to the proposed formulas:

$$S_j^2(x,y) = \sum_{(p,q) \in b^2} \left| w_j^{(m)}(p,q) \right|^2$$
$$+ \sum_{\substack{i=1 \\ i \neq m}} \left| w_j^i(x,y) \right|^2 \qquad (16)$$

In Equation 16, we sum neighboring coefficients inside a window of size b^2 in scale j and channel m. This first result is added to the sum of coefficients in the same position (x,y) but of all M channels. The threshold is defined such that $\lambda^2 = 2\sigma^2 \log b^2$ and the noise variance σ^2 is given by

$$\sigma^2 = \frac{4-\pi}{2} \left(\frac{\text{median} |W_c| + \text{median} |W_{x,y}|}{0.6745} \right)^2 , \qquad (17)$$

where median $|W_c|$ and median $|W_{x,y}|$ are the median of neighboring coefficients in the same channel m and the median of coefficients of all channels in the same spatial position, respectively.

In Equations 16 and 17, we give a new formulation of the parameters that allows us to calculate the multichannel threshold value T. The first term specified an intra-scale relationship (spatial), and the second defined an inter-channel correlation. We note that in the second term of S_j^2 and σ^2,

strategy for mono-spectral image. In multispectral image, different bands are correlated: an image discontinuity from one band is most likely to occur in at least some of the remaining bands. It should be noted that in order to avoid confusion between the spectral bands of the wavelet transform and the multiband image, the second is called multichannel.

For denoising, there are two main conceivable strategies: the first one consists of marginally applying a denoising process; the second is to devise specific non-separable multichannel denoising algorithms. Our interest is focused on the latter strategy. Therefore, we defined a *non-linear method* which generalizes a mono-channel approach by taking into account the relationship between channels (it is not a marginal approach).

the sum and the median, respectively, are made on all channels. When the number of channels is very high, e.g., for hyperspectral images, we can define two approaches: First, only the adjacent correlated channels are considered. However, when the correlated channels are not adjacent, we can search correlated bands with a block matching approach [22]. The proposed algorithm can be adapted to this second case but with an increase of complexity.

Previous multichannel magnitude thresholding is combined with linear phase regularization. It is important to notice that the multichannel phases are smoothed separately following the mono-channel strategy (median filter). Indeed, inter-correlation between the phases of different channels is not known, and the formulation of this relationship is not yet established (this work is in progress).

Proposed multichannel denoising process by the dual tree quaternionic wavelet transform and the NeighShrink/phase regularization algorithm is shown in Figure 5 (we considered a multispectral image with three channels and decomposed it into three scales).

5 Results and discussion

Different tests are accomplished to rate the effectiveness of the proposed algorithm in reducing noise and compare it with known techniques. In the following section, we present the denoising results in both single-channel and multichannel cases. This section is intended to illustrate the contribution of the quaternionic wavelet transform, the multiband information in spectral and spatial thresholding, and the phase smoothing compared to the methods based on classical real neighboring coefficient regularization.

5.1 Single-channel denoising

We compare neighborhood thresholding and the phase regularization method (proposed algorithm called *NeighShrink/phase-smooth*) with different thresholding techniques (soft shrinkage [2], neighboring shrinkage without phase regularization [18], and bivariate shrinkage [14], called *VisuShrink*, *NeighShrink*, and *BiShrink*, respectively). For implementation software of the bivariate thresholding method, we refer to the homepage [35], thanks to Shihua Cai and Keyong Li. We note that in single-channel denoising, analysis and synthesis of images over all denoising processes are made by the same dual-tree quaternionic wavelet transform with five levels of decomposition. We change only the thresholding methods listed above.

The images used in our experimentation are the second green band (left image), the first red band (middle image), and the fourth infrared band (right

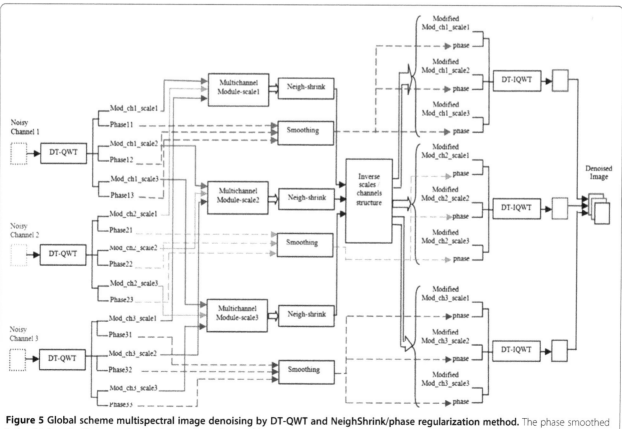

Figure 5 Global scheme multispectral image denoising by DT-QWT and NeighShrink/phase regularization method. The phase smoothed is the third angle. The two other angles remain unchangeable.

image) of satellite images [36]. The first one covers the area called *Sebkha*, part of Oran City in western Algeria, the second is one band of satellite image that covers part of Mouhammadia City in Algeria, and the last represents another area of Oran City (Figure 6). In mono-channel experiments, we have chosen three independent bands. There is no correlation between those data, and they are derived from three different areas. This choice will allow us to see the potential of our method to denoise various structures in the images. These single-channel images have the same size of 400×400. Following the model of Equation 8, normally distributed, uncorrelated, and zero-mean additive noise was generated for six levels. Then, each band is contaminated with computer-generated additive Gaussian noise $(0, \sigma_n^2)$ to simulate a noisy image. Inherent low-level noise in the original image was considered as a part of a data. More details on multispectral images are given in the next section.

The proposed approach has been evaluated using visual analysis and objective peak signal-to-noise ratio (PSNR), a criterion which is commonly used as a measure of noise suppression:

$$\text{PSNR} = 10 \log_{10} \frac{255^2 NM}{\sum_{x=1}^{N} \sum_{y=1}^{M} \left(I(x,y) - \hat{I}(x,y) \right)^2}, \tag{18}$$

where I and $\hat{I}$ are noisy and denoised images, respectively. $N \times M$ is the size of the images.

The PSNR is simple to calculate, and it is mathematically convenient in the context of optimization. However, this objective metric is not very well matched to perceived visual quality. The structural similarity index (SSIM) is a very powerful tool which is based on structural information of distorted images and converges in the same results as the visual perception. This measure was highly adapted in our algorithm. It takes into account the structural dependencies between neighboring pixels when the PSNR based on the MSE is calculated pixel by pixel.

The *SSIM* [37] between reference image I and processed image $\hat{I}$ is given by

$$\text{SSIM}(x,y) = l(x,y)c(x,y)s(x,y) \tag{19}$$

The term $l(x,y)$ stands for the luminance comparison function, $c(x,y)$ for the contrast comparison function, and $s(x,y)$ for the structure comparison.

These functions are given by the following formulas:

$$l(x,y) = \frac{2\bar{\mu}_I . \bar{\mu}_{\hat{I}} + C_1}{\left(\bar{\mu}_I\right)^2 + \left(\bar{\mu}_{\hat{I}}\right)^2 + C_1} \tag{20}$$

$$c(x,y) = \frac{2\,\sigma_I . \sigma_{\hat{I}} + C_2}{\sigma_I^2 + \sigma_{\hat{I}}^2 + C_2} \tag{21}$$

$$s(x,y) = \frac{\sigma_{I\hat{I}} + C_3}{\sigma_I . \sigma_{\hat{I}} + C_3} \tag{22}$$

with $C_1 = (LK_1)^2$, $C_2 = (LK_2)^2$, and

$$C_2 = (LK_2)^2 \tag{23}$$

where $\bar{\mu}_I$ and $\bar{\mu}_{\hat{I}}$ are the mean intensities of I and $\hat{I}$, respectively. σ_I and $\sigma_{\hat{I}}$ are the standard deviations used in the estimation of image contrast, and $\sigma_{I\hat{I}}$ corresponds to the covariance between the two images. L is the dynamic range of luminance (usually the maximum gray level). K_1 and K_2 are two constant parameters to adjust the metric variation (the Matlab implementation by the authors in [37] used the values of 0.01 and 0.03, respectively).

Tables 1 and 2 summarize the obtained results in PSNR (dB) and SSIM (%). In Table 3, we give the average gain of the two various metric comparisons.

Several conclusions can be drawn from these experiments:

1. VisuShrink does not have any denoising power or very low performance when the noise level is low (noise variance: 15, 20).
2. The effect of using only the magnitude neighboring thresholding (*NeighShrink*) for the three images is generally a considerable PSNR and SSIM gain compared to classical *VisuShrink* thresholding.

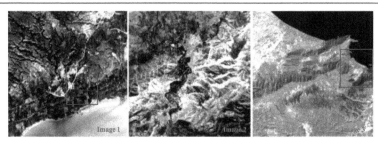

Figure 6 Test images used in the single-channel denoising experiments. Images referred to as image 1 to image 3 (left to right). Red squares represent the parts displayed in Figures 7 and 8. The images corresponding to different spectral bands are captured in gray. Additional processing gives these images false color (green, red…).

Table 1 Comparison of various denoising methods by PSNR (dB)

Methods	Noise variance					
	15	20	25	30	40	50
Image 1						
Noisy image	24.87	22.40	20.78	18.19	16.69	14.91
VisuShrink	22.93	21.51	21.49	19.71	19.90	17.90
NeighShrink	25.23	23.43	22.89	21.93	20.63	19.58
BiShrink	25.32	24.48	23.19	23.58	22.43	21.93
Proposed algorithm	26.24	25.65	25.02	24.36	23.12	22.99
Image 2						
Noisy image	24.90	22.42	20.76	18.18	16.64	14.82
VisuShrink	24.28	21.72	21.68	20.82	20.01	19.65
NeighShrink	27.37	24.95	24.02	22.31	19.80	23.12
BiShrink	26.74	25.47	25.01	20.48	23.40	23.53
Proposed algorithm	27.74	25.34	24.90	23.95	23.36	22.63
Image 3						
Noisy image	25.07	22.58	20.90	18.23	16.63	14.81
VisuShrink	24.25	22.29	25.04	22.92	22.65	21.87
NeighShrink	27.32	26.26	25.45	22.59	22.46	19.13
BiShrink	28.22	27.37	25.15	23.29	23.26	23.21
Proposed algorithm	28.02	28.42	26.55	25.02	25.03	24.92

Wavelet transform: dual-tree quaternionic wavelet transform with five levels.

Table 2 Comparison of various denoising methods by SSIM (%)

Methods	Noise variance					
	15	20	25	30	40	50
Image 1						
Noisy image	83.96	76.70	71.03	60.24	53.26	44.57
VisuShrink	84.63	65.96	66.45	53.19	55.87	36.55
NeighShrink	73.40	76.50	74.66	71.38	62.47	58.13
BiShrink	83.09	81.57	76.71	88.85	72.04	74.51
Proposed algorithm	86.53	85.57	83.61	92.80	74.93	75.78
Image 2						
Noisy image	89.28	82.84	77.25	66.08	58.24	48.22
VisuShrink	83.87	70.32	70.47	64.97	58.80	57.56
NeighShrink	92.52	87.06	84.67	79.73	71.56	82.86
BiShrink	91.53	88.23	88.27	75.59	83.88	82.15
Proposed algorithm	93.81	90.02	88.41	87.83	86.60	86.26
Image 3						
Noisy image	70.12	59.94	52.42	39.91	32.68	24.97
VisuShrink	61.30	53.84	68.96	52.23	51.75	48.07
NeighShrink	80.80	75.50	71.96	56.63	54.79	52.36
BiShrink	83.92	80.93	73.37	64.72	64.55	59.46
Proposed algorithm	84.36	84.62	77.41	69.67	74.01	68.02

Wavelet transform: dual-tree quaternionic wavelet transform with five levels.

3. *NeighShrink* is not efficient as opposed to the *bivariate* denoising method in all cases.
4. The addition of phase smoothing to the magnitude neighboring shrinkage mostly outperforms other approaches with fixed wavelet. In Table 3, the comparison for image 1 shows that the average PSNR and SSIM improvement gained by the proposed method over *NeighShrink* (without phase smoothing) are 2.45 dB and 13.78%, respectively. When our method is compared to *BiShrink*, we gain 1.07 dB and 3.73%.
5. For high levels of noise (40, 50), PSNR comparisons for image 2 and image 3 are not adequate with these conclusions. However, for the same noise variance values, the SSIM gives a better result which corresponds to visual observations. In image 1 (Figure 6), the edges of the squared vegetation are naturally very disenable over other structures. PSNR and SSIM are perfectly adapted with this image and allow very good comparisons. But, image 2 and image 3 (see Figure 6) have mixed structures and in some noise levels, only the SSIM, which is a structural metric, gives results that correspond to visual analysis.

For visual evaluation, there are two important criteria: the visibility of processing artifacts and preserving image edges. Figures 7 and 8 illustrate denoising results of single-channel image 1 and image 3, respectively, from different methods. For a better visualization of the details and differences between denoising results, only partial parts of the images are displayed (see red square in Figure 6). The *NeighShrink* approach surpasses classical *VisuShrink* thresholding for the two images, but the noise is still present (Figures 7c,d and 8c,d).

The bivariate shrinkage reduces the noise more effectively than the NeighShrink but details are very smooth

Table 3 Average PSNR and SSIM differences between denoising algorithms for the three images

		PSNR (dB)	SSIM (%)
NeighShrink/VisuShrink	Image 1	1.33	8.98
	Image 2	2.23	15.4
	Image 3	0.69	9.31
BiShrink/NeighShrink	Image 1	1.20	10.03
	Image 2	0.51	1.87
	Image 3	1.22	5.81
Proposed algorithm/NeighShrink	Image 1	2.45	13.78
	Image 2	1.05	5.75
	Image 3	2.45	11.00
Proposed algorithm/BiShrink	Image 1	1.07	3.73
	Image 2	0.39	3.88
	Image 3	1.24	5.19

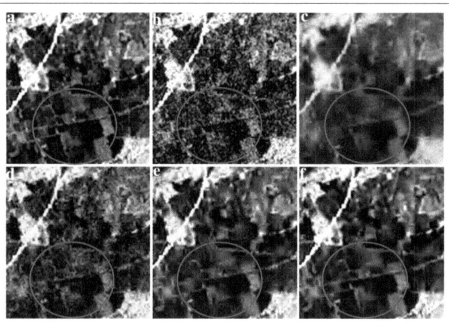

Figure 7 Single-channel denoising comparison results in PSNR/SSIM of image 1. **(a)** Partial noise-free image, **(b)** noisy image 18.19 dB/60.24%, **(c)** VisuShrink 19.71 dB/53.19%, **(d)** NeighShrink 21.93 dB/71.38%, **(e)** BiShrink 23.58 dB/88.85%, and **(f)** proposed algorithm 24.36 dB/92.80%.

(see Figures 7e and 8e). Better results are obtained with the NeighShrink/PhaseSmooth algorithm which can effectively distinguish the regions of interest from noise (square vegetation edges in Figure 7f and bottom structures in Figure 8f enclosed in red circles are more contrasted), meaning the correction of the third quaternionic angle is key to realizing the full potential of the algorithm (Figure 7f).

5.2 Multichannel satellite image denoising

We propose in this section to study the adaptation of the single-channel algorithm to multispectral satellite images. There are several sources of noise in optical satellite images (photonic, electronic, quantization error, etc.), and the additive zero-mean Gaussian noise model is a realistic approximation as shown in [24,25].

We perform the multichannel algorithm based on the DT-QWT and the NeighShrink/PhaseSmooth denoising strategy where a non-marginal aspect is highlighted. In order to compare different possible wavelet choices, the experimental results are derived from the DWT and the DT-CWT (for these representations, the thresholding approach is NeighShrink). Phase smoothing cannot be applied to the DWT (no phase) and the DT-CWT (the unique phase of this transform is a location information and phase smoothing adds nothing to denoising). In addition, the proposed algorithm is compared to the DT-QWT-Neighboring shrinkage and the DT-QWT-Bivariate shrinkage. We specify that the non-separable denoising is only done by our method. In all other

approaches, the analysis/thresholding/synthesis scheme is marginally (linearly) performed channel by channel.

The experiments in this section have been carried out on two seven-band satellite images shown in Figures 9 and 10, which represent two regions called *Sebkha* and *Sea*, parts of Oran City in western Algeria [36]. The first *Thematic Mapper* image contains a lake and vegetation with several roads. The second includes sea and mountains. The coverage areas are 30×30 km with resolution of 30 m and size of $400 \times 400 \times 7$. We note that for our comparison, denoising methods are applied to the seven bands of the satellite images. However, only three channels are used in the display of visual results (red, blue, and infrared for the Sebkha image and red, blue, and green for the Sea image; these bands allow differentiation between soil, vegetation species, coastal areas, sea, and biomass). This choice is justified by the fact that these denoising results are subsequently used in the following processes such as segmentation or compression or simply a visual interpretation of information contained in the images. In this case, we will need only three bands which correspond to areas of our interest (vegetation, lakes, sea, mountains, roads, etc.).

We measured the experimental results by the PSNR, objectively, which is an extension of the definition given by Equation 18 as

$$\text{PSNR} = 10 \log_{10} \frac{255^2 NMC}{\sum_{k=1}^{C} \left(\sum_{x=1}^{N} \sum_{y=1}^{M} \left(I(x,y) - \hat{I}(x,y) \right)^2 \right)},$$
(24)

where C is the number of channels.

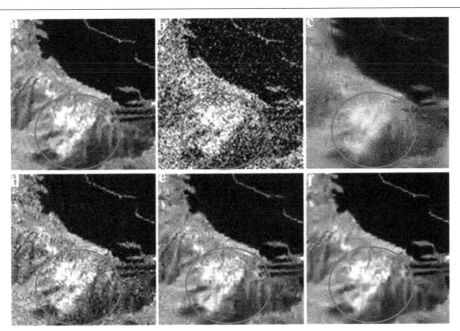

Figure 8 Single-channel denoising comparison results in PSNR/SSIM of image 3. (a) Partial noise-free image, **(b)** noisy image 14.81 dB/24.94%, **(c)** VisuShrink 21.87 dB/48.07%, **(d)** NeighShrink 19.13 dB/52.36%, **(e)** BiShrink 23.21 dB/59.46%, and **(f)** proposed algorithm 24.92 dB/68.02%.

Table 4 summarizes the obtained results. We observe the following:

1. Quaternionic and complex wavelet transforms outperform the discrete wavelet transform when the thresholding strategy (NeighShrink) is the same

(average gain 1.14 and 1.06 dB for image Sebkha and Sea, respectively).

2. DT-QWT and DT-CWT have very close results.

3. As in the single-channel experiment, the bivariate shrinkage is more efficient than the neighboring shrinkage without phase smoothing.

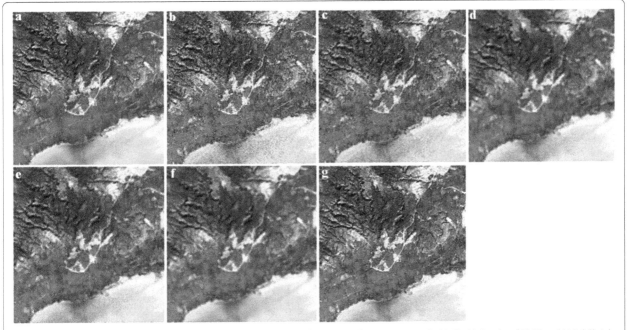

Figure 9 Multichannel Sebkha satellite image denoising. (a) Noise-free image. **(b)** Noisy image 21.26 dB. **(c)** Results of DWT and NeighShrink 22.18 dB. **(d)** Results of DT-CWT and NeighShrink 23.32 dB. **(e)** Results of DT-QWT and NeighShrink 23.36 dB. **(f)** Results of DT-QWT and BiShrink 24.57 dB. **(g)** Results of DT-QWT and NeighShrink/PhaseSmooth 26.14 dB.

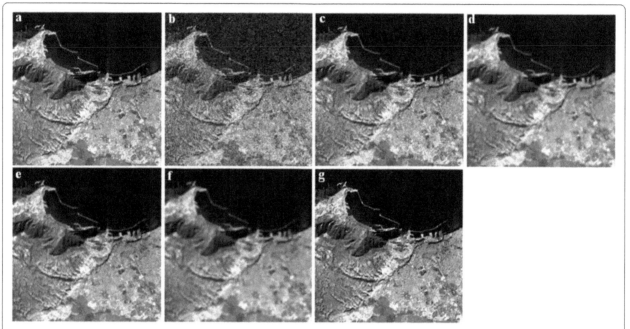

Figure 10 Multichannel Sea satellite image denoising. (a) Noise-free image. **(b)** Noisy image 15.28 dB. **(c)** Results of DWT and NeighShrink 16.12 dB. **(d)** Results of DT-CWT and NeighShrink 17.17 dB. **(e)** Results of DT-QWT and NeighShrink 17.17 dB. **(f)** Results of DT-QWT and BiShrink 19.21 dB. **(g)** Results of DT-QWT and NeighShrink/PhaseSmooth 20.87 dB.

4. Compared to the DT-QWT with neighboring channel-by-channel shrinkage, the proposed inter-channels DT-QWT NeighShrink/PhaseSmooth achieves an improved performance and yields a larger total PSNR gain (average 2.79 and 3.03 dB for the two images, respectively). The PSNR gain values are greater than the results obtained in Section 5.1 (2.45 dB).

5. When we compare our method to the DT-QWT with bivariate shrinkage, we gain 1.06 and 1.66 dB for the Sebkha and Sea images, respectively. Again, the multichannel algorithm gives better results than the single channel (1.24 dB) for the second image.

Figures 9 and 10 illustrate the comparative results among different multichannel denoising methods and proposed algorithm applied to the two images. In Figures 9c and 10c (discrete wavelet transform), the noise is very present. Noise is reduced in Figures 9d,e,f and 10d,e,f, but these three methods have the tendency to smooth discontinuities. We note that the quaternionic wavelet transform is greater than the DWT and very close to the CWT, while the thresholding strategy is only the neighboring shrinkage. The proposed methods preserve the edges of each structure near the discontinuities. This is demonstrated in Figures 9g and 10g where the algorithm incorporating inter-channel thresholding and linear phase smoothing produces a sharper image than the DT-QWT with bivariate shrinkage and neighboring shrinkage for both the Sebkha and Sea images. Vegetation and squares are identified in Figure 9g, and lines of mountains are shown in Figure 10g. In most cases, noise is not entirely removed by our method, but it is significantly reduced and the edges are sharper.

To conclude, we can say that the new formulation of the threshold factor of the quaternionic magnitude coefficients,

Table 4 PSNR (dB) comparison of multichannel image denoising algorithms

Methods	Noise variance					
	15	20	25	30	40	50
Sebkha						
Noisy image	25.14	22.89	21.26	18.73	17.06	15.56
DWT (NeighShrink)	26.09	23.79	22.18	19.63	17.94	16.45
DT-CWT (NeighShrink)	27.25	24.95	23.32	20.77	19.06	17.57
DT-QWT (NeighShrink)	27.29	24.98	23.36	20.79	19.06	17.57
DT-QWT (BiShrink)	28.50	26.19	24.57	21.99	20.25	18.75
DT-QWT (NeighShrink/ PhaseSmooth)	30.09	27.77	26.14	23.55	21.80	20.29
Sea						
Noisy image	25.87	23.16	21.18	18.91	17.14	15.28
DWT (NeighShrink)	26.74	24.03	22.04	19.76	17.97	16.12
DT-CWT (NeighShrink)	27.81	25.10	23.11	20.82	19.02	17.17
DT-QWT (NeighShrink)	27.86	25.15	23.17	20.83	19.02	17.17
DT-QWT (BiShrink)	29.09	26.38	24.39	22.07	20.26	19.21
DT-QWT (NeighShrink/ PhaseSmooth)	30.77	28.06	26.04	23.74	21.92	20.87

the estimation of noise variance based both on spatial and multichannel dependencies and the multiplication of the third-angle quaternionic phase by smoothing matrix have a great impact on satellite image denoising compared to the classical methods and advanced methods which do not use the information contained in the phase. All these experimentations demonstrate that a coherent analysis is associated with the quaternionic wavelet transformation and the potential of this multispectral representation with magnitude thresholding and phase smoothing for noise reduction and features preservation.

6 Conclusions

In this article, we introduce the 2D multiscale quaternionic wavelet transform for satellite image denoising application. We reintroduce the fact that this new representation is particularly efficient for the description of image features and more efficient for the detail representation than the discrete wavelet transform or the complex wavelet transform. As we have reviewed, quaternionic transformation generalizes 1D complex wavelet to higher dimensions and offers more information: a phase feature associated with 'texture' characteristics. Redundancy brought by the QWT phase adds complete structural information about local features of images contrary to the undecimated wavelet transform that is only associated with the translation invariance property.

The QWT is not straightforward to interpret, but here, we gave an application study crossing the gap between that framework and the way to use this tool by showing its superiority over standard wavelets in a denoising context. For this, a denoising method based on the DT-QWT with single-channel and multichannel selective neighboring coefficient thresholding and linear phase smoothing is presented. The proposed algorithm applied both in separate bands and multispectral satellite images reduces noise and keeps the edges sharp.

The obtained results confirm the efficacy of intra-channel and inter-channel dependency in thresholding and the phase regularization in comparison to the term-by-term classical shrinkage algorithm and the bivariate approach. A non-marginal strategy developed in our work outperforms existing methods, both from computational and from a quality point of view. This improvement is due to the shift invariance of the QWT magnitude together with the use of the QWT phase that contains useful structural information for image analysis. The proposed multichannel model has the potential to be extended to hyperspectral images and to introduce more information about phase.

Another question that should be investigated in a future work is the ability of the proposed method to exploit the parent-child relationship or inter-scale dependencies in addition to neighboring intra-scale and inter-channel correlations. Also, it may be possible to use a non-linear

dependency of phase and study the relationship between successive phases on different scales.

Endnotes

[a]In this article, we only analyze the invertible discrete representation in order to build a denoising method. For this, the complex continuous wavelet representation (for example, complex Morlet) is not described.

Competing interests

The authors declare that they have no competing interests.

Acknowledgements

This work is part of the Algerian National Research Project whose objective is satellite image processing, so we thank the partners which are contributing to the advancement of this project in particular the Algerian National Centre of Spatial Techniques and Algerian Center of the Satellite Development. Thanks to OSEO and the Poitou-Charentes region and the European Community that give funds for this research project.

Author details

[1]Laboratory of Telecommunications and Digital Signal Processing, Department of Electronics, Faculty of Technology, Djillali Liabes University, Sidi Bel Abbes 22000, Algeria. [2]Department of Material Science, Faculty of Sciences and Technology, University of Mascara, Mascara 29000, Algeria. [3]Laboratory of Telecommunications and Digital Signal Processing, Department of Electronics, Faculty of Technology, Djillali Liabes University, Sidi Bel Abbes 22000, Algeria. [4]XLIM-SIC Laboratory, Department of Signal, Image, and Communications, XLIM Institute, CNRS UMR 6172, UFR Sciences-SP2MI, University of Poitiers, Futuroscope Chasseneuil 86073 Poitiers CEDEX9, France.

References

1. DL Donoho, IM Johnstone, Ideal spatial adaptation by wavelet shrinkage. Biometrica **81**(3), 425–455 (1994)
2. DL Donoho, IM Johnstone, Adapting to unknown smoothness via wavelet shrinkage. J. Roy. Statist. Soc. **92**(44), 1413–1421 (1997)
3. RH Bamberger, MJT Smith, A filter bank for the directional decomposition of image: theory and design. IEEE Trans. Image Processing **40**(4), 882–893 (1992)
4. M Lang, H Guo, J Odegard, C Burrus, R Wells, Noise reduction using an undecimated discrete wavelet transform. IEEE Signal Processing Lett. **3**(1), 10–12 (1996)
5. NG Kingsbury, *The dual-tree complex wavelet transform: a new technique for shift invariance and directional filters* (IEEE Digital Signal Proc (Workshop on DSP, Bryce Canyon, USA, 1998). pp. 2543–2560
6. NG Kingsbury, *The dual-tree complex wavelet transform: a new efficient tool for image restoration and enhancement, in the 9th European Signal Processing Conference (EUSIPCO)* (Sept, Rhodes, 1998). pp. 319–322
7. NG Kingsbury, A dual-tree complex wavelet transform with improved orthogonality and symmetry properties, in *Proceedings of IEEE ICIP*, Vancouver, 10–13 Sept 2000, vol. 2, pp. 375–378
8. T Bulow, *Hypercomplex Spectral Signal Representations for the Processing and Analysis of Images* (Christian Albrechts University of Kiel, Dissertation, 1999)
9. EB Corrochano, Multi-resolution image analysis using the quaternion wavelet transform. J. Num. Algo. **39**(1), 35–55 (2005)
10. EB Corrochano, The theory and use of quaternion wavelet transform. J. Math. Imaging Vis. **24**(1), 19–35 (2006)
11. WL Chan, H Choi, R Baraniuk, Quaternion wavelets for image analysis and processing, in *The International Conference on Image Processing, Singapore, 11 Oct 2004*, vol. 5, pp. 3057–3060
12. R Soulard, *Quaternions et algèbres géométriques pour le traitement d'images* (University of Poitiers, France, Dissertation, 2009)
13. R Soulard, P Carré, Quaternionic wavelets for texture classification. Pattern Recog. Lett. **32**, 1669–1678 (2011)

14. S Gai, P Liu, J Liu, X Lang, A new image denoising algorithm via bivariate shrinkage based on quaternion wavelet transform. J. Comput. Inf. Sys. **6**(11), 3751–3760 (2010)

15. TT Cai, BW Silverman, Incorporating information on neighboring coefficients into wavelet estimation. Sankhya Series **63**(2), 127–148 (2001)

16. GY Chen, TD Bui, Multiwavelets denoising using neighboring coefficients. IEEE Signal Processing Lett. **10**(7), 211–214 (2003)

17. S Hailiang, ZI Yanyang, HE Zhengjia, W Xiaodong, Y Jing, Translation-invariant multiwavelet denoising using improved neighbouring coefficients and its application on rolling bearing fault diagnosis, in the 9th International Conference on Damage Assessment of Structures(DAMAS). J. Phys. Conf. Ser. **305**, 012012 (2011)

18. B Chinna Rao, M Madhavi Latha, Selective neighbouring wavelet coefficients approach for image denoising. Int. J. Computer Science Com. **2**(1), 73–77 (2011)

19. GY Chen, TD Bui, A Krzyak, Image denoising with neighbour dependency and customized wavelet and threshold. Pattern Recognition **38**, 115–124 (2005)

20. L Sendur, IW Selesnick, Bivariate shrinkage with local variance estimation. IEEE Signal Processing Lett. **9**(12), 438–441 (2002)

21. J Portilla, V Stela, MJ Wainwright, EP Simoncelli, Image denoising using scale mixture of Gaussians in the wavelet domain. IEEE Trans. Image Processing **12**(11), 1338–1351 (2003)

22. K Dabov, A Foi, V Katkovnik, K Egiazarian, Image denoising by sparse 3-D transform-domain collaborative filtering. IEEE Trans. Image Processing **16**(8), 2080–2095 (2007)

23. L Zhang, W Dong, D Zhang, G Shi, Two-stage image denoising by principal component analysis with local pixel grouping. Pattern Recognition **43**(4), 151–1549 (2010)

24. BR Corner, M Narayanan, SE Reichenbach, Noise estimation in remote sensing imagery using data masking. Int J Remote Sensing **24**(N4), 689–702 (2003)

25. A Jalobeanu, LB Féraud, J Zerubia, Estimation of blur and noise parameters in remote sensing, in ICASSP. Orlando, FL, USA **13–17**, 3580–3583 (May 2002)

26. F Luisier, T Blu, A new SURE approach to image denoising: interscale orthonormal wavelet thresholding. IEEE Trans. Image Processing **16**(3), 593–606 (2007)

27. F Luisier, T Blu, SURE-LET multichannel image denoising: interscale orthonormal wavelet thresholding. IEEE Trans. Image Processing **17**(4), 482–492 (2008)

28. J Saeedi, MH Moradi, K Faez, A new wavelet-based fuzzy single and multi-channel image denoising. Image Vis. Comput. **28**, 1611–1623 (2010)

29. C Chaux, AB Benyahia, JC Pesquet, Use of Stein's principle for multichannel image processing, in *IEEE-EURASIP International Symposium on Control, Communication. and Signal Processing, Marrakech, Morocco, 13–15 March 2006.*

30. C Stein, Estimation of the mean of a multivariate normal distribution. Ann. Stat. **9**(N6), 1135–1151 (1981)

31. AV Oppenheim, JS Lim, The importance of phase in signals. Proc. IEEE **69**, 529–541 (1981)

32. WL Chan, H Choi, R Baraniuk, Coherent multiscale image processing using dual-tree quaternion wavelets. IEEE Trans. Image Processing **17**(7), 1069–1082 (2008)

33. M Miller, K Kingsbury, Image denoising using derotated complex wavelet coefficients. IEEE Trans. Image Processing **17**(9), 1500–1511 (2009)

34. JA Fessler, DC Noll, Iterative image reconstruction in MRI with separate magnitude and phase regularization. Proc. IEEE Int. Symp. Biomed. Imaging **1**, 209–212 (2004)

35. S Cai, K Li, Bivariate shrinkage functions for wavelet based denoising. http://eeweb.poly.edu/iselesni/WaveletSoftware/denoise2.html

36. Algerian Space Agency. http://www.asal.dz

37. Z Wang, A Bovik, H Sheikh, E Simoncelli, Image quality assessment: from error visibility to structural similarity. IEEE Trans. Image Processing **13**(4), 600–612 (2004)

6

Patch-based local histograms and contour estimation for static foreground classification

Alex Pereira[1*], Osamu Saotome[1] and Daniel Sampaio[2]

Abstract

This paper presents an approach to classify static foreground blobs in surveillance scenarios. Possible application is the detection of abandoned and removed objects. In order to classify the blobs, we developed two novel features based on the assumption that the neighborhood of a removed object is fairly continuous. In other words, there is a continuity, in the input frame, ranging from inside the corresponding blob contour to its surrounding region. Conversely, it is usual to find a discontinuity, i.e., edges, surrounding an abandoned object. We combined the two features to provide a reliable classification. In the first feature, we use several local histograms as a measure of similarity instead of previous attempts that used a single one. In the second, we developed an innovative method to quantify the ratio of the blob contour that corresponds to actual edges in the input image. A representative set of experiments shows that the proposed approach can outperform other equivalent techniques published recently.

Keywords: Abandoned and removed object detection; Video surveillance; Video segmentation

1 Introduction

Video surveillance techniques for abandoned and removed object detection have received great attention in the last few years. Detecting suspicious objects is a central issue in the protection of public areas, such as airports, shopping malls, parks, and other mass-gathering areas.

In such applications, a sequence of computer vision methods is applied. Some approaches identify foreground blobs by applying background subtraction methods and then use an object tracker to determine whether the blob is static or not.

Other approaches avoid object tracking methods due to its flaws under crowded scenes [1]. Some alternatives have been proposed. Bayona performed a survey on stationary foreground detection [2] and concluded that approaches based on sub-sampling schemes or accumulation of foreground masks assure the best results. One year later, Bayona proposed one static foreground detection technique based on a sub-sampling scheme that outperformed other efforts mentioned in his survey. A succession of improvements has been reported in [3] and [4]. Although the stationary foreground detection issue

is far from exhausted, the present research work is not concerned with the approach applied to identify stationary foreground. Instead, the focus is on the classification of static foreground blobs as either an abandoned or removed object.

We use a well-known shared assumption described in [5]: *When a background object is removed from the scene, it is reasonable to assume that the area thus vacated will exhibit a higher degree of agreement with its immediate surroundings than before.*

Fitzsimons [6] provided a brief literature review and categorized the main mechanisms used to distinguish abandoned from removed objects into four groups: edge detection, histograms comparison, image inpainting, and region growing.

The edge detection and the histogram comparison approaches are of special interest to our research. An explanation of the other two categories can be found in [6].

The intuitive reasoning on the edge detection approach in [5], is that *placing an object in front of the background will introduce more edges to the scene around the object's boundaries, provided that the background is not extremely cluttered.*

The Sobel [5,7-12] and Canny [5,13-16] operators have been employed with greater frequency for this purpose

*Correspondence: alp@ita.br
[1]Instituto Tecnológico de Aeronáutica (ITA), Praça Mal. Eduardo Gomes, 50, São José dos Campos, BR, CEP 12.228-900
Full list of author information is available at the end of the article

than the SUSAN edge detector [17]. While edge energy was employed in [17-19].

Flaws on distinguishing abandoned from removed objects by their edges can occur when the hypothesis of not extremely cluttered background is not valid. Grigorescu [20] showed that when textures and the scale of objects are similar, a non-contextual edge detector, such as the traditional Canny operator, generates strong responses to the texture regions. Then, object contours can be difficult to identify in the output of such an operator.

In our approach the best results were achieved by combining the Sobel and SUSAN edges, which is more invariant to scale changes than the Canny operator (as reported in [21]).

Henceforth for a simpler notation, unless otherwise specified, neighborhood of foreground blobs means the corresponding neighbor region in the input frame, not in the foreground mask.

Color histogram comparison [15,22-24] is another intuitive manner to discriminate abandoned and removed objects. Researchers compare the color distributions of the interior and exterior neighborhood of foreground blobs. It makes sense to assume that if the internal and external neighbor regions are similar in color, then no object is likely to be present. The inverse is also likely to be true.

We found that the accuracy of histogram-based features relies on the choice (shape and size) of the regions to compare. Usually, a bounding box delimits the external region. However, as we show next, the color distribution comparison of whole multi-colored objects often generates wrong results.

Although both edges and histogram categories present drawbacks, we show in our results that they are complementary and an appropriate combination can take the best of both.

All these approaches rely on a hidden assumption that the foreground blob correctly outlines the objects' contour when a real object is present. Then, they define inter-

nal and external regions and extract data to compare one to the other. If the assumption fails, which often occurs, the outcome is a misleading comparison. Using bounding boxes that are smaller than the actual object and computing background pixels from the object color distribution are two examples of many possible mistakes.

Thus, the features we propose consider some degree of inaccuracy on the foreground blob. We argue that this care is essential to deal with several different video scenarios.

2   Description of the removed and abandoned blob classifier (RABC)

The first step is pre-processing each input image filtering noise and then evaluating the following two features in order to provide a reliable classification: F_h - patch-based local histogram similarity and F_c - *contour sampling*, detailed in Sections 2.2 and 2.3, respectively. The final classification using these features is detailed in Section 2.5.

2.1   Preprocessing

The artificial edges created by image compression, with the quantization of 8×8 macroblocks, are not among the edges we aim to detect. Image noise, such as noise due to sensor quality, is not of interest to our present work either.

A common low-pass filter blurs the edges while removing noise, which is inappropriate for our purpose. Tomasi [25] proposed a bilateral filtering, which smooths images while preserving edges by means of a nonlinear combination of nearby image values.

The bilateral filter uses two parameters. The geometric spread σ_d, where a large σ_d blurs more because it combines values from more distant image locations. The photometric spread σ_r, where pixels with values closer than σ_r to each other are mixed together and values more distant than σ_r are not.

We use $\sigma_r = 50$ and $\sigma_d = 20$. Figure 1 presents a sample of the bilateral filtering applied to the 1,364th frame of the Highway test case of the CDW 2014 dataset [26].

(a)   (b)

Figure 1 Bilateral filtering result. (a) Input frame 1364. **(b)** Smoothed frame.

The following presented features benefit from using smoothed input data, mainly the histogram-based feature, which computes the difference between the color distribution of two regions.

2.2 F_h - patch-based local histogram similarity

Figure 2, taken from the AB_Easy test case of the AVSS 2007 dataset [27], illustrates the intuitive reasoning of this feature. The blob from Figure 2b appears because of a bootstrap on the background model. In other words, in the first frame of the video (which was used to initialize the background model), there was a man walking. Some frames after that, the input frame (523rd) brings the uncovered background. Figure 2a presents a piece of the 523rd background frame. Figure 2b presents a segmentation where the foreground blob represents a removed object and Figure 2c shows the blob boundary projected over the corresponding input frame.

In Figure 2c, we note considerable similarity between internal and external regions of the blob. In several instances of these removed objects, the color of the external neighborhood is similar to the color of the neighborhood inside the corresponding blob. We measured this similarity by comparing the histogram of internal and external neighbor regions.

We used the multi-color observation model, by Perez [28], based on hue saturation value (HSV) color histograms. This color histogram is more accurate than a grayscale one. Our technique uses the Kolmogorov-Smirnov test [29] as a metric to evaluate the similarity between the two histograms. Blobs corresponding to

objects that differ from their neighbor region are unlikely to be classified as removed ones.

Up to this point, our proposed technique and previous ones are fairly equivalent. However, previous approaches did not tackle situations where the region behind a blob is not as homogeneous as in the example of Figure 2. For such situations, we proposed a novel approach, inspired in [29], to split the image into patches and to analyze whether each patch is homogeneous. This is discussed in Section 2.2.1.

2.2.1 Improving the similarity assessment

Color histograms can distinguish one object from another when their color distributions are distinct. However, color histograms do not differentiate objects with similar distributions but with different color locations. For example, suppose two 2×2 chess boards rotated 90° from each other. A simple color histogram comparison would evaluate that they are the same. As explained in [29], an appropriate approach would be to divide the object into regions (patches) and consider their histograms in order to take a more precise observation model of the object.

Briefly, the overall color distribution of two images might be similar, while the comparison of color distribution taken from lower scale pieces might tell us that the images are different. Lower scale pieces provide more accurate data. Therefore, the issue is how to determine the scale and shape of the pieces. In the following, we explain our method to get local color distributions.

We created rectangular patches by dividing the bounding boxes into $N \times N$ grids. The number of rows and

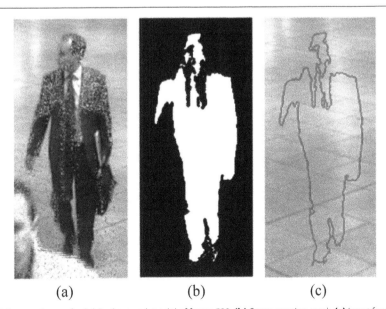

(a)   (b)   (c)

Figure 2 Removed object (person) sample. (a) Background model of frame 523. **(b)** Segmentation mask. **(c)** Input frame 523 with blob boundary.

columns N of the grid is adaptively defined according to the bounding box area A_{bb} and a goal patch area A_g, see Expression 1. This is the expression for a canonical example of a squared bounding box and works for rectangular ones as well:

$$\max\left(\sqrt{\frac{A_{bb}}{A_g}}, 1\right) \tag{1}$$

Perez [28] proposed a color histogram with 110 bins. We use the same number of bins. The number of pixels in a patch must be representative in order to get plausible quality histograms. Then, the minimum goal patch area of 300 pixels showed to be suitable.

We use a bounding box extended by 25% in area (50% in each dimension) compared to the tight bounding box of the blobs. This is necessary to get enough pixels from the external blob neighborhood. Then, from this point on, we consider that bounding box means the extended one.

We perceived that the relative position of the patches to the whole blob can affect the similarity measure. Then, we gather in a single set the patches from grids of size $N - 1$, N and $N + 1$. Some of the patches are disregarded as explained below.

The purpose here is to evaluate the color similarity in the neighborhood of the blob contour. So, only patches that cover the blob contour are used. Each patch comprises two regions, internal and external. Then, we disregard patches in which any of these regions have an area smaller than 15% of the patch area. Very few pixels cannot form representative color distributions.

Figure 3 presents the patches that cover the blob contour. This example was based on the Traffic test case from the CDW 2012 dataset [26], and the foreground mask was taken from [30]. This figure shows that using three grid sizes, we can cover a larger portion of the blob contour. Thus, the comparison accuracy does not depend on a manual selection of patch sizes.

Next, for each patch, we compare the internal and external patch regions with Kolmogorov-Smirnov test [29] as a difference metric. In order to extract the whole similarity, we could take the mean from all the differences. However, this is more appropriately modeled as a voting problem. Each patch gives valuable information about its area. No matter how close its similarity is to 100%, it must not contribute to the similarity of other patches as it would contribute by calculating a simple average. Figure 3 presents such an example. Among 22 squared patches, there are five patches that cover a wrong segmentation area (homogeneous area covering the road) and the voting scheme is able to correctly classify the blob. The following equations show the related calculations.

Consider the Kolmogorov-Smirnov test, represented by the function $KS(h_i, h_e)$ which produces a real number

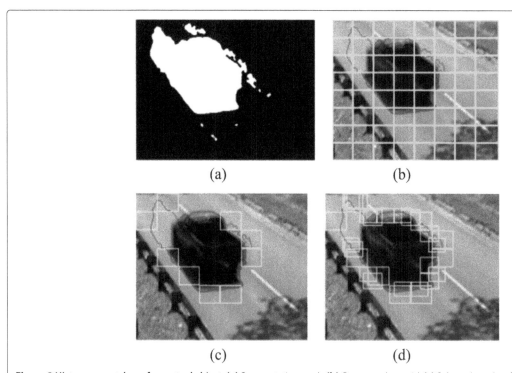

Figure 3 Histogram patches of an actual object. (a) Segmentation mask. **(b)** One complete grid. **(c)** Selected patches from one grid. **(d)** Selected patches from three grids.

in the range [0,1] corresponding to the absolute difference between two histograms, h_i and h_e. Equations 2 and 3 present the procedure to evaluate the feature F_h. The symbol τ_h is the similarity threshold, and P_a is the number of non-disregarded patches:

$$D(j) = \begin{cases} 1, & \text{if } KS(h_i, h_e) > \tau_h \\ 0, & \text{otherwise} \end{cases} \tag{2}$$

$$F_h = \frac{\sum_{j=1}^{P_a} D(j)}{P_a} \tag{3}$$

The feature value is the ratio of patches that have similar internal and external regions.

2.3 F_c - contour sampling

We developed a method to determine whether a blob region is surrounded by edges or not. The method detects the edges in the neighborhood of the blob border and evaluates the portion of the contour that is surrounded by edges. We consider that a closed/almost closed contour corresponds to an abandoned object.

Consider the sample in Figure 4 taken from Cam1 test case of the Hermes Dataset [31]. The sequence starts with a static car parked in the street (Figure 4a). After sometime, it moves and uncovers the background (Figure 4b). This situation produces a ghost because the true background data was always unavailable. At frame 1,396, the segmentation process produces two blobs with the same shape and size of the car (Figure 4c). The blob in the left represents the initial position of the car that should be classified as removed object. The other blob represents the car in frame 1,396.

Figure 5 presents the sequence of operations performed to detect the removed object. Figure 5a presents the piece of the 1,396th input frame where the car was initially parked. Figure 5b presents the corresponding foreground mask. Figure 5c presents the edges detected as explained in Section 2.4. Figure 5d shows the internal and external neighborhood of the blob border, obtained from the difference of the dilated convex hull [32] and the eroded foreground blob, henceforth referred as crown. Figure 5e

presents a binarization of the edges that lie inside the crown region.

We developed a monotonic function that quantifies the ratio of the object contour found by the edge detector in the neighborhood of the blob boundary. We call this function as contour sampling.

A geometric operation of intersecting a straight line at several (and possibly equally spaced) points of the contour can fulfill the monotonic requirement. Tracing concentric straight lines, from a point inside the contour, can perform the underlying procedure. Each line is rotated from the previous by an angle of some degrees.

Figure 5f shows the picked edges, the source point in green, the straight lines, and blue points representing the intersection. In this example, 60% of the lines intersected the edges.

In case of blobs with a complex shape, for example a U-shaped blob, a single source point is not enough to sample the whole contour because, for simplicity, we take only the first intersection point.

Then, we use several source points spaced throughout the blob region. For this, we take N_S points from the Sobol sequence [33]. This sequence is a solution to the problem of filling an area uniformly with quasi-random points.

N_S is calculated with Expression 1, setting A_g to 25 pixels. Thus, a quasi-random point is likely to be at each 5×5 piece of the bounding box.

Equation 4 is used to calculate a ratio considering the source points that lie in the black area inside the crown contour. In this equation, I_s stands for the number of intersections derived from the source point s. L represents the number of lines of each source point. Finally, the ratio is reversed to represent the missing portion of the contour:

$$F_c = 1 - \frac{\sum I_s}{N_S \times L} \tag{4}$$

As the number of traced lines increases, the value F_c approaches the actual percentage of missing contour out of the 360°. We use $L = 30$ lines for each source point, which yields a precise measurement.

Figure 6 presents an analysis of the piece of the input frame 1,396 where the car blob appears. In this example,

Figure 4 Two blobs: the actual car and the ghost. (a) Input frame 1. **(b)** Input frame 1,396. **(c)** Foreground mask.

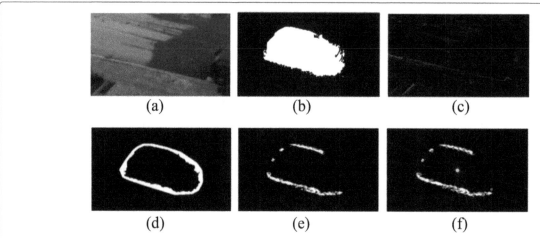

Figure 5 Removed object sample. **(a)** Piece of frame 1,396. **(b)** Foreground mask. **(c)** Edges mask. **(d)** Dilated hull/eroded foreground. **(e)** Picked edges. **(f)** Removed object contour.

86% of the lines intersected the edges. In Figure 6f, we used only two source points to simplify the presentation.

We assume that all blobs have complex shapes and always use multiple source points. This feature can identify the removed object because it is extremely unusual to find edges around the whole blob that corresponds to a removed object.

2.4 Finding the edges

We extracted the edges of each RGB channel with the SUSAN detector and the edges of the luminance (grayscale) channel with the Sobel operator and combined their results into one edge mask.

We chose the SUSAN detector because it is more invariant to scale changes than other non-contextual edge detectors [21].

Using only the luminance Y (ITU-R BT.601), as in the original experiments of SUSAN [21], is not appropriate because there are many edge samples that do not appear on the luminance channel, but only on the chrominance channels. For example, two neighboring pixels with the same luminance, but opposite extreme values of chrominance show no edges on the luminance channel.

The SUSAN detector relies on a threshold t that determines the minimum contrast of edges that will be picked up. We use a fixed threshold $t = 15$, which sometimes yields missing some edge pixels.

Using Sobel with a dynamic binarization threshold complements the SUSAN edge mask. The Sobel threshold τ_c is defined in Equation 5:

$$\tau_{sb} = \mathrm{MAX}(10, (\mathrm{mean} + 0.25 \times \mathrm{std\_dev})) \qquad (5)$$

In Equation 5, mean stands for the mean of the Sobel gradient and std_dev the corresponding standard deviation. The support at 10 is needed to not pick almost dark Sobel pixels from gradient of homogeneous images.

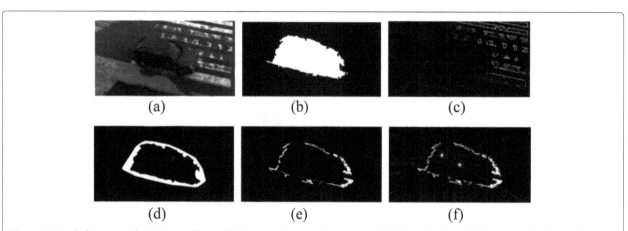

Figure 6 Actual object sample. **(a)** Piece of frame. **(b)** Foreground mask. **(c)** Edges mask. **(d)** Dilated hull/eroded foreground. **(e)** Picked edges. **(f)** Actual object contour.

The combination of the edges masks E is performed with a logic OR as shown in Equation 6:

$$E(R, G, B, Y) = \text{SUSAN}(R, t) \ \cup \ \text{SUSAN}(G, t) \ \cup$$
$$\text{SUSAN}(B, t) \ \cup \ \text{Sobel}(Y, \tau_{\text{sb}}) \quad (6)$$

2.5 Combining the two features

The target set (codomain) of both features is [0,1]. First, we evaluate each feature at the input frame ($F_h(\text{In})$ and $F_c(\text{In})$) and at the background model ($F_h(\text{Bg})$ and $F_c(\text{Bg})$). A high value of input frame features indicates that the blob is likely to correspond to a removed object. A low value indicates an abandoned one. The inverse is also true for the background features.

We subtract the input and background features; see Equations 7 and 8. The resulting sign is used as a binary rating, and the absolute value represents the corresponding confidence. This approach avoids the infeasible task of finding a single threshold to determine whether the feature values correspond to one or another classification:

$$\text{Sub}_h = F_h(\text{Bg}) - \text{F}_h(\text{In}) \quad (7)$$

$$\text{Sub}_c = F_c(\text{Bg}) - \text{F}_c(\text{In}) \quad (8)$$

A negative value of the subtraction (Sub_h or Sub_c) indicates that it is likely to exist an object in the background model and do not in the input frame, i.e., the background model does not correspond to the reality and the referred blob is a removed one. While a positive value indicates that the object is likely to be in the input frame and do not in the background model, i.e., an abandoned object.

Equation 9 models the aforementioned reasoning. Here, the underlying idea is to pick the classification of the most confident feature. If both subtractions agree in sign, the chosen Class is the corresponding class of that sign (removed for negative values). If the subtractions disagree in sign, the most confident is chosen:

$$\text{Class} = \begin{cases} \text{removed,} & \text{if } \text{Sub}_h + \text{Sub}_c < 0 \\ \text{abandoned,} & \text{otherwise} \end{cases} \quad (9)$$

3 Experimental results

One advantage of the proposed technique is that it is quite autonomous. It relies on two parameters τ_h and t,

one for each feature. The threshold τ_h is set to 0.99. In our experiments, lower values of τ_h produced undesirable false positives. Smith in [21] suggests a value between 10 and 20 to SUSAN threshold t. We set it to 15.

The classifier uses three input data: the input frames, a foreground mask, and the corresponding background model frame.

In the first experiment, we used the ASOD [34] dataset comprised of input frames, a background frame, and the corresponding ground truth (manually annotated and automatically generated inaccurate masks) of static foreground from PETS2006 [35], PETS2007 [36], AVSS2007 [27], CVSG [37], VISOR [38], CANDELA [39], and WCAM [40]. We call the manually annotated ground truth as the annotated subset, and the automatically generated masks as the real subset. The amount of blobs in both subsets is shown in Table 1.

We achieved 100% of accuracy classifying the blobs from the annotated subset (second and third column of Table 1) as either abandoned or removed. Fitzsimons [6] also achieved 100% of accuracy in the same subset. There are some reasons that we achieved a flawless result. The dataset provided canonical background frame and an annotated foreground mask. The background is a frame taken from the sequence where the only change is the presence or the absence of the object under analysis. The manually annotated foreground blobs tightly fit the border of the objects. This is the best scenario to evaluate the features. Although simple, this experiment is useful for the early validations.

The plots from Figure 7 give an overall view of this classification problem on the annotated subset. Figure 7a,b presents the Sub_h and Sub_c measures, for the abandoned and removed blobs, respectively. Note that the stepped aspect of the plots shows the beginning and ending of each scenario evaluation. The features are fairly complementary. In Figure 7a, their value alternately move away from 1, while in Figure 7b, they alternately move away from -1.

Figure 7c presents the accumulated value of Sub_h and Sub_c, and their corresponding best fitted lines (least square sense). An ideal feature would approach the line $x = y$, since in the abandoned scenarios, the subtractions Sub_h and Sub_c should always be 1. The slope of these lines are 0.61 and 0.72, for Sub_h and Sub_c, respectively. The

Table 1 ASOD dataset description

Category	Annotated		Real	
	Abandoned	Removed	Abandoned	Removed
C1	771	442	751	806
C2	574	264	497	353
C3	575	174	739	588
Total	1,920	880	1,987	1,747

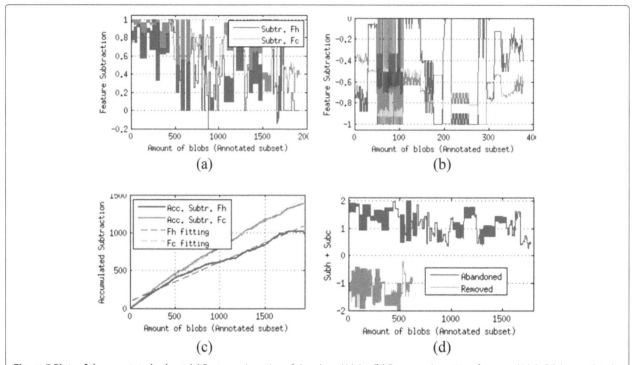

Figure 7 Plots of the annotated subset. (a) Feature subtraction of abandoned blobs. **(b)** Feature subtraction of removed blob. **(c)** Accumulated subtraction of abandoned blobs. **(d)** Plot of $Sub_h + Sub_c$.

slope is a suitable way to compare the features, since it represents the trend of the feature plot. The conclusion here is that the feature F_c is more accurate than the feature F_h.

Finally, Figure 7d shows that the feature F_c can correctly classify the whole annotated subset. By Equation 9, any sum value ($Sub_h + Sub_c$) above zero is abandoned and below zero is removed. The margin is approximately the range [-0.2,0.2].

The next experiment refers to the real subset. It is more realistic as the masks are fairly inaccurate. We disregarded blobs with less than 50 pixels. Further, we removed from the experiment the test case called *AVSSS07 indoor abandoned object easy 4cif* (comprised in the second category) because it presents misclassified blobs. The classification accuracy on the real subset is reported in Table 2. In this table, TP stands for the number of true classified abandoned object, FP stands for the misclassified abandoned objects, TN stands for true classified removed objects, and FN misclassified removed objects. The sixth column presents the recall (TP/(TP + FN)), the seventh column presents the accuracy ((TP + TN)/(FP + FN)) of the proposed technique, and the last column presents the best accuracy results achieved by the creators of this dataset [14].

Our result is 3.7% more accurate than the results from [14]. We argue that this improvement is mainly due to: 1) the diversity of patch shapes that makes the histogram feature take into consideration (most of the times) suitable regions, 2) the contour feature searching for edges in the internal neighborhood of a blob and in the external neighborhood of the blob convex hull, 3) combining the SUSAN with Sobel edges in the contour feature, and 4) replacing fixed feature thresholds for dynamic ones.

The plots in Figure 8 give an overall view of this classification problem on the real subset. Figure 8a,b presents

Table 2 Results on the real subset

Category	Abandoned		Removed		RABC	RABC	[14]
	TP	FP	TN	FN	Recall	Accuracy	Accuracy
C1	751	0	806	0	100%	100%	96.7%
C2	495	2	352	1	99.8%	99.6%	94.3%
C3	708	31	588	0	100%	97.7%	95.1%
Total	1,954	33	1,746	1	99.9%	99.1%	95.4%

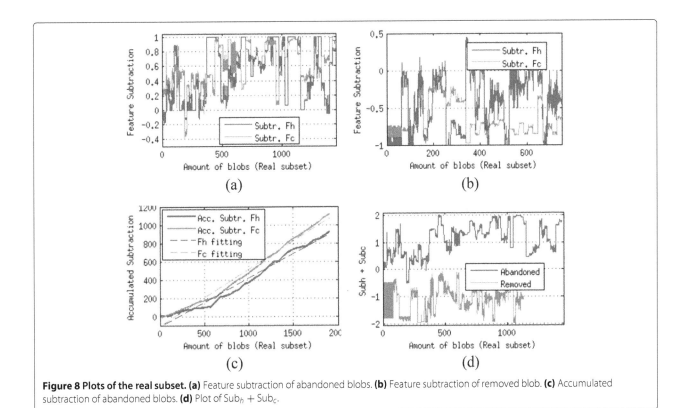

Figure 8 Plots of the real subset. (a) Feature subtraction of abandoned blobs. **(b)** Feature subtraction of removed blob. **(c)** Accumulated subtraction of abandoned blobs. **(d)** Plot of $Sub_h + Sub_c$.

the Sub_h and Sub_c measures, respectively, for the abandoned and removed blobs. These plots present a noisier appearance compared to the plots of Figure 7a,b. This appearance reflects the inaccuracy of the blobs from the real subset.

Figure 8c presents the accumulated value of Sub_h and Sub_c and their corresponding best fitted lines (least square sense). Here, we see that the classification problem is harder than the annotated one because the slope of the fitted lines is lower, 0.53 and 0.62, respectively, for Sub_h and Sub_c. The feature F_c is again more accurate than the feature F_h.

Finally, Figure 8d shows that neither the combination of the features could correctly classify the whole real subset. The mistakes were just 0.9% of the total, and the corresponding blobs barely resemble the annotated ones.

In the next experiment, we used the PETS2006 videos of the camera 3 from scenarios 1 to 7. A single event in each of these videos has been used for the accuracy evaluation on previous research [41-44]. All the seven events are abandoned bags.

In this experiment, we used the foreground mask produced with the SuBSENSE [45] segmenter. SuBSENSE does not maintain a single background model frame. Instead, it manages a set of samples for each pixel. Then, for each pixel, we extracted a background frame by choosing the sample that best fits each corresponding pixel from input frame and used it as a running average background model. This procedure was repeated for each input frame.

We correctly classified the blobs of these seven events as abandoned objects. Table 3 shows that we matched the performance of [41,43,44] and outperformed [42].

Gaetano [46] reported the detection of the blobs that appeared after the removal of the purple bins. We also classified these blobs as removed object ones.

We performed the experiments on a PC with an Intel(R) Core(TM) i5-3210M CPU @ 2.50 GHz. The performance on the PETS2006 dataset, with frames measuring 720×576, was 11 frames per second. The bilateral filter took 75% of the time to analyze each frame.

4 Conclusions

The main goal of the present research work is to develop a technique to classify static foreground blobs as abandoned or removed objects. The proposed technique, named as removed and abandoned blob classifier (RABC), is based

Table 3 Comparison on the PETS2006 dataset

Dataset	[41]	[42]	[44]	[43]	Proposed
PETS2006	6/6	6/7	6/6	7/7	7/7

on a widely used assumption that a removed region is similar to its neighborhood, while abandoned object regions usually have discontinuity, i.e., edges, defining their borders.

The RABC technique combines two features, derived from the aforementioned properties: 1) patch-based local histogram similarity and 2) contour sampling.

Both features were designed considering that some degree of inaccuracy is present in the input data. We argue that this care is essential for the classifier to deal with several different video scenarios. For example, combinations of edge operators, dynamic thresholds and patch sizes, and extended bounding boxes were designed based on this care.

The feature values are ratios in the range [0, 1]. Thus, the feature values can be understood as confidence values. The final classification compares the feature values extracted from the background with those extracted from the input frame. If the feature outcomes are the same (whether abandoned or removed), the final result is the agreed outcome. Otherwise, the most confident outcome between them is chosen. This procedure avoids the unfeasible task of defining suitable thresholds while achieving high accuracy.

The results showed that our proposed technique outperformed recent state-of-the-art techniques with the same purpose.

There is potential research that could build-on our work and our findings. One potential future work would be replacing the squared patches with superpixels in the patch-based local histogram feature. Superpixels describe image regions more precisely. Such change needs a metric like earth mover distance (EMD) metric to compare histograms. EMD has the capability of comparing two distinct sets of image pieces.

Competing interests
The authors declare that they have no competing interests.

Acknowledgements
The authors would like to thank Mr. Quanfu Fan, from the Thomas J. Watson Research Center, for sharing his ground truth data and results of his research [44]. The authors would like to thank Mr. Jack Fitzsimons, from the University of Oxford, for confirming the actual number of annotated blobs on the ASOD dataset. This work has been supported by the Coordenação de Aperfeiçoamento de Pessoal de Nível Superior (CAPES).

Author details
[1]Instituto Tecnológico de Aeronáutica (ITA), Praça Mal. Eduardo Gomes, 50, São José dos Campos, BR, CEP 12.228-900. [2]Universidade Estadual Paulista, Av. Ariberto Pereira da Cunha, 333, Guaratinguetá, BR, CEP 12.516-410.

References
1. F Porikli, Y Ivanov, T Haga, Robust abandoned object detection using dual foregrounds. EURASIP J. Adv. Signal Process. **2008**, 30 (2008)
2. Á Bayona, JC SanMiguel, JM Martínez, in *Proceedings of IEEE Conference on Advanced Video and Signal Based Surveillance (AVSS) (Genoa, 2009).* Comparative evaluation of stationary foreground object detection algorithms based on background subtraction techniques, pp. 25–30
3. D Ortego, JC SanMiguel, in *Proceedings of IEEE Conference on Advanced Video and Signal Based Surveillance (AVSS) (Kraków, 2013).* Stationary foreground detection for video-surveillance based on foreground and motion history images, pp. 75–80
4. D Ortego, JC SanMiguel, in *Proceedings of IEEE International Conference on Image Processing (ICIP).* Multi-feature stationary foreground detection for crowded video-surveillance (Paris, 2014), pp. 2403–2407
5. A Singh, A Agrawal, in *Proceedings of IEEE India Conference (INDICON).* An interactive framework for abandoned and removed object detection in video (Bombay, 2013), pp. 1–6. doi:10.1109/INDCON.2013.6725905
6. JK Fitzsimons, TT Lu, in *Proceedings of SPIE Conference on Applications of Digital Image Processing XXXVII, vol. 9217.* Markov random fields for static foreground classification in surveillance systems (San Diego, 2014), pp. 92171O–92171O-10
7. J Kim, A Ramirez Rivera, B Ryu, K Ahn, O Chae, in *Proceedings of IEEE Conference on Advanced Video and Signal Based Surveillance (AVSS).* Unattended object detection based on edge-segment distributions (Seoul, 2014), pp. 283–288. doi:10.1109/AVSS.2014.6918682
8. T Kryjak, M Komorkiewicz, M Gorgon, Real-time foreground object detection combining the PBAS background modeling algorithm and feedback from scene analysis module. Int. J. Electron. Telecommunications. **60**(1), 53–64 (2014)
9. HH Liao, JY Chang, LG Chen, in *Proceedings of IEEE Conference on Advanced Video and Signal Based Surveillance (AVSS).* A localized approach to abandoned luggage detection with foreground-mask sampling (Santa Fe, 2008), pp. 132–139
10. W Hassan, P Birch, R Young, C Chatwin, in *Proceedings of SPIE Video Surveillance and Transportation Imaging Applications, vol. 8663.* An improved background segmentation method for ghost removals, (2013), pp. 86630W–86630W-6
11. I Huerta, A Amato, X Roca, J Gonzàlez, Exploiting multiple cues in motion segmentation based on background subtraction. Neurocomputing. **100**, 183–196 (2013)
12. M Magno, F Tombari, D Brunelli, L Di Stefano, L Benini, in *Proceedings of IEEE Conference on Advanced Video and Signal Based Surveillance (AVSS).* Multimodal abandoned/removed object detection for low power video surveillance systems (Genoa, 2009), pp. 188–193
13. YJ Chai, SW Khor, YH Tay, in *Proceedings of SPIE International Conference on Digital Image Processing (ICDIP), vol. 8878.* Object occlusion and object removal detection (Beijing, 2013), pp. 88782F–88782F-5
14. J SanMiguel, L Caro, J Martinez, Pixel-based colour contrast for abandoned and stolen object discrimination in video surveillance. Electron. Lett. **48**(2), 86–87 (2012)
15. L Caro Campos, JC SanMiguel, JM Martínez, in *Proceedings of IEEE Conference on Advanced Video and Signal Based Surveillance (AVSS).* Discrimination of abandoned and stolen object based on active contours (Klagenfurt, 2011), pp. 101–106
16. RH Evangelio, T Sikora, in *Proceedings of IEEE Conference on Advanced Video and Signal Based Surveillance (AVSS).* Complementary background models for the detection of static and moving objects in crowded environments (Klagenfurt, 2011), pp. 71–76. doi:10.1109/AVSS.2011.6027297
17. P Spagnolo, A Caroppo, M Leo, T Martiriggiano, T D'Orazio, in *Proceedings of IEEE Conference on Advanced Video and Signal Based Surveillance (AVSS).* An abandoned/removed objects detection algorithm and its evaluation on pets datasets (Sydney, 2006), pp. 17–17
18. YL Tian, M Lu, A Hampapur, in *Proceedings of IEEE Conference on Computer Vision and Pattern Recognition (CVPR), vol. 1.* Robust and efficient foreground analysis for real-time video surveillance (San Diego, 2005), pp. 1182–1187
19. J Connell, AW Senior, A Hampapur, YL Tian, L Brown, S Pankanti, in *Proceedings of IEEE International Conference on Multimedia and Expo (ICME).* Detection and tracking in the IBM peoplevision system (Taipei, 2004), pp. 1403–1406
20. C Grigorescu, N Petkov, MA Westenberg, Contour and boundary detection improved by surround suppression of texture edges. Image Vision Comput. **22**(8), 609–622 (2004)
21. SM Smith, JM Brady, Susan-a new approach to low level image processing. Int. J. Comput. Vision. **23**(1), 45–78 (1997)
22. LF Tu, SD Zhong, Q Peng, Moving object detection method based on complementary multi resolution background models. J. Cent. S. University. **21**, 2306–2314 (2014)

23. B Hu, Y Li, Z Chen, G Xiong, F Zhu, in *Proceedings of IEEE International Conference on Intelligent Transportation Systems (ITSC)*. Research on abandoned and removed objects detection based on embedded system (Qingdao, 2014), pp. 2968–2971

24. S Ferrando, G Gera, C Regazzoni, in *Proceedings of IEEE Conference on Advanced Video and Signal Based Surveillance (AVSS)*. Classification of unattended and stolen objects in video-surveillance system (Sydney, 2006), pp. 21–21

25. C Tomasi, R Manduchi, in *Proceedings of IEEE International Conference on Computer Vision (ICCV)*. Bilateral filtering for gray and color images (Bombay, 1998), pp. 839–846

26. N Goyette, P Jodoin, F Porikli, J Konrad, P Ishwar, in *Proceedings of IEEE Conference on Computer Vision and Pattern Recognition Workshops (CVPRW)*. Changedetection. net: a new change detection benchmark dataset (Providence, 2012), pp. 1–8

27. IEEE International Conference on Advanced Video and Signal Based Surveillance (AVSS), London (2007). http://www.eecs.qmul.ac.uk/~andrea/avss2007_d.html, September 2014

28. P Pérez, C Hue, J Vermaak, M Gangnet, in *Proceedings of Conference on Computer Vision (ECCV)*. Color-based probabilistic tracking (Springer Copenhagen, 2002), pp. 661–675

29. A Adam, E Rivlin, I Shimshoni, in *Proceedings of IEEE Conference on Computer Vision and Pattern Recognition (CVPR)*. Robust fragments-based tracking using the integral histogram (New York, 2006), pp. 798–805

30. R Wang, F Bunyak, G Seetharaman, K Palaniappan, in *Proceedings of IEEE Conference on Computer Vision and Pattern Recognition Workshops (CVPRW)*. Static and moving object detection using flux tensor with split gaussian models (Columbus, 2014), pp. 414–418

31. J Gonzàlez, FX Roca, JJ Villanueva, in *Proceedings of Conference on Computational Vision and Medical Image Processing (VipIMAGE)*. Hermes: a research project on human sequence evaluation (Porto, 2007)

32. M De Berg, M Van Kreveld, M Overmars, O Cheong, *Computational Geometry: Algorithms and Applications*, 3rd ed. (Springer, Santa Clara, CA, USA, 2008)

33. P Bratley, BL Fox, Algorithm 659: Implementing Sobol's quasirandom sequence generator. ACM Trans. Math. Software (TOMS). **14**(1), 88–100 (1988)

34. JC San Miguel, JM Martínez, in *Proceedings of IEEE Conference on Advanced Video and Signal Based Surveillance (AVSS)*. Robust unattended and stolen object detection by fusing simple algorithms (Santa Fe, 2008), pp. 18–25

35. PETS 2006 Benchmark Data. http://www.cvg.reading.ac.uk/PETS2006/data.html, January 2015

36. PETS 2007 Benchmark Data. http://www.cvg.reading.ac.uk/PETS2007/data.html, January 2015

37. Chroma-based Video Segmentation Ground-truth (CVSG). http://www-vpu.eps.uam.es/CVSG, January 2015

38. R Vezzani, R Cucchiara, Video surveillance online repository (visor): an integrated framework. Multimedia Tools Appl. **50**(2), 359–380 (2010)

39. Candela - Surveillance. http://www.multitel.be/cantata, January 2015

40. WCAM - Surveillance. http://www.vpu.eps.uam.es/DS/ASODds/index.html, January 2015

41. A Lopez-Mendez, F Monay, JM Odobez, in *Proceedings of International Joint Conference on Computer Vision, Imaging and Computer Graphics Theory and Applications (VISIGRAPP)*. Exploiting scene cues for dropped object detection (Lisbon, 2014)

42. G Szwoch, Extraction of stable foreground image regions for unattended luggage detection. Multimedia Tools Appl., 1–26 (2014). doi:10.1007/s11042-014-2324-4

43. YL Tian, RS Feris, H Liu, A Hampapur, MT Sun, Robust detection of abandoned and removed objects in complex surveillance videos. Systems, Man, Cybernetics, Part C: App. Rev. IEEE Trans. **41**(5), 565–576 (2011). doi:10.1109/TSMCC.2010.2065803

44. Q Fan, P Gabbur, S Pankanti, in *Computer Vision (ICCV), 2013 IEEE International Conference On*. Relative attributes for large-scale abandoned object detection, (2013), pp. 2736–2743. doi:10.1109/ICCV.2013.340

45. PL St-Charles, GA Bilodeau, R Bergevin, in *Proceedings of the IEEE Computer Society Conference on Computer Vision and Pattern Recognition Workshops (CVPR Workshops), Columbus, OH, USA, 2014*. Flexible background subtraction with self-balanced local sensitivity, (2014)

46. G Di Caterina, Video analytics algorithms and distributed solutions for smart video surveillance. PhD thesis, University of Strathclyde (2013)

7

Probabilistic motion pixel detection for the reduction of ghost artifacts in high dynamic range images from multiple exposures

Jaehyun An[1†], Seong Jong Ha[2†] and Nam Ik Cho[1*†]

Abstract

This paper presents an algorithm for compositing a high dynamic range (HDR) image from multi-exposure images, considering inconsistent pixels for the reduction of ghost artifacts. In HDR images, ghost artifacts may appear when there are moving objects while taking multiple images with different exposures. To prevent such artifacts, it is important to detect inconsistent pixels caused by moving objects in consecutive frames and then to assign zero weights to the corresponding pixels in the fusion process. This problem is formulated as a binary labeling problem based on a Markov random field (MRF) framework, the solution of which is a binary map for each exposure image, which identifies the pixels to be excluded in the fusion process. To obtain the ghost map, the distribution of zero-mean normalized cross-correlation (ZNCC) of an image with respect to the reference frame is modeled as a mixture of Gaussian functions, and the parameters of this function are used to design the energy function. However, this method does not well detect faint objects that are in low-contrast regions due to over- or under-exposure, because the ZNCC does not show much difference in such areas. Hence, we obtain an additional ghost map for the low-contrast regions, based on the intensity relationship between the frames. Specifically, the intensity mapping function (IMF) between the frames is estimated using pixels from high-contrast regions without inconsistent pixels, and pixels out of the tolerance range of the IMF are considered moving pixels in the low-contrast regions. As a result, inconsistent pixels in both the low- and high-contrast areas are well found, and thus, HDR images without noticeable ghosts can be obtained.

Keywords: Exposure fusion; High dynamic range image; Image fusion; Ghost artifacts

Introduction

The dynamic ranges of most commercial image sensors and display devices are narrower than the radiance range of an actual scene, and hence, under- or over-exposure is often inevitable. In order to overcome such limitations of image sensors and displays, a number of multi-exposure capturing and processing techniques have been proposed, which can be roughly categorized into two approaches: high dynamic range imaging (HDRI) with tone mapping [1-4] and image fusion methods [5-10]. The former generates an image of higher dynamic range (i.e., higher bit depth for each pixel) from multiple images having different exposures. To obtain this image, the camera response function (CRF) must be known or estimated, and a tone mapping process is needed when showing the synthesized HDR image on a low dynamic range (LDR) display. On the other hand, the latter generates a tone-mapped-like high-quality image by the weighted addition of multiple exposure images and thus does not need CRF estimation, HDR image generation, and tone-mapping process. Hence, fusion approaches tend to require fewer computations than conventional HDRI, while providing comparable image quality for the LDR displays. Of course, HDRI is the more appropriate solution when showing images on HDR devices.

The conventional exposure fusion and the HDRI work well for the static scene when multi-exposure images are well registered and there is no moving object. But the

*Correspondence: nicho@snu.ac.kr
[†]Equal contributors
[1]Department of Electrical and Computer Engineering, INMC, Seoul National University, Seoul, Korea
Full list of author information is available at the end of the article

ghost artifact is often observed in the HDR image from the dynamic scene where the images are not aligned and/or some objects are moving. Hence, there have been much efforts to alleviate the ghosting problem in the case of HDRI approaches. Some of the existing algorithms consider misalignment of input frames and moving objects simultaneously, while others assume well-aligned input or pre-registration of misaligned frames and concentrate on the detection of moving objects that cause inconsistency. For example, the study [11] exploits the measure of local entropy differences to identify regions that might contain moving pixels, which are then excluded from the HDRI generation process. In addition, Khan et al. [12] proposed an iterative method that gives larger weights to static and well-exposed pixels, thereby diminishing the weights for pixels that can cause ghosts. Li et al. [13,14] proposed methods to detect and modify moving pixels based on the intensity mapping function (IMF) [15]. There are also patch-based methods, in which patches including moving objects are excluded [16,17]. To simultaneously deal with the misalignment and moving objects, Zimmer et al. [18] proposed an optical flow-based energy minimization method, and Hu et al. [19] used non-rigid dense correspondence and color transfer function for this task. Recently, low-rank matrix-based algorithms [20,21] have also been presented, based on the assumption that irradiance maps are linearly related to LDR exposures.

In the case of exposure fusion, there are also similar approaches for ghost removal. For example, the median threshold bitmap approach was proposed to detect clusters of inconsistent pixels [22], which are then excluded when fusing the images. In addition, a gradient domain approach was introduced that gives smaller weights to inconsistent pixels [23]. The IMF is used to exclude region of inconsistent pixels in the fusion process [24,25], where the images are over-segmented and the IMF is used to detect the inconsistent regions. In our previous work [26], we proposed a method to detect inconsistent pixels based on a test of the reciprocity law of exposure and the measure of zero-mean normalized cross-correlation (ZNCC). It is noted that the ZNCC between a region in an image and its corresponding region in the reference is close to 1 when there is no moving object. Hence, a pixel is considered to be inconsistent when the region around the pixel shows low ZNCC under a certain threshold, i.e., the hard thresholding of ZNCC was used.

In this paper, we propose a probabilistic approach to constructing a ghost map, which is a binary image depicting the pixels to be excluded in the exposure fusion process. We assume that the images are well registered, otherwise apply a registration algorithm. The basic measure is also based on the ZNCC, but probabilistic soft thresholding is used instead of the hard thresholding used in our previous work. Specifically, ZNCC histogram is modeled as a Gaussian mixture function, where the parameters are found using an expectation maximization (EM) algorithm. Generating a ghost map is then posed as a binary labeling problem based on a Markov random field (MRF) framework, where the energy to be minimized is designed as a function of the ZNCC distribution parameters. It will be shown that the proposed method provides a less noisy and more accurate binary map than the simple hard thresholding method.

However, as in other feature-based methods, the ZNCC shows meaningful differences only for well-contrasted and highly textured regions. Hence, feature-based methods often give incorrect results in low-contrast regions where the pixel values are about to be saturated due to over- or under-exposure and also in low-textured regions. For these regions, we exploit the IMF between the images, which was successfully used in [13,14,24,25]. In this paper, the IMF is estimated from regions having high ZNCC only, because other regions are saturated or moving object regions that have low credibility in estimating the IMF. Then, the pixels lying outside the IMF tolerance are considered pixels on the faint moving objects. To determine the ghost map in this region, we also develop an optimization technique, which yields less noisy results than conventional IMF-based thresholding methods. Experimental results show that the proposed method constructs plausible ghost maps and hence yields pleasing HDR images without noticeable ghost artifacts.

The rest of this paper is organized as follows: In the second section, we review the conventional weight map generation method [6]. In the third section, we describe the proposed algorithm that excludes the ghost pixels from the weight map. Then, we show some experimental results, and finally, conclusions are given in the last section.

Review of exposure fusion

Conventional exposure fusion methods create an output as a weighted sum of multiple exposure images, in which the weights reflect the quality of pixels in terms of contrast, saturation, and well-exposedness. The contrast is computed by Laplacian filtering [27], and the saturation is defined as the standard deviation of the pixels in each component. The measure of well-exposedness is designed to have the largest value when a pixel value is around the center of the dynamic range. The weight map for each exposure image is calculated by using these measures as

$$W_k(p) = (C_k(p))^{\omega_C} \times (S_k(p))^{\omega_S} \times (E_k(p))^{\omega_E} \qquad (1)$$

where p is the pixel index; k means the k-th exposure image; C, S, and E represent contrast, saturation, and well-exposedness, respectively; and ω_C, ω_S, and ω_E are corresponding weighting factors. After the weighted images are added, multi-resolution blending is performed by using pyramidal image decomposition [28]. Figure 1 presents weight maps for the corresponding multi-exposure images, as well as the output as a result of the weighted sum of images. The ghost artifacts can be observed in the red box of Figure 1c, caused by moving people.

Proposed algorithm

The core of the ghost reduction algorithm is to find inconsistent pixels that can cause artifacts, for excluding them from the fusion process. For this task, we first determine a reference frame among the multi-exposure images, one that has the largest well-contrasted region. Then, in all other input frames except for the reference frame, we find regions that have moving objects with respect to the reference. More specifically, we construct a *ghost map* (binary image) for each input frame except for the reference, which indicates which pixel to exclude or include in the image fusion process. When a pixel in the ghost map is 1, the corresponding pixel in the input frame will be included in the fusion process and vice versa.

The proposed method begins by finding the reference frame that has the largest well-contrasted region (i.e., smallest saturated region) as in conventional methods [16,24-26,29,30]. It needs to be noted that our method identifies the inconsistent pixels in high-contrast regions and low-contrast regions separately. For this, we define a *saturation map* **b**, which is also a binary matrix with the size of input image. Note that this matrix can be constructed when finding the reference frame, because we check the contrast of regions at this time. Precisely, if we denote the element of **b** at the pixel position p as $b(p)$, then it is given 1 when the p belongs to a well-contrast region in the reference frame and 0 when it belongs to the low-contrast region. In summary, for each of the input frames

Figure 1 An example of the exposure fusion. (a) A sequence of multi-exposure images. **(b)** Weight maps for the corresponding input images. **(c)** Fused image where ghost effect can be found in the red box due to moving people.

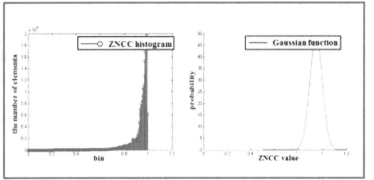

Figure 2 A pair of static images without moving objects (left) and the histogram of ZNCC for this set of images (right).

except the reference, we find the ghost maps for the region of $b(p) = 0$ and $b(p) = 1$ separately. The ghost map for the well-contrast region ($b(p) = 1$) will be denoted as $\mathbf{g}_w$ and the ghost map for the low-contrast region ($b(p) = 0$) as $\mathbf{g}_l$ in the rest of this paper. After finding these ghost maps for an input frame, the overall ghost map for the frame is constructed as $\mathbf{g} = \mathbf{g}_w \cup \mathbf{g}_l$. In this paper, finding $\mathbf{g}_w$ and $\mathbf{g}_l$ are posed as binary labeling problems, i.e., as the energy minimization problems that are solved by graph cuts [31].

Construction of $\mathbf{g}_w$

The construction of $\mathbf{g}_w$ is based on the ZNCC measure, from the observation that the ZNCC of the region containing a moving object is low when compared with the ZNCC in the static region. The energy function for this binary labeling problem is defined as

$$E_W(\mathbf{g}_w) = \sum_{p \in P_W} E_{W_D}(g_w(p)) + \gamma_W$$
$$\times \sum_{(p,q) \in N_W} E_{W_S}(g_w p), g_w(q)) \qquad (2)$$

where $g_w(p)$ is the pixel value (1 or 0) at a pixel p, P_W is the set of pixels in the well-contrasted region (all the p's with $b(p) = 1$), N_W is the set of all unordered pair of neighboring pixels over the areas of $b(p) = 1$, and γ_W is a weighting factor for balancing the data cost E_{W_D} and the smoothness cost E_{W_S}.

The data cost E_{W_D}

The ZNCC of a region R centered at a pixel p, with respect to the corresponding region of the reference image, is defined as

$$Z(p) = \frac{\sum_{p \in R} D_{\text{ref}}(p) \times D(p)}{\sqrt{\sum_{p \in R} D_{\text{ref}}(p)^2 \times \sum_{p \in R} D(p)^2}} \qquad (3a)$$

where

$$D_{\text{ref}}(p) = I_{\text{ref}}(p) - \bar{I}_{\text{ref}}(p) \qquad (3b)$$
$$D(p) = I(p) - \bar{I}(p) \qquad (3c)$$

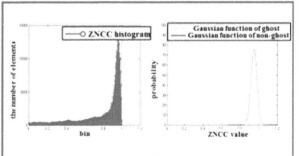

Figure 3 A pair of dynamic images with moving people (left) and the histogram of ZNCC for this set of images (right).

where I_{ref} and I mean the reference and a given frame respectively, and $\bar{I}_{\text{ref}}$ and $\bar{I}$ represent the mean values of I_{ref} and I in the region R, respectively. When there is no moving object in the scene, the histogram of ZNCC usually appears like Figure 2 because the ZNCC is close to 1 at most pixels. Hence, the histogram of ZNCC can be modeled as a left-sided normal distribution with the mean close to 1. On the other hand, Figure 3 shows another pair of images that capture a scene with some moving objects. Since the ZNCC becomes very small at the pixels of moving objects, the ZNCC distribution becomes multi-modal, which can be considered a mixture model consisting of two or more Gaussian distributions. Since the state of a pixel is just two (moving pixel or not) in our problem, we model the distribution as a sum of two Gaussian function as

$$p_r(\mathbf{x}) = \sum_{i=1}^{2} p_r(\mathbf{x}|i)P_r(i) \tag{4}$$

where i is the state and input data $\mathbf{x}$ is the ZNCC values. From the learning by EM algorithm, we find the parameters of two Gaussian density functions such as mean μ_i, variance σ_i, and weight $P_r(i)$.

With these models and parameters, the data term E_{W_D} is designed to give penalty to the mis-labeled pixels (e.g., labeled 1 while it is close to ghost). Specifically, the data cost is constructed as a negative of log-likelihoods of two Gaussian density function as

$$E_{W_D}(\text{'ghost'}) = -\ln Pr\left(x_p|G\right) \tag{5a}$$

$$E_{W_D}(\text{'non-ghost'}) = -\ln Pr\left(x_p|NG\right) \tag{5b}$$

where

$$Pr\left(x_p|G\right) = \frac{1}{\sqrt{2\pi}\sigma_1}\exp\left(-\frac{\left(x_p - \mu_1\right)^2}{2\sigma_1^2}\right) \tag{5c}$$

$$Pr\left(x_p|NG\right) = \frac{1}{\sqrt{2\pi}\sigma_2}\exp\left(-\frac{\left(x_p - \mu_2\right)^2}{2\sigma_2^2}\right). \tag{5d}$$

The smoothness cost E_{W_S}

The smoothness cost E_{W_S} is designed by Potts model [32] as

$$E_{W_S}(g_w(p), g_w(p)) = B(p,q) \times \delta(g_w(p), g_w(q)) \tag{6a}$$

where

$$\delta(g_w(p), g_w(q)) = \begin{cases} 1, & \text{if } g_1(p) \neq g_1(q) \\ 0, & \text{otherwise} \end{cases} \tag{6b}$$

$$B(p,q) = \exp\left(-\frac{(I(p) - I(q))^2}{2\sigma^2}\right) \tag{6c}$$

where $B(p,q)$ means the edge cue which represents pixel intensity difference. When the adjacent pixels are

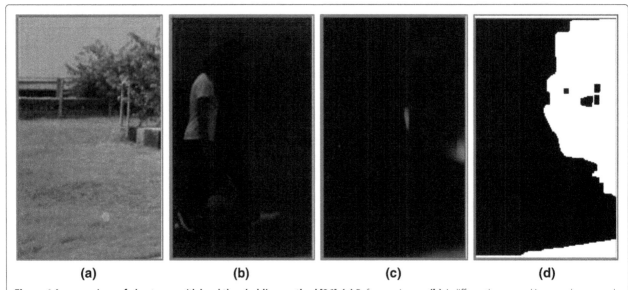

| (a) | (b) | (c) | (d) |

Figure 4 A comparison of ghost map with hard thresholding method [26]. (a) Reference image. **(b)** A differently exposed image where people appear on the left region. **(c)** Ghost map by hard thresholding method [26]. **(d)** Ghost map by the proposed method.

bordering the edge, the 'smoothness cost' is diminished by $B(p, q)$.

For each of the input frames, the binary map $\mathbf{g}_w$ is found by constructing and minimizing Equation 2. For example, Figure 4a,b shows the same area of multi-exposure images, where Figure 4a shows the crop of the reference frame and Figure 4b shows the crop of an under-exposed image where there appears moving people. The binary map resulting from the above equation is shown in Figure 4d, where the white area (labeled as 1) is the non-ghost area and the dark area (labeled as 0) contains motion pixels that are to be excluded. Figure 4c shows a binary map obtained with our previous method in [26], and the comparison with Figure 4d shows that the proposed method gives a more accurate ghost map.

Construction of $\mathbf{g}_l$

The ghost map $\mathbf{g}_w$ for the well-contrasted region is found from the above procedure, and now we find the ghost map $\mathbf{g}_l$ for the low-contrast region (for the regions with $b(p) = 0$). The problem with the low-contrast region is that there are too little textures to apply the feature-based methods (such as median pixel value [22], gradient [23], and ZNCC). Hence, we resort to intensity relationship between the frames for detecting the motion pixels in

these areas. The basic idea is that the static area shows the intensity changes according to the amount of exposure difference, whereas the areas with motion pixels will not follow that. In other words, the static area will have the luminance changes according to the IMF, whereas the dynamic areas will not.

Based on the above observation, we design the energy function for finding $\mathbf{g}_l$ as

$$E_L(\mathbf{g}_l) = \sum_{p \in P_L} E_{L_D}(g_l(p)) + \gamma_L$$
$$\times \sum_{(p,q) \in N_L} E_{L_S}(g_l(p), g_l(q)) \qquad (7)$$

where $g_l(p)$ is the pixel value (1 or 0) at a pixel p, P_L is the set of pixels in the low-contrast region (all the p's with $b(p) = 0$), N_L is the set of all unordered pair of neighboring pixels over the areas of $b(p) = 0$, and γ_L is a weighting factor for balancing the data cost E_{L_D} and the smoothness cost E_{L_S}. The smoothness cost E_{L_S} that prevents noisy result is defined the same as Equations 6a and 6c, except that g_w is replaced by g_l.

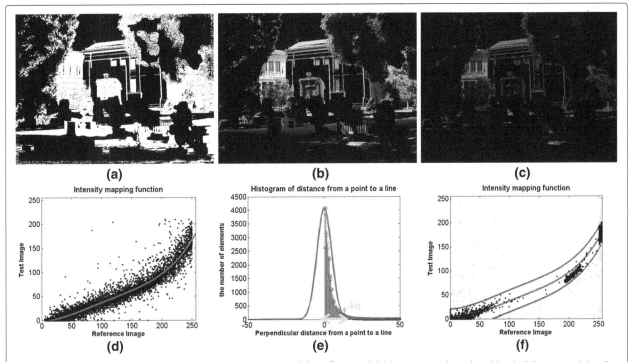

Figure 5 Estimation of IMF between a given exposure image and the reference. (a) A binary map where the white pixel denotes $g_w(p) = 1$ (well contrasted and static). **(b)** Overlap of the reference image with the binary map. **(c)** Overlap of comparing image with the binary map. **(d)** Each dot represents a pair of pixel values (only for the pair of colored pixels of (b) and (c)), and the red line is the estimated IMF by curve fitting. **(e)** Histogram of the distances of dots from the IMF. **(f)** The dots out of 4σ range are considered to include ghost pixels.

The data cost E_{L_D}

As stated above, we use the 'compliance of IMF' for detecting the moving pixels in the low-contrast region, and thus, we have to estimate the IMF. In this paper, unlike the existing IMF estimation methods in [24,25] which use all the pixels without considering the pixel quality, we use the pixels only in the areas of 'high-contrast region without moving objects,' which correspond to the region of $g_w(p) = 1$ for a given image.

The algorithm for estimating the IMF is graphically shown in Figure 5, where Figure 5a shows the binary map $g_w(p)$. That is, the white pixels denote the ones with $g_w(p) = 1$. Figure 5b shows the overlap of this map with the reference frame, i.e., the pixel-wise multiplication of the map in Figure 5a and the reference image. Likewise,

Figure 5c shows the multiplication of the map in Figure 5a with the given input image to be compared with the reference. Finally, the IMF is estimated by comparing only the colored pixels of Figure 5b,c. Figure 5d shows the plot of the pairs of pixel values from these colored regions of Figure 5b,c, and the red line is considered the IMF, which is obtained by curve fitting the dots by the fourth-order polynomial [24,25]. Then, we define the tolerance range (upper and lower blue lines in Figure 5) of intensity variation from the IMF, which means that a dot out of this range is a pair of pixels where one of the pixels possibly belongs to a moving object. Figure 5e shows how this range is determined. Specifically, it shows the histogram of the distances of dots from the IMF curve, and a dot out of 4σ range (out of blue lines in Figure 5f) is considered the ghost pixel pair.

Figure 6 Ghost maps obtained by the IMF-based methods. (a) Reference image. **(b)** Differently exposed image. **(c)** Ghost map by hard thresholding method [29]. **(d)** Ghost map by the proposed method. **(e)** Magnification of (c). **(f)** Magnification of (d).

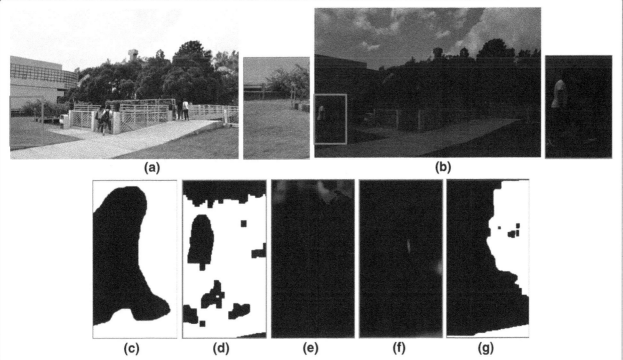

Figure 7 Comparison of the overall ghost maps. (a) Reference image and the magnification of the red box region. **(b)** Under-exposed image and the magnification of the red box region. **(c)** Ground truth ghost map for the red box region. **(d)** Motion map by [22]. **(e)** Consistency map by [23]. **(f)** Ghost map by [26]. **(g)** Ghost map by the proposed method.

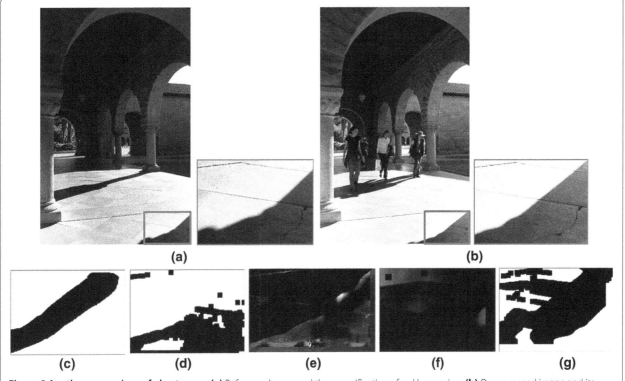

Figure 8 Another comparison of ghost maps. (a) Reference image and the magnification of red box region. **(b)** Over-exposed image and its magnification in the red box. **(c)** Ground truth ghost map for the red box region. **(d)** Motion map by [22]. **(e)** Consistency map by [23]. **(f)** Ghost map by [26]. **(g)** Ghost map by our method.

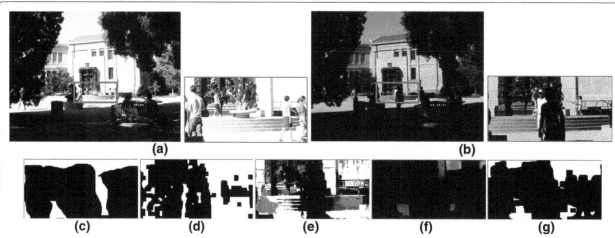

Figure 9 Comparison of ghost maps for other set of images. (a) Reference image and the magnification of red box region. **(b)** Under-exposed image and its magnification in the red box. **(c)** Ground truth ghost map for the red box region. **(d)** Motion map by [22]. **(e)** Consistency map by [23]. **(f)** Ghost map by [26]. **(g)** Ghost map by the proposed method.

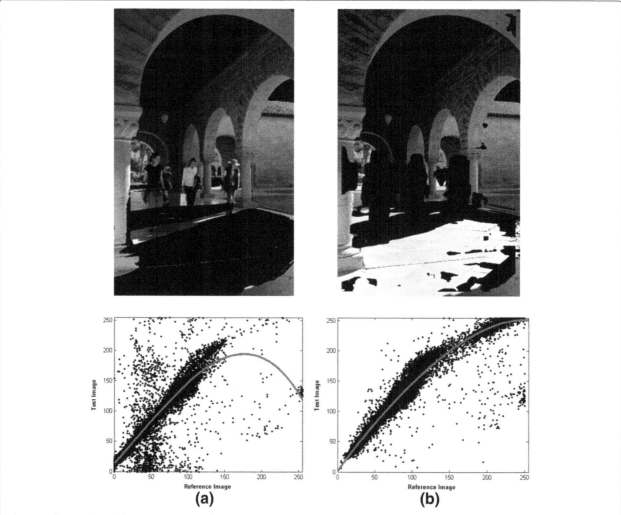

Figure 10 Comparison with Raman and Chaudhuri [25]. (a) (top) Detected static region of over-exposed source image in Figure 8b by [25] and (bottom) estimation of IMF (the red line which is obtained by curve fitting the dots by the fourth-order polynomial) using the static region. **(b)** The result by the proposed method.

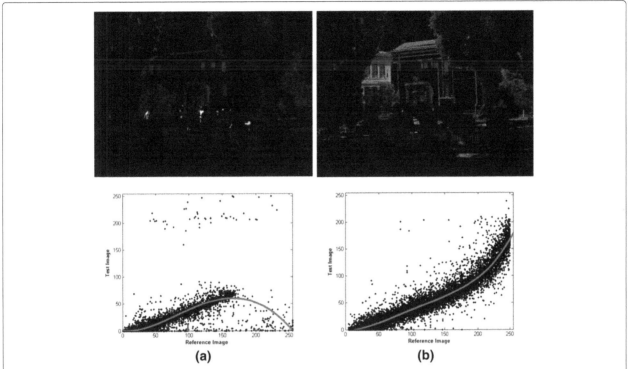

Figure 11 Another comparison with Raman and Chaudhuri [25]. (a) Detected static region of under-exposed source image in Figure 9b by [25] and (bottom) estimation of IMF (the red line which is obtained by curve fitting the dots by the fourth-order polynomial) using the static region. (b) Result by the proposed method.

Based on the estimated IMF, we design the data cost of energy function as

$$E_{L_D}(g_l(p)) = \begin{cases} 0, & \text{if } \{g_l(p) = 0 \cap G(p) > 4\sigma\} \\ & \text{or } \{g_l(p) = 1 \cap G(p) \leq 4\sigma\} \\ 1, & \text{otherwise} \end{cases} \quad (8a)$$

where

$$G(p) = |I(p) - \mathrm{IMF}(I_{ref}(p))| \quad (8b)$$

where $I(p)$ is the intensity of pixel p of the given frame and $\mathrm{IMF}(I_{\mathrm{ref}}(p))$ is the mapping of $I_{\mathrm{ref}}(p)$ according to the IMF. Then, minimizing the total energy by graph cuts gives a binary map $\mathbf{g}_l$ for the given input frame. Figure 6 compares the binary maps that represent ghost pixels as black, which are generated by hard thresholding method [29] and the proposed optimization method. Figure 6a,b shows the reference image and a differently exposed image, respectively, and Figure 6c,d shows the ghost maps of the thresholding and probabilistic methods, respectively. Also, Figure 6e,f shows the crops of the above images for better comparison.

It can be observed that the optimization leads to less map.

Experimental results

In the previous section, we have seen that each of the steps provides a less noisy and/or more plausible ghost map than the hard thresholding methods [26,29]. In this section, we compare the accuracy of the overall ghost map $\mathbf{g} = \mathbf{g}_w \cup \mathbf{g}_l$ with those of the existing methods. First, we compare the accuracy of the ghost map with [22,23,26], for the pair of the reference image in Figure 7a and a differently exposed image in Figure 7b. It can be seen that people appear in Figure 7b in the red box area. Hence, the ground truth ghost map for this area should be like in Figure 7c, and the ghost maps produced by [22,23,26] and the proposed method appear in Figure 7d,e,f,g, respectively. As can be observed in the figures, the median threshold bitmap approach [22] fails to detect the moving object, and the gradient domain method [23] determines the non-ghost region as a ghost region. The reason for this seems that the brightness/gradient difference between the moving object and the background is too small. Our previous work [26] used weight factor for ZNCC measure to extremely diminish ghost effect, so this method also regards the non-ghost pixels as ghost. On the other hand, the ghost map produced by the proposed algorithm is closest to the ground truth. Figures 8 and 9 show another results that the proposed method provides better ghost map.

Figures 10 and 11 show the comparison of [25] and the proposed method for detecting the static region and estimating the IMF between the reference and a given frame. Figure 10a shows the static region detected by [25] (the dynamic region is denoted as black and only the static region remains) for the pair of images in Figure 8a,b and also the estimated IMF from this result. It can be seen that the moving people (dynamic region) are not removed and conversely the floor is detected as moving pixels. In the case of the result of our method (Figure 10b), it can be seen that dynamic regions are successfully detected, and hence, we can obtain more plausible IMF that should be a monotonically increasing function [15]. Figure 11

shows a similar result for the multi-exposure images in Figure 9a,b.

Figures 12,13,14 show the comparison of final fusion results for the eight existing methods [16,17,20-23,26,30] and the proposed method. Specifically, Figure 12a shows the sequence of multi-exposure images, and Figure 12b,c,d shows the comparisons of [16,22] and [26] with the proposed method. The first row of these figures shows the area for the comparison in the red boxes, the second row are the results of these compared methods in the order [16,22,26], and the bottom row shows our results for the corresponding areas. In these figures, it can be seen that the compared methods show some noticeable ghosts, whereas the proposed method does not. Figure 12f shows the overall area of fusion result of our method, and Figure 12e shows the result by [20]. Comparison shows that our method yields comparable

Figure 12 Comparison of results for a set of multi-exposure images. (a) Multi-exposure images. **(b)** Result by the patch-based algorithm based on the HDRI method [16]. **(c)** Result by the median threshold bitmap approach [22]. **(d)** Result by our previous method [26]. **(e)** Result by the low-rank matrix-based approach [20]. **(f)** Result by the proposed method.

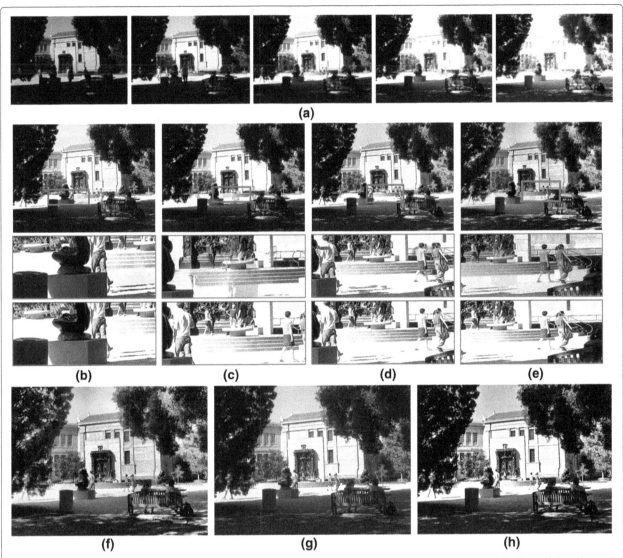

Figure 13 Another comparison of results for a set of multi-exposure images. (a) Multi-exposure images. **(b)** Result by the patch-based algorithm based on the HDRI method [16]. **(c)** Gradient domain approach [23]. **(d)** PatchMatch-based method [30]. **(e)** Low-rank approach in [20]. **(f)** Low-rank matrix-based approaches in [21]. **(g)** Hybrid patch-based approach [17]. **(h)** The proposed method.

output as the HDRI approach by Oh et al. [20], which also yields almost no noticeable artifacts for the given image sequence. Likewise, Figure 13 shows the comparison of [16,20,21,23,30] and [17] with the proposed method. The photos of Figure 13a are the input images, and the second rows of Figure 13b,c,d,e show the results by [16,23,30] and [20], respectively, where the images in the third row are the results of the proposed method at the same area. It can be observed that the method of Gallo et al. [16] removes ghost successfully; however, when the difference of brightness among the neighboring patch is large, this causes some visible seam as shown in Figure 13b. In Figure 13c,d,e, we can see ghost artifacts in the existing methods, whereas the artifact is not noticeable in the case of our algorithm (third row). Also, Figure 13f,g,h shows the results of [17,21] and the proposed method for this set of images, where the ghost artifact is not noticeable in the overall area. Figure 14 shows another comparison of [22,23,30] and [21] with the proposed method. Figure 14a shows the set of input images, and the second row of Figure 14b,c,d,e shows the result of [22,23,30] and [21], respectively, in the red box area of images in the first row. The images in the third row are the results by the proposed method in the same area, and Figure 14f shows the result of our method in the overall area. It can be observed that the proposed method shows almost no ghost artifacts, while others have a little noticeable artifacts as in the second row.

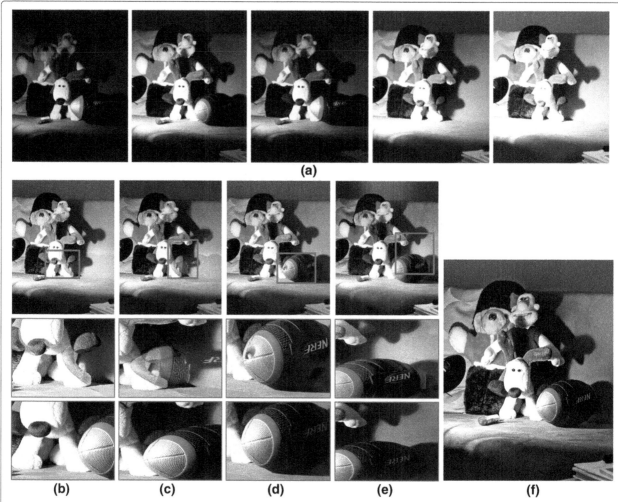

Figure 14 Another comparison of results for a set of multi-exposure images. **(a)** Multi-exposure images. **(b)** Result by the median threshold bitmap approach [22]. **(c)** Gradient domain approach [23]. **(d)** PatchMatch-based method [30]. **(e)** Low-rank matrix-based approach [21]. **(f)** The proposed method.

It is noted that our method has some limitations when the selected reference has 'saturated and moving' foreground object. For example, Figure 15a shows a set of multi-exposure images where the third image is selected as the reference frame because it has the largest area of well-contrast region in the background. In this case, the proposed algorithm yields the fusion result as shown in Figure 15c because the foreground object is moving and hence excluded from the fusion process. On the other hand, since the algorithm in [17] sets the first image as the reference and tries to track the inconsistent pixels, it keeps the foreground object very well as shown in Figure 15b. When we wish to keep the contrast of foreground object, we have to select the reference manually in this case. If we also select the reference as the first frame, then we obtain the result shown in Figure 15d. Finally, it is worth to comment that the fusion results can be enhanced by any conventional histogram equalization or edge-preserving

enhancement method such as [33], like the HDRI performs tone mapping process for the optimal display of HDR on the LDR display devices. The executables for our algorithm and full resolution results with this postprocessing are available at http://ispl.snu.ac.kr/~jhahn/deghost/, which are also available as Additional files 1 and 2.

Conclusions

We have proposed an HDR image fusion algorithm with reduced ghost artifacts, by detecting inconsistent pixels in the high-contrast and low-contrast regions separately. To detect inconsistent pixels in high-contrast areas, a ZNCC measure is used based on the observation that the ZNCC histogram displays a unimodal distribution in static regions, whereas it has a multimodal shape in dynamic regions. A cost function based on the parameters of these probability distributions is designed, whose

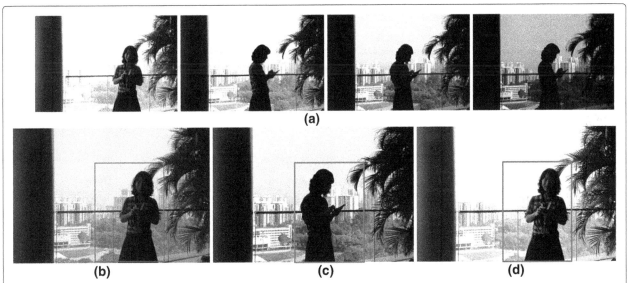

Figure 15 Another comparison of results. (a) Multi-exposure images. **(b)** Result by the hybrid patch-based approach [17]. **(c)** The proposed method. **(d)** The proposed method with the manual selection of the reference frame.

minimization yields the ghost map for the highly contrasted region. To detect the ghost map in the low-contrast region, the IMF is first estimated using pixels from the high-contrast regions having no moving objects. Next, a cost function that encodes the IMF compliance of the pixel pairs is designed, whose minimization gives the ghost map for the low-contrast areas. The overall ghost map is defined as the logical operation of these two maps, and the ghost pixels are excluded from the fusion process. Since the proposed algorithm can find faint moving objects in areas where the pixel values are about to be saturated due to over- and under-exposure, it provides satisfactory HDR outputs with no noticeable ghost artifacts. However, the proposed method has limitations in correcting moving foreground object when it is saturated in the reference frame (Figure 15), because they are simply excluded from the fusion process. In this case, we have to manually select a reference frame that has well-exposed foreground objects, which can degrade the fusion results due to the narrower well-exposed background region than in the reference. Otherwise, we need to correct the inconsistent pixels instead of simply excluding them, which is a very challenging problem, especially when the moving foreground object is not consistently detected in each frame due to saturation, noise, or non-rigid motion.

Additional files

Additional file 1: Results. This file contains the final full-size fusion results for several sets of multi-exposure images.

Additional file 2: Codes. This file contains MatLab codes for running the proposed algorithm.

Competing interests
The authors declare that they have no competing interests.

Acknowledgements
This research was supported by the Basic Science Research Program through the National Research Foundation of Korea (NRF) funded by the Ministry of Science, ICT and Future Planning (2009-0083495).

Author details
[1]Department of Electrical and Computer Engineering, INMC, Seoul National University, Seoul, Korea. [2]Samsung SDS, Seoul, Korea.

References
1. PE Debevec, J Malik, Recovering high dynamic range radiance maps from photographs, in *Proceedings of the 24th Annual Conference on Computer Graphics and Interactive Techniques (SIGGRAPH'97)* (Los Angeles, Aug 1997), pp. 369–378
2. E Reinhard, G Ward, S Pattanaik, P Debevec, *High Dynamic Range Imaging: Acquisition, Display, and Image-Based Lighting (The Morgan Kaufmann Series in Computer Graphics)* (Morgan Kaufmann, San Francisco, 2005)
3. S Mann, R Picard, S Mann, RW Picard, On being 'undigital' with digital cameras: extending dynamic range by combining differently exposed pictures, in *Proceedings of the 48th IS&T's Annual Conference* (Washington, DC, May 1995), pp. 442–448
4. K Devlin, *A review of tone reproduction techniques. Technical report CSTR-02-005.* (Department of Computer Science, University of Bristol, 2002)
5. AA Goshtasby, Fusion of multi-exposure images. Image Vis. Comput. **23**(6), 611–618 (2005)
6. T Mertens, J Kautz, FV Reeth, Exposure fusion: a simple and practical alternative to high dynamic range photography. Comput. Graph Forum. **28**(1), 161–171 (2009)
7. S Raman, S Chaudhuri, A matte-less, variational approach to automatic scene compositing, in *IEEE International 11th Conference on Computer Vision* (Los Alamitos, Oct 2007), pp. 1–6
8. MH Malik, S Asif, M Gilani, Wavelet based exposure fusion, in *Proceedings of the World Congress on Engineering* (London, July 2008), pp. 688-693

9. S Raman, S Chaudhuri, Bilateral filter based compositing for variable exposure photography, in *Proceeding of Eurographics Short Papers* (Munich, Mar 2009), pp. 1–4

10. J Shen, Y Zhao, Y He, Detail-preserving exposure fusion using subband architecture. Vis. Comput. **28**(5), 463–473 (2012)

11. K Jacobs, C Loscos, G Ward, Automatic high-dynamic range image generation for dynamic scenes. IEEE Comput. Graph. Appl. **28**(2), 84–93 (2008)

12. E Khan, A Akyuz, E Reinhard, Robust generation of high dynamic range images, in *Proceedings of the IEEE International Conference on Image Processing* (Atlanta, Oct 2006), pp. 2005–2008

13. Z Li, S Rahardja, Z Zhu, S Xie, S Wu, Movement detection for the synthesis of high dynamic range images, in *Proceedings of the IEEE International Conference on Image Processing* (Hong Kong, Sept 2010), pp. 3133-3136

14. S Wu, S Xie, S Rahardja, Z Li, A robust and fast anti-ghosting algorithm for high dynamic range imaging, in *Proceedings of the IEEE International Conference on Image Processing* (Hong Kong, Sept 2010), pp. 397–400

15. MD Grossberg, SK Nayar, Determining the camera response from images: what is knowable. IEEE Trans.Pattern Anal. Mach. Intell. **25**(11), 1455–1467 (2003)

16. O Gallo, N Gelfand, W Chen, M Tico, K Pulli, Artifact-free high dynamic range imaging, in *IEEE International Conference on Computational Photography* (San Francisco, Apr 2009), pp. 1–7

17. J Zheng, Z Li, Z Zhu, S Wu, S Rahardja, Hybrid patching for a sequence of differently exposed images with moving objects. IEEE Trans. Image Process. **22**(12), 5190–5201 (2013)

18. H Zimmer, A Bruhn, J Weickert, Freehand HDR imaging of moving scenes with simultaneous resolution enhancement. Comput. Graph. Forum. **30**(2), 405–414 (2011)

19. J Hu, O Gallo, K Pulli, Exposure stacks of live scene with hand-held cameras, in *12th European Conference on Computer Vision* (Firenze, Oct 2012), pp. 499–512

20. T-H Oh, J-Y Lee, IS Kweon, High dynamic range imaging by a rank-1 constraint, in *IEEE International Conference on Image Processing* (Melbourne, Sept 2013), pp. 790–794

21. C Lee, Y Li, V Monga, Ghost-free high dynamic range imaging via rank minimization. IEEE Signal Process. Lett. **21**(9), 1045–1049 (2014)

22. F Pece, J Kautz, Bitmap movement detection: HDR for dynamic scenes, in *The 11th European Conference on Visual Media Production* (London, Nov 2010), pp. 1–8

23. W Zhang, W-K Cham, Gradient-directed composition of multi-exposure images, in *IEEE Conference on Computer Vision and Pattern Recognition* (San Francisco, June 2010), pp. 530–536

24. S Raman, S Chaudhuri, Bottom-up segmentation for ghost-free reconstruction of a dynamic scene from multi-exposure images, in *Proceedings of the Seventh Indian Conference on Computer Vision, Graphics and Image Processing* (Chennai, Dec 2010), pp. 56–63

25. S Raman, S Chaudhuri, Reconstruction of high contrast images for dynamic scenes. Vis. Comput. **27**(12), 1099–1114 (2011)

26. J An, SH Lee, JG Kuk, NI Cho, A multi-exposure image fusion algorithm without ghost effect, in *IEEE International Conference on Acoustics, Speech, and Signal Processing* (Prague, May 2011), pp. 1565-1568

27. J Malik, P Perona, Preattentive texture discrimination with early vision mechanisms. J. Opt. Soc. Am. **7**(5), 923–932 (1990)

28. P Burt, E Adelson, The Laplacian pyramid as a compact image code. IEEE Trans. Comm. **31**(4), 532–540 (1983)

29. J An, SJ Ha, JG Kuk, NI Cho, Reduction of ghost effect in exposure fusion by detecting the ghost pixels in saturated and non-saturated regions, in *IEEE International Conference on Acoustics, Speech, and Signal Processing* (Kyoto, Mar 2012), pp. 1101–1104

30. J Hu, O Gallo, K Pulli, X Sun, HDR deghosting: how to deal with saturation?, in *IEEE Conference on Computer Vision and Pattern Recognition* (Portland, June 2013), pp. 1163–1170

31. YY Boykov, MP Jolly, Interactive graph cuts for optimal boundary & region segmentation of objects in n-d images, in *Proceedings of Internation Conference on Computer Vision* (Vancouver, July 2001), pp. 105–112

32. Y Boykov, O Veksler, R Zabih, Markov random fields with efficient approximations, in *IEEE Conference on Computer Vision and Pattern Recognition* (Santa Barbara, June 1998), pp. 648–655

33. K He, J Sun, X Tang, Guided image filtering. IEEE Trans. Pattern Anal. Mach. Intell. **35**(6), 1397–1409 (2013)

8

Structure-based level set method for automatic retinal vasculature segmentation

Bekir Dizdaroğlu[1,2]*, Esra Ataer-Cansizoglu[2], Jayashree Kalpathy-Cramer[3], Katie Keck[4], Michael F Chiang[4,5] and Deniz Erdogmus[2]

Abstract

Segmentation of vasculature in retinal fundus image by level set methods employing classical edge detection methodologies is a tedious task. In this study, a revised level set-based retinal vasculature segmentation approach is proposed. During preprocessing, intensity inhomogeneity on the green channel of input image is corrected by utilizing all image channels, generating more efficient results compared to methods utilizing only one (green) channel. A structure-based level set method employing a modified phase map is introduced to obtain accurate skeletonization and segmentation of the retinal vasculature. The seed points around vessels are selected and the level sets are initialized automatically. Furthermore, the proposed method introduces an improved zero-level contour regularization term which is more appropriate than the ones introduced by other methods for vasculature structures. We conducted the experiments on our own dataset, as well as two publicly available datasets. The results show that the proposed method segments retinal vessels accurately and its performance is comparable to state-of-the-art supervised/unsupervised segmentation techniques.

Keywords: Color retinal fundus images; Phase map; Segmentation of retinal vasculature; Structure and texture parts of retinal fundus image; Structure-based level set method

1 Introduction

Published ophthalmology studies reveal that there are often significant differences in clinical diagnosis of retinal diseases among medical experts [1]. Some of these approaches involve tedious processes. Manual segmentation has become more and more time consuming with the increasing amount of patient data. An automatic retinal vasculature segmentation method may become an integral part of a computer-based image analysis and diagnosis systems with improved accuracy and consistency [2].

Considering the conducted research, literature is full of examples [3-10] on vasculature segmentation, detection, and other kinds of analysis employing especially supervised/unsupervised classification of pixels in retinal fundus images [11-19]. Marin et al. [14] and Soares et al. [15] presented two different supervised methods for segmentation of retinal vasculature by using moment invariant-based features and 2-D Gabor filters, respectively. Staal et al. [16] proposed a retinal vasculature segmentation method using centerlines of a vessel base that are extracted by using image ridges. Budai et al. [17] presented an improved approach using Frangi's method [18]. Other studies have employed centerline tracing methods and principal curves [19,20]. The reader may refer to [21] for more related studies in the literature.

Level set-based methods have been widely used for image segmentation [22-34]. In general, these methods can be classified under two categories: (i) edge-based [22-30] and (ii) region-based [31-34] methods. However, level set-based methods have not been extensively employed in retinal vasculature segmentation. To the best of our knowledge, there have been only a few studies in the literature proposing methods based on level sets to trace vasculature in retinal fundus images. This is due to challenges of vessel shapes in level set-based image segmentation methods [24]. Major challenges posed by the very thin and elongated structure of retinal vessels are further compounded by poor contrast in regions of interest for level set-based segmentation

* Correspondence: bekir@ktu.edu.tr
[1]Department of Computer Engineering, Karadeniz Technical University, Trabzon 61080, Turkey
[2]Cognitive Systems Laboratory, Northeastern University, Boston, MA 02115, USA
Full list of author information is available at the end of the article

methods. In one of those studies [24], the level set-based method is applied only on a selected region of images by implementing a non-automatic initialization of zero-level contours. These regions do not have any non-uniform intensity values. The method in [24] also employs edge information based on phase map and uses a re-initialization process to regularize the level set function, which is a problem in level set-based framework [25]. Moreover, this process requires complex discretization especially for re-initialization of the level set function. In addition, the method employs fixed filter coefficients to generate image features such as edges by using the log-Gabor filter, which does not generate a proper output to trace extremely thin retinal vessels in fundus images smoothly. The level set segmentation method [26] proposed by Pang et al. requires the selection of initial contour in the form of long strips in the vertical direction, and this is not an optimal selection. This selection leads to an increase in the number of iterations to generate the results. According to the accuracy metric, the method produces poor results quantitatively on a non-pathological fundus image. Although they claim to present a fully automated method, the system requires mask images from the user. There are other level set approaches [27-29,31-34] that focus on segmenting other vasculature structures in different image modalities such as ultrasound images and magnetic resonance images (MRIs). However, these region-based methods [32,33] cannot be used extensively in segmentation of retinal fundus images due to the form of vascular structures. Another method presented for retinal vessel segmentation [34] employs region-based level sets and region growing approaches, simultaneously.

In this paper, we present an improved and automatic level set-based method for retinal vasculature segmentation. The presented method utilizes a robust phase map to determine image structures and seed points around the vessels in the initialization of the level set function. The performed tests on pathological and non-pathological fundus images demonstrate that the proposed method performs better than the existing approaches based on level sets.

The organization of the paper is structured as follows. 'Section 2' introduces the general information about retinal fundus images and level set-based methods developed for segmentation. 'Section 3' explains the proposed method and compares it with the existing approaches in the literature. Experimental results are given in 'Section 4.' Finally, 'Section 5' presents a conclusion and possible future work in the field.

2 Background

Let $\mathbf{I}: \Omega \rightarrow \mathbb{R}^3$ be a color image defined on domain $\Omega \rightarrow \mathbb{R}^2$, and let $I_i: \Omega \rightarrow \mathbb{R}$ represent the ith color channel of the image $\mathbf{I}$. Let $\mathbf{p} = (x, y) \in \Omega$, denote any point in Ω. Digital images have two additive components: structure part and texture part. These can be visualized as the cartoon version with sharp edges and noisy/textured version of the original image, respectively [35-37].

2.1 Characteristics of retinal fundus images

Retinal fundus images can be generated in color or grayscale format in digital media. The pixels of a retinal fundus image are represented as color values in RGB color space as seen in Figure 1a,b. In terms of representation of retinal vessels, these images have mostly structure information but also a texture part (noise, defects, etc.). The retinal fundus images can be split into two categories, namely the pathological retinal fundus images and the non-pathological ones. The aim of segmentation methods for retinal fundus images is to separate vasculatures from other regions as can be seen in Figure 1c,d. However, due to the structure of the optic disk and macula, segmentation of blood vessels of retinal images is difficult. These regions have a more prominent intensity inhomogeneity compared to other parts of retinal images. Furthermore, pathological images may contain defects and disorders such as drusen, geographic atrophy (GA), and non-uniform intensities. Such disorders also make the process of segmentation complicated.

As shown in Figure 2, each color channel in RGB color space can be separated and treated as an independent grayscale image. Considering those channels, the green channel component of the retinal image gives the best structure information to be processed [15,19] even though some regions such as the optic disk and macula in this channel component have non-uniform intensity levels. Let us use I instead of I_2 to represent the green channel component of the given image. In this case, the model would be as in $I = bJ$ + noise (defects) [33], where bJ and noise are considered as the structure component and the texture component, respectively. The green channel of the given image has some noises but no defects such as drusen, GA, etc.; the noise can be reduced using a convolution with a Gaussian filter G_σ of standard deviation σ. In the above equation, J is the true image, which consists of almost all constant values in an image region such as the optic disk, and b is referred to as the intensity inhomogeneity (shading artifact), which changes slowly throughout that image region.

2.2 Edge-based level set segmentation approach

In this section, we give brief information about segmentation of object and background using edge-based level set methods. Let C be a closed subset of Ω, that is, the union of a finite set of smooth Jordan curves C_i. Let Ω_i be the connected regions of $\Omega \backslash C$ bounded by C_i. C can be expressed as the zero-level contour of some scalar

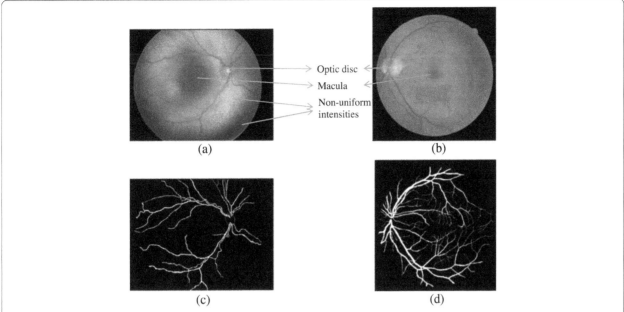

Figure 1 Sample retinal fundus images and manual segmentations. A pathological image (of size 640 × 480 pixels) from our own dataset ([2,19]) given in **(a)**, a non-pathological image (of size 565 × 584 pixels) from the DRIVE dataset ([3]) given in **(b)**, the manual segmentation image of **(a)** given in **(c)**, and the manual segmentation image of **(b)** given in **(d)**.

Lipschitz continuous function $\Phi: \Omega \to \mathbb{R}$ [22]. The level set evolution equation of the curve C with the speed function F is as given in Equation 1:

$$\frac{\partial \Phi}{\partial t} = F(||\nabla \Phi||). \tag{1}$$

Iterations of level set evolution are adversely affected by numerical errors and other factors that cause irregularities. Therefore, a frequent re-initialization process, formulated as $\partial \Phi / \partial t = \text{sign}(\Phi_0)\ (1 - ||\nabla \Phi||)$, could be included to restore the regularity of the level set function, establishing a stable level set evolution. Here, Φ_0

is the level set function to be re-initialized and sign(.) stands for signum function. Re-initialization is performed by interrupting the evolution periodically and correcting irregularities of the level set function using a signed distance function. Even with a re-initialization process, in most of the level set methods such as the geodesic active counters (GAC) model [23], irregularities can still emerge [25]. Therefore, Li et al. introduced a new energy term called level set function regularization [25].

Image segmentation based on level set methods typically consists of two additively combined energy terms, which are the length regularization term and the speed

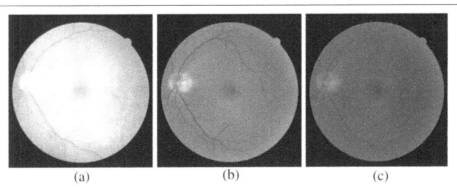

Figure 2 Color channel components of the non-pathological retinal fundus image presented in Figure 1b. Red **(a)**, green **(b)**, and blue **(c)** channel components.

term related to the weighted area. The model is defined as $E(\Phi) = \mu R(\Phi) + \vartheta L(\Phi) + \alpha A(\Phi)$, where $R(.)$, $L(.)$, and $A(.)$ are the level set function regularization term, the zero-level contour regularization term, and the term adjusting the speed of motion to zero-level contour, respectively. Here, μ, ϑ, and α are weighting parameters.

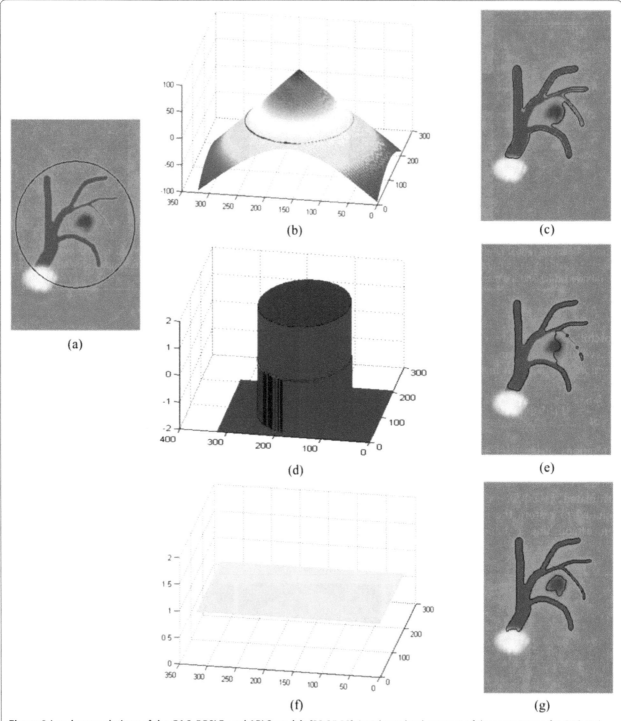

Figure 3 Level set evolutions of the GAC, DRSLE, and ARLS models [23,25,28]. Initial zero-level contours of the given image for GAC and DRSLE **(a)**, initial level set function with a signed distance function **(b)**, final zero-level contour of the given image for the GAC model **(c)**, initial level set function with a binary function **(d)**, final zero-level contour of the given image for the DRSLE model **(e)**, initial level set function with a constant function **(f)**, and final zero-level contour of the given image for the ARLS model **(g)**. Note that the given image can be segmented, if the level set function is re-initialized properly for the GAC model.

The level set function can be initialized in three different ways. In order to demonstrate the effect to the segmentation results, instead of a retinal fundus image, we employ a synthetic image that comprises artificially similar vessels and defects (Figure 3).

1. Initialization with a signed distance function, $d(.)$ (GAC model [23]) (Figure 3a,b,c):

$$\Phi_{initial}(\mathbf{p}) = \begin{cases} -d(\mathbf{p}, C) & \text{in } \Omega_0 \text{ where } \Omega_0 \text{ (marked by the} \\ 0 & \text{on } C \text{ user or selected automatically)} \\ d(\mathbf{p}, C) & \text{in } \Omega \backslash \Omega_0 \text{ is an initial region in } \Omega. \end{cases}$$

2. Initialization with a binary function (distance regularized level set evolution (DRLSE) model [25]) (Figure 3a,d,e): $\Phi_{initial} = \begin{cases} -c_0 & \text{in } \Omega_0 \\ c_0 & \text{in } \Omega \backslash \Omega_0 \end{cases}$, where c_0 is a small valued constant.

3. Initialization with a constant function (adaptive regularized level set (ARLS) model [28]) (Figure 3f,g): $\Phi_{initial} = \mp c_0$ in Ω.

Edge-based level set methods have some drawbacks. Sometimes, a global minimum cannot be found and the methods tend to be slower than other segmentation methods. The global minimum can be correctly obtained if the initial contour is set properly. Level set-based methods also run faster when a narrow band approach is employed in the segmentation process.

3 The proposed method

Our method can be considered in three main steps as outlined in Figure 4:

1. Preprocessing
2. Modified phase map estimation
3. Structure-based level set segmentation

More details about these steps are given in the following subsections of 3.1, 3.2, and 3.3.

3.1 Preprocessing for correction of non-uniform intensity

A preprocessing step is employed for the correction of intensity inhomogeneity of retinal fundus images. Firstly, we apply a trace-based method to reduce noise and then a shock filter is applied to sharpen the image. Both filters work based on color information and give more robust results compared to the scalar approaches presented in [19,38]. Secondly, the green channel of the filtered image is extracted. Thirdly, two different images are generated by applying adaptive histogram equalization on the green channel image and then by applying a classical median filter on the equalized histogram image [19]. Lastly, depending on the case (intensity inhomogeneity),

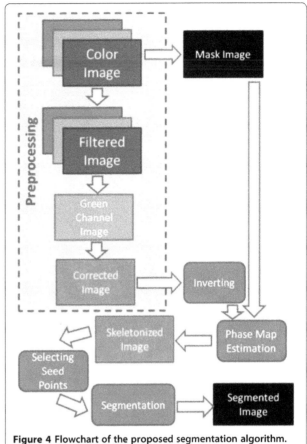

Figure 4 Flowchart of the proposed segmentation algorithm.

one of the following is executed to produce the corrected image:

1. If the input image does not have intensity inhomogeneity, only the histogram-equalized green channel image in the previous step is taken into account as a corrected image.
2. Otherwise, the corrected image is produced by division of those generated images.

To apply the trace-based method on color images, the local geometry for the color image $\mathbf{I}$ is obtained by computing the field $\mathbf{K}$ of geometry tensors. $\mathbf{K}$ is the gradient of $\mathbf{I}$, $\mathbf{K} = \sum_{i=1}^{3} \nabla I_i \nabla I_i^T$, where $\nabla I_i = [\partial I_i / \partial x, \quad \partial I_i / \partial y]^T$. Moreover, $\mathbf{K}$ is expressed as the following for $\mathbf{I}$ in *RGB* color space [39]:

$$\mathbf{K} = \begin{bmatrix} k_{11} & k_{12} \\ k_{21} & k_{22} \end{bmatrix} = \begin{bmatrix} R_x^2 + G_x^2 + B_x^2 & R_x R_y + G_x G_y + B_x B_y \\ R_y R_x + G_y G_x + B_y B_x & R_y^2 + G_y^2 + B_y^2 \end{bmatrix}, \text{ where }$$

$$R_x = \partial I_1 / \partial x, \ G_x = \partial I_2 / \partial x \text{ and } B_x = \partial I_3 / \partial x$$
$$R_y = \partial I_1 / \partial y, \ G_y = \partial I_2 / \partial y \text{ and } B_y = \partial I_3 / \partial y$$

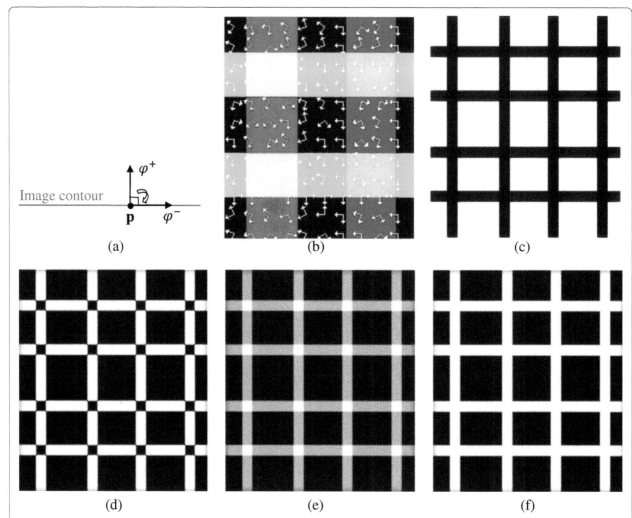

Figure 5 Color image with vector geometries. Graphical representation of two orthogonal eigenvectors on a current point **p (a)**. Some two orthogonal eigenvectors depicted **(b)**, vector edge indicator function $g = (1 + \lambda^{+}\lambda^{-})^{-1}$ **(c)**, vector gradient norm calculated by $\sqrt{\lambda^{+}}$ **(d)**, vector gradient norm calculated by $\sqrt{\lambda^{+}-\lambda^{-}}$ **(e)**, and vector gradient norm calculated by $||\nabla\mathbf{I}|| = \sqrt{\text{trace}(\mathbf{K})} = \sqrt{\sum_{i=1}^{3}||\nabla I_{i}||} = \sqrt{\lambda^{+} + \lambda^{-}}$ **(f)**.

The positive eigenvalues $\lambda^{\pm}$ and the orthogonal eigenvectors $\varphi^{\pm}$ of $\mathbf{K}$ are calculated as

$$\lambda^{\pm} = \left(k_{11} + k_{22} \pm \sqrt{(k_{11}-k_{22})^2 + 4k_{12}^2}\right)/2, \text{ and}$$

$$\varphi^{\pm} = \left[2k_{12} , \quad k_{22}-k_{11} \pm \sqrt{(k_{11}-k_{22})^2 + 4k_{12}^2} \right]^T.$$

$\mathbf{K}_{\sigma} = \mathbf{K} * G_{\sigma}$ is obtained by eliminating noise via the Gaussian filter G_{σ}, and a more stable geometry is generated. Here, * is the convolution operator. $\mathbf{K}_{\sigma}$ is a good predictor of the local geometry of $\mathbf{I}$. The spectral elements of $\mathbf{K}_{\sigma}$ give the color-valued variations such as edge strength by means of the eigenvalues $\lambda^{\pm}$, and they also give the

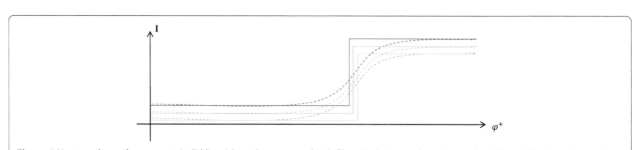

Figure 6 Vector edge enhancement (solid lines) based on vector shock filter. Each image channel smoothed (dashed lines) is sharpened without blurring artifact.

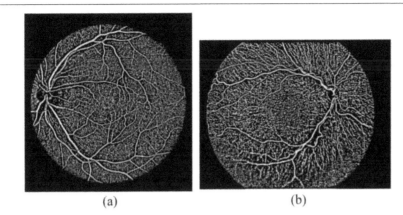

Figure 7 Image features of the green channel components for retinal fundus images in Figure 1. Edges from phase map [24] **(a, b)**. Note that extremely slim vessel could not be smoothly estimated.

corners and edge directions of the local image structures by means of the eigenvectors $\varphi^- \perp \varphi^+$ (Figure 5). More clearly, eigenvalues $\lambda^\pm$ give some information about the active point as follows:

1. If $\lambda^+ \cong \lambda^- \cong 0$, then the point may be in a homogenous region.

2. If $\lambda^+ \gg \lambda^-$, then the point may be on an edge.
3. If $\lambda^+ \cong \lambda^- \gg 0$, then the point may be on a corner.

Tschumperlé et al. [39] suggested designing a particular field $\mathbf{T}: \Omega \to P(2)$ of diffusion tensors to define the specification of the local smoothing method for the regularization process. It should be noticed that $\mathbf{T}$,

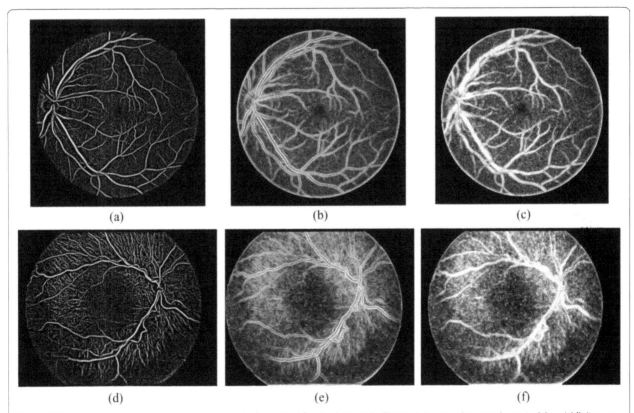

Figure 8 Features of the green channel components for retinal fundus images in Figure 1. Image edges are shown in **(a)** and **(d)**, lines are shown in **(b)** and **(e)**, and structures from our modified phase map approach are shown in **(c)** and **(f)**. Note that our preprocessing step is not applied on these test images.

depended on the local geometry of **I**, can be defined in terms of the spectral elements $\lambda^{\pm}$ and $\varphi^{\pm}$ of $\mathbf{K}_{\sigma}$.

$$\mathbf{T} = s^{-}\left(\lambda^{+}, \lambda^{-}\right)\varphi^{-}\varphi^{-T} + s^{+}\left(\lambda^{+}, \lambda^{-}\right)\varphi^{+}\varphi^{+T}.$$

Here, $s^{\pm}: \mathbb{R}^{2} \rightarrow \mathbb{R}$ are smoothing functions (along $\varphi^{\pm}$), and they change depending on the type of application. Sample functions for image smoothing are proposed in [39] as $s^{-}\left(\lambda^{+}, \lambda^{-}\right) = \left(1 + \lambda^{+} + \lambda^{-}\right)^{-a_{1}}$ and $s^{+}\left(\lambda^{+}, \lambda^{-}\right) =$

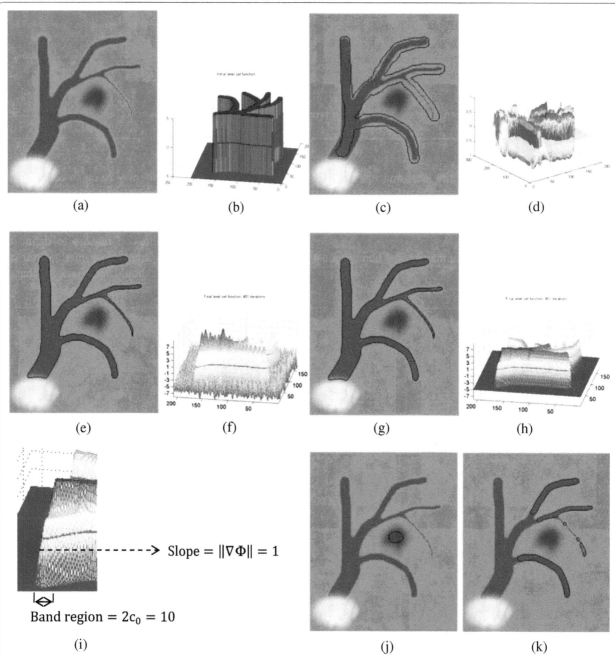

Figure 9 Level set evolution. Synthetic image **(a)**, initialization of the level set function with a binary function using $c_{0} = 5$ **(b)**, and its initial zero-level contour **(c)**, image edges from modified phase map **(d)**, final level set contours based on the proposed method using the potential function P_{1} **(e)**, and its level set function **(f)**, final level set contours based on the proposed method using the potential function P_{2} **(g)**, and its level set function after 451 iterations **(h)**, slope of final level set function in a band region with size of $2c_{0}$ **(i)**, final zero-level contours of the given image based on DRLSE [25] using the potential function P_{2} and set by a negative-valued a **(j)** and a positive-valued a **(k)**. In **(g)**, with area functional $A(.)$, the initial contour is shrunk and expanded automatically to match the boundary of vessels. With the length functional $L(.)$, this fitting has become smooth. The initial level set function in **(b)** is regularized using the regularization functional $R(.)$, and the final, regularized level set function in **(h)** is obtained.

$\left(1 + \lambda^+ + \lambda^-\right)^{-a_2}$, where $a_1 < a_2$. The goals of smoothing operation are

1. To process pixels on image edges along the φ^- direction (anisotropic smoothing)
2. To process pixels on homogeneous regions on all possible directions (isotropic smoothing). In this case, T $\cong$ identity matrix and then the method behaves as a heat equation

The regularization approach presented by Tschumperlé et al. [39] is used to obtain the local smoothing geometry T, based on the trace operator:

$$\partial I / \partial t = \partial I_i / \partial t = \text{trace}(\mathbf{T} \mathbf{H}_i) \tag{2}$$

where $\mathbf{H}_i$ is the Hessian matrix of I_i: $\mathbf{H}_i = \begin{bmatrix} \partial^2 I_i / \partial x^2 & \partial^2 I_i / \partial x \partial y \\ \partial^2 I_i / \partial y \partial x & \partial^2 I_i / \partial y^2 \end{bmatrix}$.

To sharpen the color images, the shock filter is applied on each image channel I_i only in one direction φ^+ of the vector discontinuities [39]. Moreover, a weighting function is added to enhance color image structure without changing the flat regions. As depicted in Figure 6, such a filter is formulized as follows [39]:

$$\partial I_i / \partial t = \left(s^+ \left(\lambda^+, \lambda^-\right) - 1\right) \text{sign}\left(\varphi^{+T} \mathbf{H}_i \varphi^+\right) \left| I_{i_{(\varphi^-)}} \right|, \text{ where}$$

$$I_{i_{(\varphi^+)}} = \varphi^- E^- + \varphi^+ E^+,$$

$$E^- = \begin{cases} 0 & \text{if } \dfrac{\partial I_{i(b)}}{\partial x} \times \dfrac{\partial I_{i(f)}}{\partial x} < 0 \\ \min\left(\dfrac{\partial I_{i(b)}}{\partial x}, \dfrac{\partial I_{i(f)}}{\partial x}\right) & \text{else} \end{cases}$$

$$E^+ = \begin{cases} 0 & \text{if } \dfrac{\partial I_{i(b)}}{\partial y} \times \dfrac{\partial I_{i(f)}}{\partial y} < 0 \\ \min\left(\dfrac{\partial I_{i(b)}}{\partial y}, \dfrac{\partial I_{i(f)}}{\partial y}\right) & \text{else} \end{cases}$$

$$\tag{3}$$

Here, $s^+: \mathbb{R}^2 \to \mathbb{R}$, $s^+(.) = (1 + \lambda^+ + \lambda^-)^{-0.5}$ is a decreasing function, and sub-indexes b and f stand for backward and forward finite differences, respectively.

The methods based on color information are compatible with all local geometric properties expressed above: $\mathbf{I}_{(t+1)} = \mathbf{I}_{(t)} + \tau_1 \partial \mathbf{I}_{(t)} / \partial t$, where τ_1 is an adapting time step. The adapting time step τ_1 is set by the following inequality: $\tau_1 \leq 20/\max(\max_{\mathbf{p}}(\partial \mathbf{I}_{(t)}(\mathbf{p})/\partial t), \min_{\mathbf{p}}(\partial \mathbf{I}_{(t)}(\mathbf{p})/\partial t))$.

3.2 Modified phase map estimation

Another important step followed in preprocessing retinal fundus images is developing an efficient method for estimation of the image structures in cases, for instance, where retinal vessel network contains slim and lengthy vessels with weak edge intensities. According to our experiment, edge-based level set image segmentation methods give the best results on images that have only structure information in the segmented regions. Although the method [25] described above could segment objects in MRIs and other common medical image formats with reasonable success, it may fail to segment retinal vasculature successfully, due to vessels with weak edge properties. Therefore, an alternative image structure based on the phase map of the image is employed. It should be noted that neither the phase congruency-based method [40] nor the phase map-based approach [24] (see Figure 7) generates adequate structure information for segmentation of vasculature in fundus images [30]. Therefore, we combine these two methods as described below to improve the phase map.

The log-Gabor filter can efficiently extract image features such as edges and corners without missing any weak object boundaries. This filter, generated in frequency domain, is a version of logarithmic transformation of the

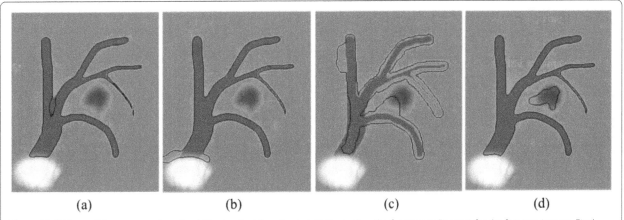

(a) (b) (c) (d)

Figure 10 Failure of the proposed method. The level set function is initialized using the function in Figure 8 for the first two images. Final level set contours based on the proposed method using heat equation as a potential function **(a)**, final level set contours based on the proposed method using the potential function P_2 without preprocessing **(b)**, binary mask for initialization of the level set function **(c)**, and final level set contours based on the proposed method using the potential function P_2 **(d)**.

Table 1 Formulas of some variational image segmentation methods

Group	Method	Formula
Edge-based	GAC [23]	$\vartheta\|\nabla\Phi\|\mathrm{div}\left(g\frac{\nabla\Phi}{\|\nabla\Phi\|}\right) + ag\|\nabla\Phi\|$
	PBLS [24]	$\vartheta\|\nabla\Phi\|\mathrm{div}\left(\frac{\nabla\Phi}{\|\nabla\Phi\|}\right) - a\|\nabla\Phi\|\Re(\hat{q}_{PBLS})$
	DRLSE [25]	$\mu\,\mathrm{div}(D(\|\nabla\Phi\|)\nabla\Phi) + \vartheta\delta_\varepsilon(\Phi)\mathrm{div}\left(g\frac{\nabla\Phi}{\|\nabla\Phi\|}\right) + ag\delta_\varepsilon(\Phi)$
	ARLS [28]	$\mu\left(\nabla^2\Phi - \mathrm{div}\left(\frac{\nabla\Phi}{\|\nabla\Phi\|}\right)\right) + \vartheta\delta_\varepsilon(\Phi)\mathrm{div}\left(\|\nabla\Phi\|^{s(\nabla(I*G_\sigma))-2}\nabla\Phi\right) + a\delta_\varepsilon(\Phi)\nabla^2(I*G_\sigma)$
Region-based	RBLSE [33]	$\mu\,\mathrm{div}(D(\|\nabla\Phi\|)\nabla\Phi) + \vartheta\delta_\varepsilon(\Phi)\mathrm{div}\left(\frac{\nabla\Phi}{\|\nabla\Phi\|}\right) - a\delta_\varepsilon(\Phi)(e_1 - e_2),$

where e_i is the data fitting function of/in region Ω_i. See [33] for more details.

Gabor filter [4], and it has no DC component. In polar coordinates, the filter consists of two components, the radial part and the angular part. These two components are combined to create the log-Gabor filter, which is the transfer function formulated as follows [40]:

$$G_l(r,\theta) = \exp\left(-\frac{(\log(r/f_0))^2}{2\sigma_r{}^2} - \frac{(\theta-\theta_0)^2}{2\sigma_\theta{}^2}\right).$$

Here, (r, θ) stands for the polar coordinates, f_0 is the center frequency, θ_0 is the orientation angle (direction), $\sigma_r = \log(v/f_0)$ defines the scale bandwidth, and σ_θ defines the angular bandwidth. In order to keep the shape ratio of the filter constant, the term v/f_0 must also be kept constant for varying f_0 [40].

The log-Gabor filter can be efficiently used to generate the phase map instead of the gradient norm in image segmentation [24,40]. The image is filtered at different scales in at least three uniformly distributed directions to grab the poor contrast and vasculature with varying width [24]. The filter output is complex in the time domain, where real and imaginary parts consist of line and edge information, respectively. Filter responses in each scale for all directions must be combined to obtain a rotationally invariant phase map. The absolute value of the imaginary parts is taken to avoid an elimination [24].

With these in mind, the modified phase map q is obtained as in Equation 4:

$$q = \frac{\sum_{k=1}^{O}\sum_{l=1}^{S}\|\bar{q}_{k,l}\|^\beta\bar{q}_{k,l}}{\sum_{k=1}^{O}\sum_{l=1}^{S}\|\bar{q}_{k,l}\|^\beta}. \qquad (4)$$

Here, $\bar{q}_{k,l} = \Re\left(q_{k,l}\right) + \left|\Im\left(q_{k,l}\right)\right|\sqrt{-1}$, O is the number of the orientation angles, S is the number of the scales, $\bar{q}_{k,l}$ is the filter response based on the corrected phase, and β is a weighting parameter. The normalization $\hat{q} = q\|q\|/\left(\|q^2 + \sigma_q{}^2\right)$ is also used to regularize the phase map. Here, σ_q stands for a threshold used to reduce noise effect [24]. Since edges align with the zero crossings of the real part of the phase map, the function $\Re(\hat{q})$ can be used to estimate image edges as in [24]. Moreover, $\Im(\hat{q})$ gives image lines, and the norm of the filter response, formulated as $\|\hat{q}\| = \sqrt{\Re(\hat{q})^2 + \Im(\hat{q})^2}$, gives the strength of the image structure. So, the image structures of the green channel of retinal fundus images are estimated efficiently and correctly by using the log-Gabor filter as seen in Figure 8.

3.3 Structure-based level set segmentation method
A novel structure-based variational method is proposed in this study in order to trace retinal vasculature. The level set function in [25] can be discretized more easily compared to

Table 2 Parameter values of the methods

Method	Parameters
Proposed preprocessing	Amplitude of the trace-based filter is 30, amplitude of the shock filter is 45, $\tau_1 =$ updated at each iteration, other parameters of these filters are kept as in the related study [39], and kernel size of median filter is 25×25.
Log-Gabor filter [40] and modified phase map	$f_0(x) = \left(3 \times 2.1^{(x-1)}\right)^{-1}$, $1 \leq x \leq S = 3$, $\sigma_r = \log(0.55)$, $\sigma_\theta = 1.2$, $\theta_0(x)$, $1 \leq x \leq O = 8$, $\beta = 1$, and $\sigma_q = 3$.
GAC [23]	$\tau_2 = 0.2$, $\vartheta = 1$, and $a = 0.3$
PBLS [24]	$\tau_2 =$ updated at each iteration, $\vartheta = 0.07$, and $a = 1$
DRLSE [25]	$\tau_2 = 5$, $\sigma = 1.5$, $\mu = 0.04$, $\vartheta = 5$, $a = \pm 1.5$, and $c_0 = 2$
ARLS [28]	$\tau_2 = 5$, $\sigma = 1.4$, $\mu = 0.04$, $\vartheta = 2.7$, $a = \pm 1$, and $c_0 = \pm 1$
Proposed segmentation	$\tau_2 = 1$, $\mu = 0.2$, $\vartheta = 0.6$, $a = 3$, and $c_0 = \{2, 5\}$
RBLSE [33]	$\tau_2 = 0.1$, $\sigma = 4$, $\mu = 1$, $\vartheta = 0.01 \times 255^2$, and $c_0 = 1$

other methods in the literature since it has a level set regularization term. The discretization process uses center/forward difference model instead of other complex discretization schemes [23,24]. For instance, in the GAC model in [23], the upwind method is used for the calculation of the gradient norm of the level set function Φ, and for the re-initialization of the level set function Φ, essentially non-oscillatory (ENO) scheme is employed. Therefore, the same level set function regularization term of the DRLSE method [25] is used in the proposed method.

In the DRLSE method [25], the formulas of $R(\Phi) = \int_{\Omega} P(\Phi)d\mathbf{p}$, $L(\Phi) = \int_{\Omega} g\delta_{\varepsilon}(\Phi)||\nabla\Phi||d\mathbf{p}$ and $A(\Phi) = \int_{\Omega} gH_{\varepsilon}(-\Phi)d\mathbf{p}$ are employed for segmentation. Here, $P(.)$ is a potential function. The length functional $L(.)$ smoothes the zero-level contour. The area functional $A(.)$ helps accelerate the level set evolution when the initial contour is located far away from the object boundaries. For demonstration, see Figure 9.

In edge-based level set approaches, a smooth edge indicator function is generally obtained from the gradient norm of the Gaussian-filtered image. One choice is $g = (1 + ||\nabla(G_{\sigma} * I)||^2)^{-1}$. The edge indicator function

g carries key information to locate the zero-level contour. H_{ε} and $\delta_{\varepsilon} = H'_{\varepsilon}$ are finite-width approximations of the Heaviside function and Dirac-delta for ε:

$$H_{\varepsilon}(x) = \begin{cases} \frac{1}{2}\left[1 + \frac{\pi}{\varepsilon} + \frac{1}{\pi}\sin\left(\frac{\pi x}{\varepsilon}\right)\right], & |x| \le \varepsilon \\ 1, & x > \varepsilon \\ 0, & x < -\varepsilon \end{cases} \quad \text{and}$$

$$\delta_{\varepsilon}(x) = \begin{cases} \frac{1}{2\varepsilon}\left[1 + \cos\left(\frac{\pi x}{\varepsilon}\right)\right], & |x| \le \varepsilon \\ 0, & |x| > \varepsilon \end{cases}$$

where, in general, the parameter ε is set to 1.5.

The level set function regularization term should have a minimum to maintain the signed distance property of $||\nabla\Phi|| = 1$ in a band region around the zero-level contour as depicted in Figure 9i, instead of the heat equation [25] that enforces $||\nabla\Phi|| = 0$, eventually. So, the solution, based on the potential function $P_1(||\nabla\Phi||) = 0.5(||\nabla\Phi|| - 1)^2$, is formulated as follows [25]:

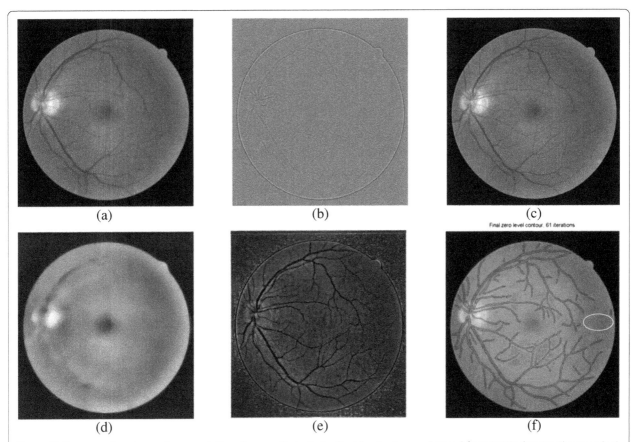

Figure 11 Preprocessing step and segmentation of non-pathological retinal fundus image obtained from DRIVE dataset. The smoothed image using the scalar approach [19,38] **(a)**, the image generated by subtracting the original green channel image from the smoothed one **(b)**, the sharpened image **(c)**, the estimated intensity inhomogeneity image obtained by using the median filter **(d)**, the corrected image **(e)**, and segmented image using the proposed structure-based level set segmentation method after 61 iterations **(f)**.

$$\frac{\partial \Phi_R}{\partial t} = \mu \mathrm{div}(D(||\nabla\Phi||)\nabla\Phi) = \mu\left(\nabla^2\Phi - \mathrm{div}\left(\frac{\nabla\Phi}{||\nabla\Phi||}\right)\right)$$

$$(5)$$

The sign of $D(||\nabla\Phi||) = 1 - (1/||\nabla\Phi||)$, where $D(x) = x^{-1}$ $\partial P(x)/\partial x$ indicates the property of the diffusion term

based on anisotropic regularization in the following two cases [25]:

1. For $||\nabla\Phi|| > 1$, the diffusion rate $\mu D(.)$ is positive and the diffusion is forward, which decreases the term $||\nabla\Phi||$

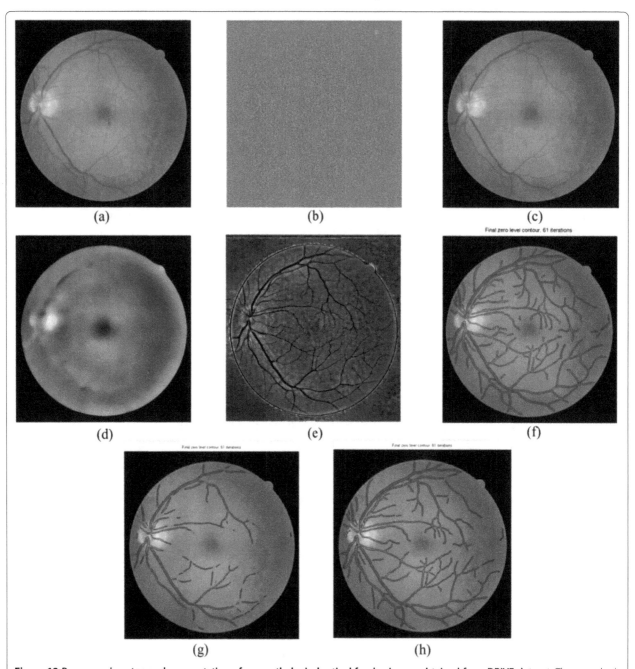

(a)   (b)   (c)

(d)   (e)   (f)

(g)   (h)

Figure 12 Preprocessing step and segmentation of non-pathological retinal fundus image obtained from DRIVE dataset. The smoothed image using the trace-based approach [39] **(a)**, the image generated by subtracting the original green channel image from the smoothed one **(b)**, the sharpened image [39] **(c)**, the estimated intensity inhomogeneity image obtained by using the median filter **(d)**, the corrected image based on our approach **(e)**, segmented image using the proposed structure-based level set segmentation method **(f)**, segmented result using only green channel of the given image based on the proposed structure-based level set segmentation method without preprocessing **(g)**, and segmented result using only green channel of the histogram-equalized given image based on the proposed structure-based level set segmentation method without preprocessing after 61 iterations **(h)**.

2. For $||\nabla\Phi|| < 1$, the diffusion is backward, which increases the term $||\nabla\Phi||$

However, this regularization term may cause an unsatisfactory result on the level set function when $||\nabla\Phi||$ is close to 0 outside the band region as shown in Figure 9e,f. So, as given in Figure 9g,h, a corrected potential function is given as follows [25]:

$$P_2(x) = \begin{cases} \dfrac{1}{(2\pi)^2}(1 - \cos(2\pi x)) & \text{if } x \leq 1 \\ \dfrac{1}{2}(x-1)^2 & \text{if } x \geq 1. \end{cases}$$

In the proposed method, the initial contours have to be set automatically around vessels in order to find the global minimum in a segmented image correctly. Sometimes, there is a risk of getting stuck in a local minimum due to the fact that retinal fundus images include defects such as drusen, GA, etc. So, seed points should be chosen around vessel regions to generate a desirable result. Note that the seed points can be set in or out of vessel areas, but they should be very close to the vessel structures (compare Figures 9 and 10). There is another approach, called the ARLS method [28] in the literature, utilizing automatic initial contours based on Laplacian of Gaussian (LoG) filter. This method is not proper for segmenting retinal vasculature, as the filter is very sensitive to noise, and there is a risk in the automatic initial contours if the retinal fundus image contains pathological regions. On the contrary, in the proposed method, the real part of the modified phase map has zero-crossing boundaries, and the method ensures to find the global minimum if the initial contour is selected around vasculature

regions (Figure 9a,b,c,d,e,f,g,h). Therefore, we improve the speed term based on the area functional $A(.)$ as follows:

$$\frac{\partial\Phi_A}{\partial t} = -\alpha\delta_\varepsilon(\Phi)\Re(\hat{q}). \tag{6}$$

In our method, iso-contours automatically shrink when the contour is outside the object due to the functional of $A(.)$ returning a positive contribution, or they automatically expand with a negative value in $A(.)$ when the contour is inside, regardless of the sign of α values as in the existing method [25] (Figure 9j,k).

To eliminate staircasing effect [41] and not to miss weak object boundaries [28], a potential function based on weighted total variation (WTV) model is used as $P_3(\Phi) = \frac{\nabla^{s(\nabla(I*G_\sigma))}}{s(\nabla(I*G_\sigma))}$. Here, $s: \mathbb{R} \rightarrow [1,2)$ is a monotonically decreasing function [27,28,41]. Such a function used in the ARSL method [28] is not capable of regularizing zero-level contours because of the smoothed gradient norm which cannot generate image structure. Furthermore, the total variation (TV) model, presented in the PBLS method [24], will not smooth zero-level contours completely, generating unsatisfactory results. Therefore, we suggest a modified oriented Laplacian flow as in Equation 7, originally employed in image denoising [39,42], in order to regularize the zero-level contour:

$$\frac{\partial\Phi_L}{\partial t} = \vartheta\delta_\varepsilon(\Phi)\left(\Phi_{\xi\xi} + s(||\hat{q}||)\Phi_{\eta\eta}\right) \tag{7}$$

where $s(||\hat{q}||) = \left(1 + ||\hat{q}||^2\right)^{-1}$, $\Phi_{\zeta\zeta} = \zeta^T\mathbf{H}\zeta$, $\Phi_{\eta\eta} = \eta^T\mathbf{H}\eta$, and $\mathbf{H}$ is the Hessian of Φ. The unit vectors η and ζ are represented by the gradient direction and the tangential

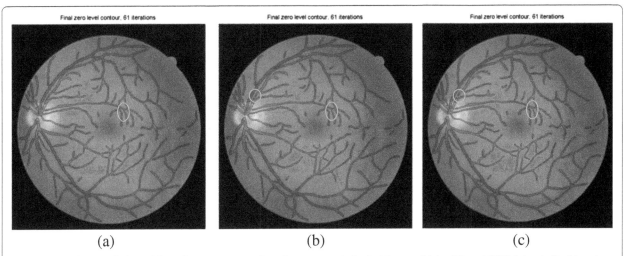

| (a) | (b) | (c) |

Figure 13 Level set evolution with setting parameter values for a non-pathological image obtained from DRIVE dataset. $\vartheta = 0.4$ and $\alpha = 1.5$ **(a)**, $\vartheta = 0.8$ and $\alpha = 2.5$ **(b)**, and $\vartheta = 1$ and $\alpha = 3$ **(c)**.

(its orthogonal) direction, respectively. Here, $\eta = \nabla\Phi/ ||\nabla\Phi||$ and $\zeta = \eta^{\perp}$. $s(.)$ depends on the value of the strength of the image structure $||\hat{q}||$, which is generated from phase map. So, along the zero-level contour, the oriented Laplacian flow has a strong smoothing effect. As a result, our approach is more efficient compared to the PBLS method [24] to regularize zero-level contours.

3.4 Proposed segmentation method

The proposed method accepts a retinal fundus image in *RGB* color space as input. Firstly, a simple mask is obtained to exclude the exterior parts of the fundus where the color is in the 0-U interval in all three channels (generally very dark regions). Also, an iterated erosion operator whose structure element is $\mathbf{B} = [0,\ 1,\ 0;\quad 1\ ,1,\ 1;$

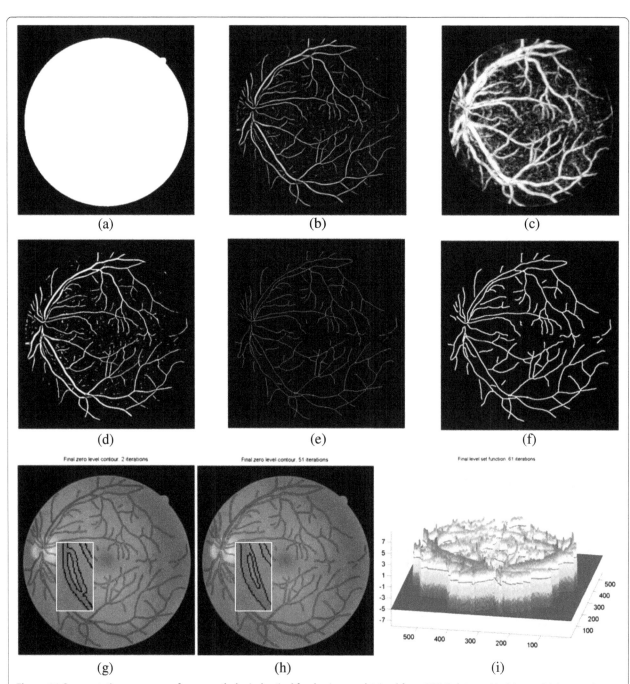

Figure 14 **Segmentation processes of a non-pathological retinal fundus image obtained from DRIVE dataset.** Mask image **(a)**, image edge obtained using the proposed phase map **(b)**, image structure obtained using the phase map **(c)**, binary image obtained from (b) using Otsu thresholding [43] **(d)**, skeletonized version of (d) after eliminating outliers **(e)**, dilated version of (e) **(f)**, segmented image using the proposed method after 2 iterations **(g)**, segmented image using the proposed method after 51 iterations **(h)**, and the level set function after 61 iterations **(i)**.

0, 1, 0$]^T$ is applied on the mask for proper execution. Secondly, a preprocessing step is employed to obtain a corrected image in terms of intensity inhomogeneity. Thirdly, we compute the phase map by using the corrected image as input. Afterwards, to eliminate some small non-blood vessels region, Otsu's method [43] is applied on the processed image. As a result of these processes, a skeleton-based image giving the centerlines of the vasculature is generated with the following steps: (i) remove disconnected pixels, (ii) obtain skeleton-based image, (iii) find junctions, (iv) trace lines (centerlines) and label them, and (v) clean short lines. Here, a threshold value is used to eliminate tiny little short lines called artifacts.

In order to set the optimum initialization of the zero-level contour, seed points have to be selected around the vasculature according to the centerline obtained based on phase map properties. Here, a morphological dilation operator whose structure element is $\mathbf{B} = [1, 1, 1; \ 1, 1, 1; \ 1, 1, 1]^T$, is performed on the centerlines to generate a proper initial contour. Finally, the proposed method creates the output by using the structure-based level set method. Our level set function is minimized by using Euler Lagrange and the iterative gradient descent procedure as follows:

$$\frac{\partial \Phi}{\partial t} = \mu \text{div}(D(||\nabla\Phi||)\nabla\Phi) + \vartheta\delta_\varepsilon(\Phi)$$
$$\times \left(\Phi_{\zeta\zeta} + s(||\hat{q}||)\Phi_{\eta\eta}\right) - \alpha\delta_\varepsilon(\Phi)\mathcal{R}(\hat{q}). \quad (8)$$

Note that values of the edge indicator function g, used in [25], are in the [0,1] interval. In the proposed method, the sign of the coefficient α in the level set energy functional can always remain positive in contrast to the earlier method [25] since the function $\mathcal{R}(\hat{q})$ obtained from the phase map has a different sign around object boundaries.

The proposed level set evolution equation culminates in $\Phi_{(t+1)} = \Phi_{(t)} + \tau_2\partial\Phi_{(t)}/\partial t$ where τ_2 is a time step, which is set by $\tau_2 \leq (4\mu)^{-1}$ based on Courant-Friedrichs-Lewy (CFL) condition with 4-neighbor connectivity [25,44].

The initialization of level set function is important. If the seed points are selected away from the vessel centers and close to pathological regions, the proposed method can fail (wrongly segmenting the pathological region, as well) as shown in Figure 10d.

4 Experimental results

The proposed method is tested on DRIVE [3], STARE [11], and our own datasets [2,19] for this study. Our 34 wide-angle fundus images are grabbed from premature infants supplied by the RetCam II camera and delineated by medical experts. The images from different experts are combined to create one ground truth image for each one of the fundus image [1,2]. Some methods used in this study are summarized in Table 1. The chosen parameters of the algorithm are given in Table 2. Eight uniformly distributed angle directions and three image re-sampling scales for the log-Gabor filter are used in the method. The maximum number of iterations for the

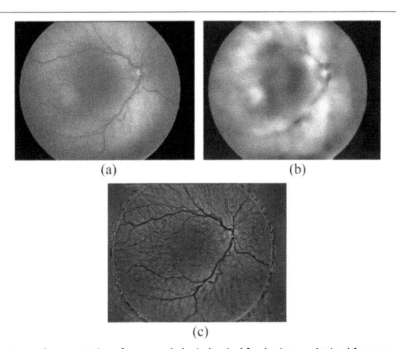

(a)

(b)

(c)

Figure 15 Preprocessing step and segmentation of a non-pathological retinal fundus image obtained from our dataset. Green channel of the given image in Figure 1a **(a)**, estimated intensity inhomogeneity image that is obtained by using the median filter **(b)**, and the corrected image that is obtained by our method **(c)**.

main algorithm depends on the radii of the vessel, and for this study, it is experimentally set as 60 + 1 (extra regularization of the zero-level contour via level set evolution with $\alpha = 0$). The threshold values of U for creating mask images are set to 40, 40, and 45, for DRIVE dataset, our dataset, and STARE dataset, respectively. Moreover, small gaps in the created mask image for STARE dataset are filled using a morphological closing operator whose structure element is a disk of radius 10. In order to eliminate the out of fundus image region, the numbers of iterated erosion operator are set to 8, 8, and 2 for DRIVE dataset, our dataset, and STARE dataset, respectively. The threshold values of short line length are set as 15, 35, and 15 for DRIVE dataset, our dataset, and STARE dataset, respectively. c_0 values for initializing of level set functions are set to 5, 5, and 2 for DRIVE

dataset, our dataset, and STARE dataset, respectively. Here, in all cases except for the 20th image from STARE dataset, second selection is used for preprocessing. First selection is used for preprocessing on 20th image from STARE dataset because this image does not have intensity inhomogeneity. The Neumann boundary condition is employed [25] to solve Equation 8.

The results of the preprocessing step for some test images from DRIVE dataset are seen in Figures 11 and 12. Using the segmented image, on which a scalar approach [19,38] is applied for the preprocessing step, the vasculature cannot be traced truly. This does not happen in our method because we use a trace-based method to smoothen and then a shock filter to sharpen the given image. Both filters work based on the color information unlike the ones in the scalar approach presented in

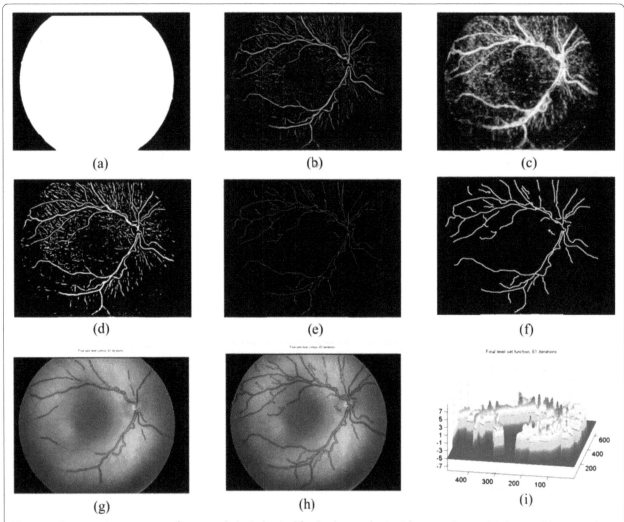

Figure 16 Segmentation processes of a non-pathological retinal fundus image obtained from our dataset. Mask image **(a)**, image edge obtained using the proposed phase map **(b)**, image structure obtained using the phase map **(c)**, binary image obtained from (b) using Otsu thresholding [43] **(d)**, skeletonized version of (d) after eliminating outliers **(e)**, dilated version of (e) **(f)**, segmented result using only green channel of the given image based on the proposed structure-based level set segmentation method without preprocessing **(g)**, segmented image using the proposed method **(h)**, and the level set function after 61 iterations **(i)**.

[19,38]. Therefore, the image, obtained by our method, is denoised more efficiently and segmented more correctly. While our method produces promising results, we should also indicate that there are still missed retinal vessels. Those missed vessels are very thin with weak edge properties. There are regular retinal vessels with normal dimensions wholly missed with the preprocessing step presented in [19]. Such a region is marked with a blue circle as shown in Figure 11f. In Figure 12b, a difference image between input color image and smoothed version of the input image is shown. The blue channel

has noise and seems to contain higher frequencies compared to Figure 11b. Furthermore, images that could not be segmented using the proposed structure-based level set segmentation method without preprocessing are shown in Figure 12g,h.

Figure 13 demonstrates the results of the level set function evolution based on setting the coefficient values ϑ and α used in the length term regularizing zero-level contour and the speed term accelerating the level set function evolution. ϑ is set to 0.4, 0.8, and 1, and α is set to 1.5, 2.5, and 3, respectively, as shown Figure 13a,b,c.

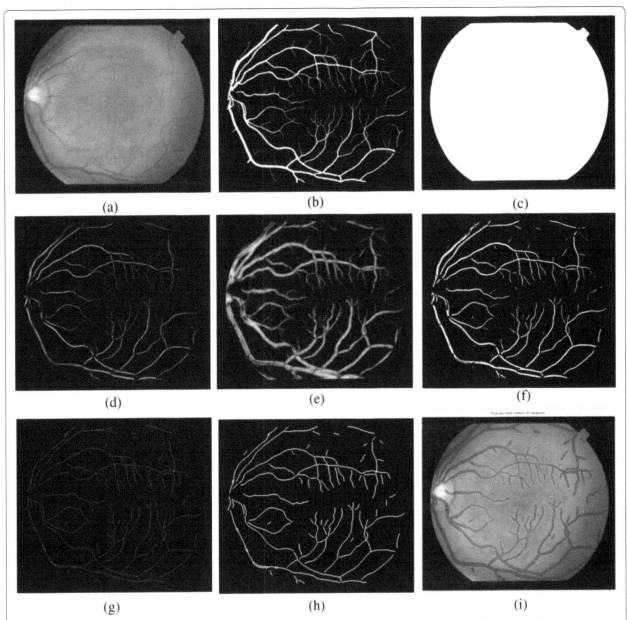

(a) (b) (c)

(d) (e) (f)

(g) (h) (i)

Figure 17 Segmentation processes of a 700 × 605-pixel non-pathological retinal fundus image obtained from STARE dataset. Input image **(a)**, manual segmentation (first observer) **(b)**, mask image **(c)**, image edge obtained using the proposed phase map **(d)**, image structure obtained using the phase map **(e)**, binary image obtained from **(d)** using Otsu thresholding [43] **(f)**, skeletonized version of **(f)** after eliminating outliers **(g)**, dilated version of **(g)** **(h)**, segmented image using the proposed method after 61 iterations **(i)**.

However, some retinal vessels (marked with a blue circle) are still not connected. Therefore, in order to generate a good result as seen in Figure 12f, ϑ and α are set to 0.6 and 3, respectively.

Our segmentation process illustrated in Figure 14 employs the skeletonized version of the input image on which a morphological dilation operator is performed only once to initialize the level set function. The proposed method generates good results; some very thin retinal vessels with poor contrast are still missed due to the fact that our method is unable to produce a proper phase map. However, unlike previous works [24,25], the

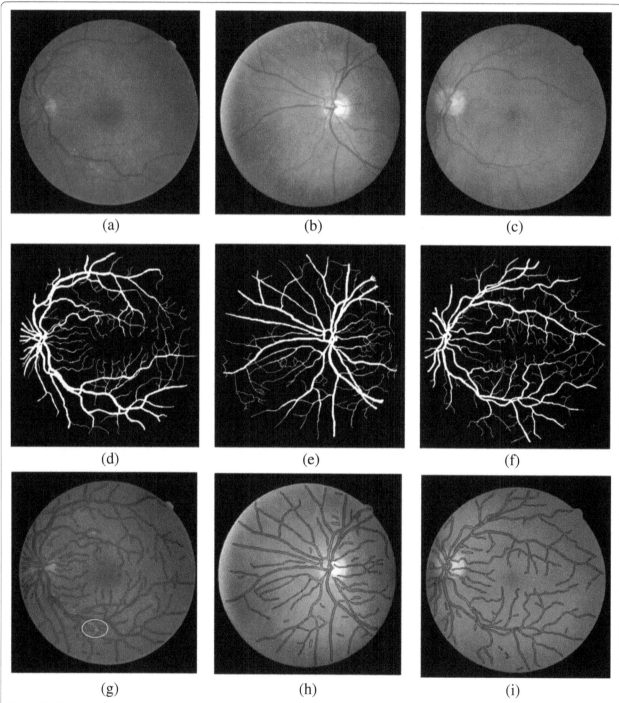

Figure 18 Vessel segmentation results for 565 × 584-pixel pathological and non-pathological images obtained from DRIVE dataset.
Pathological image **(a)**, non-pathological image **(b)**, and another non-pathological image **(c)** (row 1). Manual segmentations of images in row 1 (row 2). Segmented images (row 3).

method can trace retinal vessels efficiently, since the structure-based level set segmentation method is able to shrink or expand automatically as displayed in Figure 14h where the level set function is initialized inside the vessels in some regions and outside the vessels in some regions.

The test results of preprocessing operations on our dataset are shown Figure 15. The non-uniform intensities in the given image are estimated and corrected properly.

A sample vessel segmentation result for a non-pathological fundus image from our dataset is shown in Figure 16. Here, the approach cannot trace some vessels with poor contrasts as seen in Figure 16h. Also, the image could not be segmented employing the proposed segmentation method without preprocessing as depicted in Figure 16g.

Another sample vessel segmentation result for a non-pathological fundus image from STARE dataset is depicted in Figure 17. Here, the vessels can be traced properly using the method.

The results of other test images in DRIVE, our images, and STARE datasets are given in Figures 18, 19 and 20. Some segmentation results for pathological images include artifact, and they are marked with blue circles. These regions have also poor contrast, and retinal vessels in these regions are very thin.

Figure 21 depicts another case, for which both methods described in earlier work [24,25] failed especially at regions with poor contrast. However, the proposed method is able to properly track the vessels in those regions as shown in Figure 21e. Although the

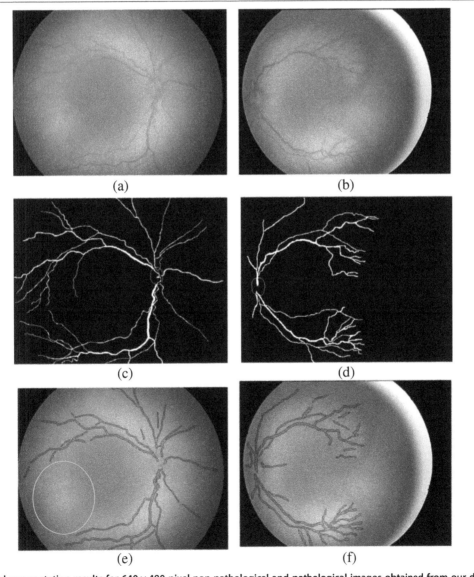

Figure 19 Vessel segmentation results for 640 × 480-pixel non-pathological and pathological images obtained from our dataset.
Non-pathological image **(a)**, and pathological image **(b)** (row 1). Manual segmentations of images in row 1 (row 2). Segmented images (row 3).

PBLS method presented in [24] runs faster than ours since it employs a narrow band implementation, that faster method is unable to trace retinal vessels properly due to the fact that the phase map of the method is not estimated correctly in the regions with thin vessels and poor contrasts. Also, the DRLSE method proposed in [25] does not expand the vessels if the initialization starts inside the vessel. On the other hand, if initialization starts outside the vessel and the image is in poor contrast, the DRLSE method over-segments the vessels because it uses the image gradient instead of the phase map. Instead of a TV approach, $\partial \Phi_L / \partial t = \vartheta \delta_\varepsilon(\Phi)$ $\text{div}\left(g\frac{\nabla \Phi}{\|\nabla \Phi\|}\right)$, if an oriented Laplacian flow approach, $\partial \Phi_L / \partial t = \vartheta \delta_\varepsilon(\Phi)(\Phi_{\zeta\zeta} + g\Phi_{\eta\eta})$, proposed in our work, is employed in the DRLSE method to smooth zero-level contours, the results may visually seem to be like over-smoothing as displayed in Figure 21b,c. But, as depicted

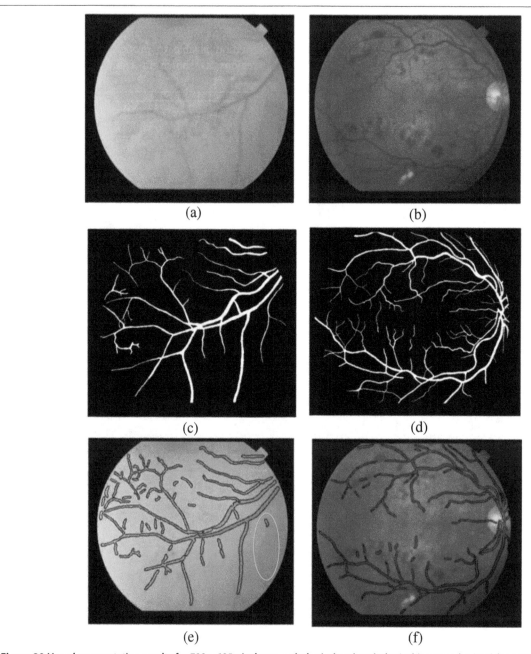

(a)

(b)

(c)

(d)

(e)

(f)

Figure 20 Vessel segmentation results for 700 × 605-pixel non-pathological and pathological images obtained from STARE dataset.
Non-pathological image **(a)**, and pathological image **(b)** (row 1). Manual segmentations of images (first observer) in row 1 (row 2), and segmented images (row 3).

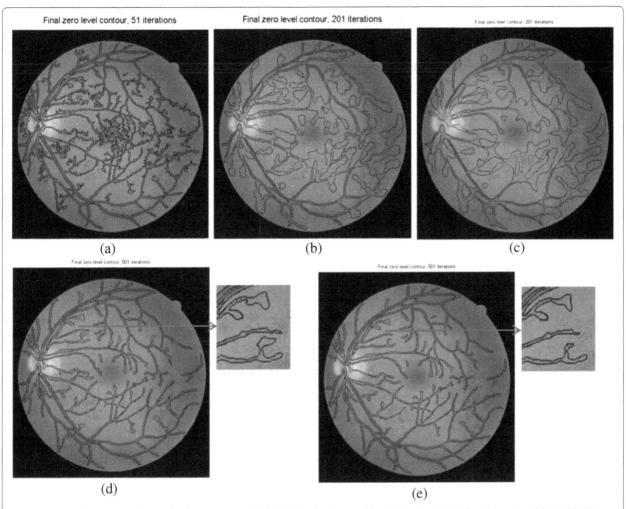

Figure 21 Vessel segmentation results for the non-pathological fundus image. The PBLS method [24] after 51 iterations **(a)**, the DRLSE method [25] based on TV approach after 201 iterations **(b)**, the DRLSE method [25] based on oriented Laplacian flow approach after 201 iterations **(c)**, the proposed method based on modified TV approach after 501 iterations **(d)**, and the proposed method based on modified oriented Laplacian flow approach after 501 iterations **(e)**.

in Figure 21e, this disadvantage turns into an advantage if the modified oriented Laplacian flow approach, $\partial\Phi_L/\partial t = \vartheta\delta_\varepsilon(\Phi)\left(\Phi_{\eta\eta} + s(||\hat{q}||) \; \Phi_{\eta\eta}\right)$, is employed in our method, since it eliminates the expansion of segmented vessel areas. As shown in Figure 21d, the expansion is not completely eliminated if a modified TV approach, $\partial\Phi_L/\partial t = \vartheta\delta_\varepsilon(\Phi)\mathrm{div}(s(||\hat{q}||)\nabla\Phi/||\nabla\Phi||)$, is used in our method. Also, the vessels could be traced more properly in the proposed method, if the iteration number is increased, but this increases the cost. The result of our method seems to be more efficient compared to the existing methods [24,25] in the literature since it has a novel zero-level contour regularization term and it employs a modified phase map.

Lastly, the segmentation results of the non-pathological image generated by the region-based level set evolution method (RBLSE) [33] are given in Figure 22. The most important advantage of this method is that the initialization may start on any region of the fundus image instead of around vessels by a simple selection. The segmentation of vessels can be done in the fundus images without poor contrast in the initialization phase. After that, while some segmented vessels are combined, some gradually disappeared in later iterations. But surprisingly, after the 42nd iteration, all segmented vessels are gone and only the boundary of the retina remains as segmented as presented in Figure 22c.

Quantitative results are obtained for both datasets where manual vessel segmentation labeling was performed and verified by medical experts. Comparing the results with manual delineations, we obtain overall statistical quality metrics such as sensitivity Se, specificity

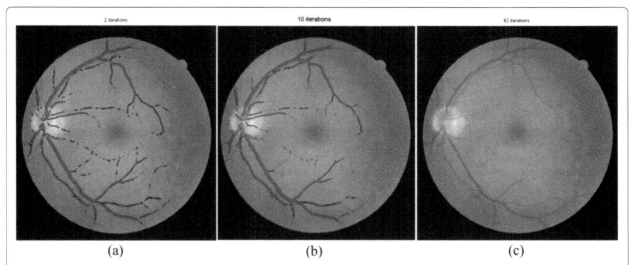

Figure 22 Vessel segmentation results obtained by the RBLSE method [33] for the non-pathological fundus image. After 2 iterations **(a)**, after 10 iterations **(b)**, and after 42 iterations **(c)**.

Sp, positive predictive value Ppv, negative predictive value Npv, accuracy Acc [14], and kappa κ [45]. These measures are given as follows:

$$Se = \frac{TP}{TP + FN}, \quad Sp = \frac{TN}{TN + FP}, \quad Ppv = \frac{TP}{TP + FP},$$

$$Npv = \frac{TN}{TN + FN}, \quad Acc = \frac{TP + TN}{TP + FP + TN + FN},$$

$$\text{and} \quad \kappa = \frac{2(TP \times TN - FP \times FN)}{(TP + FP)(FP + TN) + (TP + FN)(FN + TN)}.$$

$$(9)$$

Here, TP refers to a pixel labeled as vessel by both the algorithm and the medical experts' ground truth data, while TN refers to a pixel that is deemed to be non-vessel by both. FN refers to pixels of vessels (according to ground truth data) missed by the algorithm, and FP refers to pixels falsely categorized by the algorithm as vessel. In order to compare the proposed method, the same statistical metrics for supervised and unsupervised methods [11,14-17] on DRIVE dataset, our dataset, and STARE dataset are also reported in Tables 3, 4, 5, and 6. Here, it should be addressed that, although vascular segmentation has been achieved in countless studies, some of which even have better results in the literature, it has not been done so far using structure-based level set approach. In addition, for instance, while the unsupervised method [17] has good accuracy metric results, it generates occasional artifacts, such as false vessels, next to the optic disks. The results of our method are promising due to the fact that the method does not use any training algorithm compared to the supervised methods presented in [14-17]. As can be seen in Table 6 from the

Acc and κ metrics, for instance, when compared with PBLS method, our method fairs better quantitatively.

The methods are implemented using MATLAB R2010a. The programs are executed on a laptop with a Pentium 2.20-GHz processor and a 2-GB RAM. The segmentation of the retinal fundus image with a size of 565×584 pixels, as depicted in Figure 12f, lasts 61 iterations and 92.69 s. Note that the run time of the program may vary according to structure and size of the retinal fundus image.

5 Conclusions

We present a structure-based level set method with automatic seed point selection for segmentation of retinal vasculature in fundus images. Extensive experiments employing the proposed algorithms using datasets indicate that the algorithm performs well and favorably compared to the already existing level set-based methods in the literature. Developing strategies to improve inconsistencies in clinical diagnosis is an important challenge in ophthalmology. The segmentation methods described in this study may provide a basis for the development of computer-based image analysis algorithms. Future work will involve quantitative feature extraction from segmented retinal vessels, followed by implementation of these image analysis algorithms for image-based diagnostic assistance.

We plan to extend the study in order to improve the results especially for pathological regions such as drusen, GA, etc. Moreover, we will investigate how to use all color channels of the given image interactively in an efficient manner in order to trace retinal vasculature more properly. In addition to this, we plan to do a narrow band implementation in order to accelerate the run time of the proposed method.

Table 3 Statistical results of our method for test images of 1 to 20 from DRIVE dataset

Dataset	Image number	Se	Sp	Ppv	Npv	Acc	κ
DRIVE	1	0.8182	0.9581	0.7461	0.9723	0.9398	0.7457
	2	0.7764	0.9654	0.7982	0.9608	0.9371	0.7502
	3	0.7387	0.9513	0.7218	0.9551	0.9202	0.6834
	4	0.7456	0.9677	0.7826	0.9607	0.9378	0.7279
	5	0.7419	0.9682	0.7878	0.9593	0.9371	0.7279
	6	0.7142	0.9726	0.8126	0.9534	0.9358	0.7233
	7	0.7507	0.9466	0.6846	0.9609	0.9204	0.6699
	8	0.7285	0.9619	0.7332	0.9610	0.9325	0.6923
	9	0.7223	0.9738	0.7880	0.9630	0.9439	0.7221
	10	0.7535	0.9656	0.7507	0.9661	0.9400	0.7179
	11	0.7456	0.9512	0.6972	0.9613	0.9243	0.6768
	12	0.7932	0.9594	0.7391	0.9697	0.9383	0.7297
	13	0.7165	0.9665	0.7811	0.9533	0.9307	0.7073
	14	0.7940	0.9573	0.7130	0.9720	0.9380	0.7160
	15	0.7867	0.9463	0.6321	0.9742	0.9296	0.6616
	16	0.7880	0.9697	0.7989	0.9677	0.9457	0.7621
	17	0.7581	0.9715	0.7900	0.9660	0.9451	0.7425
	18	0.8407	0.9517	0.6965	0.9784	0.9388	0.7271
	19	0.8696	0.9599	0.7504	0.9815	0.9489	0.7764
	20	0.8254	0.9604	0.7162	0.9785	0.9458	0.7364

Table 4 Statistical results of our method for test images of 1 to 20 from our dataset

Dataset	Image number	Se	Sp	Ppv	Npv	Acc	κ
Ours	1	0.4821	0.9905	0.7483	0.9702	0.9623	0.5676
	2	0.3471	0.9887	0.6680	0.9586	0.9494	0.4330
	3	0.5745	0.9786	0.5802	0.9781	0.9589	0.5557
	4	0.5617	0.9695	0.5911	0.9657	0.9398	0.5437
	5	0.5699	0.9872	0.7537	0.9708	0.9602	0.6284
	6	0.3527	0.9879	0.6416	0.9613	0.9511	0.4318
	7	0.8109	0.9566	0.5234	0.9885	0.9485	0.6098
	8	0.3134	0.9887	0.6280	0.9594	0.9499	0.3950
	9	0.3966	0.9857	0.5666	0.9719	0.9591	0.4461
	10	0.4290	0.9878	0.5958	0.9764	0.9654	0.4814
	11	0.2789	0.9901	0.6119	0.9607	0.9523	0.3619
	12	0.5497	0.9840	0.6101	0.9796	0.9651	0.5602
	13	0.6942	0.9783	0.6056	0.9852	0.9653	0.6288
	14	0.4028	0.9844	0.5128	0.9759	0.9616	0.4316
	15	0.5848	0.9849	0.5977	0.9840	0.9700	0.5756
	16	0.3300	0.9877	0.6573	0.9539	0.9440	0.4133
	17	0.7426	0.9731	0.5785	0.9870	0.9622	0.6308
	18	0.5550	0.9762	0.5149	0.9797	0.9578	0.5122
	19	0.7238	0.9712	0.6101	0.9826	0.9567	0.6392
	20	0.6576	0.9680	0.4891	0.9838	0.9542	0.5373

Table 5 Statistical results of our method for test images of 1 to 20 from STARE dataset

Dataset	Image number	Se	Sp	Ppv	Npv	Acc	κ
STARE	1	0.6449	0.9731	0.7455	0.9574	0.9374	0.6570
	2	0.5754	0.9836	0.7795	0.9584	0.9464	0.6336
	3	0.8036	0.9519	0.5973	0.9820	0.9398	0.6527
	4	0.3117	0.9972	0.9275	0.9271	0.9271	0.4376
	5	0.8084	0.9466	0.6803	0.9723	0.9296	0.6985
	6	0.7759	0.9666	0.6912	0.9781	0.9498	0.7035
	7	0.8567	0.9631	0.7412	0.9820	0.9514	0.7674
	8	0.7758	0.9644	0.7125	0.9742	0.9451	0.7121
	9	0.7814	0.9698	0.7569	0.9736	0.9495	0.7406
	10	0.7568	0.9722	0.7711	0.9700	0.9485	0.7349
	11	0.8000	0.9629	0.7004	0.9780	0.9470	0.7175
	12	0.8446	0.9665	0.7490	0.9814	0.9537	0.7679
	13	0.7743	0.9710	0.7881	0.9687	0.9470	0.7510
	14	0.7611	0.9739	0.8055	0.9663	0.9474	0.7528
	15	0.6239	0.9796	0.8031	0.9512	0.9376	0.6680
	16	0.4445	0.9916	0.8961	0.9165	0.9150	0.5528
	17	0.7238	0.9803	0.8372	0.9621	0.9488	0.7477
	18	0.5669	0.9931	0.8594	0.9685	0.9635	0.6647
	19	0.4183	0.9934	0.8001	0.9646	0.9595	0.5304
	20	0.8035	0.9512	0.6234	0.9797	0.9377	0.6679

Table 6 Statistical average results for test images of 1 to 20 from the datasets

Dataset		Method	Se	Sp	Ppv	Npv	Acc	κ
DRIVE	Unsupervised	PBLS [24]	0.7754	0.9348	0.6403	0.9655	0.9140	0.6494
		Jiang et al. [12]	-	-	-	-	0.9212	-
		Martinez-Perez et al. [13]	0.7246	0.9655	-	-	0.9344	-
		Proposed	0.7704	0.9613	0.7460	0.9658	0.9365	0.7198
		Budai et al. [17]	0.6440	0.9870	-	-	0.9572	-
	Supervised	Staal et al. [16]	0.7194	0.9773	-	-	0.9442	-
		Marin et al. [14]	0.7067	0.9801	0.8433	0.9582	0.9452	-
		Soares et al. [15]	0.7283	0.9788	-	-	0.9466	-
Ours	Unsupervised	PBLS [24]	0.6600	0.9482	0.4380	0.9804	0.9328	0.4754
		Proposed	0.5179	0.9810	0.6042	0.9737	0.9567	0.5192
STARE	Unsupervised	PBLS [24]	0.8268	0.9117	0.5227	0.9803	0.9035	0.5822
		Hoover et al. [11]	0.6751	0.9567	-	-	0.9267	-
		Martinez-Perez et al. [13]	0.7506	0.9569	-	-	0.9410	-
		Proposed	0.6926	0.9726	0.7633	0.9656	0.9441	0.6779
	Supervised	Soares et al. [15]	0.7103	0.9737	-	-	0.9480	-
		Staal et al. [16]	0.6970	0.9810	-	-	0.9516	-
		Marin et al. [14]	0.6944	0.9819	-	-	0.9526	-

Competing interests

The authors declare that they have no competing interests.

Acknowledgements

This work is partially supported by grants from TUBITAK (grant no. 1059B191000548), NSF, and NIH.

Author details

[1]Department of Computer Engineering, Karadeniz Technical University, Trabzon 61080, Turkey. [2]Cognitive Systems Laboratory, Northeastern University, Boston, MA 02115, USA. [3]Martinos Imaging Center, Massachusetts General Hospital, Boston, MA 02129, USA. [4]Department of Ophthalmology, Oregon Health & Science University, Portland, OR 97239-3098, USA. [5]Department of Medical Informatics, Oregon Health & Science University, Portland, OR 97239-3098, USA.

References

1. MF Chiang, L Jiang, R Gelman, YE Du, JT Flynn, Interexpert agreement of plus disease diagnosis in retinopathy of prematurity. Arch. Ophthalmol **125**, 875–880 (2007)

2. R Gelman, L Jiang, YE Du, ME Martinez-Perez, JT Flynn, MF Chiang, Plus disease in retinopathy of prematurity: pilot study of computer-based and expert diagnosis. JAAPOS **11**(6), 532–540 (2007)

3. A Osareh, B Shadgar, An automated tracking approach for extraction of retinal vasculature in fundus images. J. Opthalmic. Vis. Res. **5**, 20–26 (2010)

4. D Wu, M Zhang, JC Liu, W Bauman, On the adaptive detection of blood vessels in retinal images. IEEE Trans. Biomed. Eng. **53**, 341–343 (2006)

5. MZC Azemin, DK Kumar, TY Wong, R Kawasaki, P Mitchell, JJ Wang, Robust methodology for fractal analysis of the retinal vasculature. IEEE Trans. Med. Imaging **2**(30), 243–250 (2011)

6. V Mahadevan, H Narasimha-Iyer, B Roysam, HL Tanenbaum, Robust model-based vasculature detection in noisy biomedical images. IEEE Trans. Inf. Technol. Biomed. **8**(3), 360–376 (2004)

7. H Narasimha-Iyer, V Mahadevan, JM Beach, B Roysam, Improved detection of the central reflex in retinal vessels using a generalized dual-Gaussian model and robust hypothesis testing. IEEE Trans. Inf. Technol. Biomed. **3**(12), 406–410 (2008)

8. KW Tobin, E Chaum, VP Govindasamy, TP Karnowski, Detection of anatomic structures in human retinal imagery. IEEE Trans. Med. Imaging **26**(12), 1729–1739 (2007)

9. M Niemeijer, X Xu, AV Dumitrescu, P Gupta, B van Ginneken, JC Folk, MD Abramoff, Automated measurement of the arteriolar-to-venular width ratio in digital color fundus photographs. IEEE Trans. Med. Imaging **11**(30), 1941–1950 (2011)

10. L Wang, A Bhalerao, R Wilson, Analysis of retinal vasculature using a multiresolution Hermite model. IEEE Trans. Med. Imaging **2**(26), 137–152 (2007)

11. A Hoover, V Kouznetsova, M Goldbaum, Locating blood vessels in retinal images by piecewise threshold probing of a matched filter response. IEEE Trans. Med. Imaging **19**(3), 203–210 (2000)

12. X Jiang, D Mojon, Adaptive local thresholding by verification-based multithreshold probing with application to vessel detection in retinal images. IEEE Trans. Pattern. Anal. Mach. Intell. **25**(1), 131–137 (2003)

13. ME Martinez-Perez, AD Hughes, SA Thom, AA Bharath, KH Parker, Segmentation of blood vessels from red-free and fluoresce in retinal images. Med. Image Anal. **11**(1), 47–61 (2007)

14. D Marin, A Aquino, GME Arias, JM Bravo, A New supervised method for blood vessel segmentation in retinal images by using gray-level and moment invariants-based features. IEEE Trans. Med. Imaging **30**(1), 146–158 (2011)

15. JVB Soares, JJG Leandro, RM Jr Cesar, HF Jelinek, MJ Cree, Retinal vessel segmentation using the 2-D Gabor wavelet and supervised classification. IEEE Trans. Med. Imaging **25**(9), 1214–1222 (2006)

16. J Staal, MD Abramoff, M Niemeijer, MA Viergever, B van Ginneken, Ridge-based vessel segmentation in color images of the retina. IEEE Trans. Med. Imaging **23**, 501–509 (2004)

17. A Budai, R Bock, A Maier, J Hornegger, G Michelson, Robust vessel segmentation in fundus images. Int. J Biomed. Imaging **2013**, (2013)

18. AF Frangi, WJ Niessen, KL Vincken, MA Viergever, *Multiscale Vessel Enhancement Filtering (Springer* (Germany, Heidelberg, 1998)

19. S You, E Bas, D Erdogmus, J Kalpathy-Cramer, Principal curve based retinal vessel segmentation towards diagnosis of retinal diseases. Proc. Healthcare Inform, Imaging Sys. Biol. (HISB) 331–337 (2011). San Jose, California, USA, (2011)

20. D Erdogmus, U Ozertem, Self-consistent locally defined principal surfaces. Proc. ICASSP **Vol. 2**, II.549–II.552 (2007). Honolulu, Hawaii, USA

21. C Kirbas, F Quek, *Vessel Extraction Techniques and Algorithms: a Survey.* Proceedings of the Third IEEE Symposium on BioInformatics and BioEngineering (BIBE'03), 238-245 (Bethesda, Maryland, USA, 2003)

22. L Vese, T Chan, A multiphase level set framework for image segmentation using the Mumford and Shah model. Int. J. Comput. Vis. **50**(3), 271–293 (2002)

23. V Caselles, R Kimmel, G Sapiro, Geodesic active contours. Int. J. Comput. Vis. **22**(1), 61–79 (1997)

24. G Lathen, J Jonasson, M Borga, Blood vessel segmentation using multi-scale quadrature filtering. Pattern Recogn. Lett. **31**, 762–767 (2010)

25. C Li, C Xu, C Gui, MD Fox, Distance regularized level set evolution and its application to image segmentation. IEEE Trans. Image Process. **19**(12), 3243–3254 (2010)

26. KY Pang, L Iznita, A Fadzil, AN Hanung, N Hermawan, SA Vijanth, *Segmentation of Retinal Vasculature in Colour Fundus Images* (Conference on Innovation Technologies in Intelligent Systems and Industrial Applications (CITISIA, Malaysia, 2009), pp. 398–401

27. B Zhou, C Mu, Level set evolution for boundary extraction based on a p-Laplace equation. Appl. Math. Mod **34**(12), 3910–3916 (2010)

28. L Meng, H Chuanjiang, Z Yi, Adaptive regularized level set method for weak boundary object segmentation. Math. Probl. Eng **2012**(369472), 16 (2012). doi:10.1155/2012/369472

29. A Belaid, D Boukerroui, Y Maingourd, J-F Lerallut, Phase based level set segmentation of ultrasound images. IEEE Trans. Inform. Tech. Biomed **15**(1), 138–147 (2011)

30. B Dizdaroglu, E Ataer-Cansizoglu, J Kalpathy-Cramer, K Keck, MF Chiang, D Erdogmus, *Level Sets for Retinal Vasculature Segmentation Using Seeds from Ridges and Edges from Phase Maps.* 2012 IEEE International Workshop On Machine Learning For Signal Processing (Santander, Spain, 2012)

31. G Yu, P Lin, P Li, Z Bian, Region-based vessel segmentation using level set framework. Int. J. Control. Autom. Syst. **4**(5), 660–667 (2006)

32. C Li, C Kao, JC Gore, Z Ding, Minimization of region-scalable fitting energy for image segmentation. EEE Trans. Image Proc. **17**(10), 1940–1949 (2008)

33. C Li, R Huang, Z Ding, C Gatenby, DN Metaxas, JC Gore, A level set method for image segmentation in the presence of intensity inhomogeneities with application to MRI. IEEE Trans. Image Proc. **20**(7), 2007–2016 (2011)

34. YQ Zhao, XH Wang, XF Wang, FY Shih, Retinal vessels segmentation based on level set and region growing. Pattern Recognition. **47**(7), 2437–2446 (2014)

35. M Bertalmio, L Vese, G Sapiro, S Osher, Simultaneous structure and texture image inpainting. IEEE Trans. Image Process. **12**, 882–889 (2003)

36. A Buades, TM Le, J-M Morel, LA Vese, Fast cartoon + texture image filters. IEEE Trans. Image Process. **19**(8), 1978–1986 (2010)

37. B Dizdaroğlu, An image completion method using decomposition. EURASIP J. Advanc. Signal Proc **2011**(831724), 15 (2011). doi:10.1155/2011/831724

38. MJ Black, G Sapiro, DH Marimont, D Heeger, Robust anisotropic diffusion. IEEE Trans. Image Process. **7**(3), 421–432 (1998)

39. D Tschumperlé, *PDE's based regularization of multi-valued images and applications, PhD thesis* (Université de Nice-Sophia Antipolis, France, 2002)

40. P Kovesi, Phase congruency: a low-level image invariant. Psychological Research **64**(2), 136–148 (2000)

41. P Blomgren, TF Chan, CK Wong, Total variation image restoration: numerical methods and extensions. Proc. IEEE Int. Conf Image Proc **3**, 384–387 (1997)

42. P Kornprobst, R Deriche, G Aubert, *Image Restoration via PDE's* (First Annual Symposium on Enabling Technologies for Law Enforcement and Security - SPIE Conference 2942: Investigative Image Processing, Boston, Massachusetts, USA, 1996)

43.   N Otsu, A threshold selection method from gray-level histogram. IEEE Trans. Syst. Man Cybern **9**(1), 62–66 (1979)
44.   R Courant, K Friedrichs, H Lewvy, Über die partiellen Differenzengleichungen der mathematischen Physik. Math. Ann. **100**(1), 32–74 (1928)
45.   J Landis, G Koch, The measurement of observer agreement for categorical data. Biometrics **33**, 159–174 (1977)

9

Noise reduction of continuous wave radar and pulse radar using matched filter and wavelets

Md Saiful Islam and Uipil Chong[*]

Abstract

This paper analyzes noise reduction using matched filter and wavelet transform in the signals of continuous wave radar and pulse radar. The denoising application of wavelets has been used in spectrum cleaning of atmospheric radar signals. Matched filter has a strong anti-noise ability; it can also achieve accurate pulse compression in a very noisy environment. This paper analyzes the algorithms of matched filter and wavelets that are used in radar signal processing to reduce the noise. The simulation results indicate that matched filter has a strong anti-noise ability for pulse radar and wavelet for continuous wave radar.

Keywords: Denoising; Matched Filter; Radar Noise; SNR; Wavelets

1 Introduction

Chaos is the very complicated behavior of a low-order dynamical system, because it is both nonlinear and deterministic [1,2]. It demonstrates a strong notion, permitting the use of a simple deterministic system to illustrate highly irregular fluctuations exhibited by physical phenomena encountered in nature. Recently, some engineering applications of chaos have been reported in literature [3-6]. These can be grouped under two broadly defined categories [3,4]. One group is synthesis of chaotic signals, which includes signal masking and spread-spectrum communications. Another is analysis of chaotic signals. It exploits the fact that some physical phenomena allow the use of a chaotic model.

For more than 20 years, many methods for smoothing denoising filters have been proposed. Various standard spatial domain filters have been proposed to reduce noise [7]. The 2-D Gaussian filter [8] and the median filter [9] have also been widely applied. The most commonly used is the Lee filter [10], but it requires knowledge of interferometric coherence. The adaptive contoured-window filter method [11] and the two-stage filtering method [12] can also reduce noise effectively.

Wavelet analysis [5] and matched filter [6] are two of the most significant tools in the field of signal processing

in the last few decades. We analyze both techniques and show how such an individual can improve the quality of radar-received signals in a noisy environment for both types of radar, i.e., continuous wave radar (radars continuously transmit a high-frequency signal and the reflected energy is also received and processed continuously) and pulse radar (transmits high power, high-frequency pulses toward the target, and it waits for the echo of the transmitted signal before it transmits a new pulse). The problem addressed here concerns the denoising of the radar-received signal immersed in noise. Several simulations have been performed to verify the algorithm for both types of radar. All of the simulations give the same time delay, and even the received signal is attenuated more than 90%. The simulation results indicate that the algorithm is effective and robust even when the receiver receives a very weak signal.

The remainder of the paper is organized as follows: In Section 2, we briefly describe the literature of matched filter and the characteristics of matched filter related to radar noise reduction. Section 3 presents wavelets denoising technique, while the simulations and data analysis are described in Section 4. Finally, we make some conclusions about our comparison related to noise reduction.

---

* Correspondence: upchong@ulsan.ac.kr
Department of Electrical and Computer Engineering, University of Ulsan,
Bldg. #7, Room #318, 93 Daehak-ro, Nam-gu, Ulsan 680-749, South Korea

2 Noise reduction by matched filter

2.1 Theory of matched filter

Matched filter is not a specific type of filter, but a theoretical frame work. It is an ideal filter that processes a received signal to minimize the effect of noise. Therefore, it optimizes the signal-to-noise ratio (SNR) of the filtered signal [13].

The original matched filter was proposed by D. O. North [14]. Later, many authors [15-17] tried to improve the performance of matched filter. However, the conventional matched-filter detector has some drawbacks [18]. To reduce the drawbacks, the exhaustive-search matched filter (EMF) detector and the near-optimal MF (NMF) detector are proposed in [19]. Recently, [20] proposed a developed NMF (D-NMF) to improve the performance of NMF.

The radar-received signal $r(t)$ contains two components $s_i(t)$ and $n_i(t)$ that represent the certain signal (e.g., targets) and noise, respectively, i.e., $r(t) = s_i(t) + n_i(t)$. The matched filter $h(t)$ yielding the output $y(t) = s_o(t) + n_o(t)$ is to generate the maximal ratio of $s_o(T)$ and $n_o(T)$ in the sampling values at time T. Where $s_o(t)$ and $n_o(t)$ are the outputs of $s_i(t)$ and $n_i(t)$, respectively, after the matched filter shown in Figure 1.

In Figure 1, $s_i(t)$ represents the target signal we are attempting to detect and $n_i(t)$ represents the additive white Gaussian noise in the system. $s_o(t)$ and $n_o(t)$ represent the outputs of the matched filter by $s_i(t)$ and $n_i(t)$. Matched filter maximizes the SNR, the ratio of the power of $s_o(t)$, and the power of $n_o(t)$ according to the Schwarz inequality.

Here, we suppose that the noise $n_i(t)$ additive white Gaussian noise, whose power spectrum is $N/2$, and the spectrum of the target's signal $s_i(t)$ is [13]

$$F_{s_i}(\omega) = \int_{-\infty}^{+\infty} s_i(t)e^{-j\omega t}dt \tag{1}$$

The above equation is the Fourier transform of $s_i(t)$. The output of the matched filter $y(t)$ also contains two components representing the target's signal and noise, $y(t) = s_o(t) + n_o(t)$, where

$$s_o(t) = \frac{1}{2\Pi} \int_{-\infty}^{+\infty} [H(\omega)F_{s_i}(\omega)]e^{j\omega t}dt \tag{2}$$

The average power of the noise equals the value of autocorrelation function, which is

$$E[n^2{}_o(t)] = \frac{1}{2\Pi}\frac{N}{2}\int_{-\infty}^{+\infty} |H(\omega)|^2 dt \tag{3}$$

Now, according to the definition of SNR, time T is

$$\mathrm{SNR} = \frac{|s_o(T)|^2}{E(n^2{}_o)}$$

$$= \frac{\left|\frac{1}{2\Pi}\int_{-\infty}^{+\infty}[H(\omega)F_{\mathrm{target}}(\omega)]e^{j\omega t}d\omega\right|^2}{\frac{1}{2\Pi}\frac{N}{2}\int_{-\infty}^{+\infty}|H(\omega)|^2 d\omega} \tag{4}$$

Using the Schwarz inequality, we get

$$\left|\frac{1}{2\Pi}\int_{-\infty}^{+\infty}[H(\omega)F_{\mathrm{target}}(\omega)]e^{j\omega t}dt\right|^2 ,$$

$$\leq \frac{1}{4\Pi^2}\int_{-\infty}^{+\infty}|H(\omega)|^2 d\omega \int_{-\infty}^{+\infty}|F_{\mathrm{target}}(\omega)|^2 d\omega$$

Hence,

$$\mathrm{SNR} \leq \frac{\frac{1}{4\Pi^2}\int_{-\infty}^{+\infty}|H(\omega)^2|d\omega\int_{-\infty}^{+\infty}F_{\mathrm{target}}(\omega)^2 d\omega}{\frac{1}{2\Pi^2}\frac{N}{2}\int_{-\infty}^{+\infty}|H(\omega)|^2 d\omega}$$

$$= \frac{\frac{1}{2\Pi}\int_{-\infty}^{+\infty}|F_{\mathrm{target}}(\omega)|^2}{\frac{N}{2}} \tag{5}$$

The numerator of the above equation denotes power of the signal according to Parseval's theorem. From Equation 5, the matched filter maximizes the SNR of the filtered signal and has an impulse response that is a reverse time-shifted version of the input signal. So, to obtain the maximum SNR, we need the time delay, D. With the use of this time delay, D, we obtain the output of the cross-correlation between transmitted signals and received signals.

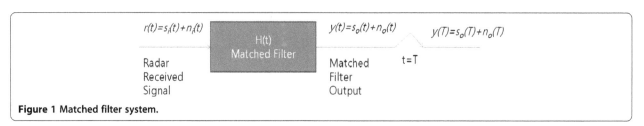

Figure 1 Matched filter system.

2.2 Cross-correlation to find time delay D

Correlation is the process to determine degree of 'fit' between two waveforms and to determine the time at which the maximum correlation coefficient or 'best fit' occurs [21-23]. For the radar system, if we correlate between the transmitted signal and the received signal, then we get the time difference between the transmitted and received signals. We consider the transmitted signal to be $x(n)$, and then the returned signal $r(n)$ may be modeled as:

$$r(n) = \alpha x(n - D) + w(n) \tag{6}$$

where $w(n)$ is assumed to be the additive noise during the transmission, α is the attenuation factor, and D is the delay which is the time taken for the signal to travel from the transmitter to the target and back to the receiver.

The cross-correlation between the transmitted signal, $x(n)$, and the received signal, $r(n)$, is [21]

$$C_{xr}(l) = \alpha C_{xx}(l - D) \tag{7}$$

From Equation 7, the maximum value of the cross-correlation will occur at $l = D$, which is our interest in cross-correlation from which we can get the time delay, D. For the multiple targets, we get the multiple number of D from Equation 7. For example, if there are n targets then we can get n number of delays such as $D_1, D_2, D_3,..., D_n$.

2.3 Matched filter for radar

For pulse radars, consider pulse width τ_ρ and τ_κ is the time that a target is illuminated by the radars. Thus, we can write $r(t)$ as

$$r(t) = V \text{rect} \left[\frac{t - \tau_\rho}{\tau_\kappa} \right] \tag{8}$$

From Equation 5, and for Equation 8, we can write the pulse radar as [24]

$$(\text{SNR})_{\text{pulse}} = \frac{P_t G^2 \lambda^2 \sigma \tau_\rho}{(4\pi)^3 K T_0 BFLR^4} \tag{9}$$

where P_t is the peak transmitted power of radar, G is the antenna gain, σ is the radar cross section (RCS), R is the range which electromagnetic wave transmits, λ is the wavelength, $K = 1.38 \times 10^{-23}$ J/K is Boltzmann's constant, B is bandwidth, $T_0 = 290$ K is the operating temperature of antenna, F is the noise figure of receiver, and L denotes as radar losses.

For continuous wave radars, radar equation can be written as [24]

$$(\text{SNR})_{\text{cw}} = \frac{P_{\text{CW}} T_{\text{DWELL}} G^2 \lambda^2 \sigma}{(4\pi)^3 K T_0 BFLR^4} \tag{10}$$

where P_{CW} is the continuous wave average transmitted power and T_{DWELL} is the dwell interval.

3 Wavelet denoising

For removing noise and extracting signal from any data, wavelet analysis is one of the most important methods. The wavelet denoising application has been used in spectrum cleaning of the atmospheric signals. There are different types of wavelets available like Morlet, Coiflet, Mexican hat, Symlet, Biorthogonal, and Haar, which have their own specifications such as filter coefficients and reconstruction filter coefficients. In this paper, to eliminate noise embedded in the radar signal 'sym8', wavelets have been used. The goal of this study is to denoise the radar signal. One often encounters the term 'denoising' in recent wavelet literature, described in an informal way with various schemes that attempt to reject noise by damping or thresholding in the wavelet domain [25,26]. The threshold of wavelet coefficient has near optimal noise reduction for different kinds of signals. Wavelets have many advantages over fast Fourier transform. Fourier analysis has a major drawback, which is that time information is lost, when transforming to the frequency domain. Thus, it is impossible to tell when a particular event took place under Fourier analysis. Wavelet analysis is capable of revealing aspects of data that other signal analysis techniques, aspects such trends, breakdown points, discontinuities in higher derivatives, and self-similarity, are unable to reveal. Wavelet analysis can often denoise a signal without appreciable degradation. Wavelet transform performs a correlation analysis. Therefore, the output is expected to be maximal when the input signal most resembles the mother wavelet.

3.1 Wavelet transform

According to the definition of wavelet transform [27], for function $f(t)$, wavelet transform coefficient $W_f(a, \tau)$

$$W_f(a, \tau) = \left\langle f(t), \psi_{(a,\tau)}(t) \right\rangle = \frac{1}{\sqrt{a}} \int f(t) \psi^* \left(\frac{t - \tau}{a} \right) dt \tag{11}$$

Here, $f(t)$, $\psi_{(a,\tau)}(t)$ is the wavelet basis function, $\psi^* \left(\frac{t-\tau}{a} \right)$ is a conjugate of wavelet basis function, τ is the amount of shift, and a is scale.

3.2 Wavelet denoising

The wavelet denoising procedure proceeds in three steps:

Step 1 Signal decomposing: Choose the wavelet basis function, and to determine the decomposition level N, get the coarse and detail coefficients by DWT.

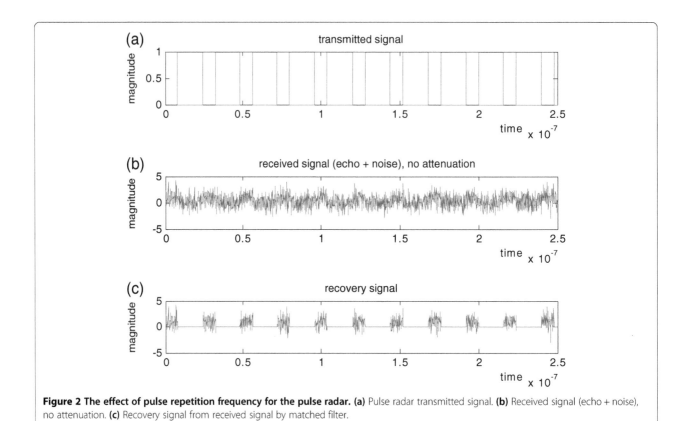

Figure 2 The effect of pulse repetition frequency for the pulse radar. (a) Pulse radar transmitted signal. **(b)** Received signal (echo + noise), no attenuation. **(c)** Recovery signal from received signal by matched filter.

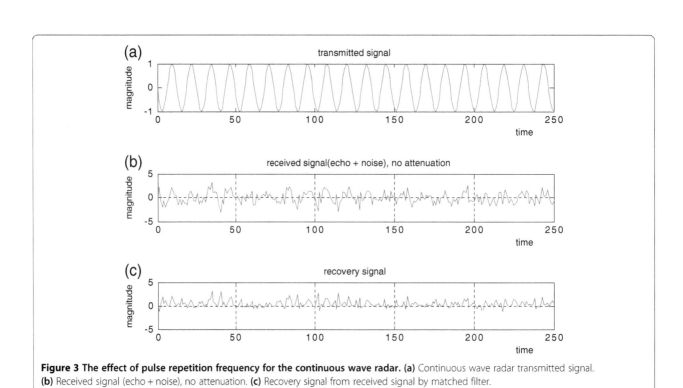

Figure 3 The effect of pulse repetition frequency for the continuous wave radar. (a) Continuous wave radar transmitted signal.
(b) Received signal (echo + noise), no attenuation. **(c)** Recovery signal from received signal by matched filter.

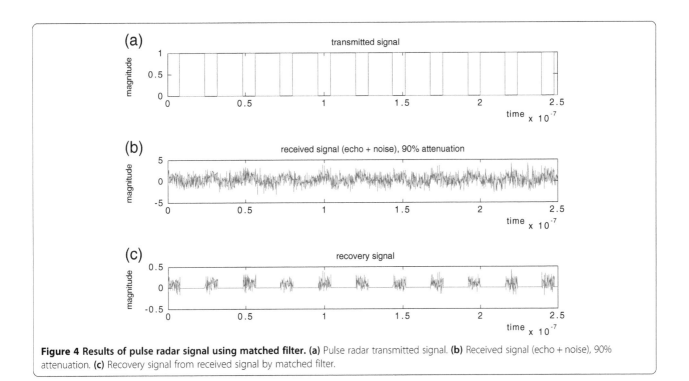

Figure 4 Results of pulse radar signal using matched filter. (a) Pulse radar transmitted signal. **(b)** Received signal (echo + noise), 90% attenuation. **(c)** Recovery signal from received signal by matched filter.

Step 2 Threshold detail coefficients: For each level from 1 to N, compare the detail coefficients to threshold values.

Step 3 Reconstructing the signal: Reconstruct the denoised signal based on the original approximation coefficients of level N and the modified detail coefficients of levels from 1 to N.

3.3 Traditional threshold function

The major signal information mainly concentrates in the low frequency sub-band of wavelet transform domain.

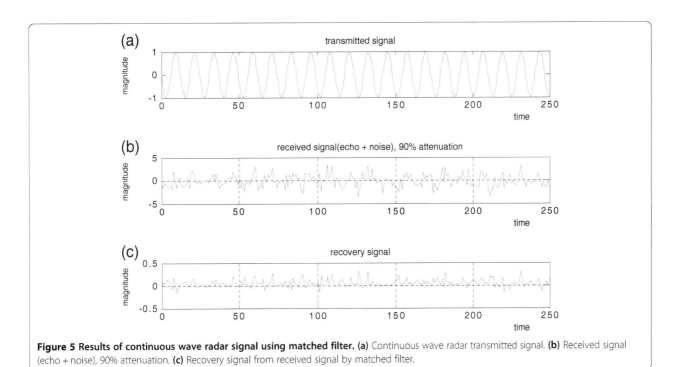

Figure 5 Results of continuous wave radar signal using matched filter. (a) Continuous wave radar transmitted signal. **(b)** Received signal (echo + noise), 90% attenuation. **(c)** Recovery signal from received signal by matched filter.

Table 1 SNR of pulse radar and continuous wave radar

Range in km	SNR (dB)			
	Pulse radar (matched filter)	CW radar (matched filter)	CW radar (traditional wavelet)	CW radar (proposed wavelet)
0	117	107	114	119
20	42	30	40	45
40	32	17	22	25
60	24	10	14	16
80	18	6	9	11
100	15	1	4	5
120	12	−3	1	2

Noise equally distributes in all wavelet coefficients, so the wavelet transform factor should be larger than the wavelet transform factor of the noises after wavelet decomposition. Therefore, the selection of wavelet threshold is an important step, which also directly impacts on the effect of noise reduction. Different methods have been proposed to choose the threshold. The frequently used thresholding of wavelet coefficients is governed mainly by either soft or hard thresholding function, proposed by Donoho [28]. The soft thresholding is generally referred to as wavelet shrinkage, since it 'shrinks' the coefficients with high amplitude toward zero, whereas the hard thresholding is commonly referred to simply as wavelet thresholding. Given that d_{jk} indicates the value of wavelet coefficient, $\tilde{d}_{jk}$ implies the value of d_{jk} after thresholding function, and T is the threshold value.

The soft thresholding function is defined as

$$\tilde{d}_{jk} = \begin{cases} 0 & \text{if } |d_{jk}| \leq T \\ d_{jk}-T & \text{if } |d_{jk}|\rangle T \\ d_{jk}+T & \text{if } |d_{jk}|\langle -T \end{cases} \tag{12}$$

T is the threshold and generally can be a function of J and K. The hard thresholding function is defined as

$$\tilde{d}_{jk} = \begin{cases} 0 & \text{if } |d_{jk}| \leq T \\ d_{jk} & \text{if } |d_{jk}|\rangle T \end{cases} \tag{13}$$

Soft thresholding provides smoother results in comparison with the hard thresholding whereas thresholding technique provides better edge preservation in comparison with the soft thresholding technique.

Soft thresholding and hard thresholding have some limitations in denoising of signal [29,30]. The Equation 12 indicates that the reconstructed signal faces oscillation, since the estimated wavelet coefficients are not continuous at position $\pm T$ [31]. Although the estimated wavelet coefficients of Equation 13 have good continuity, these coefficients include constant errors [31], which directly influence the accuracy of the reconstructed signal.

3.4 An improved threshold function
To overcome the limitations of hard thresholding and soft thresholding denoising methods, an improved thresholding is proposed as follows:

$$\tilde{d}_{jk} = \begin{cases} 0 & \text{if } |d_{jk}|\langle T \\ d_{jk}+\dfrac{T(e^{-t}-1)}{2(e^{-t}+1)} & \text{if } |d_{jk}|\geq T \end{cases} \tag{14}$$

Equation 14 improves the reconstruction precision, since it reduces the constant errors. Hence, it enhances the denoising effect. This thresholding function also assures the continuity of estimated wavelet coefficients.

4 Simulation and performance assessment
The denoising of the received radar signal is simulated in the presence of white Gaussian noise. The effect of

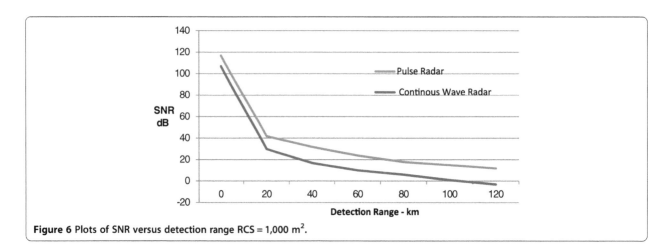

Figure 6 Plots of SNR versus detection range RCS = 1,000 m².

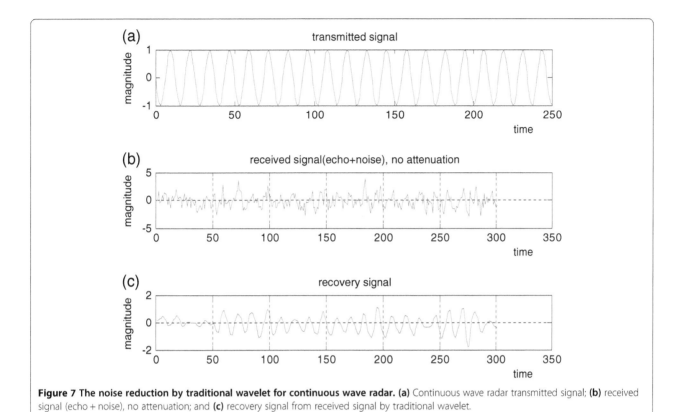

Figure 7 The noise reduction by traditional wavelet for continuous wave radar. (a) Continuous wave radar transmitted signal; **(b)** received signal (echo + noise), no attenuation; and **(c)** recovery signal from received signal by traditional wavelet.

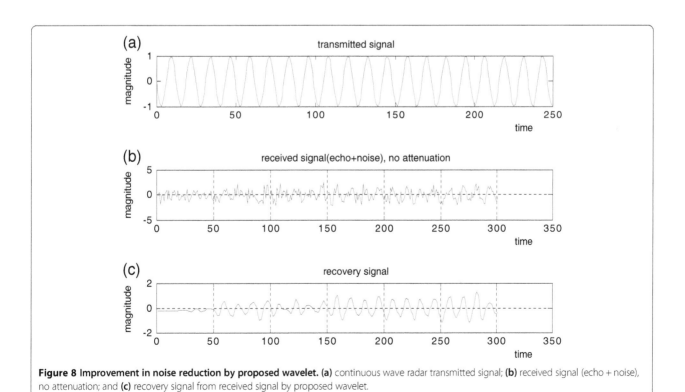

Figure 8 Improvement in noise reduction by proposed wavelet. (a) continuous wave radar transmitted signal; **(b)** received signal (echo + noise), no attenuation; and **(c)** recovery signal from received signal by proposed wavelet.

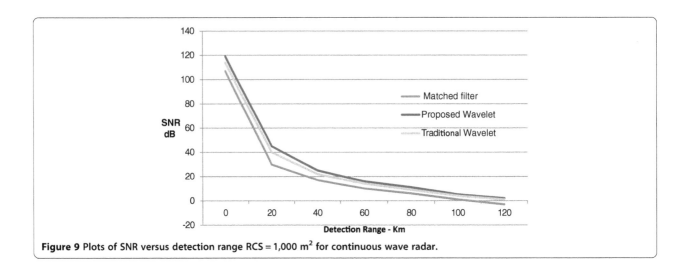

Figure 9 Plots of SNR versus detection range RCS = 1,000 m² for continuous wave radar.

signal parameter changes on the algorithm has been investigated. These parameters include the SNR of the signal. The SNR is defined as the ratio of the signal power to the noise power in the entire period. The following parameters are assumed: sampling frequency = 10 GHz, pulse duration = 8 ns, pulse repetition frequency = 0.24 GHz for the pulse radar (Figure 2) and transmitted frequency = 10 GHz for the continuous wave radar (Figure 3) The receiver receives the return from the targets in the present of AWGN.

We recover our transmitted signal from the received signal using the matched filter for both pulse radar and continuous wave radar. For the pulse radar, the recovery signal is almost similar to transmitted signal shown in Figure 2c. But in the case of continuous wave radar, it is almost impossible to understand the shape of the transmitted signal from the recovery signal (Figure 3). Figures 4 and 5 are similar to Figures 2 and 3, respectively, except the received signals are attenuated more than 90%. Figure 4 indicates that the matched filter has a strong advantage in anti-noise ability for pulse radar. Unfortunately, the matched filter for continuous wave radar is not superior to recover the transmitted signal (Figure 5c). The reason for this is that the transmitted average power of the continuous wave radar is lower, and the thermal noise relevant to the operating bandwidth and the radar's structure design, so the signal detection threshold of continuous wave radar is lower, and this demands higher receiver sensitivity (Table 1). This is shown in Figure 6 using Equations 9 and 10. Also, applying the matched filter for continuous wave radar limits the performance in three major areas [32]: the effect of nonlinearities in the frequency transmission and the matched filter, variations in the transmitted frequency, and relative velocity of target.

We also apply the wavelet denoising technique to remove the noise from received signal. This technique overcomes the problem of continuous wave radar. Figure 7c shows the noise reduction by traditional wavelet for continuous wave radar. By comparing this with Figure 3c, we can say that more noise is reduced in Figure 7c. Figure 8c shows the improvement in noise reduction by our proposed method. The reason for this is that the SNR is increased (Table 1) when we use the wavelet denoising technique for continuous wave radar. Our proposed wavelet threshold function even further reduced more noise for continuous wave radar. This is shown in Figure 9.

5 Conclusions

This paper presented a comprehensive comparison between matched filter and wavelet in terms of noise reduction abilities of pulse radar and continuous wave radar. The simulation results show that a significant reduction in noise is achieved for pulse radar by matched filter, but employing matched filter for continuous wave radar increases the difficulty of detection. The use of wavelet denoising technique instead of matched filter for continuous wave radar reduced more noise. Our proposed wavelet threshold function even further reduced more noise for continuous wave radar.

Competing interests
The authors declare that they have no competing interests.

Acknowledgements
This work was supported by 2014 Special Research Fund of Electrical Engineering at University of Ulsan.

References

1. H Simon, L Xiao, Bo, Detection of signals in chaos. Proc. IEEE **83**, 1 (1995)
2. TS Parker, LO Chua, Chaos: a tutorial for engineers. Proc. IEEE **75**(8), 982–1008 (1987)
3. AV Oppenheim, GW Womell, SH Isabelle, KM Cuomo, Signal processing in the context of chaotic signals, in *Proc ICASSP-92, vol. 4* (San Francisco, 1992), pp. 117–120
4. S Haykin, Chaotic signal processing: new research directions and novel applications, in *IEEE Workshop on SSAP* (Victoria, 1992)
5. AS Grispino, GO Petracca, AE Domínguez, Comparative analysis of wavelet and EMD in the filtering of radar signal affected by brown noise. IEEE Lat. Am. Trans. **11**, 1 (2013)
6. MA Govoni, LI Hongbin, Range-Doppler resolution of the linear-Fm noise radar waveform. IEEE Trans. Aerosp. Electron. Syst. **49**, 1 (2013)
7. G Kingsbury, Complex wavelets for shift invariant analysis and filtering of signals. J. Appl. Comput. Harmonic. Anal. **10**(3), 234–253 (2011)
8. D Geudtner, M Schwabisch, R Winter, SAR-interferometry with ERS-1 data. Proc. PIERS, 11–15 (1994)
9. ALB Candeias, LV Dutra, JR Moreira, JC Mura, Interferogram phase noise reduction using morphological and modified median filters. Proc. IGARSS **1**, 166–168 (1995)
10. JS Lee, Digital image enhancement and noise filtering by use of local statistics. IEEE Trans. Pattern Analysis Machine Intell. **2**(2), 165 (1980)
11. Q Yu, X Yang, S Fu, X Liu, X Sun, An adaptive contoured window filter for interferometric synthetic aperture radar. IEEE Geosci. Remote Sens. Lett. **4**(1), 23–26 (2007)
12. D Meng, V Sethu, E Ambikairajah, L Gr, A novel technique for noise reduction in InSAR images. IEEE Geosci. Remote Sens. Lett. **4**(2), 165 (1980)
13. MD Saiful Islam, H Hyungseob, L Myung, J Gook, Small target detection and noise reduction in marine radar systems. IERI Procedia **51**, 168–173 (2013)
14. DO North, An analysis of the factors which determine signal/noise discrimination in pulsed carrier systems. Proc. IEEE **51**, 1016–1027 (1963)
15. WS Chen, IS Reed, A new CFAR detection test for radar. Digital Signal Process **1**, 198–214 (1991)
16. FC Robey, DR Fuhrmann, EJ Kelly, R Nitzberg, A CFAR adaptive matched filter detector. IEEE Trans. Aerosp. Electron. Syst. **28**(1), 208–216 (1992)
17. JR Roman, M Rangaswamy, DW Davis, Q Zhang, B Himed, JH Michels, Parametric adaptive matched filter for airborne radar applications. IEEE Trans. Aerospace Electron. Syst. **36**, 2 (2000)
18. J Jeganathan, A Ghrayeb, L Szczecinski, Spatial modulation: optimal detection and performance analysis. IEEE Commun. Lett. **12**(8), 545–547 (2008)
19. S Sugiura, C Xu, SX Ng, L Hanzo, Reduced-complexity coherent versus non-coherent QAM-aided space-time shift keying. IEEE Trans. Commun. **59**(11), 3090–3101 (2011)
20. Y Ping, X Yue, L Lei, T Qian, L Shaoqian, An improved matched-filter based detection algorithm for space-time shift keying systems. IEEE Signal Process Lett. **19**, 5 (2012)
21. MD Saiful Islam, C Uipil, Detection of uncooperative targets using cross-correlation in oceanic environment. Int. J. Digital Content Technol. Appl. **7**, 12 (2013)
22. H Sheng, Y Hongqi, T Wenhui, Z Zheng, Study on the auto-correlation and cross-correlation properties of hybrid bridge function sequence. Adv. Inf. Sci. Ser. Sci. **4**, 7 (2012)
23. S Kirill, V Ekaterina, S Boris, Echo delay estimation using algorithms based on cross- correlation. J. Convergence Inf. Technol. **6**, 4 (2011)
24. MA Richards, *Fundamentals of Radar Signal Processing*, 1st edn. (McGraw-Hill, New York, 2005), pp. 88–91
25. L Yuan, *Wavelet Analysis for Change Points and Nonlinear Wavelet Estimates in Time Series* (Statistics Press, Beijing, 2001)
26. D Yinfeng, L Yingmin, X Mingkui, M Lai, Analysis of earthquake ground motions using an improved Hilbert–Huang transform. Soil Dyn. Earthq. Eng. **28**(1), 7–19 (2008)
27. Z Zhi Qiang, Z Guo Wei, P Yu, S Wei, L Cheng, L Jin Zhao, Study on pulse wave signal noise reduction and feature point identification. J. Convergence Inf. Technol. **8**, 9 (2013)
28. DL Donoho, Denoising by soft-thresholding. IEEE Trans. Inf. Theory **41**(3), 613–627 (1995)
29. RR Coifman, DL Donoho, Translation-invariant de-noising, in *Wavelets and Statistics, Springer Lecture Notes in Statistics 103* (Springer, New York, 1994), pp. 125–150
30. S Qin, C Yang, B Tang, S Tan, The denoise based on translation invariance wavelet transform and its applications. Conf. Struct. Dyn. Los Angeles **1**, 783–787 (2002)
31. G Song, R Zhao, *Three novel models of threshold estimator for wavelet coefficients, 2nd International Conference on Wavelet Analysis and its Applications* (Springer, Berlin, 2001), pp. 145–150
32. MJ Withers, Matched filter for frequency-modulated continuous wave radar systems. Proc. IEEE **113**, 3 (1966)

10

Simplified spiking neural network architecture and STDP learning algorithm applied to image classification

Taras Iakymchuk[*], Alfredo Rosado-Muñoz, Juan F Guerrero-Martínez, Manuel Bataller-Mompeán and Jose V Francés-Víllora

Abstract

Spiking neural networks (SNN) have gained popularity in embedded applications such as robotics and computer vision. The main advantages of SNN are the temporal plasticity, ease of use in neural interface circuits and reduced computation complexity. SNN have been successfully used for image classification. They provide a model for the mammalian visual cortex, image segmentation and pattern recognition. Different spiking neuron mathematical models exist, but their computational complexity makes them ill-suited for hardware implementation. In this paper, a novel, simplified and computationally efficient model of spike response model (SRM) neuron with spike-time dependent plasticity (STDP) learning is presented. Frequency spike coding based on receptive fields is used for data representation; images are encoded by the network and processed in a similar manner as the primary layers in visual cortex. The network output can be used as a primary feature extractor for further refined recognition or as a simple object classifier. Results show that the model can successfully learn and classify black and white images with added noise or partially obscured samples with up to ×20 computing speed-up at an equivalent classification ratio when compared to classic SRM neuron membrane models. The proposed solution combines spike encoding, network topology, neuron membrane model and STDP learning.

Keywords: Spiking neural networks - SNN; STDP; Visual receptive fields; Spike coding; Embedded system; Artificial neuron; Image classification

1 Introduction

In the last years, the popularity of spiking neural networks (SNN) and spiking models has increased. SNN are suitable for a wide range of applications such as pattern recognition and clustering, among others.There are examples of intelligent systems, converting data directly from sensors [1,2], controlling manipulators [3] and robots [4], doing recognition or detection tasks [5,6], tactile sensing [7] or processing neuromedical data [8]. Different neuron models exist [9] but their computational complexity and memory requirements are high, limiting their use in robotics, embedded systems and real-time or mobile applications in general.

Existing simplified bio-inspired neural models [10,11] are focused on spike train generation and real neuron modeling. These models are rarely applied in practical tasks. Some of the neuronal models are applied only for linearly separable classes [12] and focus on small network simulation.

Concerning hardware implementation, dedicated ASIC solutions exist such as SpiNNaker [13], BrainScaleS [14], SyNAPSE [15] or others [16], but they are targeted for large-scale simulations rather than portable, low-power and real-time embedded applications. The model we propose is mainly oriented for applications requiring low-power, small and efficient hardware systems. It can also be used for computer simulations with up to ×20 speed-up compared to classic SRM neuron membrane model. Nowadays, due to a continuous decrease in price and increase in computation capabilities, combined with

*Correspondence: taras.yakymchuk@uv.es
GPDS, ETSE, University of Valencia, Av. Universitad, 46100 Burjassot, Valencia, Spain

the progress in high-level hardware description language (HDL) synthesis tools, configurable devices such as FPGA can be used as efficient hardware accelerators for neuromorphic systems. A proposal was made by Schrauwen and Van Campenhout [17] using serial arithmetic to reduce hardware resource consumption, but no training or weight adaptation was possible. Other solution, presented by Rice et al. [18] used full-scale Izhikevich neurons with very high resource consumption (25 neurons occupy 79% of logic resources in a Virtex4 FPGA device), without on-line training.

Computation methods used for FPGA dramatically differ from classic methods used in Von Neumann PCs or even SIMD processing units like GPUs or DSPs. Thus, the required SNN hardware architecture must be different for reconfigurable devices, opening new possibilities for computation optimization. FPGA are optimal for massive parallel and relatively simple processing units rather than large universal computational blocks as is in case of SNN, including lots of multiply-add arithmetic blocks and vast quantities of distributed block RAM [19]. This work describes computation algorithms properly modeling the SNN and its training algorithm, specifically targeted to benefit from reconfigurable hardware blocks. The proposed solution combines spike encoding, topology, neuron membrane model and spike-time dependent plasticity (STDP) learning.

2 Spiking neural networks model

Spiking neural networks are considered to be the third generation of artificial neural networks (ANN). While classic ANN operate with real or integer-valued inputs, SNN process data in form of series of spikes called spike trains, which, in terms of computation means that a single bit line toggling between logical levels '0' and '1' is required. SNN are able to process temporal patterns, not only spatial, and SNN are more computationally powerful than ANN [20]. Classic machine learning methods perform poorly for spike coded data, being unsuitable for SNN. As a consequence, different training and network topology optimization algorithms must be used [9,21].

The SNN model used in this work is the feed-forward network, each neuron is connected to all the neurons in the next layer by a weighted connection, which means that the output signal of a neuron has a different weighted potential contribution [22]. Input neurons require spike trains and input signals (stimuli) need to be encoded into spikes (typically, spike trains) to further feed the SNN.

An approximation to the functionality of a neuron is given by electrical models which reproduce the functionality of neuronal cells. One of the most common models is the spike response model (SRM) due to the close approximation to a real biological neuron [23,24]; the SRM is a generalization of the 'integrate and fire' model [9]. The main characteristic of a spiking neuron is the membrane potential, the transmission of a single spike from one neuron to another is mediated by synapses at the point where neurons interact. In neuroscience, a transmitting neuron is defined as a presynaptic neuron and a receiving neuron as a postsynaptic neuron. With no activity, neurons have a small negative electrical charge of -70 mV, which is called resting potential; when a single spike arrives into a postsynaptic neuron, it generates a post synaptic potential (PSP) which is excitatory when the membrane potential is increasing and inhibitory when decreasing. The membrane potential at an instant is calculated as the sum of all present PSP at the neuron inputs. When the membrane potential is above a critical threshold value, a postsynaptic spike is generated, entering the neuron into a refractory period when the membrane remains overpolarized, preventing neurons from generating new spikes temporarily. After a refractory period, the neuron potential returns to its resting value and is ready to fire a new spike if membrane potential is above the threshold.

The PSP function is given by Equation 1, where τ_m and τ_s are time constants to control the steepness of rise and decay, and t is the time after the presynaptic spike arrived.

$$PSP(t) = e^{\left(\frac{-t}{\tau_m}\right)} - e^{\left(\frac{-t}{\tau_s}\right)}, \tag{1}$$

Figure 1A shows different PSP as a function of time (ms) and weight value, being excitatory in case of red and blue lines, and inhibitory in case of a green line.

Let us consider the example shown in Figure 1B where spikes from two presynaptic neurons trigger an excitation PSP in a postsynaptic neuron. The spike train generated by the presynaptic neurons will change the membrane potential calculated as the sum of individual PSPs generated by incoming spikes. When membrane potential reaches the threshold, the neuron fires a spike at the instant t_s. Graphically it is shown on Figure 1C. If we denote the threshold value as υ, the refractory period η is defined according to Equation 2 [24]. This equation describes a simple exponential decay of membrane charge, being $H(t)$ the Heavyside step function, $H(t) = 0$, for $t < 0$ and $H(t) = 1$ for $t > 0$; τ_r is a constant defining the steepness of the decay.

$$\eta(t) = -\upsilon e^{\left(\frac{t}{\tau_r}\right)} H(t) \tag{2}$$

Being $t_i^{(g)}$ the time when a spike is fired by a presynaptic neuron, this spike changes the potential of a postsynaptic

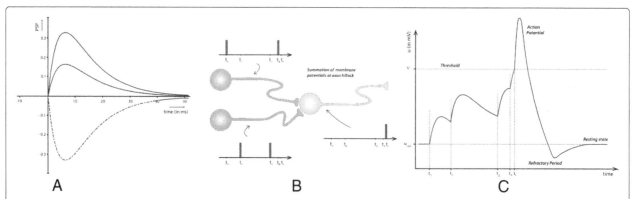

Figure 1 Postsynaptic potential function (PSP) with weight dependency. (A) Red line is for $\omega = 1$, green for $\omega = -1$ and blue is for $\omega = 0.5$. **(B)** Two neurons (yellow) generate spikes, which are presynaptic for next layer neuron (green). **(C)** Membrane potential graph for green neuron. Presynaptic spikes raise the potential; when the potential is above threshold, a postsynaptic spike is generated and the neuron becomes overpolarized.

neuron j at time t and the time difference between these two events is $t - t_i^{(g)}$. The travelling time between two neurons for a spike is defined by Equation 3 where d_{ji} is the delay of synapse value.

$$\Delta t_{ji} = t - t_i^{(g)} - d_{ji} \qquad (3)$$

When a sequence of spikes $F_i = \left\{ t_i^{(g)}, \ldots, t_i^K \right\}$ arrives to a neuron j, the membrane potential changes according to the PSP function and refractory period, and thus, an output spike train is propagated by neuron j as $F_j = \left\{ t_j^{(f)}, \ldots, t_j^N \right\}$. The equation for the j-th neuron potential

P_j is obtained according to Equation 4, where the refractory period is also considered.

$$P_j(t) = \sum_i^K \sum_{t_i^{(g)} \in F_i} w_{ij} PSP(\Delta t_{ji}) + \sum_{t_j^{(f)} \in F_j} \eta \left(t - t_j^{(f)} \right) \qquad (4)$$

These equations define the SRM, which can be modeled by analog circuits since the PSP function can be seen as a charging and discharging RC circuit. However, this model is computationally complex when used in digital systems. We propose to use a simplified model

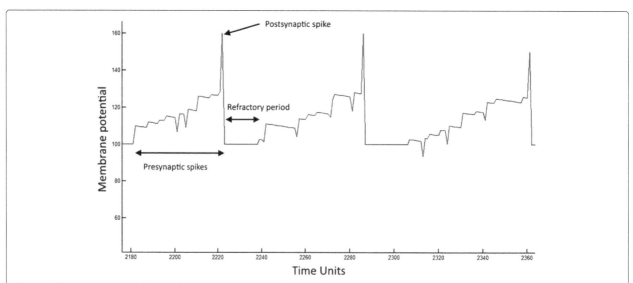

Figure 2 Membrane potential dynamics of a single neuron with simplified membrane model. After several incoming spikes, the membrane potential surpasses threshold and neuron fires a postsynaptic spike. For better visibility, neuron potential is increased twice for one TU after spiking. During refractory period, neuron does not change its potential. For visibility, neuron potential is shown with offset +100.

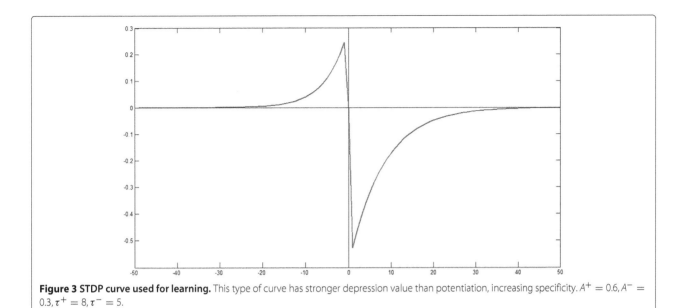

Figure 3 STDP curve used for learning. This type of curve has stronger depression value than potentiation, increasing specificity. $A^+ = 0.6, A^- = 0.3, \tau^+ = 8, \tau^- = 5$.

with linear membrane potential degradation with similar performance and learning capabilities as the classic SRM.

3 Simplified spiking neural model

The classic leaky integrate-and-fire (LIF) model [9] and its generalized form (SRM) are widely used as a neuron model. However, LIF spiking neuron models are computationally complex since non-linear equations are used to model the membrane potential. However, simplification might be defined in order to reduce computational complexity by proposing a simplified membrane model. Let us describe the membrane potential P_t as a function of time and incoming spikes. Time units are counted in discrete time form as the model is intended to be used in digital circuits. For an n-input SNN, during the non-refractory period, each incoming spike $S_{it}, i = [1..n]$ increases the membrane potential P_t by a value of synapse weight W_i. In addition, the membrane potential is decreasing by a constant value D, every time instant. This process can be described by Equation 5, which corresponds to a simplified version of Equation 4 in a LIF model.

$$P_t = \begin{cases} P_{t-1} + \sum_{i=1}^{n} W_i S_{it} - D, & \text{if } P_{min} < P_{t-1} < P_{threshold} \\ P_{refract}, & \text{if } P_{t-1} \geq P_{threshold} \\ R_p, & \text{if } P_{t-1} \leq P_{min} \end{cases}$$

(5)

Thus, instead of an initial postsynaptic potential ramp in the spike response model, the instant change of membrane potential allows a neuron to fire immediately in the next clock cycle after the spike arrives.

At each time instant t, if membrane potential P_t is bigger than the resting potential $R_p = 0$, it degrades by a fixed value $P_t = P_{t-1} - D$. The resulting PSP function will be a saw-like linear function, which is easily implemented by a register and a counter, contrary to classic non-linear PSP models based on look-up tables or RAM/ROM for non-linear equations. The value of constant D is chosen relevant to the maximum presynaptic spike rate and the number of inputs. An example of membrane potential dynamics is shown in Figure 2. When $P_t > P_{threshold}$, the neuron fires a spike, the membrane potential becomes $P_t = P_{refract}$ (resting potential) and a refractory period

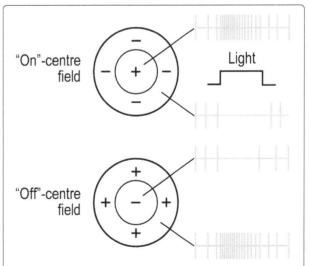

Figure 4 Off-centered and on-centered neural receptive field and corresponding spike trains. *Source: Millodot: Dictionary of Optometry and Visual Science, 7th edition. ©2009 Butterworth-Heinemann.*

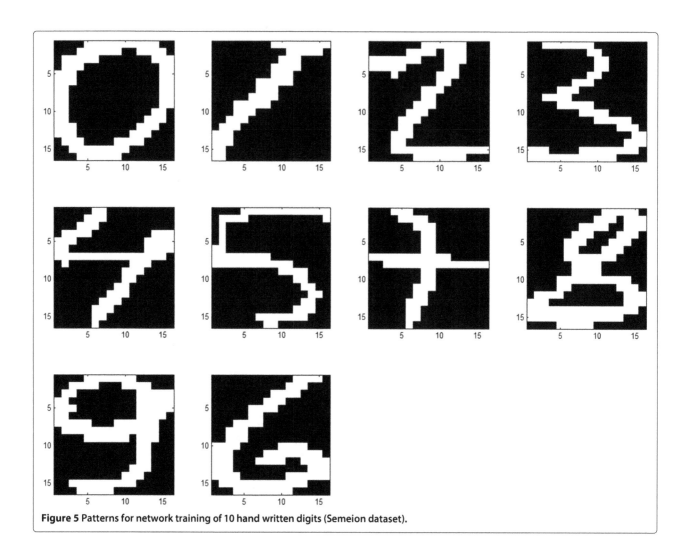

Figure 5 Patterns for network training of 10 hand written digits (Semeion dataset).

counter starts. Instead of a slow repolarization of membrane after the spike, the neuron is blocking its inputs for time T_{refract}, and holds membrane potential at P_{refract} level during this time. To avoid strong negative polarization of membrane, its potential is limited by P_{min}. Despite the model of the neuron is linear, the network can produce non-linear response by tuning the weights of previous layer inputs.

3.1 Spike-time dependent plasticity learning

STDP is a phenomenon discovered in live neurons by Bi and Poo [25] and adapted for learning event-based networks. STDP learning is an unsupervised learning algorithm based on dependencies between presynaptic and postsynaptic spikes. In a given synapse, when a postsynaptic spike occurs in a specific time window after a presynaptic spike, the weight of this synapse

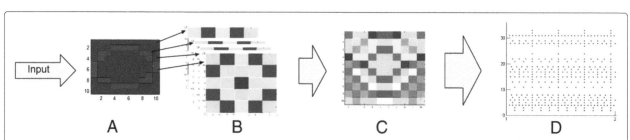

Figure 6 Image to spike train encoding dataflow. Input image **(A)** is processed with RFs of encoding neurons **(B)**, and the result **(C)** is received by encoding neurons, generating the spike trains **(D)** where spike frequency is proportional to the intensity of corresponding pixel and its surroundings.

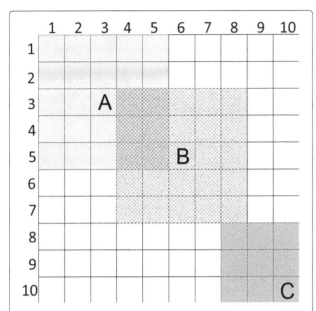

Figure 7 Three receptive fields on the 10 × 10 input space. Blue field corresponds to the neuron **(A)** (3,3 in input matrix). Green field corresponds to neuron **(B)** (6,5) and orange corresponds to neuron **(C)** (10,10). Note that only active part or RF is shown.

postsynaptic spike events. The used function is shown on Figure 3.

For STDP learning, The classic asymmetric reinforcement curve is used, taking time units (TUs) as argument. The learning function is described in Equation 6 where A^- and A^+ are constants for negative and positive values of time difference Δt between presynaptic and postsynaptic spikes, determining the maximum excitation and inhibition values; τ^-, τ^+ are constants characterizing the steepness of the function.

$$\text{STDP}(\Delta t) = \Delta w = \begin{cases} A^- \exp^* \left(\frac{\Delta t}{\tau^-} \right), & \text{if } \Delta t \leq -2 \\ 0, & \text{if } -2 < \Delta t < 2 \\ A^+ \exp^* \left(\frac{\Delta t}{\tau^+} \right), & \text{if } \Delta t \geq 2 \end{cases}$$

(6)

The learning rule (weight change) is described by Equation 7. The weights are always limited by $w_{\max} \geq w \geq w_{\min}$. The desired distance between presynaptic and postsynaptic spike is unity and the STDP window is [2..20] TUs in both directions. The weight change rate σ controls the weight adaptation speed.

is increased. If the postsynaptic spike appears before the presynaptic spike, a decrease in the weight occurs assuming that inverse dependency exists between pre- and postsynaptic spikes. The strength of the weight change is a function of time between presynaptic and

$$w_{\text{new}} = \begin{cases} w_{\text{old}} + \sigma \Delta w (w_{\max} - w_{\text{old}}), & \text{if } \Delta w > 0 \\ w_{\text{old}} + \sigma \Delta w (w_{\text{old}} - w_{\min}), & \text{if } \Delta w \leq 0 \end{cases}$$

(7)

Since unsupervised learning requires competition, lateral inhibition was introduced and thus, the weights of

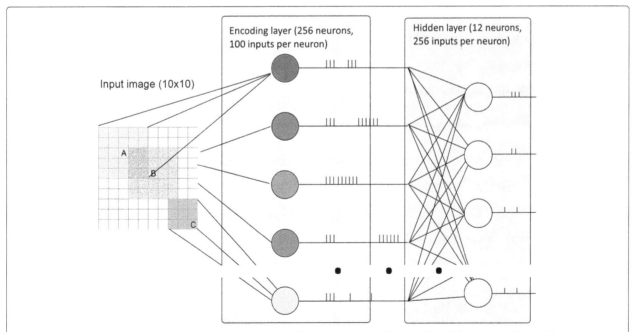

Figure 8 Network structure used in the simulation. Input space of 10 × 10 is converted into a spike train by a matrix of 10 × 10 input neurons with 5 × 5 receptive field. The generated spike train is fed to the hidden layer of 9 simplified LIF neurons with training. Lateral inhibition connections are shown in red. Not all connections between the input space and encoding layer are shown.

the winner neurons (first spiking neurons) are increased while other neurons suffer a small weight reduction value. Tests showed that depressing the weights of the non firing neurons decrease the amount of noise in the network. The depression of synapses that do not fire at all was added in order to eliminate 'mute' synapses (inactive synapses), reducing the network size and improving robustness against noise. This training causes a side effect since, for weight increase, spike-intense patterns require a higher membrane threshold, avoiding the patterns with low spike intensity to be recognized by the network. This is solved by introducing negative weights, preventing neurons from reacting on every pattern and increasing the specificity of classifier.

4 Visual receptive fields

The visual cortex is one of the best studied parts of the brain. The receptive field (RF) of a visual neuron is an area of the image affecting the neural input. The size and shape of receptive fields vary depending on the neuron position and neuron task. A variety of tasks can be done with RFs: edge detection, sharpening, blurring, line decomposition, etc. In each subsequent layer of the visual cortex, receptive fields of the neurons cover bigger and bigger regions, convolving the outputs of the previous layer.

Mammalian retinal ganglion cells located at the center of vision, in the fovea, have the smallest receptive fields, and those located in the visual periphery have the largest receptive fields [26]. The large receptive field size of neurons in the visual periphery explains the poor spatial resolution of human vision outside the point of fixation, together with photoreceptor density and optical aberrations. Only a few cortical receptive fields resemble the structure of thalamic receptive fields, some fields have elongated subregions responding to dark or light spots,

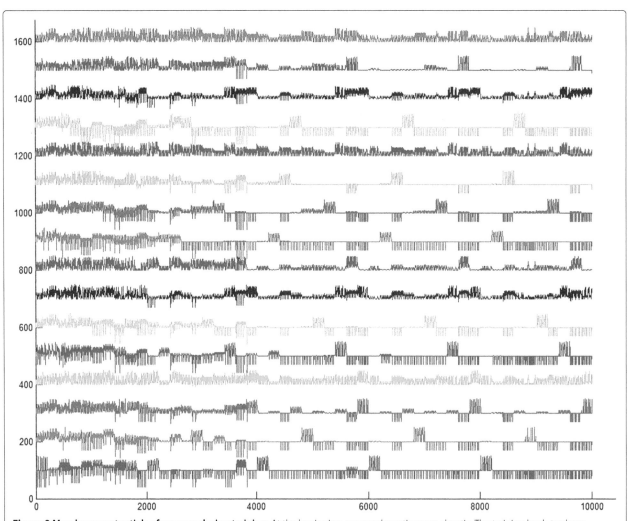

Figure 9 Membrane potentials of neurons during training. At the beginning, neuronal reactions are chaotic. The training leads to sharp individual neuronal reactions, neurons become specific to one pattern. The most intensive weight shaping occurs between 3,000 and 4,000 TUs.

while others do not respond to spots at all. In addition, the implementation of a receptive field is a first stage of sparse coding [27] where the neurons are reacting to shapes, not single pixels. The receptive field model proposed here shows a good approximation to the real behavior of primary visual cortex.

4.1 Receptive field neuron response

The neurons in the receptive or sensory layer generate a response R_{RF} defined by Equation 8, as the calculation of Frobenious inner product of the input image S with the receptive field F of the neuron and calculation of the sum of input stimuli. This operation is similar to normal 2D convolution, the only difference that in convolution kernel is rotated by 180°.

$$R_{RF} = \sum_{i}^{I}\sum_{j}^{J} S_{ij}F_{ij} \qquad (8)$$

The matrix F defines a receptive field (RF) of the neuron, being I the X axis and J the Y axis sizes of input image S. While the shape and size of receptive field can be arbitrary, in the mammalian visual cortex, there are several distinct types of receptive fields. Two common types are off-centered and on-centered as shown in Figure 4. These RFs can be used as line detectors, small circle detectors or perform basic feature extraction for higher layers. Simple classification tasks such as the inclination of a line, circle or non-circle object and others can be performed by this type of single-layer receptive field neurons. Once input and weights are normalized, the maximum excitation of a certain output neuron will be achieved when the input exactly matches the weight matrix, providing pattern classification when weights are properly adjusted.

Sensory layer neurons generate spikes at a frequency proportional to their excitation. As the frequency of a firing neuron cannot be infinite, the maximum firing rate is limited, and thus, the membrane potential is normalized.

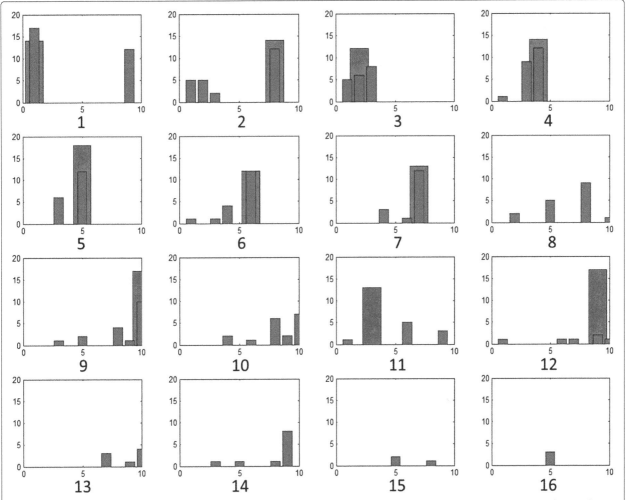

Figure 10 Spike rate per sample before and after training. Blue bars are spike rate before training and red ones represent the spike rate after the training.

The spiking response firing rate (FR_n) is described by Equation 9, where RPmax is the defined minimum refractory period and $\max(R)$ is the maximum possible value of membrane potential.

$$FR_n = \begin{cases} \dfrac{1}{RP\text{max}*\frac{R_{RF}}{\max(R)}}, & \text{if } R_{RF} > 0 \\ 0, & \text{if } R_{RF} \leq 0 \end{cases} \qquad (9)$$

5   Software simulation and results

A subset of Semeion handwritten digit dataset [28] was used to test the new algorithms and proof the validity of simplifications. Matlab software was used. The dataset consists on 1,593 samples of black and white images of handwritten digits 0 to 9 (160 samples per digit), 16×16 pixels size as shown in Figure 5. The training set consisted of 20 samples for each class (each digit) with 5% of uniform random noise added to every sample fed into the SNN.

5.1   Image encoding

In the described experiment, a 5×5 on-centered receptive field was used. This receptive field was weighted in a $[-0.5,..,1]$ range according to Manhattan distance to the center of the field. A 16×16 pixel input is processed by a 16×16 encoding neuron layer (256 neurons), obtaining a potential value for each input which will be further converted into spikes. The coding process using the 5×5 receptive field is shown in Figure 6A,B. The neural response, shown in Figure 6C is the membrane potential map, further converted into spike trains whose spiking frequency is proportional to such potential, as shown in Figure 6D. The same procedure is repeated for all input neurons. The receptive fields of the neurons are over-

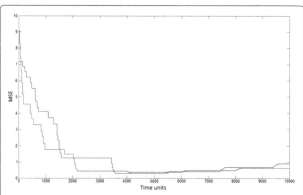

Figure 12 MSE for single pattern during learning. Red line represents simplified model, and blue represents classic SRM. It can be seen that, after 5,000 TU, neuron becomes overtrained for both models.

lapping; an example of three receptive fields is shown in Figure 7 where, in case C, a part of the RF lay outside the input space, and thus, that part is not contributing to membrane potential.

5.2   Network architecture

The proposed SNN consists of 2 layers, an encoding layer of 256 neurons with an on-centered 5×5 pixel RF and second layer of 16 neurons using the simplified SRM. Experimental testing showed that, for proper competitiveness in the network, the number of neurons should be at least 20% greater than the number of classes and thus, 16 neurons were implemented. If the number of neurons is insufficient, only the most spike-intensive patterns are learnt. Each sample was presented to the network during 200 time units (TUs). With a refractory period of encoding neurons of 30 TUs, the maximum possible amount of spikes is $200/30 = 6$. STDP parameters for learning were $A^+ = 0.6, A^- = 0.3, \tau^+ = 8, \tau^- = 5$. The maximum weight change rate σ was fixed to $0.25 * \max(\text{STDP}) = 0.25 * 0.25 = 0.0625$.

Instead of using a 'winner-takes-all' strategy, a modification is done by using a 'winner-depresses-all' strategy, where the first spiking neuron gets a weight increase and all other neuron potentials are depressed by 50% of the

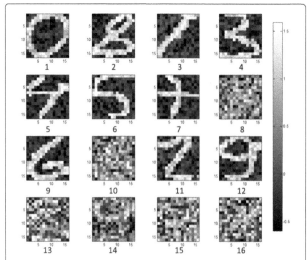

Figure 11 Neurons weights representation after STDP training. Ten out of sixteen neurons learnt to discriminate all ten numbers in the SEMEION dataset.

Table 1 Simulation speed of classic and simplified networks

	Classic (s)	Simplified (s)
5 classes, 8 neurons, 15,000 time units	48.1	2.25
6 classes, 9 neurons, 15,000 time units	48.9	2.4
6 classes, 16 neurons, 15,000 time units	66.1	3.9
6 classes, 100 neurons, 15,000 time units	137.1	13.03
12 classes, 50 neurons, 96,000 time units	1327.12	80.28

All data are obtained on synthetic datasets taking the mean values of five runs.

spike threshold value. Thus, strongly stimulated neurons can fire immediately after the winner, which adds plasticity to the network. The whole network structure is shown on Figure 8.

For the classic SRM algorithm, a table-based PSP function of 30 points was used (simplified model uses constant decrease as PSP and does not require table-based functions). For both SRM and simplified models, STDP function was also table-based with 30 positive and 30 negative values. All algorithms (classic and simplified model) were written using atomic operations without the usage of Matlab vector and matrix arithmetic. Such coding style provides more accurate results in performance tests when modeling hardware implementation.

5.3 Results

In order to prove noise robustness, input spike trains were corrupted by randomly inverting the state of 5% from all spike trains. Thus, some spikes were missing and some other random spikes were injected into the spike trains. Five training epochs were run before the evaluation. The implemented network successfully learned all patterns. In Figure 9, the membrane potential change is shown, having small values at the beginning. During the training, the membrane potential becomes more and more polarized with strong negative values on the classes that are not recognized by the selected neuron. It can also be appreciated that six neurons (numbered 8,10,13,14,15,16) remained almost untrained, with random weights.

Training evolution can be observed by the spike rate diagrams shown in Figure 10. Each graph represents one neuron, with classes along X axis. Before training, every neuron is firing in several classes, and after the training, each neuron has a discriminative high spike rate only in one class. As a result, the final weight maps of neurons become similar to the presented stimuli as Figure 11 depicts. The successful separation of patterns 2 to 5 and 1 to 6 proves that a network can solve problems with partially overlapping classes. The performance of learning between classic SRM and simplified SRM models can be measured with the mean square error (MSE) for normalized weights after training. The training error for a single pattern (class 0) can be seen in Figure 12. The graph shows very similar learning dynamics and performance of both models. Starting from 5,000 TU, both models tend to increase the error showing over-training.

For comparing time of simulation, three synthetic datasets from Semeion samples with 5, 6 and 12 classes were prepared (12 classes dataset as digits 1 and 0 were represented with 2 classes each). Every class was repeated 30 times to test different network sizes (8, 9, 16 and 50 SNN neuron size in hidden layer were tested). Time of Matlab simulation in Table 1 shows an improvement over 20 times when comparing the simplified and classic SRM.

Simulation was done on a 64-bit OS system with 6 GB of RAM and an Intel i7-2620M processor.

6 Conclusions

In this paper, we describe a simplified spiking neuron architecture optimized for embedded systems implementation, proving the learning capabilities of the design. The network preserves its learning and classification properties while computational and memory complexity is reduced dramatically - by eliminating the PSP table in each neuron. Learning is stable and robust, the trained network can recognize noisy patterns. A simple, yet effective visual input encoding was implemented for this network. The simplification is beneficial for reconfigurable hardware systems, keeping generality and accuracy. Furthermore, slight modifications would allow to be used with Address-Event Representation (AER) data protocol for frameless vision [29]. The proposed system could be further implemented in FPGAs for low-power embedded neural computation.

Competing interests
The authors declare that they have no competing interests.

Authors' contributions
All authors are with Digital Signal Processing Group, Electronic Eng. Dept., ETSE, University of Valencia. Av. Universitat s/n, 46100 Burjassot, Spain.

References
1. Lovelace JJ, Rickard JT, Cios KJ. A spiking neural network alternative for the analog to digital converter. In: Neural Networks (IJCNN), The 2010 International Joint Conference On. New Jersey, USA: Institute of Electrical and Electronics Engineers-IEEE; 2010. p. 1–8.
2. Ambard M, Guo B, Martinez D, Bermak A. A spiking neural network for gas discrimination using a tin oxide sensor array. In: Electronic Design, Test and Applications, 2008. DELTA 2008. 4th IEEE International Symposium On. New Jersey, USA: Institute of Electrical and Electronics Engineers-IEEE; 2008. p. 394–397.
3. Bouganis A, Shanahan M. Training a spiking neural network to control a 4-dof robotic arm based on spike timing-dependent plasticity. In: Neural Networks (IJCNN), The 2010 International Joint Conference On. New Jersey, USA: Institute of Electrical and Electronics Engineers-IEEE; 2010. p. 1–8.
4. Alnajjar F, Murase K. Sensor-fusion in spiking neural network that generates autonomous behavior in real mobile robot. In: Neural Networks, 2008. IJCNN 2008. (IEEE World Congress on Computational Intelligence). IEEE International Joint Conference On. New Jersey, USA: Institute of Electrical and Electronics Engineers-IEEE; 2008. p. 2200–2206.
5. Perez-Carrasco JA, Acha B, Serrano C, Camunas-Mesa L, Serrano-Gotarredona T, Linares-Barranco B. Fast vision through frameless event-based sensing and convolutional processing: Application to texture recognition. Neural Networks IEEE Trans. 2010;21(4):609–620.
6. Botzheim J, Obo T, Kubota N. Human gesture recognition for robot partners by spiking neural network and classification learning. In: Soft Computing and Intelligent Systems (SCIS) and 13th International Symposium on Advanced Intelligent Systems (ISIS), 2012 Joint 6th International Conference On. New Jersey, USA: Institute of Electrical and Electronics Engineers-IEEE; 2012. p. 1954–1958.
7. Ratnasingam S, McGinnity TM. A spiking neural network for tactile form based object recognition. In: The 2011 International Joint Conference on

Neural Networks (IJCNN). New Jersey, USA: Institute of Electrical and Electronics Engineers-IEEE; 2011. p. 880–885.

8. Fang H, Wang Y, He J. Spiking neural networks for cortical neuronal spike train decoding. Neural Comput. 2009;22(4):1060–1085.

9. Gerstner W, Kistler WM. Spiking Neuron Models: Single Neurons, Populations, Plasticity. Cambridge, United Kingdom: Cambridge University Press; 2002, p. 494.

10. Arguello E, Silva R, Castillo C, Huerta M. The neuroid: A novel and simplified neuron-model. In: 2012 Annual International Conference of the IEEE Engineering in Medicine and Biology Society (EMBC). New Jersey, USA: Institute of Electrical and Electronics Engineers-IEEE; 2012. p. 1234–1237.

11. Ishikawa Y, Fukai S. A neuron mos variable logic circuit with the simplified circuit structure. In: Proceedings of 2004 IEEE Asia-Pacific Conference on Advanced System Integrated Circuits 2004. New Jersey, USA: Institute of Electrical and Electronics Engineers-IEEE; 2004. p. 436–437.

12. Lorenzo R, Riccardo R, Antonio C. A new unsupervised neural network for pattern recognition with spiking neurons. In: International Joint Conference on Neural Networks, 2006. IJCNN 06. New Jersey, USA: Institute of Electrical and Electronics Engineers-IEEE; 2006. p. 3903–3910.

13. Painkras E, Plana LA, Garside J, Temple S, Galluppi F, Patterson C, Lester DR, Brown AD, Furber SB. Spinnaker: A 1-w 18-core system-on-chip for massively-parallel neural network simulation. IEEE J. Solid-State Circuits. 2013;48(8):1943–1953.

14. Schemmel J, Grubl A, Hartmann S, Kononov A, Mayr C, Meier K, Millner S, Partzsch J, Schiefer S, Scholze S, et al. Live demonstration: A scaled-down version of the brainscales wafer-scale neuromorphic system. In: 2012 IEEE International Symposium on Circuits and Systems (ISCAS). New Jersey, USA: Institute of Electrical and Electronics Engineers-IEEE; 2012. p. 702–702.

15. Hylton T. 2008. Systems of neuromorphic adaptive plastic scalable electronics. http://www.scribd.com/doc/76634068/Darpa-Baa-Synapse.

16. Schoenauer T, Atasoy S, Mehrtash N, Klar H. Neuropipe-chip: a digital neuro-processor for spiking neural networks. Neural Networks, IEEE Trans. 2002;13(1):205–213.

17. Schrauwen B, Campenhout JV. Parallel hardware implementation of a broad class of spiking neurons using serial arithmetic. In: Proceedings of the 14th European Symposium on Artificial Neural Networks. Evere, Belgium: D-side conference services; 2006. p. 623–628.

18. Rice KL, Bhuiyan MA, Taha TM, Vutsinas CN, Smith MC. Fpga implementation of izhikevich spiking neural networks for character recognition. In: International Conference on Reconfigurable Computing and FPGAs, 2009. ReConFig 09. New Jersey, USA: Institute of Electrical and Electronics Engineers-IEEE; 2009. p. 451–456.

19. Xilinx. Spartan-6 family overview. Technical Report DS160, Xilinx, Inc. October 2011. http://www.xilinx.com/support/documentation/data_sheets/ds160.pdf.

20. Maass W. Networks of spiking neurons: The third generation of neural network models. Neural Networks. 1997;10(9):1659–1671.

21. MCWV Rossum, Bi GQ, Turrigiano GG. Stable hebbian learning from spike timing-dependent plasticity. J. Neurosci. 2000;20(23):8812–8821.

22. Pham DT, Packianather MS, Charles EYA. A self-organising spiking neural network trained using delay adaptation. In: Industrial Electronics, 2007. ISIE 2007. IEEE International Symposium On. New Jersey, USA: Institute of Electrical and Electronics Engineers-IEEE; 2007. p. 3441–3446.

23. Paugam-Moisy H, SM Bohte. Computing with Spiking Neuron Networks In: G Rozenberg, JK T Back, editors. Handbook of Natural Computing. Heidelberg, Germany: Springer; 2009.

24. Booij O. Temporal pattern classification using spiking neural networks. (August 2004). Available from http://obooij.home.xs4all.nl/study/download/booij04Temporal.pdf.

25. Bi G-Q, Poo M-M. Synaptic modifications in cultured hippocampal neurons: dependence on spike timing, synaptic strength, and postsynaptic cell type. J. Neurosci. 1998;18(24):10464.

26. Martinez LM, Alonso J-M. Complex receptive fields in primary visual cortex. Neuroscientist: Rev. J Bringing Neurobiology, Neurology Psychiatry. 2003;9(5):317–331. PMID: 14580117.

27. Foldiak P, Young MP. The Handbook of Brain Theory and Neural Networks. Cambridge, MA, USA: MIT Press; 1998, pp. 895–898. http://dl.acm.org/citation.cfm?id=303568.303958.

28. Repository UML. Semeion Handwritten Digit Dataset. 2014. http://archive.ics.uci.edu/ml/datasets/Semeion+Handwritten+Digit Accessed 2014-10-30.

29. Perez-Carrasco JA, Zhao B, Serrano C, Acha B, Serrano-Gotarredona T, Chen S, Linares-Barranco B. Mapping from frame-driven to frame-free event-driven vision systems by low-rate rate coding and coincidence processing–application to feedforward convnets. Pattern Anal. Machine Intelligence, IEEE Trans. 2013;35(11):2706–2719.

11

Tumor segmentation in brain MRI using a fuzzy approach with class center priors

Moumen T El-Melegy[1*] and Hashim M Mokhtar[2]

Abstract

This paper proposes a new fuzzy approach for the automatic segmentation of normal and pathological brain magnetic resonance imaging (MRI) volumetric datasets. The proposed approach reformulates the popular fuzzy c-means (FCM) algorithm to take into account any available information about the class center. The uncertainty in this information is also modeled. This information serves to regularize the clusters produced by the FCM algorithm thus boosting its performance under noisy and unexpected data acquisition conditions. In addition, it also speeds up the convergence process of the algorithm. Experiments using simulated and real, both normal and pathological, MRI volumes of the human brain show that the proposed approach has considerable better segmentation accuracy, robustness against noise, and faster response compared with several well-known fuzzy and non-fuzzy techniques reported in the literature.

Keywords: Prior information; MRI segmentation; Fuzzy c-means; Fuzzy algorithms; Brain MRI; Tumor segmentation

1 Introduction

Magnetic resonance imaging (MRI) of the brain is often used to monitor tumor response to treatment process. The segmentation of the brain tumor from the magnetic resonance images is important in medical diagnosis because it provides information associated to anatomical structures as well as potential abnormal tissues necessary to treatment planning and patient follow-up. It can also be helpful for general modeling of pathological brains and the construction of pathological brain atlases [1]. One example is to analyze and estimate quantitatively the growth process of brain tumors, and to assess the response to treatment and in guiding appropriate therapy in serial studies [2,3]. In spite of numerous efforts and promising results in the medical imaging community, accurate and reproducible segmentation and characterization of abnormalities are still a challenging and difficult task because of the variety of the possible shapes, locations and image intensities of various types of tumors. This task involves various disciplines including medicine, MRI physic, radiologist's perception, and image analysis based on intensity and shape.

Brain tumor segmentation process consists of separating the different tumor tissues, such as solid tumor, edema, and necrosis from the normal brain tissues, such as gray matter (GM), white matter (WM), and cerebrospinal fluid (CSF). Although manual segmentation by qualified professionals remains superior in quality to automatic methods, it has two drawbacks. The first drawback is that producing manual segmentations or semi-automatic segmentations is extremely time-consuming, with higher accuracies on more finely detailed volumes demanding increased time from medical experts. The second problem with manual and semiautomatic segmentations is that the segmentation is subject to variations both between observers and within the same observer. For example, a study by Mazzara et al. [1] quantified an average of 28% ± 12% variation in quantified volume between individuals performing the same brain tumor segmentation task, and quantified a 20% ± 15% variation within individuals repeating the task three times at one month intervals. This statistic demonstrates that the manual segmentation has no confidence in tracking the tumor volume during the patient follow-up process and the automatic methods that could achieve a sufficient level of accuracy would be highly desirable for their ability to perform high-throughput segmentation. On the other hand, automatic methods would be advantageous since they are not subject to this variation, and thus,

* Correspondence: moumen@aun.edu.eg
[1]Electrical Engineering Department, Assiut University, Assiut 71516, Egypt
Full list of author information is available at the end of the article

the significance of changes in volumes could be more easily assessed.

In addition to tumor volume calculation, accurate automatic segmentation methods additionally have the potential to reduce the variability and increase the standardization of other measurements and protocols, including the quantification of edema or necrosis. Also, automatic segmentation could lead to new applications, including effective content-based image retrieval in large medical databases. This could allow clinicians to find similar images in historical data based on tumor location, grade, size, enhancement, extent of edema, similar patterns of growth, or a variety of other factors. This information could help clinicians in making decisions, in addition to being a useful research tool for exploring patterns in the historical data. In a similar vein, accurate high-throughput segmentations could be used in combination with relevant features and machine learning methods to improve tumor grading in cases where grading is ambivalent (or to discover potentially useful distinctions within grades), and to provide a more accurate and patient-specific prognosis [4].

Due to the above advantages of the automatic segmentation, it becomes a necessary issue for clinicians. Nevertheless, automatic tumor segmentation is still a difficult problem for two key reasons: (1) There is a large number of tumor types which differ greatly in size, shape, location, tissue composition and tissue homogeneity [5]. In some cases, their border with normal tissues cannot be very well defined on images; therefore, they are even difficult for radiology experts to delineate. (2) The consequence of the phenomenon of partial volume effect (PVE), where 1 pixel/voxel may belong to multiple tissue types, in addition to noise due to the MRI acquisition system.

In this paper, we address these difficulties using a soft computing approach based on fuzzy concepts. This fuzzy approach provides several advantages. First, it inherently has the attractive property of the soft classification model, where each point can belong to more than one class. This is consistent with the partial volume effect observed in MR images and thus eliminates the need for explicit modeling of mixed classes (which is required - for example - by segmentation methods based on the finite Gaussian mixture [5]). Another key advantage of the fuzzy approach is that it can segment several tissues at the same time. Therefore, this approach can be used to segment all brain tissues of interest, such as tumor and other abnormal tissues (e.g., edema and necrosis) in addition to the normal brain tissues (e.g., WM, GM, and CSF). This is in contrast to some popular methods for medical image segmentation, such as deformable models [6,7] and level sets [8,9], where only one object or tissue of interest can be typically segmented at any time. Moreover, while these latter segmentation methods often need careful (sometimes even manual) close-enough initialization to ensure the method

convergence to a proper solution, the proposed approach can start with random initial values.

In particular, the fuzzy approach that we propose is based on the fuzzy c-means (FCM) algorithm [10,11]. Indeed, this fuzzy clustering algorithm has been already used for MRI segmentation (e.g., Ahmed et al. [12], Caldairou et al. [13], Cai et al. [14]). One key contribution of this paper is that the proposed approach, unlike the earlier ones, is able to utilize prior information in the segmentation process. It incorporates available information about the class centers of the data. This can be as simple as the rough knowledge of the mean intensity (class center in FCM terminology) of a class (a particular tissue in the MRI data). The uncertainty in this information is also modeled. This information serves to regularize the clusters produced by the FCM algorithm thus boosting its performance under noisy and unexpected data acquisition conditions. In addition, it speeds up the convergence process of the algorithm. To the best of our knowledge, the idea, mathematical formulation, and derivation of incorporating this information have not been reported before in the wide literature of fuzzy clustering and its applications.

We apply the proposed approach to the automatic segmentation of the human brain from two popular benchmark MR datasets: the simulated BrainWeb MR datasets [15], and normal real MR datasets obtained from the Internet Brain Segmentation Repository (IBSR) [16]. We compare these results with those of the standard FCM and several well-known fuzzy and non-fuzzy MRI segmentation techniques found in the literature. We also apply the proposed approach to pathological T1-weighted MRI databases obtained from IBSR and from a local MRI scan center to detect hyper-intense tumors. The results on the pathological MRI are evaluated by expert radiologists from Assiut University Medical Hospital.

The remainder of this paper is organized as follows: Section 2 briefly reviews related work. Section 3 gives a concise description of the standard FCM algorithm. In section 4, a full explanation of the proposed approach for MRI segmentation is given. Our approach for tumor segmentation is developed in section 5. Section 6 presents the experimental results and some comparisons with other methods. Finally, the paper is concluded in section 7.

2 Related work

Many techniques for MRI segmentation have been developed over the years based on several techniques. These techniques can be divided into four major classes [17]: threshold-based techniques, region-based techniques, pixel classification techniques, and model-based techniques. In this section, we give a brief overview on these methods. The interested reader is referred to the recent survey in [17] for more details.

One of the earliest and classical methods is thresholding, in which the objects of the image are classified by comparing their intensities with one or more intensity thresholds. These thresholds can be either global or local. For example, Gibbs et al. [18] presented a semi-supervised approach for the segmentation of enhancing tumor pixels from T1-weighted post-contrast images. It first applied an intensity threshold to a manually selected region of interest, and represents a clearly justified approach for segmenting image objects that are different in intensity from their surroundings. Their method does not effectively take into account the presence of hyper-intense pixels representing normal structures in T1 post-contrast images. Other segmentation methods based on thresholding include those in [19,20]. However, generally threshold-based segmentation methods, either local or global, are unable to exploit all the information provided by MRI and are often used as a first step in the segmentation process.

Region-based segmentation approaches (e.g. [21-23]) examine pixels in an image and form disjoint regions by merging neighborhood pixels with homogeneity properties based on a predefined similarity criterion. One example is the work of Salman [21] who presented a comparative analysis of the traditional region growing segmentation and a modified region growing method, addressed to brain tumor segmentation in 3D T1 MR images. Other approaches incorporate the region growing process as a refinement step [22] or in an adaptive fashion [23]. While the advantage of region growing is its capability of correctly segmenting regions that have similar properties and generating connected region, it suffers from the partial volume effect which limits the accuracy of MR brain image segmentation. Partial volume effect blurs the intensity distinction between tissue classes at the border of the two tissues types, because the voxel may represent more than one kind of tissue types.

In brain tumor segmentation, the methods based on pixel classification are constrained to the use of supervised or unsupervised classifiers to cluster pixels in the feature space. While the supervised methods include Bayes classifiers and artificial neural networks, unsupervised methods include k-means, fuzzy clustering techniques [10,11], and statistical methods such as Markov random fields (MRF). Fuzzy methods will be discussed in more detail later in this section. The unsupervised method of MRF provides a way to integrate spatial information into the clustering process, reducing the overlapping of clusters and the effect of noise on the result [24]. A major difficulty in MRF is the selection of the parameters that control the strength of spatial interactions, which can result in very soft segmentation and a loss of structural details.

In model-based segmentation, a connected and continuous model is built for a specific anatomic structure by incorporating *a priori* knowledge of the object such as shape, location, and orientation. The key methods in this class often employ active contour models or snakes [6,7] and level set methods [8,9]. While the former generally suffers from the difficulty of naturally handling topological changes for the splitting and merging of contours, level set handles this in a natural fashion. Segmenting tumors by geometric deformable models or level sets permits the development of fully automatic and highly accurate segmentation approaches [17]. Unfortunately, these methods are still computationally expensive [9,17], and sometimes hard to initialize [8].

One of the clustering algorithms that have enjoyed considerable success in image clustering and segmentation is the well-known FCM [10,11] and its variants. This fuzzy approach provides several advantages. First, it inherently offers a soft classification model, which is consistent with the partial volume effect observed in MR images and thus eliminates the need for explicit modeling of mixed classes (which is required - for example - by segmentation methods based on the finite Gaussian mixture [5]). Another key advantage of the fuzzy approach is that it can segment several tissues at the same time. Therefore, this approach can be used to segment all brain tissues of interest, such as tumor and other abnormal tissues (e.g., edema and necrosis) in addition to the normal brain tissues (e.g., WM, GM, and CSF). This is in contrast to deformable models [6,7] and level sets [8,9], where only one object or tissue of interest can be typically segmented at any time.

A lot of work has been developed in order to further improve the FCM performance for MRI segmentation. Almost all these efforts have focused on imposing spatial constraints into the clustering algorithm [12-14,25-29]. Some notable examples of these methods follow.

Liew et al. [25] proposed a fuzzy algorithm that incorporates the local spatial context. Kang et al. [30] improved FCM with adaptive weighted average filter. Ahmed et al. [12] modified the objective function of FCM to allow the labeling of a pixel to be influenced by the labels in its immediate neighborhood. But the main disadvantage is that it computes the neighborhood term in each iteration step, which is time-consuming. Chen and Zhang [27] proposed two variant algorithms, which simplified the neighborhood term of the objective function of [12]. Chuang et al. [28] proposed averaging the fuzzy membership function values and reassigning them according to a tradeoff between the original and averaged membership values. This approach can produce accurate clustering if the tradeoff is well adjusted empirically, but it is enormously time-consuming. Cai et al. [14] proposed a fast generalized FCM algorithm which incorporates the spatial information, the intensity of the local pixel neighborhood and the number of gray levels in an image. This algorithm forms a nonlinearly weighted sum image from both original image and its local spatial and gray level neighborhood.

Hoppner and Klawonn [31] introduced a new way to constrain the membership functions and proposed a FCM-based algorithm with improved fuzzy partitions. They modified the objective function so that the FCM algorithm worked on distances to the Voronoi cell of the cluster rather than using distances to the cluster proto-types. Zhu et al. [32] improved on the algorithm of [31] and proposed a generalized FCM clustering algorithm with the fuzziness index being set by the users so as to achieve more effective clustering performance. Both the algorithms of [31] and [32] rewarded the crisp member-ship degrees and made the FCM-based algorithm faster with fewer iteration steps. Unfortunately, this kind of method makes FCM lose its attractive soft classification nature rendering it no longer suitable to take PVE into account.

Ji et al. [33] constructed a regular energy term to deal with the effect of noise by using the non-local patch in-formation. This method needs to choose different pa-rameters of the regular energy term when segmenting different images. More recently, along the same line, the fuzzy local [28] and non-local [13,22,34] information c-means algorithms have been proposed.

The previous methods have been developed for image and/or MRI segmentation. There are several methods that are crafted for the particular sake of tumor segmentation from MRI, including level sets [8,9], expectation-maximization algorithm [17,35] and fuzzy techniques [33,36-38].

The above methods for normal and/or pathological MRI segmentation have some known limitations. On the one hand, the majority of them has focused on imposing some sort of spatial constraints over a local neighborhood, and requires a tunable parameter to weigh the importance of these constraints relative to the data-driven objective function. This parameter has a crucial impact on the performance of those methods, and its selection is generally difficult and needs some trial-and-error experiments. Some few methods (e.g. [13]) have however tried to get around this problem by making the determination of this parameter adaptive and data-dependent. On the other hand, some of these methods (e.g. [33]) need user intervention one way or the other.

The approach proposed in this paper goes around these issues by following a different, novel methodology. The approach makes use of available information about the mean intensities of the various MR tissues and their uncertainty to guide the minimization of the data-driven objective function. Such prior information can be easily extracted from some training MRI samples of these tissues. The incorporation of this information

allows the automatic segmentation of these tissues from the MRI datasets, without the need for any parameters or weighting factors to be tuned. This also enhances the approach performance in terms of accuracy, noise robust-ness and speed, as will be demonstrated in our experimen-tal results.

3 Standard FCM

In this section, we give a brief overview of the standard FCM clustering algorithm. It was first introduced by Dunn [10] and later extended by Bezdek [11]. Its object-ive is to partition data in such a way that the data points within one cluster are as similar to each as possible and as far away as it can be from the data points of other clusters. In the context of our work, the FCM approach can be formulated as follows. Let us consider an image (or MRI data volume) composed of a set of N points (voxels). Let us suppose that this volume has to be seg-mented into K ($K \geq 2$) classes, in a fuzzy fashion. This means that a point i does not necessarily belong to one of the K classes, but can partially belong to several ones. For each point $i \in N$, let $(u_{ic})_{c=1}^{K} = (u_{i1}, u_{i2}, \ldots, u_{iK})$ be the memberships of the point i with respect to these K classes, such that $\sum_{c=1}^{K} u_{ic} = 1$ and $u_{ic} \in [0, 1]$. For each class c let v_c be the centroid (class center) of this class (this usually corresponds to the mean value of this class's points). In the FCM approach, the segmentation process of the image (volume) can be defined as the minimization of the energy function

$$J_{FCM} = \sum_{c=1}^{K} \sum_{i=1}^{N} u_{ic}^{m} \|y_i - v_c\|^2. \tag{1}$$

The parameter m is a weighting exponent on each fuzzy membership and determines the amount of fuzzi-ness of the resulting classification (typically set to 2). This function in (1) can be easily minimized using the Lagrange multiplier (λ), so the constrained optimization becomes

$$F_{FCM} = \sum_{c=1}^{K} \sum_{i=1}^{N} u_{ic}^{2} \|y_i - v_C\|^2 + \lambda(1 - \sum_{c=1}^{K} u_{ic}). \tag{2}$$

A solution can be obtained by alternatively computing the membership ratios u_{ic} and the centroids v_c until convergence as follows:

$$v_c = \frac{\sum_{i=1}^{N} u_{ic}^2 y_i}{\sum_{i=1}^{N} u_{ic}^2}, \tag{3}$$

$$u_{ic} = \frac{1/d_{ic}}{\sum_{j=1}^{K} 1/d_{ij}}, \tag{4}$$

where $d_{ic} = \|y_i - v_C\|$.

The memberships are often initialized with random values between 0 and 1, such that the constraint of the membership is satisfied. The FCM objective function is minimized when high membership values are assigned to points whose intensities are close to the centroid of its particular class, and low membership values are assigned when a point's intensity is far from the centroid.

4 Proposed approach

The proposed method is based on a new formulation of the objective function of the standard FCM algorithm in (1) in order to incorporate *a priori* information. The new objective function is given by

$$J = \sum_{c=1}^{K} \sum_{i=1}^{N} g(v_c; \theta_c)\, u_{ic}^m \|y_i - v_c\|^2. \tag{5}$$

The functional term $g(v_c; \theta)$ models the available prior information about the class center v_c with any necessary parameters encapsulated in θ_c. A general solution of this objective function is explored in the following subsection. Then a proper form of the functional term $g(v_c; \theta_c)$ is devised in order to derive the exact formulae for the solution parameters.

4.1 Solution estimation

The objective function (5) can be minimized in a fashion similar to the standard FCM algorithm. First, a constrained minimization function using the Lagrange multiplier is constructed as

$$F = \sum_{c=1}^{K} \sum_{i=1}^{N} g(v_c; \theta_c)\, u_{ic}^m \|y_i - v_C\|^2 + \lambda\left(1 - \sum_{c=1}^{K} u_{ic}\right). \tag{6}$$

Taking the first derivatives of F with respect to u_{ic} and setting it to zero results in

$$\frac{\partial F}{\partial u_{ic}} = 0 \Rightarrow 2g(v_c; \theta_c)u_{ic}d_{ic}^2 - \lambda = 0 \tag{7}$$

Solving for u_{ic} we have

$$u_{ic} = \frac{\lambda}{2g(v_c; \theta_c)d_{ic}^2}. \tag{8}$$

Since $\sum_{j=1}^{K} u_{ij} = 1 \;\forall\; i$, then

$$\lambda = \frac{2}{\sum_{j=1}^{K} \dfrac{1}{g(v_j; \theta_j)d_{ij}^2}}. \tag{9}$$

Substituting (9) in (8) gives the final formula of the membership as

$$u_{ic} = \frac{\dfrac{1}{g(v_c; \theta_c)d_{ic}^2}}{\sum_{j=1}^{K} \dfrac{1}{g(v_j; \theta_j)d_{ij}^2}}. \tag{10}$$

The condition of the zero gradient of F with respect to v_c leads to

$$\frac{\partial F}{\partial v_C} = 0 \;\Rightarrow\; \sum_{i=1}^{N} u_{ic}^2 \Big[-2(y_i - v_C)g(v_c; \theta_c) + (y_i - v_c)^2 \frac{\partial}{\partial v_c} g(v_c; \theta_c) \Big] = 0. \tag{11}$$

The solution of this equation relies on the specific form of the prior information term $g(v_c; \theta_c)$ which will be devised next. Once this is done, the exact formulae to obtain the memberships and class centers can be derived.

4.2 Prior information guided solution

The class centers in the intensity domain are the central parameters that all different FCM algorithms consume most of the time in searching for their optimal values. Thus, incorporating any available information about them can guide the algorithm to find the optimal values at a reduced search time. This available information can be encapsulated in a certain distribution of the class center. If uniform distributions are assumed for all the class centers, the proposed algorithm boils down to the exact standard FCM algorithm. However, if more informative distributions can be safely assumed, the algorithm will exhibit a different behavior leading to improved results.

One may assume the typical (and often logical) Gaussian distribution of the class centers, i.e., $v_c \sim N(\mu_c, \sigma_c^2)$, where μ_c is the mean of the class center, and σ_c^2 is the variance of this center, which represents the uncertainty of our information about this center. The prior information term $g(v_c; \theta_c)$ for each class is to be taken to reflect the information about this class center distribution. One way to do this is to take it as the reciprocal of this distribution. That is,

$$g(v_c; \theta_c) = \sigma_c \sqrt{2\pi} \exp\left(\frac{(v_c - u_c)^2}{2\sigma_c^2} \right), \tag{12}$$

where $\theta_c = \{\mu_c, \sigma_c\}$ represents the class's own parameters. The intuition here behind using the reciprocal is that the more likely a class center is, the smaller the objective function (5) becomes.

Having formulated an explicit form of $g(v_c; \theta_c)$, we are ready now to draw more light on (11). Substituting from (12) in (11) and doing some manipulation will lead to a cubic polynomial in the center of each class:

$$a_3 v_c^3 + a_2 v_c^2 + a_1 v_c + a_0 = 0, \tag{13}$$

where the coefficients of this cubic polynomial are given by

$$a_3 = \sum_{i=1}^{N} u_{ic}^2,$$

$$a_2 = -\sum_{i=1}^{N} u_{ic}^2 (2y_i + \mu_c),$$

$$a_1 = \sum_{i=1}^{N} u_{ic}^2 (y_i^2 + 2\mu_c y_i + 2\sigma_c^2), \text{ and}$$

$$a_0 = -\sum_{i=1}^{N} u_{ic}^2 (2\sigma_c^2 y_i + \mu_c y_i^2).$$

The solution of the cubic polynomial (13) for each class generally gives three roots. Logically, one should consider only real roots. If, however, three such real roots are obtained, we choose the one nearest to the mean μ_c.

Now we are ready to give the complete prior-information-guided FCM (PIGFCM) algorithm, which can be summarized in the following steps:

Step 1: Set the number of the classes K and the stopping condition ε.

Step 2: Based on available prior information, set $\{\mu_c, \sigma_c\}$, $c = 1, ..., K$.

Step 3: Initialize the memberships for all points with random values between 0 and 1 such that the constraint on the memberships is satisfied.

Step 4: Set loop counter $b = 0$.

Step 5: Calculate the class center v_c, $c = 1, ..., K$, solving (13).

Step 6: Calculate the new memberships of all points in all the classes using (10).

Step 7: If max $\left| V_c^{(b)} - V_c^{(b-1)} \right| < \varepsilon$, then stop, otherwise, set $b = b + 1$ and go to Step 5. $V_c^{(b)}$ denotes the vector of all class centers v_c, $c = 1, ..., K$, obtained at iteration b.

Note that in the algorithm, the memberships are initialized randomly such that the constraint on the sum of memberships per each point is satisfied. However, other possibilities do exist. For example, the memberships of a point in all classes can start with equal values.

An even better possibility is to use the class center means from the prior information to initialize the class centers (i.e., $v_c = \mu_c$, $c = 1, ..., K$, at $b = 0$) and then use them to obtain the starting values of the memberships from (10). However, in our implementation, we follow the random initialization scenario (as exactly given in the PIGFCM algorithm outlined above) in order to make the starting point of our algorithm consistent with the standard FCM algorithm and other FCM-based methods for the sake of comparison in the experimental results section.

5 Tumor segmentation

The proposed PIGFCM algorithm segments the brain MRI volume into the main tissues. Often, the tissues related to gray matter (GM), white matter (WM), and cerebrospinal fluid (CSF), in addition to the background (BG), are the ones of interest. The user provides the prior information, $\{\mu_c, \sigma_c\}$, $c = 1, ..., K$, of these tissues based on the expertise or after analyzing sample (training) MRI datasets. Typically, the BG class center's mean and variance are assumed to be small numbers close to zero.

For pathological brain MRI, the additional class corresponding to tumor (and maybe other abnormal tissues, such as edema and necrosis) is also taken into account. The prior information about the tumor class can be gathered from tumors pre-segmented by experts from training datasets. In this work, we focus on the particular type of hyper-intense tumors (tumors that have the highest intensity among the other tissues in T1 weighted MRI), but it is easy to extend it to segment other types by incorporating information about their characteristics.

When the PIGFCM algorithm has converged, a defuzzification process takes place in order to convert the fuzzy memberships to crisp. The maximum membership procedure is typically the method employed for this purpose, assigning a point i to the class C with the highest membership: $C_i = \arg_c \max\{u_{ic}\}$, $c = 1, ..., K$.

The resulting segmented volume of the tumor class is then subjected to some post-processing in order to isolate the tumor. First, morphological operations (opening followed by hole filling) are employed to remove the isolated voxels and very small objects throughout the volume. Then a connecting component technique is applied to extract all the connected shapes in the volume. The largest component is finally presented as the desired tumor isolated from the input pathological MRI volume.

6 Experimental results

In this section, the performance of the proposed PIGFCM is evaluated for the segmentation of normal and pathological brain MRI volumes. As there are publically available standard benchmark datasets of normal synthetic and real human brain MRI volumes with known ground truth, our first series of experiments are directed to the automatic segmentation of normal brain tissues. The proposed algorithm is first applied to 3D synthetic MRI phantoms from the BrainWeb [15]. These phantoms are T1-weighted-type MRI datasets that are realistic simulations of MRI acquisition with different levels of noise and intensity non-uniformity. They also have a ground truth volume which is used to quantify the performance of different segmentation algorithms. The algorithm is then applied to real human brain MRI volumes from the Internet Brain Segmentation Repository (IBSR) [16]. This segmentation repository provides real datasets along with their ground truth segmentation as obtained by human experts. Several experiments are conducted to demonstrate the performance of the proposed algorithm in terms of accuracy, robustness against noise, and convergence speed.

The performance of the proposed algorithm on both BrainWeb and IBSR datasets is compared with some reported fuzzy approaches: the standard FCM algorithm and the FCM algorithm with incorporated neighborhood information (NFCM) [12]. The latter algorithm is selected because it is one of the most notable FCM-based algorithms imposing spatial constraints. It is implemented and run using its best working parameters. In addition, the proposed algorithm is compared with the recent non-local FCM family of algorithms [13] (NLFCM, NL-R-FCM, and NL-Reg), and Robust Fuzzy C-means algorithm (RFCM) [39], as well as the non-fuzzy methods of expectation-maximization segmentation (EMS) [40], hidden Markov chains (HMC) [41], and statistical parametric mapping (SPM5) [42].

The second series of our experiments are carried out to evaluate the proposed algorithm performance in detecting tumors from pathological brain MRI datasets. In this case, to the best of our knowledge, there are no publically available benchmark datasets of brain MRI with tumors along with their ground truth segmentations. Thus, in order to evaluate our algorithm, we use a real MRI dataset from IBSR [16] and another from a local MRI scan center in Luxor, Egypt. The performance on these datasets is assessed by two expert radiologists from Assiut University Medical Hospital.

6.1 Simulated normal MRI segmentation

Here, the brain web datasets [15] are used. Volumes in these datasets are defined at a 1-mm isotropic voxel grid, with dimensions $217 \times 181 \times 181$. The BrainWeb site provides a fuzzy tissue membership volume that represents the ground truth for each tissue class. Twenty different T1-weighted MRI volumes with noise levels ranging from 0% to 9%, and bias field from 0% to 40% are used for the experiment here. Out of those, 10 volumes are used to collect the prior information. The obtained information includes the mean μ_c and its variance σ_c of each class center. Figure 1 shows a slice of one such volume and the obtained segmentation result using the proposed algorithm.

The performance of the algorithm is assessed using two accuracy metrics: The first is the RMSE between the obtained segmentation memberships and the ground truth memberships, computed for all classes and over all the volume voxels. The second is the popular Kappa Index or (Dice similarity coefficient) [43] defined as

$$D = \frac{2|M \cap G|}{(|M| + |G|)}, \qquad (14)$$

where M refers to the segmented tissue, and G refers to the ground truth tissue. Note that the Dice metric is defined for hard memberships. Therefore, to apply it, we employ the maximum membership rule on each point's memberships as obtained from the fuzzy algorithm. The value of Dice ranges from [0,1], with 0 for no similarity, and 1 for full similarity.

The proposed algorithm is compared against a collection of algorithms, including the standard FCM, NFCM, the recent non-local FCM family of algorithms [13] (NLFCM, NL-R-FCM, and NL-Reg), and Robust Fuzzy C-means algorithm (RFCM) [39], as well as the non-fuzzy methods

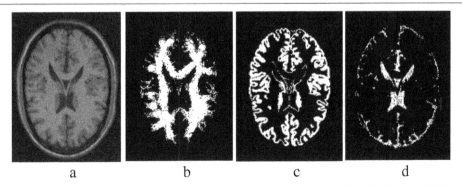

Figure 1 Evaluation of the proposed algorithm on a simulated normal MRI volume. (a) One slice of a volume with 9% noise and 40% RF bias. **(b)** Segmented WM. **(c)** Segmented GM. **(d)** Segmented CSF.

Table 1 Comparison between various methods and proposed PIGFCM on the BrainWeb database

Algorithm	Noise level (%)											
	WM						GM					
	0	1	3	5	7	9	0	1	3	5	7	9
SPM5 [20]	0.91	0.95	0.95	0.93	0.90	0.86	0.91	0.94	0.93	0.92	0.88	0.85
EMS [42]	0.87	0.91	0.93	0.92	0.90	0.85	0.83	0.91	0.92	0.92	0.89	0.87
HMC [19]	0.97	0.97	0.93	0.94	0.92	0.92	0.97	0.97	0.96	0.94	0.93	0.92
FCM [11]	0.87	0.86	0.84	0.81	0.79	0.75	0.87	0.85	0.84	0.81	0.80	0.77
NFCM [12]	0.95	0.94	0.93	0.92	0.90	0.87	0.93	0.90	0.89	0.87	0.86	0.84
NL-Reg [13]	0.73	0.73	0.73	0.73	0.73	0.73	0.65	0.65	0.64	0.64	0.63	063
NL-R_FCM [13]	0.97	0.95	0.95	0.94	0.92	0.91	0.96	0.95	0.94	0.93	0.9	88
NL-FCM [13]	0.98	0.96	0.95	0.93	0.90	0.82	0.94	0.93	0.92	0.90	0.88	0.78
PIGFCM	0.98	0.98	0.97	0.95	0.94	0.93	0.96	0.95	0.94	0.92	0.90	0.87

of expectation-maximization segmentation (EMS) [40], hidden Markov chains (HMC) [41], and statistical parametric mapping (SPM5) [42]. Table 1 lists the average Dice metric on the segmented WM and GM classes for all these algorithms on the T1 BrainWeb database with 20% inhomogeneity under various noise levels.

From these results one can notice that the proposed PIGFCM algorithm has the best overall performance among all algorithms in terms of accuracy thanks to incorporating the class center prior information. This clearly shows that the proposed algorithm outperforms not only well-known fuzzy approaches, such as the standard FCM, NFCM, and NLFCM algorithms, but also key non-fuzzy approaches, such as EMS and HMC.

As previously outlined in the PIGFCM algorithm, the initialization of the class centers was done randomly thus making the starting point of our algorithm consistent with those of the standard FCM and NFCM algorithms. It is however of interest to study the effect of initialization on the three algorithms. As such, another experiment has been conducted to compare the effect of initialization on PIGFCM and the other fuzzy algorithms: standard FCM and NFCM. The average Dice and RMSE metrics over all the three brain tissues and all the test volumes for the three algorithms are tabulated in the upper part of Table 2. The three algorithms are also compared in terms of convergence speed using a pc with a 1.7-Hz P4 processor and 1-GB RAM. The running times are also given in Table 2.

From these results, one can notice that the NFCM has better results than the standard FCM algorithm. However, the proposed PIGFCM algorithm provides the best accuracy (smallest RMSE and highest Dice). Although the NFCM corrects for the effect of the MRI bias field on the segmentation accuracy [12], the proposed algorithm (which does not) provides considerably superior performance. Moreover, it has a faster trend to converge; it needs less than 0.17 of the time needed by the NFCM algorithm, and about 0.81 of the FCM algorithm. NFCM

takes rather a long time due to the more complicated calculations needed to be made at each iteration. Clearly the incorporation of the prior information about the class centers has indeed improved the segmentation accuracy of the brain tissues, and guided the algorithm to reach the proper solution faster.

The same experiment is repeated for the algorithms: FCM, NFCM, and the proposed PIGFCM after being initialized using the prior information about the class centers (i.e., $v_c = \mu_c$, $c = 1, ..., K$, at $b = 0$). Again, the segmentation accuracy and the time performance are recorded for the three algorithms; see the lower part of Table 2. One can clearly notice that the initialization has no significant effect on the accuracy, which is a good feature of the three algorithms. On the other hand, the different (and better) initialization has indeed affected the time performances positively, where the time consumed by each algorithm has dropped considerably (about three to four times of improvement).

The robustness against the noise levels is evaluated using a simulated brain MRI volume from the Brain-Web with 0% noise level and 0% bias field to produce a number of noisy volumes by adding a normal noise with zero mean and standard deviation ranging from 0 to 50. At each noise standard deviation, the three algorithms are applied and the two accuracy measures are recorded. This

Table 2 Comparison between FCM, NFCM, and PIGFCM algorithms concerning initialization

Initialization	Algorithm	Average dice	Average RMSE	Average time (s)
Random	FCM [11]	0.86	0.115	135
	NFCM [12]	0.91	0.100	670
	PIGFCM	0.95	0.075	110
Prior information	FCM [11]	0.86	0.111	41
	NFCM [12]	0.92	0.098	221
	PIGFCM	0.97	0.060	25

is repeated 10 times for each noise standard deviation. Figure 2a graphs the average RMSE for the three algorithms, while Figure 2b plots the average Dice metric. The NFCM algorithm demonstrates somewhat better robustness against noise than FCM due to the inclusion of the neighborhood constraint that has a noise-smoothing effect. However, it is clear that the PIGFCM algorithm is the most robust among the three algorithms due to incorporating the class center priors that has a regularization effect on the algorithm output. Even at a high noise standard deviation of 50, the average RMSE of PIGFCM is only 0.8 of that of the NFCM algorithm.

6.2 Real normal MRI segmentation

The proposed algorithm is applied to 20 real MRI volumes obtained from IBSR [16] for different subjects. The volumes in these datasets are defined at a 1-mm isotropic voxel grid, with dimensions $256 \times 256 \times Z$, where Z ranges from 55 to 67 with 3.1-mm slice thickness. The ground truth segmentation of each volume as obtained by expert radiologists is also available. The prior information for each class center of the three main brain tissues is estimated from 10 volumes. The outputs of the proposed algorithm and several algorithms are assessed using the 10 remaining MRI volumes. The algorithms under

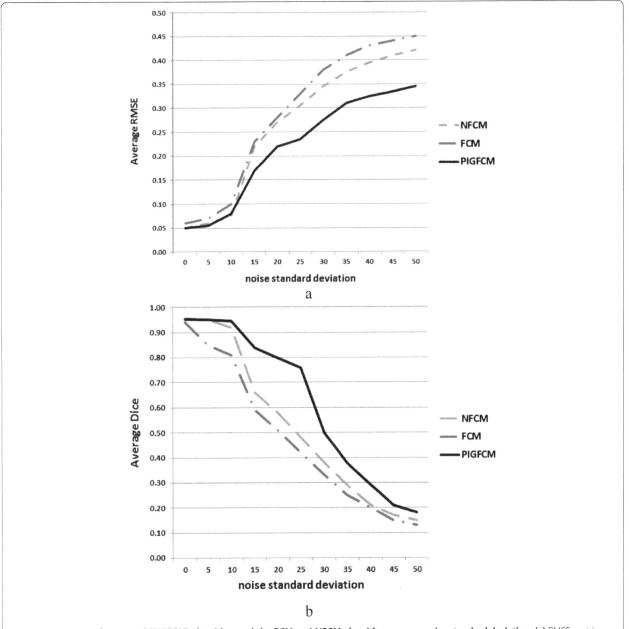

Figure 2 Accuracy of proposed (PIGFCM) algorithm and the FCM and NFCM algorithms versus noise standard deviation. (a) RMSE metric. **(b)** Dice metric.

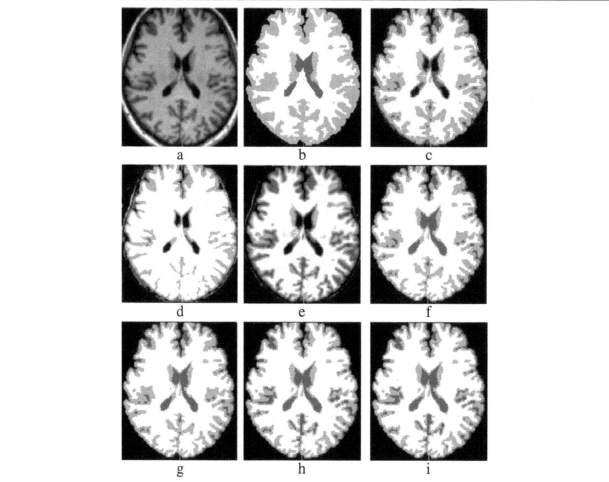

Figure 3 Results of several algorithms on the IBSR database. **(a)** A brain MRI slice of case 11 from IBSR. **(b)** Ground truth. Results using **(c)** PIGFCM, **(d)** NFCM [12], **(e)** FCM [11], **(f)** RFCM [41], **(g)** NL-Reg [13], **(h)** NL-FCM [13], and **(i)** NL-R-FCM [13].

comparison include the standard FCM, NFCM, the recent non-local FCM family of algorithms [13] (NLFCM, NL-R-FCM, and NL-Reg), and Robust Fuzzy C-means algorithm (RFCM) [39], as well as the non-fuzzy methods of expectation-maximization segmentation (EMS) [40], hidden Markov chains (HMC) [41] and statistical parametric mapping (SPM5) [42]. Figure 3 shows the segmentation results of the three main tissues: WM, GM, and CSF for one axial T1-weighted brain MRI slice using several of these algorithms.

The accuracy of the segmentation is assessed using the RMSE and Dice metrics. Table 3 gives the averages of the two metrics for the WM and GM tissues over the dataset volumes for the various algorithms as well as the time consumed by each algorithm. The results show that the proposed algorithm has the best overall performance among all algorithms in terms of accuracy thanks to incorporating the class center prior information. Additionally, the proposed algorithm has demonstrated the fastest performance among all algorithms. This clearly shows that

Table 3 Comparison in terms of Dice and RMSE measures and consumed times for different segmentation methods

Algorithm	Dice		RMSE		Average time (min)
	WM	GM	WM	GM	
HMC [19]	0.8653	0.7994	0.4013	0.4452	20
EMS [42]	0.8587	0.7894	0.3254	0.3978	21
SPM5 [20]	0.8527	0.7870	0.2832	0.2949	22
NL-R-FCM [13]	0.8435	0.8322	0.3072	0.4002	28
NL-FCM [13]	0.8468	0.7884	0.3650	0.4420	29
NL-Reg [13]	0.8631	0.8318	0.2352	0.4294	28
RFCM [41]	0.8609	0.8408	0.3823	0.4146	36
FCM [11]	0.8560	0.8321	0.2930	0.3111	4
NFCM [12]	0.8372	0.6057	0.2822	0.3742	11
PIGFCM	0.9672	0.8405	0.2442	0.2843	3

the proposed algorithm outperforms not only well-known fuzzy approaches, such as the standard FCM, NFCM, and NLFCM algorithms, but also key non-fuzzy approaches, such as EMS and HMC.

6.3 Tumor segmentation from pathological MRI

In this part of our experimental results, we evaluate the proposed approach for automatic tumor segmentation from pathological brain MRI. Assessing the performance on such a task is not trivial due to the lack of standard benchmark datasets. Here, we test our approach on two different 3D T1-weighted datasets: (1) Tumor-Dataset-1 obtained from IBSR [16] consisting of four ($256 \times 256 \times 28$) axial scans, taken at roughly 6-month intervals over 3.5 years for a 59-year-old female at the first scan. (2) Tumor-Dataset-2 for two subjects, consisting of two axial ($256 \times 256 \times 22$) scans obtained from a local MRI scan center located in Luxor, Egypt. The two datasets exhibit

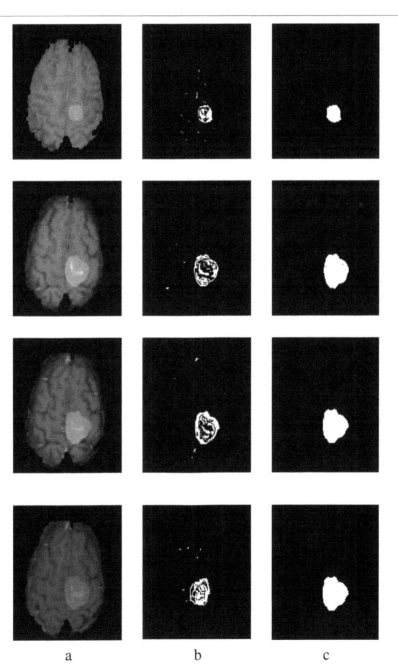

a   b   c

Figure 4 An example of tumor segmentation from Tumor-Dataset-1 volumes (each row shows volume at different scan time). (a) A slice of MRI volume after removing non-brain tissues such as skull. **(b)** The tumor class memberships from the PIGFCM algorithm in that slice. **(c)** The final segmented tumor after applying morphological operations.

tumors with different sizes and at different locations. For quantitative evaluation of the segmentation results; unfortunately, these datasets lack any ground truth segmentation. Therefore, we resort to two expert radiologists from Assiut University Medical Hospital to assess the algorithm outputs.

The datasets also have the skull as part of the imaged volume, so it is important to remove it in a separate pre-process. This is achieved using the Brain suite [30] automated software package for skull removing. Then the proposed approach is applied on the volumes of the datasets to segment each into the five classes (WM, GM, CSF, BG, and tumor). For all these datasets, we use the same prior information for the class centers of WM, GM, and CSF as constructed in the previous experiment using real normal IBSR datasets. The BG class center's mean and variance are assumed to be small numbers close to zero. The radiologists were independently asked to manually segment a small part of the tumor MR images of the first volume of each dataset, which is used to obtain coarse *a priori* information about the tumor class center. Figure 4 shows some slices from Tumor-Dataset-1 volumes for one subject at different scan times, along with the results of the PIGFCM algorithm. Shown on the right are the final segmented tumors after applying the post-processing morphological operations on the hardened tumor class memberships. Figure 5 illustrates analogous results on two volumes from Tumor-

Dataset-2. Both figures show good segmentations of tumors of various shapes, sizes, and locations.

All the outputs from the proposed approach are assessed by our two expert radiologists. Each radiologist was independently asked to examine each 3D output of the algorithm and assign a score out of 10. Given the limited time availability of the two radiologists, we managed to have them assess the outputs of the NFCM algorithm on all these volumes as well. The average score of the two radiologists for each volume (four volumes from Tumor-Dataset-1 and two from Tumor-Dataset-2) for the two algorithms is given in Table 4. The scores in the table surely demonstrate the high performance of the proposed algorithm as assessed by the experts. Moreover, the scores reflect its better performance over the NFCM algorithm.

7 Conclusions

In this paper, a new soft computing approach based on the fuzzy c-means algorithm is proposed for the automatic segmentation of MRI volumetric datasets. These datasets are classified to three main classes (WM, GM, CSF). The main key contribution here is that the proposed approach, for the first time in the literature, is able to utilize available prior information about the MRI tissues in the estimation process. In particular, the knowledge about the mean values of these tissues (the class centers in FCM terminology) is exploited. The uncertainty in this information is

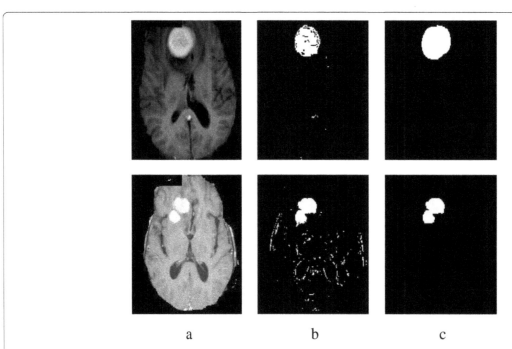

a   b   c

Figure 5 An example of tumor segmentation from Tumor-Dataset-2 volumes (one per row). (a) A slice of MRI volume after removing non-brain tissues such as skull. **(b)** The tumor class memberships from the PIGFCM algorithm in that slice. **(c)** The final segmented tumor after applying morphological operations.

Table 4 Average scores of two expert radiologists for outputs of PIGFCM and NFCM algorithms (out of 10)

Volume	PIGFCM	NFCM
Tumor-Dataset-1_1	9.5	9.1
Tumor-Dataset-1_2	9.0	9.0
Tumor-Dataset-1_3	9.5	8.5
Tumor-Dataset-1_4	9.8	9.0
Tumor-Dataset-2_1	8.7	8.1
Tumor-Dataset-2_2	8.5	8.0

also modeled in the proposed approach. Compared to other popular techniques for MRI segmentation, such as deformable models [6,7] and level sets [8,9], the proposed approach can automatically segment several tissues simultaneously starting from random initialization. Moreover, it deals in a straight-forward manner with the problem of partial volume effect in MRI.

We have applied the algorithm to the segmentation of several simulated and real brain normal MRI volumes. From the experimental results and the comparisons with other well-known techniques in the literature, we have shown that the incorporation of such prior information in the formulation and derivation of the standard FCM algorithm has indeed offered a considerable enhancement in the performance of the algorithm even at high degrees of noise. The new prior-information-guided FCM (PIGFCM) algorithm has resulted in not only increasing the segmentation accuracy, but also in speeding up the algorithm convergence. It does not require the tuning of any weighting factors to properly balance constraints with the data-driven objective function. In addition, the algorithm has demonstrated significant lower sensitivity to noise and non-homogeneity intensity bias. The new algorithm outperformed the performance of other fuzzy methods, such as the FCM algorithm with incorporated neighborhood information (NFCM) [12] and the non-local FCM algorithm [13], as well as other non-fuzzy methods, such as the expectation-maximization segmentation (EMS) method [40] and the hidden Markov chains (HMC) method [41].

Furthermore, we have developed an approach based on the proposed PIGFCM algorithm for the segmentation of tumors from pathological brain MRI datasets. The application of this approach on several brain T1-weighted MRI volumes with hyper-intense tumors of various sizes and different locations has demonstrated high-quality tumor segmentation as assessed by expert radiologists.

Our current research is directed to further improving the proposed algorithm by taking into account intensity non-uniformity in MRI data [5], which is often referred to as bias field. This inherent artifact in MRI is produced due to imperfection in radio frequency coil and also patient electrodynamics interactions. The bias field causes smooth variations in tissue intensities across MRI datasets. Although the bias field has little effect on visual interpretation, it may affect the accuracy of automatic processing tools, such as segmentation and registration. Therefore, reformulating the algorithm proposed here to account for bias field will further improve the MRI segmentation accuracy. In addition, the number of classes into which a given dataset is segmented is determined in the proposed algorithm in a supervised manner based on the expertise of the user (typically the radiologist). As there are a number of methods available in the literature (e.g., [44-46]) to determine this number automatically, seeking full algorithm automation, we are also investigating the employment of some of these methods in our algorithm.

Competing interests
The authors declare that they have no competing interests.

Acknowledgement
The authors like to thank Dr. Ehab Mansour and Dr. Mohamed Mostafa of Assiut University Medical Hospital, for their help and efforts to assess the tumor segmentation results.

Author details
[1]Electrical Engineering Department, Assiut University, Assiut 71516, Egypt.
[2]Computer and Information Systems Department, Sadat Academy, Assiut 71111, Egypt.

References
1. G Mazzara, R Velthuizen, J Pearlman, H Greenberg, H Wagner, Brain tumor target volume determination for radiation treatment planning through automated MRI segmentation. Int. J. Radiat. Oncol. Biol. Phys. **59**(1), 300–312 (2004)
2. D Weibei, S Ruan, C Yanping, D Bloyet, J Constans, A framework of fuzzy information fusion for the segmentation of brain tumor tissues on MR images. Image Vis. Comput. **25**, 164–171 (2007)
3. K Michael, K Simon, A Nabavi, M Peter, A Ferenc, R Jolesz, Automated segmentation of MRI of brain tumors. Radiology **218**, 586–591 (2001)
4. Y Zhu, H Yan, Computerized tumor boundary detection using a Hopfield neural network. IEEE Trans. Med. Imag. **16**, 55–67 (1997)
5. V Uros, P Franjo, L Bostjan, A review of methods for correction of intensity inhomogeneity in MRI. IEEE Trans. Med. Imag. **26**(3), 405–421 (2007)
6. S Luo, R Li, S Ourselin, A new deformable model using dynamic gradient vector flow and adaptive balloon forces, in APRS Workshop on Digital Image Comp (APRS, Brisbane, 2003), pp. 9–14
7. T McInerney, D Terzopoulos, Deformable models in medical image analysis: a survey. Med. Image Anal. **1**(2), 91–108 (1996)
8. AE Lefohn, JE Cates, RT Whitaker, Interactive, GPU-based level sets for 3D segmentation. Med. Image Comput. Computer-assisted Intervention Conference - MICCAI. Lect. Notes Comput. Sci. **2878**, 564–572 (2003)
9. S Ho, E Bullitt, G Gerig, Level set evolution with region competition: automatic 3D segmentation of brain tumors. Int. Conf. Patt. Recog. **16**(1), 532–535 (2002)
10. J Dunn, A fuzzy relative of the ISODATA process and its use in detecting compact well separated clusters. J. Cybern. **3**, 32–57 (1974)
11. J Bezdek, Pattern Recognition with Fuzzy Objective Function Algorithms (Plenum, New York, 1981)
12. MN Ahmed, SM Yamany, N Mohamed, AA Farag, T Moriarty, A modified fuzzy c-means algorithm for bias field estimation and segmentation of MRI data. IEEE Trans. Med. Imag. **21**(3), 193–199 (2002)
13. B Caldairou, N Passat, P Habas, C Studholme, F Rousseau, A non-local fuzzy segmentation method: application to brain MRI. Pattern Recogn. **44**(9), 1916–1927 (2011)

14. W Cai, S Chen, D Zhang, Fast and robust fuzzy c-means clustering algorithms incorporating local information for image segmentation. Pattern Recogn. **40**(3), 825–838 (2007)

15. Online simulated brain web. http://brainweb.bic.mni.mcgill.ca/brainweb/. Accessed 26 Sept 2011

16. Internet Brain Segmentation Repository (IBSR). http://www.nitrc.org/projects/ibsr. Accessed 26 Feb 2011

17. N Gordillo, E Montseny, P Sobrevilla, State of the art survey on MRI brain tumor segmentation. Mag. Resonance Imag. (31), 1426–1438 (2013)

18. P Gibbs, D Buckley, S Blackb, A Horsman, Tumour determination from MR images by morphological segmentation. Phys. Med. Biol. **41**(11), 2437–46 (1996)

19. A Stadlbauer, E Moser, S Gruber, R Buslei, C Nimsky, R Fahlbusch, O Ganslandt, Improved delineation of brain tumors: an automated method for segmentation based on pathologic changes of H-MRSI metabolites in gliomas. Neuro Imag. **23**(2), 454–461 (2004)

20. KJ Shanthi, MS Kumar, Skull stripping and automatic segmentation of brain MRI using seed growth and threshold techniques, in *the International Conference on Intelligent and Advanced Systems (ICIAS 2007)* (IEEE, Kuala Lumpur, 2007), pp. 422–426

21. Y Salman, Modified technique for volumetric brain tumor measurements. J. Biomed. Sci. Eng. **2**, 16–19 (2009)

22. W Dou, S Ruan, Y Chen, D Bloyet, J Constans, A framework of fuzzy information fusion for the segmentation of brain tumor tissues on MR images. Imag. Vision Comput. **25**, 164–171 (2007)

23. W Deng, W Xiao, H Deng, J Liu, MRI brain tumor segmentation with region growing method based on the gradients and variances along and inside of the boundary curve, in *the 3rd International Conference on Biomedical Engineering and Informatics (BMEI), vol.1* (IEEE, Yantai, 2010), pp. 393–396

24. T Tran, R Wehrens, L Buydens, Clustering multispectral images: a tutorial. Chemometrics and Intelligent Laboratory Systems, Volume 77. Issues **1–2**(28), 3–17 (2005)

25. AWC Liew, H Yan, N Law, Image segmentation based on adaptive cluster prototype estimation. IEEE Transact. Fuzzy Syst. **13**(4), 444–453 (2005)

26. S Chen, D Zhang, Robust image segmentation using FCM with spatial constraints based on new kernel-induced distance measure. IEEE Transact. Syst. Man Cybern. **34**(4), 1907–1916 (2004)

27. S Krinidis, V Chatzis, A robust fuzzy local information C-means clustering algorithm. IEEE Transact. Imag. Process. **19**(5), 1328–1337 (2010)

28. KS Chuang, HL Tzeng, S Chen, J Wu, TJ Chen, Fuzzy c-means clustering with spatial information for image segmentation. Comp. Med. Imag. Graph. **30**, 9–15 (2006)

29. M Clark, L Lawrence, D Golgof, R Velthuizen, F Murtagh, M Silbiger, Automatic tumor segmentation using knowledge-based techniques. IEEE Transact. Med. Imag. **17**(2), 187–201 (1998)

30. JY Kang, LQ Min, QX Luan, X Li, JZ Liu, Novel modified fuzzy c-means algorithm with applications. Digital Signal Process. **19**(2), 309–319 (2009)

31. F Hoppner, F Klawonn, Improved fuzzy partitions for fuzzy regression models. Int. J. Approx. Reason. **32**, 85–102 (2003)

32. L Zhu, FL Chung, S Wang, Generalized fuzzy c-means clustering algorithm with improved fuzzy partitions, IEEE Transactions on Systems, Man, and Cybernetics. Part B. Cybernetics **39**(3), 578–591 (2009)

33. Z Ji, Q Sun, D Xia, A framework with modified fast FCM for brain MR images segmentation. Pattern Recognition. **44**(5), 999–1013 (2011)

34. Y Chen, J Zhang, S Wang, Y Zheng, Brain magnetic resonance image segmentation based on an adapted non-local fuzzy c-means method. IET Comput. Vision **6**(6), 610–625 (2012)

35. K Wong, Medical image segmentation: methods and applications in functional imaging, in *Handbook Biomed Image Anal, Topics in Biomedical Engineering International Book Series* (Springer, Berlin, 2005), pp. 111–182

36. H Khotanloua, O Colliotb, J Atifc, I Blocha, 3D brain tumor segmentation in MRI using fuzzy classification, symmetry analysis and spatially constrained deformable models. Fuzzy Sets and Syst. **160**, 1457–1473 (2009)

37. G Moonis, J Liu, J Udupa, D Hackney, Estimation of tumor volume with fuzzy-connectedness segmentation of MR images. Am. J. Neuro. Radiol. **23**, 352–363 (2002)

38. J Ashburner, K Friston, Unified segmentation. Neuro Imag. **26**(3), 839–851 (2005)

39. LR Dice, Measures of the amount of ecologic association between species. Ecology **26**(3), 297–302 (1945)

40. K Leemput, F Maes, D Vandermeulen, P Suetens, Automated model-based bias field correction of MR images of the brain. IEEE Transact. Med. Imag. **18**, 885–896 (1999)

41. S Bricq, C Collet, J-P Armspach, Unifying framework for multimodal brain MRI segmentation based on hidden Markov chains. Med. Imag. Anal. **12**(6), 639–652 (2008)

42. DL Pham, Spatial models for fuzzy clustering. Comput. Vision Imag. Understanding **84**(2), 285–297 (2001)

43. D Shattuck, R Leahy, BrainSuite: an automated cortical surface identification tool. Med. Imag. Anal. **6**(2), 129–142 (2002)

44. H Sun, S Wang, Q Jiang, FCM-based model selection algorithms for determining the number of clusters. Pattern Recogn. **37**(10), 2027–2037 (2004)

45. M El-Melegy, E Zanaty, W Abd-Elhafiez, A Farag, On cluster validity indexes in fuzzy and hard clustering algorithms for image segmentation, in *IEEE International Conference on Image Processing (ICIP'07), Vol.6* (IEEE, San Antonio, TX, 2007), p. VI - 5–VI - 8

46. Y Li, Y Shen, An automatic fuzzy c-means algorithm for image segmentation. Soft Comput. **14**(2), 123–128 (2010)

12

Suboptimal threshold estimation for detection of point-like objects in radar images

Zoran P Đorđević[1*†], Stevica G Graovac[2†] and Srđan T Mitrović[3†]

Abstract

There are many methods for detection of point-like features in gray-leveled bitmap images. The problem of defining a threshold for acceptance or rejection of the results is usually neglected or left to experts. In this paper, a novel method of estimating suboptimal detection threshold values is proposed. It is based on overlapping the results of two or three different methods parametrized with respective thresholds. The quality functions (of two or three variables), whose global extrema (maximum) approximately correspond to the suboptimal levels of thresholds for the used methods, are defined. This method was applied to a series of the bitmaps generated by a radar sensor and by simulated bitmaps.

Keywords: Image processing; Auto-correlation and correlation methods; Template matching; Automatic threshold; Point detection

1 Introduction

To alleviate the problem of detection and identification of potentially problematic structures in maritime traffic, the Automatic Identification System (AIS) has been introduced into service 15 years ago. However, not all objects at sea have an AIS transceiver; moreover, some deliberately avoid using it, trying to squeeze through a network of radars. There is a great probability that some of these vehicles have been designed to be difficult for detection and localization in space by any sensor (e.g., visual, radar, sonar, or infrared sensor systems). The speed of these vehicles can be below 5 knots, making them hard to detect even with radars with moving target indication (MTI, Doppler) processing. Merchant ships are equipped with classic maritime radars, which usually do not include any kind of MTI processing. This kind of system is commonly used in maritime traffic control centers. The radar operator has to adjust various parameters: gain, brilliance, anti-clutter sea, anti-clutter rain, and tune (manually or in automatic mode) without any guarantee that these objects will be detected.

Many papers deal with image enhancement methods in the form of clutter-reduction techniques. They can be divided in three main categories: based on image processing, based on statistical signal processing [1,2] and constant false alarm rate (CFAR) systems [3,4], and based on artificial neural networks (ANNs), like in [5,6], which are relatively new.

The clutter-reduction methods usually delete objects with small reflections and with high fluctuations. Several classical methods of processing and detecting objects in radar images are presented in [7].

The approach in this paper is an attempt to deal with a raw, nonfiltered radar image in order to do detection of problematic objects. Enhanced detection of small, point-like objects in gray-leveled bitmaps from radar images is a focus of this research.

Reflection of electromagnetic energy from small objects is very low and has large fluctuations in the intensity and distribution around the object. This phenomenon leads to a situation where small objects are hard to be detected by classical methods. It is likely that such objects would not be noticed or detected (i.e., declared as a plot).

Methods based on image processing techniques are used in this paper. The problem of selecting point-like objects in bitmaps belongs to the class of fundamental problems in computer vision systems. In [8], it is pointed at several categories of approaches to this problem. One

*Correspondence: dzoran1@gmail.com
†Equal contributor
[1]Horizon Systems - workshop for HW/SW development, Pirot, Serbia, Knjaza Milosa 2 ulaz 2 stan 27, 18300 Pirot, Serbias
Full list of author information is available at the end of the article

category is based on the methods of gradient analysis, i.e., changes in the intensities of the resolution elements (pixels) are analyzed. The second category includes methods based on search procedures based on the template matching.

In a series of papers, Kenney et al. [9,10] performed a detailed comparative analysis of these methods. In [10], axiomatic approach to several algorithms of detection is shown. The original proposal was made to compare the methods for detecting characteristic points (corners). Methods like Harris-Stephens, Forstner, Shi-Tomasi, and Rohr are generalized so that the data on position can be in one, two, or N dimensions, and intensity can be from one to M dimensions.

The research in [11] is an example of using normalized cross-correlation (NCC) methods of identification and registration of images. Brunelli and Poggio [12] compared NCC with other methods of searching for patterns in the image and identified the method of localization of characteristic points in the tasks of human face recognition. An example of recent work that deals with the methods of template matching is the work of Lamberti et al. [13].

One of the practical examples of its implementation is given inside the open computer library sponsored by Intel under the name Open Computer Vision (OPENCV). Bouguet [14] in his detailed technical description used the Shi and Tomasi method to detect point-like features and follow up these features by using the method of pyramidal implementation based on the work of Lukas and Kanade [15].

All of the abovementioned methods in some part utilize a threshold associated with a decision to accept the result or to refuse. In many studies in the field of characteristic point detection (corners), the threshold question is ignored or it is taken as a predefined constant.

By doing the original experiments described in the papers [16-19], two methods are used: normalized cross-correlation and the Shi-Tomasi method. By experimenting with these two methods, it was observed (by a human operator) that the threshold values should have to be changed periodically for obtaining good detection results. The threshold values depend on atmospheric phenomena, sea conditions, and so on. It has been observed that when the thresholds were fine adjusted manually by the experienced operator, the detections of the first and second methods were close as regards the position.

This paper is an attempt to propose a new method which is based on comparing the results of different detection methods.

The present research deals with three different methods where the resulting detections depend on separate thresholds. The results of all three methods are compared. The overlapping quality functions are defined. The maximum value of those functions correspond to new automatic threshold determination. By doing so, need for human operator intervention is eliminated.

The proposed method is tested by a bitmap produced by a maritime radar located on the coast. This radar is working in amplitude/noncoherent mode. In order to do better testing of this method, simulations are made. A certain number of locations are selected to test this method. Around these positions, the intensity values of neighbor pixels are simulated to look like they originate from highly fluctuating objects. By changing the statistical parameters of the simulation, it is possible to test the new proposed method.

The paper is organized as follows: Section 2 presents the methods used in this paper. The Harris and Stephens method is introduced, and the threshold expressed in percent is defined. In a similar way, the Shi-Tomasi method and the appropriate threshold are introduced. After a brief introduction, the normalized cross-correlation method, which belongs to a different category than the first two methods, is presented. Similarly to the first two methods, the threshold is defined. Section 3 explains how the new overlapping quality measure is defined based on counting detections resulting from the application of three different methods. The quality measure gives positive numbers, the bigger values corresponding to better overlapping. In order to find the global maximum of the quality function, two approaches are made. One is brutal force, calculating the results for all discrete threshold values and a more sophisticated one using the well-known hill climbing algorithm. Section 4.1 presents the results of this novel method applied to the recorded radar image of a radar surveillance station. To deeply test this procedure, the simulation model described in Section 4.3 is made. The final conclusions are given in Section 5.

2 The methods

This section gives a brief overview of the three known methods for detection of characteristic points in an image. These are the Harris-Stephens and Shi-Tomasi, as representatives of the auto-correlation method, and the normalized cross-correlation, which belongs to another category of methods.

The example of a radar bitmap image, which is within the focus of this research, is given in Figure 1. This bitmap is a part of the maritime radar screen. The observed range is 18 nautical miles from the coastal radar station position. The radar screen is north up oriented. The values are 8-bit gray leveled and correspond to the power level of the amplitude of the returned signal which is reflected from the space under surveillance. The pixel's X and Y coordinates represent the east and north positive locations from the location of the radar sensor. The sample cell is 75 m and 450 cells to full range. The original bitmap is 900 × 900 pixels, and in this paper, only some parts are shown.

Figure 1 Raw radar image. Part of a bitmap image produced by radar sensor. The bitmap is taken from a maritime radar screen and presents only the value of amplitude reflections. Image is north up oriented, with a north east positive direction. The exact coordinates are irrelevant.

The call of each of the methods produces a result that is a matrix of the same dimensions as the matrix representing the starting bitmap. Auto-correlation methods at locations corresponding to the corners give the results that have higher values.

In practice, there is no procedure which defines the threshold, when to accept or reject the result. The threshold is usually selected from case to case relying on the opinion of an expert. There is no clear boundary. The situation is similar when using the normalized cross-correlation method. Auto-correlation methods produce a similar resulting matrix. The results are invariant with respect to the changes in light intensity, rotation, translation, affine transformations, and scaling. Featuring normalized cross-correlation is invariant with respect to changes in the intensity of the image, but not to the other image transformations. The introduced template matrix is an attempt to ensure the invariance to the other transformations.

The basic idea exploited in this paper is that the most significant (good) results of all applied methods have best overlap only for certain levels of thresholds. Thresholds for each of the methods and functions of overlapping quality are defined.

If there is a maximum of the quality function, there is the best match of the results of the applied methods.

In other words, the optimal thresholds are obtained for all three methods.

2.1 Harris-Stephens auto-correlation method

This auto-correlation method is proposed in [20]. Revisiting the research of Moravec [21], a function designed to detect both edges and corners as a linear combination of determinant and trace of μ squared is proposed. Starting from a bitmap image represented by matrix $A(x, y)$, matrix $G(p)$ is calculated as:

$$G(p) = G(p_x, p_y) = \sum_{x=p_x-\omega_x}^{p_x+\omega_x} \sum_{y=p_y-\omega_y}^{p_y+\omega_y} \begin{bmatrix} I_x^2 & I_xI_y \\ I_xI_y & I_y^2 \end{bmatrix}, \quad (1)$$

observing conditions:

- $(\min(x) + \omega_x) < p_x < (\max(x) - \omega_x)$ and
- $(\min(y) + \omega_y) < p_y < (\max(y) - \omega_y)$.

I_x and I_y from Equation 1 are defined in Equations 2 and 3, respectively:

$$I_x = I_x(x, y) = \frac{A(x+1, y) - A(x-1, y)}{2}, \quad (2)$$

$$I_y = I_y(x, y) = \frac{A(x, y+1) - A(x, y-1)}{2}. \quad (3)$$

Matrix $G(p)$ can be represented in the form:

$$G(p) = \begin{bmatrix} a & c \\ c & b \end{bmatrix}. \quad (4)$$

The measure of corner (or edge) quality is calculated according to [20] as:

$$R(p_x, p_y) = \det(G(p)) - k \cdot \text{trace}^2(G(p)) = ab - c^2 - k(a+b)^2, \quad (5)$$

where k is the empirical constant. Threshold T_h for the Harris-Stephens auto-correlation method can be defined as:

$$T_h = R_{\min} + \frac{(R_{\max} - R_{\min}) \cdot T_H}{100}, \quad (6)$$

where T_H represents the relative threshold expressed in percents. It is required for Equation 6 to find the minimal and maximal values of $R(p)$, labeled as $R_{\min}$ and $R_{\max}$, respectively. When threshold is applied to $R(p)$, values greater than T_h are taken as detections, and values of

$R(p)$ less than T_h are assigned a zero value. After application of the threshold matrix, R is the subject of spatial filtering, where R is divided into submatrices and only the local maximums are kept, while all other values are set to zero. The total number of local maximums corresponds to the number of detected point-like objects. From these locations, a set of detected features O_H is formed.

2.2 Shi-Tomasi auto-correlation method

The second analyzed and modified method for detection of point-like object detection is proposed in [22]. In essence, the Shi-Tomasi method is similar to Harris-Stephens, where, from the bitmap image represented with matrix $A(x, y)$, matrix $G(p_x, p_y)$ is calculated by (1). Matrix $G(p)$ can be represented in the same way as in (4).

The main difference with regard to the Harris-Stephens method is the calculation of matrix G eigenvalues (7), followed by the smaller value of λ selection (8), which is assigned to all points of matrix $L(p)$:

$$\lambda_{1,2} = \frac{a+b}{2} \pm \frac{\sqrt{4c^2 + (a-b)^2}}{2}, \tag{7}$$

$$L(p) = \min(\lambda_1(p), \lambda_2(p)). \tag{8}$$

Standard implementations of this procedure require the sorting of $L(p)$ values in ascending order, followed by selection of the first N_j locations, where N_j is a previously defined constant. Sorting of a large number of points is a time-consuming operation, and it can significantly affect the time of execution of this method.

As an efficient alternative to using the first N_j-sorted elements, a relative threshold T_S is suggested. The relative threshold represents a ratio in percents compared to the extremal values of $L(p)$, and the appropriate absolute threshold value is:

$$T_s = L_{\min} + \frac{(L_{\max} - L_{\min}) \cdot T_S}{100}. \tag{9}$$

Values of matrix $L(p)$ smaller than T_s are assigned a zero value, and then, spatial filtering is performed on the modified matrix $L(p)$, resulting in its division into submatrices whose local maximum locations correspond to the point-like object locations. From these locations, a set of detected features O_S is formed.

2.3 Normalized cross-correlation-based method

The third method used for detecting and locating point-like objects is the search pattern method based on normalized cross-correlation. A matrix of dimensions $(2\omega_x + 1) \times (2\omega_y + 1)$ is used as a template for this search. Further, with $\omega_x = \omega_y = 3$, the template bitmap is a square 7×7 matrix, and it is used as a point-like object template Equation 10.

This type of matrix was chosen because dimensions of the objects that look like points are about six to seven

pixels. The selected mean value of gray intensity is 127, between the minimum 0 and maximum 255 of each pixel. Distribution of the pixels corresponds roughly to a circle. This was intended to bridge the fact that normalized cross-correlation is not invariant to rotation, translation, affine transformations, and scaling. Martin and Crowley [23] compared the correlation techniques and emphasized this fact:

$$T(k,l) = \begin{bmatrix} 0 & 0 & 0 & 0 & 0 & 0 & 0 \\ 0 & 0 & 127 & 127 & 127 & 0 & 0 \\ 0 & 127 & 127 & 127 & 127 & 127 & 0 \\ 0 & 127 & 127 & 127 & 127 & 127 & 0 \\ 0 & 127 & 127 & 127 & 127 & 127 & 0 \\ 0 & 0 & 127 & 127 & 127 & 0 & 0 \\ 0 & 0 & 0 & 0 & 0 & 0 & 0 \end{bmatrix}. \tag{10}$$

The initial task is to solve the problem by minimizing the sum of square differences (MSSD) between the image in bitmap form represented by matrix $A(x, y)$ and the template matrix T in the well-known form given by Equation 11. The main goal is to find locations in matrix $A(x, y)$ with minimum $\varepsilon(p_x, p_y)$:

$$\varepsilon(p_x, p_y) = \sum_{m_x=-\omega_x}^{\omega_x} \sum_{m_y=-\omega_y}^{\omega_y} \big[A(p_x + m_x, p_y + m_y) \tag{11}$$
$$- T(\omega_x + m_x, \omega_y + m_y) \big]^2.$$

Dimensions of the bitmap $A(x, y)$ are N_x and N_y, and the region of $\varepsilon(p_x, p_y)$ values is computed over $\omega_x < p_x < (N_x - \omega_x)$, $\omega_y < p_y < (N_y - \omega_y)$. A good match between pattern T and image $A(x, y)$ is achieved at the positions with the smallest value of $\varepsilon(p_x, p_y)$. Another known form for $\varepsilon(p_x, p_y)$ computation is given by Equation 12, known as the normalized cross-correlation. This form is independent of intensity fluctuation and is given as:

$$\varepsilon(p_x, p_y) = K(p) =$$
$$= \frac{\displaystyle\sum_{m_x=-\omega_x}^{\omega_x} \sum_{m_y=-\omega_y}^{\omega_y} \big[(A(p_x + m_x, p_y + m_y) - \overline{A}(p_x, p_y))(T(\omega_x + m_x, \omega_y + m_y) - \overline{T}) \big]}{\sqrt{\displaystyle\sum_{m_x=-\omega_x}^{\omega_x} \sum_{m_y=-\omega_y}^{\omega_y} \big[(A(p_x + m_x, p_y + m_y) - \overline{A}(p_x, p_y))^2 (T(\omega_x + m_x, \omega_y + m_y) - \overline{T})^2 \big]}},$$
$$\tag{12}$$

where $\overline{A}(p_x, p_y)$ is the mean window value of size $(2\omega_x + 1, 2\omega_y + 1)$, and centered at (p_x, p_y), while $\overline{T}$ is the mean value of pattern T. To unify symbols with the previous section relation, $K(p) = K(p_x, p_y) = \epsilon(p_x, p_y)$ is made.

The outcome of Equation 12 is in the range $K(p) \in (-1, 1)$. The maximum negative values of $K(p)$ correspond to a good match with the original pattern, while large positive values implicate matching with the inverted pattern. Threshold T_C is introduced in a similar way like in the above two methods, and relative threshold T_c is defined as:

$$T_c = K_{\min} + \frac{(K_{\max} - K_{\min}) \cdot T_C}{100}. \tag{13}$$

Similarly, as in the previous section, values greater than T_c are taken into consideration while all other values are assigned a zero value. Spatial filtering (like in Sections 2.1 and 2.2) is carried out within matrix $K(p)$ where the local maximum value is selected inside each submatrix of dimensions 7×7. Thus, detected positions form a set O_C.

3 Novel procedure for suboptimal threshold value estimation

The main goal of this research is to propose a procedure for finding the optimal values for thresholds T_H, T_S, and T_C to obtain the maximum of the quality function. For the purpose of this work, these thresholds were chosen to be integer percentage values. For each of discrete threshold values T_H, T_S, and T_C, sets of appropriate detected positions O_H, O_S, and O_C are generated. Elements of these three sets are locations of the point-like objects obtained as a result of the detection procedures described in Sections 2.1, 2.2, and 2.3, respectively. The proposed optimization procedure is based on the so-called overlapping of elements in sets O_H, O_S, and O_C. Denote the number of elements of each set by hu, su, and cu, respectively.

The assumption is that the best overlapping results of the comparison of an element of O_H, O_S, and O_C lead to approximately optimally selected thresholds. To determine the quality (the goodness of overlap), Euclidean distance between elements of sets O_H, O_S, and O_C is calculated. When the distance is less than some preassigned value, it can be considered that there is a good fit.

In this paper, the approach is chosen whereby the main matrix is divided into uniformly spaced submatrices where detections are counted. The selected dimensions of submatrices are 12×12. The number of detections inside each of the submatrices for the respective method is labeled by hm, sm, and cm. If any of these numbers is larger than zero then the number of detected objects hu, su, and cu is incremented for all methods (Equation 14). When the resulting detections come from two methods in every one of the submatrices, the two methods overlap (Equation 15). Equation 16 shows how the resulting detections are counted for all three methods:

$$\text{hu} = \begin{cases} 0, & \text{hm} = 0 \\ \text{hu} + 1, & \text{hm} > 0 \end{cases}$$

$$\text{su} = \begin{cases} 0, & \text{sm} = 0 \\ \text{su} + 1, & \text{sm} > 0 \end{cases}, \tag{14}$$

$$\text{cu} = \begin{cases} 0, & \text{cm} = 0 \\ \text{cu} + 1, & \text{cm} > 0 \end{cases}$$

$$\text{hsu} = \begin{cases} 0, & (\text{hm} = 0) \vee (\text{sm} = 0) \\ \text{hsu} + 1, & (\text{hm} > 0) \wedge (\text{sm} > 0) \end{cases}$$

$$\text{scu} = \begin{cases} 0, & (\text{sm} = 0) \vee (\text{cm} = 0) \\ \text{scu} + 1, & (\text{sm} > 0) \wedge (\text{cm} > 0) \end{cases}, \tag{15}$$

$$\text{hcu} = \begin{cases} 0, & (\text{hm} = 0) \vee (\text{cm} = 0) \\ \text{hcu} + 1, & (\text{hm} > 0) \wedge (\text{cm} > 0) \end{cases}$$

$$\text{hscu} = \begin{cases} 0, & (\text{hm} = 0) \vee (\text{sm} = 0) \vee (\text{cm} = 0) \\ \text{hscu} + 1, & (\text{hm} > 0) \wedge (\text{sm} > 0) \wedge (\text{cm} > 0) \end{cases}. \tag{16}$$

The number of successful Harris-Stephens vs Shi-Tomasi methods overlapping is denoted by hsu; scu stands for the overlapping Shi-Tomasi vs normalized cross-correlation (CC); and the Harris-Stephens vs normalized CC successful hits is marked by hcu Equation 15. The number hscu represents successful overlapping of all three methods (Equation 16).

The overlapping quality for each combination of these methods is obtained by Equations 17 to 20 where Q_{hs}, Q_{sc}, Q_{hc}, and Q_{hsc}, respectively, represent the quality measure for overlapping Harris-Stephens vs Shi-Tomasi, Shi-Tomasi vs normalized CC, Harris-Stephens vs normalized CC, and Harris-Stephens vs Shi-Tomasi vs normalized CC.

$$Q_{hs} = Q_{hs}(T_H, T_S) = \frac{\text{hsu}(T_H, T_S)}{\text{hu}(T_H) + \text{su}(T_S)}, \tag{17}$$

$$Q_{sc} = Q_{sc}(T_S, T_C) = \frac{\text{scu}(T_S, T_C)}{\text{su}(T_S) + \text{cu}(T_C)}, \tag{18}$$

$$Q_{hc} = Q_{hc}(T_H, T_C) = \frac{\text{hcu}(T_H, T_C)}{\text{hu}(T_H) + \text{cu}(T_C)}, \tag{19}$$

$$Q_{hsc} = Q_{hsc}(T_H, T_S, T_C) = \frac{\text{hscu}(T_H, T_S, T_C)}{\text{hu}(T_H) + \text{su}(T_S) + \text{cu}(T_C)}. \tag{20}$$

The intervals for thresholds T_H, T_S, and T_C can be changed within the values for which the number of detection is greater than zero and less than the maximum number of filtered results. For example, if the image has dimension 900×900 and spatial filter window is 9×9, the thresholds make sense if the number of detections is from 0 to $100 \times 100 = 10,000$. In the case that both methods give the maximum number of overlapping detections, the proposed method does not give useful results.

If the two thresholds are varied from the minimum to maximum meaningful values, one can form a surface which may have one or more local peaks, but only one of them is global and represents the solution for selection of optimal thresholds.

3.1 Hill climbing optimization

'Hill climbing' is a mathematical optimization technique for the iterative searching of local or global extreme value of functions of one or more variables. These procedures belong to the widely used methods in artificial intelligence systems [24]. For the experiment in this work, a brutal force method is used to locate the global maximum for the case where two variables are considered. The 'Hill climbing' procedure is developed following the recommendations from [25] and [24], for finding the global extreme in the case of the function of three variables. In this way, automatic finding of suboptimal values of thresholds T_H, T_S, and T_C was made. The main idea about this suboptimal solution is to choose random values of thresholds and then to search for the maximum in the neighborhood. This procedure is repeated for a limited number of times. The number of necessary calculations done in this way is greatly reduced compared to the brutal force method. There is a possibility that this algorithm ends up in a local extremum. The hill climbing method belongs to a special area of research and, in these experiments, is used as is.

4 The experiments

The idea about the proposed procedure was borne through the solving of the tasks of detecting objects at sea by radar which produces bitmap images. On these bitmap-based images, small objects are shown like small points. Implementing the method proposed by Shi/Tomasi has given satisfactory results, but parameter T_S in this method should be determined with the help of experts in interpreting radar image. As an alternative, the normalized cross-correlation method could be implemented in which experts also have to adjust the threshold T_C. The same situation is with the Harris-Stephens method. By one radar system, the first two methods were implemented to work in parallel. In the first experiment thresholds of the first and second methods according to the procedures described in Sections 2.1 and 2.2 were left to the operator by choice. When the thresholds were varied, it was observed that for certain values of the thresholds the results of both methods came to a good overlap. For small values of the thresholds, it has been observed that the number of detections increases, but the new detections did not overlap well. A large number of newly detected locations cannot overlap - they diverge. In other words, besides overlapped detections, the number of those which cannot overlap also increases.

As a measure of goodness of the overlap, the criteria In Equations 17 to 20 are defined. In order to test this method, an attempt was made to develop a simulation model. In this newly created test model, it is possible to set up new point-like objects with different statistical parameters which can be varied in a controlled way. By doing this, the whole newly proposed model can be deeply tested.

4.1 Real marine radar image

The proposed procedure was tested by the radar images with locations of detections as shown in Figure 1. The same figure with marked regions is shown in Figure 2. Two regions are selected in Figure 2. A large circle at the right of the image marks the region with well-visible objects. These objects may be detected by classical methods like sliding window. A large rectangle covers the area where one small boat shows reflections with high fluctuation. Figure 3 shows six successive bitmap images (successive radar scans) inside the area of the big rectangle.

The brutal force method (i.e., calculation of the quality functions for all values of the thresholds) to find the global extremes of Equations 17, 18, and 19 over the bitmap shown in Figure 1 gives the results presented by the surf diagrams in Figures 4, 5, and 6. These diagrams clearly

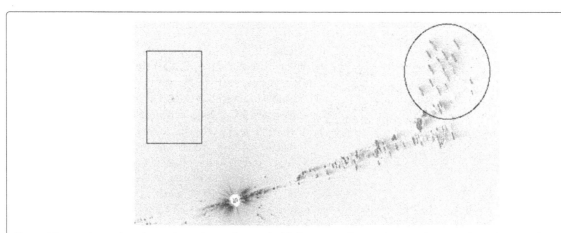

Figure 2 Interesting regions. Interesting regions in Figure 1: highly fluctuating object is shown in the rectangle; inside the circle are well-detected objects.

Figure 3 Object with high fluctuations. Object with high fluctuations in the rectangle in Figure 2 presented as a sequence of the same region registered during a 10-min period.

show the existence of existing global extrema. Figure 7 shows objects detected by all three methods with low-threshold values. The results of different methods are marked by different colors. The main principle used in this study is that when reducing the threshold, one can observe scattering detections of different methods. Finding the optimal thresholds described in Section 3 results in the image with detections shown in Figure 8. It may be noted that the structure from the center of the rectangle of Figure 2 is detected by all three methods.

To simplify the proposed method, the choice is made to use integer values for the thresholds. In this example, meaningful ranges (where the number of detections is greater than zero and less than the maximum, i.e., one per each submatrix filter) are chosen. Thresholds T_H, T_S, and T_C in this example may have 72, 52, and 88 discrete values, respectively. In order to find the global maximum of Equation 20, it is necessary to combine all detections 329,472 times.

By using the hill climbing method, the suboptimal solution is tested. The computing time has now been drastically reduced, as mentioned in Section 3.1. In this case, random numbers with uniform distribution between the minimal and maximal threshold values are selected for T_H, T_S, and T_C, and the results for Q_{hsc} are compared. If a new value of $Q_{hsc}(T_H, T_S, T_C)$ is greater than the previous value, the search is continued to find if there is any higher value of Q_{hsc} in the neighborhood. The whole procedure is repeated thousands of times, which decreases possibility of ending up at one of the local extrema. In the experiments made while preparing this paper, typical number of attempts was around 15,000 to obtain an approximate location of a global extremum. Figure 8 shows a situation where the thresholds are nearly optimal. Circles of different colors which symbolize the results obtained by separate methods show a relatively good overlapping.

4.2 Discussion of the results

The resulting surf diagrams show the existence of global extrema. The diagram in Figure 4 shows that the extremum is noticed for thresholds $T_C \approx 32$ i $T_H \approx 8$.

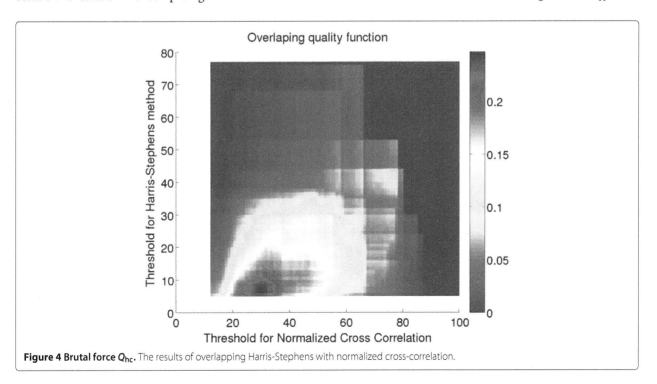

Figure 4 Brutal force Q_{hc}. The results of overlapping Harris-Stephens with normalized cross-correlation.

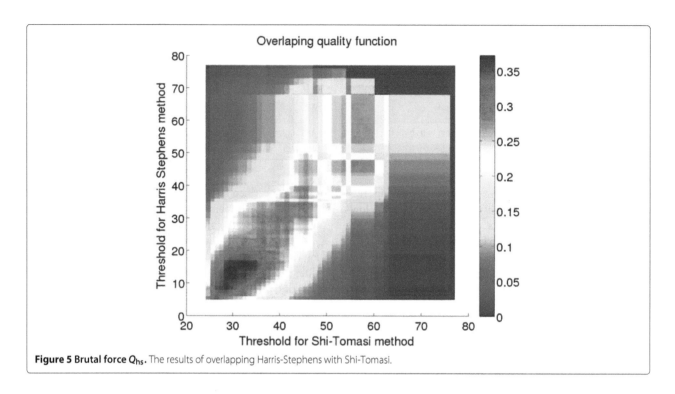

Figure 5 Brutal force Q_{hs}. The results of overlapping Harris-Stephens with Shi-Tomasi.

The diagram of Figure 5 shows an approximate location of the global extremum for values $T_S \approx 28 - 35$ and $T_H \approx 8 - 15$. The existence of the fuzzy locations can be explained that, even though both methods belong to the class of auto-correlation, the terms given by Equation 5 for Harris-Stephens and by Equation 7 and 8 for Shi-Tomasi are different. Figure 6 shows the location of maximum overlapping of quality functions for thresholds $T_S \approx 27 - 30$ and $T_C \approx 30 - 35$. From these diagrams, it can be concluded that there is an approximate range of thresholds for each method where the defined quality functions give maximum.

Equation 20 was introduced to calculate the overlapping quality for all three methods. The maximum was found by

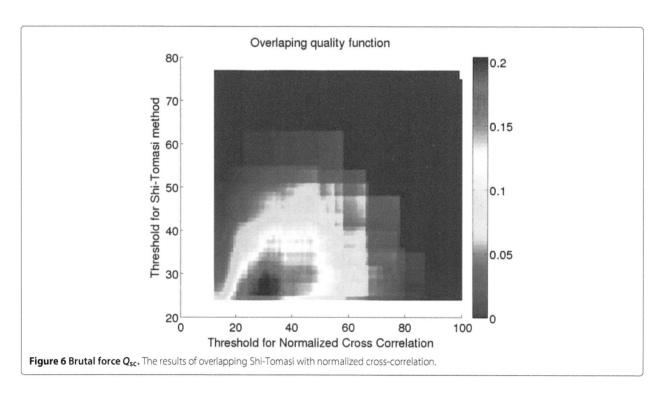

Figure 6 Brutal force Q_{sc}. The results of overlapping Shi-Tomasi with normalized cross-correlation.

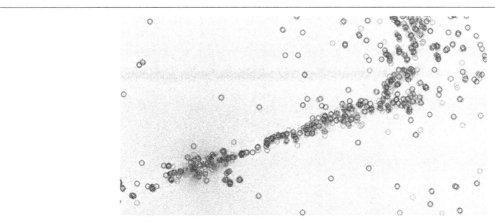

Figure 7 Detection with low threshold. The image shows detections over Figure 1, with low values of thresholds. Green circles are detection results when Harris- Stephens method is used; blue circles are detection results when Shi-Tomasi method is used; and red circles are detection results when normalized cross-correlation method is used.

using the hill climbing method. Like in the previous brutal force methods, similar threshold values are obtained.

In Figure 8, the resulting detection locations are marked by different colors. Thresholds for all three methods are calculated with the hill climbing method. The object with a big fluctuation located at the upper left part of the image was detected by all three methods. There is a chance for misinterpretation when there is only one object. To overcome this possibility, a series of simulations is made.

4.3 Simulation

Simulation is made in order to test the proposed procedure. The mean value and standard deviation are calculated for the bitmap shown in Figure 1. The mean value of 45 and standard deviation of 6 are calculated. Then, 50 new objects are placed over the original bitmap. It is assumed that their intensities and densities have big fluctuations. Simulated objects were generated using a pseudorandom generator with normal distribution supposing that real objects are small, with weak radar reflexive surface and that they have echoes which look similar to additive white Gaussian noise (AWGN) with some mean value and variance.

Over Figure 1, by using the pseudorandom number generator with Gaussian distribution, a group of pixels, of elliptical shape, with bigger axis tangentially directed to the sensor position is generated. Length of the major axis was chosen to be seven pixels and the small axis a length of four pixels. Values of the pixel intensity in the groups with the simulated object are created by varying the mean value with a standard deviation of 50. If there are values produced with the pseudorandom generator with Gaussian distribution that are less than 0, then they are made equal to 0, and if greater than 255, they are limited to 255. The positions of the simulated objects are assigned to the set Os (defined previously). Part of the whole bitmap is shown

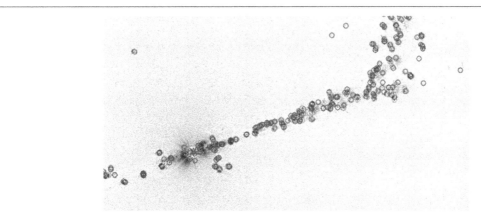

Figure 8 Detection with suboptimal threshold. The image shows detections over Figure 1, with nearly optimal values of thresholds - maximum overlap. Green circles are detection results when Harris-Stephens method is used; blue circles are detection results when Shi-Tomasi method is used; and red circles are detection results when normalized cross-correlation method is used.

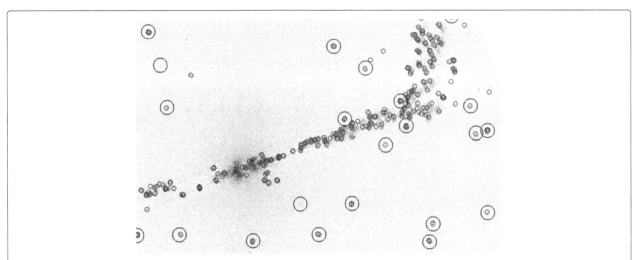

Figure 9 The original image with added simulations. The result of the procedure using optimal threshold selection over Figure 1 with added simulated objects. Green circles are detection results when Harris-Stephens method is used; blue circles are detection results when Shi-Tomasi method is used; and red circles are detection results when normalized cross-correlation method is used. Centers of black circles represent positions of the simulated objects.

in Figure 9. In this figure, the bigger black circles represent locations of the simulated objects, and the smaller colored circles represent detections produced by different methods.

Amplitude variations of the simulated objects are so specific that these locations are sometimes hard to be noticed by the human eye. They are marked with big black circles like in Figure 9.

Figure 10 summarizes the results of ten successive tests generating 50 objects and a varying mean value from 40 to

120 with a standard deviation of 50 (it is considered to be a big fluctuation). Values bigger than 120 lead to almost 100% detection. Then point-like objects are possible to be detected by using a constant threshold. The average line shows a tendency for better hitrate as the mean value increases. It can be seen that even near the mean value of the whole picture, it is possible to detect many simulated objects.

When the simulated object intensity mean value is 45, there are about 45% detection hits. It can be noticed

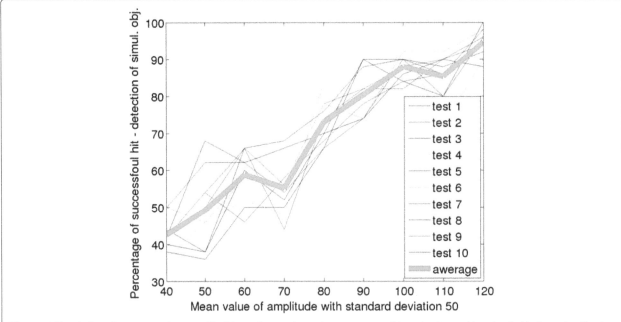

Figure 10 Simulation of ten successive tests. The hitrate diagram shows the percentage of detection by applying thresholds determined by the proposed procedure to the image with simulated objects. Standard deviation is 50 and mean value is varied from 40 to 120.

that the percentage of hits grows when the mean value increases. In the region around 70, there is a fall of the percentage of hits. It is possible that coastal objects produce this effect, or imprecision of the random generator, or maybe the hill climbing method ended in a region of local extrema.

The results of detection in the real and simulated scenarios confirmed the efficiency of the proposed automatic threshold adjustment.

Simulation of real radar signals is complex. Image processing methods are usually tested by a predefined set of test images. The simulation is made in order to test this method. It shows that the maxima of our quality functions exist even for objects which are hard to be noticed by the human/operator's eye.

5 Conclusions

The task of selecting a threshold level in a number of methods is done manually and is based on the opinions of individual experts in particular fields of interests. This paper is an attempt to automate the process of decision making on the threshold levels.

The starting point is the assumption that each of the methods for a certain threshold of acceptance of the results gives detections that are valid. By lowering the threshold of acceptance, the method starts to detect details that do not correspond to the actual small objects. It has been observed that the detection of almost insignificant objects by all three methods do not match. By using the proposed procedure and function of the quality of overlap, it was possible to detect this moment, and the results are suboptimal threshold values. This paper combined the detections of the methods of Shi-Tomasi, Harris-Stephens, and normalized cross-correlation. It is believed that, in a similar way, other methods can be combined and that they will produce similar overlap.

In practice, it is proven by the mentioned experiments that in the case of coastal radar stations this approach provides satisfactory results. The proposed procedure does not work if the image has the maximum number of objects obtained by filtering. There is a need for existence of a part of the picture in which the results of all methods diverge. The application of hill climbing optimization used in this method makes the results close to real time. On the other hand, theoretical comparative analysis of these three methods is not a trivial process. This proposed overlapping procedure gave satisfactory results. Testing by simulations of this proposed method by a radar image yielded good results. The eventual implementation of the proposed method in the FPGA environment to work faster is one possibility. This method has to be tested in a real dense navigational area with a lot of small boats equipped with AIS transceivers. This will have true positions obtained by AIS and the measured data with high fluctuations produced by radar. By this test, the proposed model will be subjected to further proofs.

Abbreviations

AIS: automatic identification system; CC: cross-correlation; CFAR: constant false alarm rate; FPGA: field-programmable gate array; MTI: moving target indication; NCC: normalized cross-correlation; OPEN-CV: Open Computer Vision.

Competing interests

The authors declare that they have no competing interests.

Author details

[1] Horizon Systems - workshop for HW/SW development, Pirot, Serbia, Knjaza Milosa 2 ulaz 2 stan 27, 18300 Pirot, Serbias. [2] School of Electrical Engineering, University of Belgrade, Bulevar kralja Aleksandra 73, 11120 Belgrade, Serbia. [3] University of Defence in Belgrade, Military Academy, Pavla Jurisica Sturma 33, 11000 Belgrade, Serbia.

References

1. A Ghosh, NS Mishra, S Ghosh, Fuzzy clustering algorithms for unsupervised change detection in remote sensing images. Inf. Sci. **181**(4), 699–715 (2011). doi:10.1016/j.ins.2010.10.016
2. PK Verma, AN Gaikwad, D Singh, MJ Nigam, Analysis of clutter reduction techniques for through wall imaging in UWB range. Prog. Electromagnetics Res. B. **17**, 29–48 (2009)
3. G Gao, L Liu, L Zhao, G Shi, G Kuang, An adaptive and fast CFAR algorithm based on automatic censoring for target detection in high-resolution SAR images. IEEE Trans. Geoscience Remote Sensing. **47**(6), 1685–1697 (2009). doi:10.1109/TGRS.2008.2006504
4. G Gao, A parzen-window-kernel-based CFAR algorithm for ship detection in SAR images. IEEE Geoscience Remote Sensing Lett. **8**(3), 557–561 (2011)
5. R Vicen-Bueno, R Carrasco-Alvarez, M Rosa-Zurera, JC Nieto-Borge, Sea clutter reduction and target enhancement by neural networks in a marine radar system. Sensors. **9**(3), 1913–1936 (2009). doi:10.3390/s90301913
6. R Vicen-Bueno, R Carrasco-Alvarez, M Rosa-Zurera, JC Nieto-Borge, MP Jarabo-Amores, Artificial neural network-based clutter reduction systems for ship size estimation in maritime radars. EURASIP J. Adv. Signal Process. **2010**, 1–15 (2010). doi:10.1155/2010/380473
7. P Tait, in *IEE Radar, Sonar, Navigation, and Avionics Series*. Introduction to Radar Target Recognition (IET Institution of Engineering and Technology Stevenage, 2005). http://digital-library.theiet.org/content/books/ra/pbra018e
8. JK Kearney, WB Thompson, DL Boley, Optical flow estimation: an error analysis of gradient-based methods with local optimization. Pattern Anal Machine Intelligence, IEEE Trans. on. **PAMI-9**(2), 229–244 (1987). doi:10.1109/TPAMI.1987.4767897
9. M Zuliani, C Kenney, BS Manjunath, in *Conf. Computer Vision and Pattern Recognition Workshop*. A mathematical comparison of point detectors (IEEE Piscataway, NJ, USA, 2004), p. 172. doi:10.1109/CVPR.2004.8
10. CS Kenney, M Zuliani, BS Manjunath, in *IEEE Conf. Computer Vision and Pattern Recognition, vol. 1*. An axiomatic approach to corner detection (IEEE Piscataway, NJ, USA, 2005), pp. 191–197. doi:10.1109/CVPR.2005.68
11. DI Barnea, HF Silverman, A class of algorithms for fast digital image registration. IEEE Trans. Comput. **C-21**(2), 179–186 (1972). doi:10.1109/TC.1972.5008923
12. R Brunelli, T Poggio, Face recognition: features versus templates. IEEE Trans. Pattern Anal. Machine Intelligence. **15**(10), 1042–1052 (1993). doi:10.1109/34.254061
13. F Lamberti, A Sanna, G Paravati, Improving robustness of infrared target tracking algorithms based on template matching. IEEE Trans. Aerospace Electron. Syst. **47**(2), 1467–1480 (2011). doi:10.1109/TAES.2011.5751271
14. J Bouguet, Pyramidal implementation of the Lucas Kanade feature tracker. Intel Corporation, Microprocessor Research Labs (2000)
15. BD Lucas, T Kanade, in *Proceedings of the 7th International Joint Conference on Artificial Intelligence - Volume 2*. An iterative image registration technique with an application to stereo vision (Morgan Kaufmann Publishers Inc. San Francisco, CA, USA, 1981), pp. 674–679

16. Z Djordjevic, in *IEEE 8th Int. Symp. on Intelligent Systems and Informatics –
     SISY*. Intelligent system for automatic maritime traffic control (IEEE
     Piscataway, NJ, USA, 2010), pp. 497–500. doi:10.1109/SISY.2010.5647305
17. Z Djordjevic, A Jovanovic, A Perovic, in *Proc. 54 ETRAN Conf*. Models of
     intelligent marine surveillance systems (ETRAN, Belgrade, Serbia, 2010)
18. Z Djordjevic, in *Proc. 55 ETRAN Conf*. Modeling intelligent radar echo
     classificatory system (ETRAN, Belgrade, Serbia, 2011)
19. Z Djordjevic, in *IEEE 9th International Symposium on Intelligent Systems and
     Informatics – SISY*. Intelligent real time GIS based classificatory method for
     maritime surveillance systems (IEEE Piscataway, NJ, USA, 2011),
     pp. 223–226. doi:10.1109/SISY.2011.6034327
20. C Harris, M Stephens, in *Proc. of Fourth Alvey Vision Conference*. A
     combined corner and edge detector, (1988), pp. 147–151
21. H Moravec, in *Tech. Report CMU-RI-TR-80-03*. Obstacle avoidance and
     navigation in the real world by a seeing robot rover (Robotics Institute,
     Carnegie Mellon University & Doctoral Dissertation Stanford University,
     1980)
22. J Shi, C Tomasi, in *IEEE Conf. Computer Vision and Pattern Recognition*.
     Good features to track (IEEE Piscataway, NJ, USA, 1994), pp. 593–600.
     doi:10.1109/CVPR.1994.323794
23. J Martin, JL Crowley, in *IAS-4, International Conference on Intelligent
     Autonomous Systems*. Experimental comparison of correlation techniques,
     (1995)
24. S Russell, P Norvig, *Artificial Intelligence: A Modern Approach (2nd Edition)*,
     vol. 2. (Prentice Hall, Englewood Cliffs, NJ, 2002)
25. KA Sullivan, SH Jacobson, A convergence analysis of generalized hill
     climbing algorithms. IEEE Trans. Autom. Control. **46**(8), 1288–1293 (2001).
     doi:10.1109/9.940936

13

Automatic image-based segmentation of the heart from CT scans

Jorge Larrey-Ruiz[*], Juan Morales-Sánchez, María C Bastida-Jumilla, Rosa M Menchón-Lara, Rafael Verdú-Monedero and José L Sancho-Gómez

Abstract

The segmentation of the heart is usually demanded in the clinical practice for computing functional parameters in patients, such as ejection fraction, cardiac output, peak ejection rate, or filling rate. Because of the time required, the manual delineation is typically limited to the left ventricle at the end-diastolic and end-systolic phases, which is insufficient for computing some of these parameters (e.g., peak ejection rate or filling rate). Common computer-aided (semi-)automated approaches for the segmentation task are computationally demanding, and an initialization step is frequently needed. This work is intended to address the aforementioned problems by providing an image-driven method for the accurate segmentation of the heart from computed tomography scans. The resulting algorithm is fast and fully automatic (even the region of interest is delimited without human intervention). The proposed methodology relies on image processing and analysis techniques (such as multi-thresholding based on statistical local and global parameters, mathematical morphology, and image filtering) and also on prior knowledge about the cardiac structures involved. Segmentation results are validated through the comparison with manually delineated ground truth, both qualitatively (no noticeable errors found after visual inspection) and quantitatively (mass overlapping over 90%).

1 Introduction

Cardiovascular disease is the leading direct or contributing cause of non-accidental deaths in the world [1]. As a consequence, the current research is particularly focused on its early diagnosis and therapy. An example of this effort is the delineation of the left ventricle (LV) of the heart, which turns out to be an important tool in the assessment of cardiac functional parameters such as ejection fraction, myocardium mass, or stroke volume. Fully automatic and reliable segmentation methods are desirable for the quantitative and massive analysis of these clinical parameters, because the traditional practice of manual delineation of the heart's ventricles is subjective, prone to errors, tedious, hardly reproducible, and very time-consuming - typically between 1 and 2 h per cardiac study, thus exhausting the radiologist's capacity and resources. Even though the most relevant medical information can be extracted from the left heart, a segmentation of the whole heart (and eventually also

the great vessels) can be useful to extract a model of the organ before surgery or to facilitate diagnosis [2,3].

Compared with other imaging modalities (such as ultrasound and magnetic resonance imaging), cardiac computed tomography (CT) can provide detailed anatomical information about the heart chambers, great vessels, and coronary arteries [4,5]. Actually, CT is often preferred by diagnosticians since it provides more accurate anatomical information about the visualized structures, thanks to its higher signal-to-noise ratio and better spatial resolution. Although computed tomography was at one time almost absent in cardiovascular examinations, recent technological advances in X-ray tubes, detectors, and reconstruction algorithms, along with the use of retrospectively gated spiral scanning, have opened the doors to new diagnostic opportunities [6], enabling the non-invasive derivation of the aforementioned functional parameters [7,8]. Therefore, computed tomography becomes an important imaging modality for diagnosing cardiovascular diseases [9].

In the recent literature, one can find many papers which tackle the (semi-)automated segmentation of the

---
[*] Correspondence: jorge.larrey@upct.es
Departamento de Tecnologías de la Información y las Comunicaciones, Universidad Politécnica de Cartagena, 30202 Cartagena, Murcia, Spain

heart from CT or MRI scans. These works deal with different strategies for approaching the segmentation task, including image-driven algorithms [10-13], probabilistic atlases [14,15], fuzzy clustering [16], deformable models [17-19], neural networks [20], active appearance models [21,22], anatomical-based landmarks [23], or level set and its variations [24,25]. A comprehensive review of techniques commonly used in cardiac image segmentation can be found in Kang et al. [5]. Nevertheless, many published methods have various disadvantages for routine clinical practice: they are either computationally demanding [6,14,16,22], potentially unstable for subjects with pathology [25,26], limited to the left ventricle [11,24,25,27], require additional images to be acquired [28,29], or need complex shape and/or gray-level appearance models constructed (or 'learned') from many manually segmented images - which is labor intensive and of limited use due to both anatomical and image contrast inconsistencies [14,22,26-28]. Moreover, most prior work has been devoted to segmenting cardiac data given a reasonable initialization [25,30] or an accurate manual segmentation of a subset of the image data [31,32]. For full automation, and with the purpose of eliminating the inter- and intra-observer variability, initialization should also be automatic.

In this work, we propose an efficient image-driven method for the automatic segmentation of the heart from CT scans. The methodology relies on image processing techniques such as multi-thresholding based on statistical local and global features, mathematical morphology, or image filtering, but it also exploits the available prior knowledge about the cardiac structures involved. The development of such a segmentation system comprises two major tasks: initially, a pre-processing stage in which the region of interest (ROI) is delimited and the statistical parameters are computed; and next, the segmentation procedure itself, which makes use of the data obtained during the previous stage. Our fully automatic approach improves on the state of the art through both computation speed and simplicity of implementation.

The paper is organized as follows: in Section 2, the proposed methodology is presented; along subsections 2.1 and 2.2, the pre-processing and segmentation stages, respectively, are detailed; Subsection 2.3 deals with the extraction of the left ventricle from the outcome of the previous segmentation. Next, the validity of our approach is tested through the segmentation of different cardiac CT scans and the subsequent comparison of the results with manually delineated ground truth. Finally, the conclusions close the paper.

2 Proposed methodology

As commented before, the segmentation algorithm is based on the information available about the cardiac structures and tissues. This knowledge allows us to separate the region

of interest from the rest of the image (such as bones of the rib cage) and to obtain the statistically derived thresholds which are needed in order to define the binary masks that will be used along the procedure. In the following subsection is explained how to calculate these thresholds, which depend on the distribution of the image histogram. An important feature of the proposed algorithm is that it uses the same type of thresholds for all the slices of the scan, not an *ad hoc* set for each image.

2.1 Pre-processing stage
In this stage, all the variables needed to perform the segmentation (statistical parameters, position of the spine, etc.) are determined, and a preliminary cleaning of the images (which basically selects the ROI) is performed.

2.1.1 Statistical parameters
Let us consider the volume which results of the CT scan as a scalar function $f(x,y,z)$, where $x =1,...,N$, $y =1,...,M$, and $z =1,...,P$, being N, M, and P the number of discrete elements (voxels) in each of the spatial dimensions. For each of the axial slices (i.e., for a fixed value k of the z coordinate) the following parameters are computed:

a) Mean value of the intensity of the pixels, $\mu(k)$:

$$\mu(k) = \frac{1}{NM}\sum_{x=1}^{N}\sum_{y=1}^{M}f(x,y,k) \qquad (1)$$

This value allows us to automatically separate the air and the background from the rest of the image. Indeed, the histogram of images which result from a standard CT scan always present five to seven well-delimited distributions of gray levels. The lowest intensity levels are related to the air and the highest to the bones. Consequently, the first (i.e., leftmost) and second peaks of the histogram correspond to the image background and the air in the lungs, respectively. This can be seen in Figure 1, where the image is thresholded with an intensity value laying in the valley which separates the two leftmost maxima from the remaining peaks (five, in this example). This value is the parameter $\mu(k)$.

b) Mean intensity value of the pixels with an intensity level higher than $\mu(k)$ in the kth slice, $\mu_{\text{sup}}(k)$:

$$\mu_{\text{sup}}(k) = \frac{1}{R_k}\sum_{i=1}^{R_k}(X_iY_ik) \qquad (2)$$

where R_k is the number of pixels $(X_i Y_i)$ in the kth slice which satisfy $f(X_i,Y_i,k) > \mu(k)$. This value is used when computing the global mean μ_{global}, which is the parameter

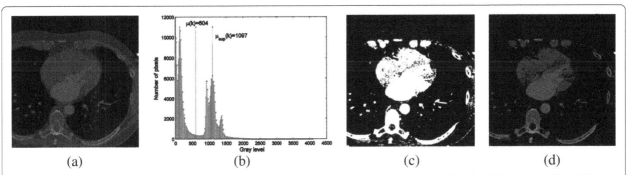

Figure 1 Example of thresholding with μ(k). (a) Original slice, **(b)** histogram, **(c)** binary mask computed by thresholding with μ(k), and **(d)** masked slice.

that the algorithm requires in the segmentation stage in order to separate cardiac structures from the rest of the image. Moreover, it is also used for obtaining a binary mask which determines the position of the spine in each image. The gray level represented by the parameter $\mu_{\text{sup}}(k)$ belongs to the interval of intensities in which deoxygenated blood and bone marrow are included. Hence, masks obtained from this parameter would contain the outer layer of bones and tissues where oxygenated blood flows, whose intensity levels are higher than the value of $\mu_{\text{sup}}(k)$. However, as shown in Figure 2, this parameter is not a suitable threshold for segmenting cardiac structures, since the resulting mask does not include some tissues where deoxygenated blood flows, such as right atrium and right ventricle. Therefore, in order to accomplish our goal, a lower threshold is needed. More precisely, the required threshold has to be located in the interval of gray levels which corresponds to muscular tissues.

c) Standard deviation of intensities of pixels in the kth slice with an intensity level higher than $\mu(k)$, $\sigma(k)$:

$$\sigma(k) = \sqrt{\frac{1}{R_k-1}\sum_{i=1}^{R_k}\Big(f(X_i X_i k) - \mu_{\text{sup}}(k)\Big)^2} \qquad (3)$$

The threshold $\mu_{\text{sup}}(k) + \sigma(k)$ allows us to obtain a binary mask which is used later in the segmentation stage in order to locate the descending aorta in all the slices of the volumetric scan. The resulting gray level is useful for separating the outer layer of the bones and the structures where oxygenated blood flows from the rest of the image, as shown in Figure 3.

d) Mean of the parameter $\mu_{\text{sup}}(k)$ minus the standard deviation of $\mu_{\text{sup}}(k)$ (in the following *global mean*), μ_{global}:

$$\mu_{\text{global}} = \left(\frac{1}{P}\sum_{k=1}^{P}\mu_{\text{sup}}(k)\right) - \sqrt{\frac{1}{P-1}\sum_{i-1}^{P}\Big(\mu_{\text{sup}}(i)\Big) - \frac{1}{P}\sum_{k-1}^{P}\mu_{\text{sup}}(k)^2} \qquad (4)$$

This is a global parameter, since it depends on the whole CT scan. It belongs to the interval of intensities which characterize muscular tissues. The reason for not using the mean of $\mu_{\text{sup}}(k)$ as a threshold is that this value is located on the edge of two distributions, one representing muscular tissues and the other representing deoxygenated blood, thus occasionally causing an overfitting to the

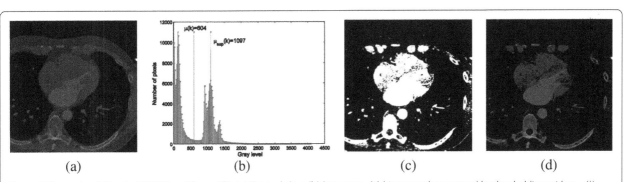

Figure 2 Example of thresholdi006Eg with $\mu_{\text{sup}}(k)$. (a) Original slice, **(b)** histogram, **(c)** binary mask computed by thresholding with $\mu_{\text{sup}}(k)$, and **(d)** masked slice.

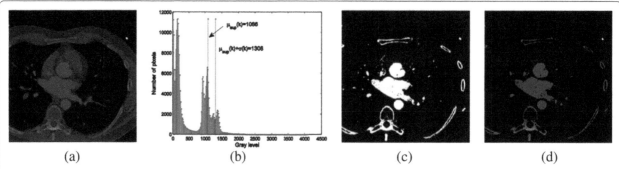

Figure 3 Example of thresholding with $\mu_{sup}(k) + \sigma(k)$. (a) Original slice, **(b)** histogram, **(c)** binary mask computed by thresholding with $\mu_{sup}(k) + \sigma(k)$, and **(d)** Masked slice.

structures of interest and consequently yielding the appearance of holes in the mask. In order to avoid this problem, a less restrictive threshold, i.e., μ_{global}, is used instead. Figure 4 shows the difference of thresholding with μ_{global} and $\mu_{sup}(k)$. Anyway, the resulting binary mask is yet inadequate for separating the structures of interest, since pulmonary veins and part of the bones are still present after the thresholding. This is addressed further in Section 2.2.

2.1.2 Position of the spine and the aorta

Once the statistical parameters are computed, a later step (which will be performed in the segmentation stage) is to remove the spine from the dataset. For doing so, we exploit the fact that both the spine and the descending aorta are present in all the slices of the (axial) scan. Firstly, P binary masks are obtained by thresholding each CT slice

with its corresponding parameter $\mu_{sup}(k)$. If the area which is common to all these masks is computed (e.g., by means of a logical AND), the resulting pixels with a value of 1 certainly belong to either the spine or the aorta. More precisely, the common object with the highest number of pixels should belong to the spine. Nevertheless, it is possible that the pixels which belong to the spine are non-connected, and as a result, the object with the highest number of pixels actually represents the aorta, which would be falsely labeled as spine. In order to avoid such an error, a morphological dilation with a horizontal structuring element is previously performed, as shown in Figure 5b. The object of highest area after the dilation is used as the mask for selecting the spine in all the slices.

During the process of removing the spine, a portion of the descending aorta can also be incorrectly deleted (e.g., if it overlaps with the mask computed through

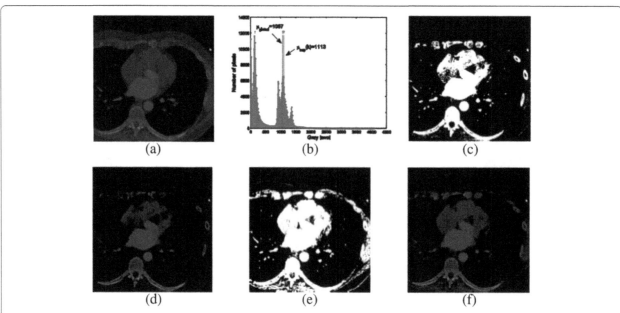

Figure 4 Example of thresholding with μ_{global}. (a) Original slice, **(b)** histogram, **(c)** binary mask computed by thresholding with $\mu_{sup}(k)$, **(d)** original slice masked with **(c)**, **(e)** binary mask computed by thresholding with μ_{global}, and **(f)** original slice masked with **(e)**.

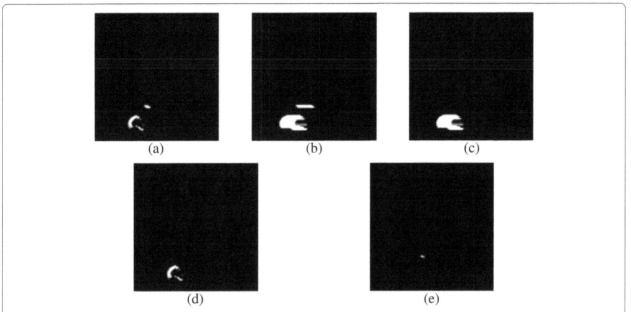

Figure 5 Position of the spine and the aorta. (a) Common area to all masks computed by thresholding with $\mu_{\sup}(k)$, **(b)** morphological horizontal dilation of the common area, **(c)** object of highest area, **(d)** masked common area (i.e., pixels belonging to the spine), and **(e)** common area to all masks computed by thresholding with $\mu_{\sup}(k) + \sigma(k)$ (i.e., pixels belonging to the aorta).

the dilation of the common area). Therefore it becomes necessary to previously locate the aorta in order to restore it after the deletion procedure. With this purpose, we first compute the common area to all the superimposed masks which are obtained by thresholding each slice with its corresponding value $\mu_{\sup}(k) + \sigma(k)$. As explained in the previous subsection, the threshold $\mu_{\sup}(k) + \sigma(k)$ allows us to select the structures where oxygenated blood flows: aorta and left atrium and ventricle. Among these structures, the only one which is common to all slices is

the descending aorta. As shown in Figure 5e, the resulting image exclusively contains pixels belonging to the aorta, which will be used to select and restore the latter in the segmentation stage. It should be noted that the logical AND (Figure 5e) would likely result in an empty mask in cases of severe scoliosis or tortuous aorta. In order to prevent such a problem, the algorithm includes a rigid registration stage, which finds the relative displacement (in pixels) between each binary mask and the following one. The P masks are then correctly

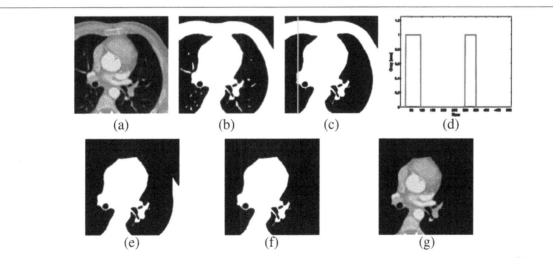

Figure 6 Automatic selection of the ROI. (a) Original slice, **(b)** binary mask computed by thresholding with $\mu(k)$, **(c)** object of highest area (column #70 highlighted), **(d)** one-dimensional profile corresponding to the column #70, **(e)** outcome of the proposed algorithm, **(f)** object of highest area, and **(g)** masked slice (region of interest).

aligned (i.e., shifted an integer number of pixels in the x- and/or y-axis) prior to the computation of the logical AND.

2.1.3 Automatic selection of the region of interest

This procedure determines, through the analysis of the columns of each image (considered as a matrix of size $N \times M$), which regions have to be removed. For each image, M one-dimensional profiles (i.e.; M arrays of N elements, corresponding to the M columns of the slice) are obtained from the binary mask computed by thresholding with $\mu(k)$; as commented before, this parameter is suitable for separating the air and the background from the rest of the image, as shown in Figure 1. Additionally, all the objects, but that with the highest number of pixels, are removed after the thresholding, as shown in Figure 6c.

Each profile (i.e., each column of the binary mask) consists in a number of 'pulses' of amplitude 1 (the number of pulses may vary from none to more than one), as shown in Figure 6d. These pulses represent the pixels with a value of 1 in the corresponding column of the binary mask. The proposed algorithm, which automatically selects the ROI depending on the number and width of the pulses which appear in each one-dimensional profile, is summarized in the following pseudo-code:

1. DO initialize the mean width: $w_{\mathrm{mean}} = 0.1*N$
2. DO initialize the maximum width to be removed: $w_{\max} = 0.3*N$
3. FOR $j = 1:M$
   DO compute the jth one-dimensional profile
   IF width w_j of the leftmost pulse of the jth profile satisfies $w_j < w_{\max}$ (i.e., the corresponding pixels belong to the rib cage)
   THEN update the mean width w_{mean} with the value w_j and remove (i.e., set to 0) the upmost w_j pixels with a value of 1 in the jth column of the binary mask
   ELSE remove the upmost w_{mean} pixels with a value of 1 in the jth column of the binary mask (i.e., remove only the pixels which belong to the rib cage, not the ones which belong to the heart)
4. IF after the processing there is more than one object in the resulting mask, select the largest one and discard the rest.

An example of the results obtained with this procedure can be seen in Figure 6.

2.2 Segmentation stage

In this stage, the segmentation itself is performed, using for this purpose the data collected through the previous subsection: the local and global statistical parameters (which will serve as thresholds), some pixels which

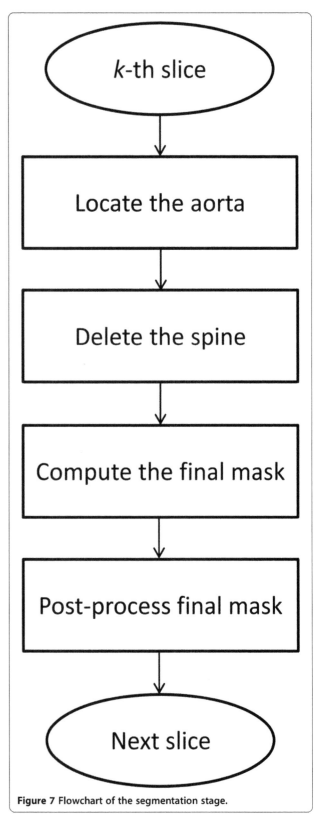

Figure 7 Flowchart of the segmentation stage.

belong to the spine and some pixels which belong to the descending aorta, and the particular region of interest which will be processed in each slice of the scan.

In the following, the sequential steps of the proposed segmentation algorithm (whose flowchart is shown in Figure 7) are detailed.

2.2.1 Location of the aorta

This procedure consists of two tasks. Firstly, each one of the P slices of the scan is thresholded with its corresponding value $\mu_{\text{sup}}(k) + \sigma(k)$. Next, the objects which appear in the resulting binary mask are labeled; the object which contains the pixels extracted in the process described in Subsection 2.1.2 is the descending aorta in the kth image. Figure 8 illustrates this procedure. The reason for locating the aorta is twofold: it is the only object of interest in the slices with *too much* liver (i.e., slices in which the liver takes up a large area), as shown Figure 8d; additionally, since there exists the possibility of deleting part or even the totality of the aorta during the removal of the spine (as explained in Subsection 2.1.2), it becomes necessary to know the position of this artery in order to restore it at the end of the following procedure.

2.2.2 Deletion of the spine

This process consists of four steps. First, the P slices of the scan are thresholded with their corresponding values $\mu_{\text{sup}}(k)$, thus allowing us to isolate bones and tissues where oxygenated blood flows from the rest of the image. At this point, the objects of the resulting binary mask are labeled, and the spine is then selected as the

object which contains the pixels obtained by the process described in Subsection 2.1.2. Next, the binary mask defined by the spine is dilated with a horizontal structuring element, and the outcome is used as a mask for separating cardiac structures from the posterior part of the chest wall (since the process described in Subsection 2.1.3 does not remove the lower part of the image). Finally, the descending aorta is added, and the object in which it is contained is selected as the resulting mask. Figure 9 illustrates this procedure.

2.2.3 Computation of the final mask

In order to segment the structures of interest (i.e., ventricles, atria, aorta, and vena cava vein), a threshold belonging to the interval of intensities which represent muscular tissues is needed. As explained in Subsection 2.1.1, this value is the parameter μ_{global}. Obviously, the use of μ_{global} as a threshold results in a binary mask which contains all the aforementioned structures, since the gray level of the cardiac muscles is lower than the gray level of the blood (either oxygenated or not). The bone marrow, which also has an intensity level higher than μ_{global}, does not appear in this final mask (shown in Figure 10b) because of the cleaning process previously performed (i.e., selection of the ROI and deletion of the spine).

2.2.4 Post-processing of the final mask

As can be appreciated in Figure 10b, the outcome of the previous step still shows slight imperfections. Therefore,

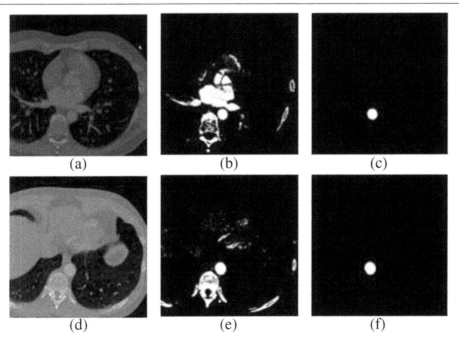

(a)　　　　　　　　(b)　　　　　　　　(c)

(d)　　　　　　　　(e)　　　　　　　　(f)

Figure 8 Location of the aorta. (a) Original slice, **(b)** binary mask computed by thresholding with $\mu_{\text{sup}}(k) + \sigma(k)$, **(c)** object which contains the pixels belonging to the aorta, **(d)** original slice with too much liver, **(e)** binary mask computed by thresholding with $\mu_{\text{sup}}(k) + \sigma(k)$, and **(f)** object which contains the pixels belonging to the aorta.

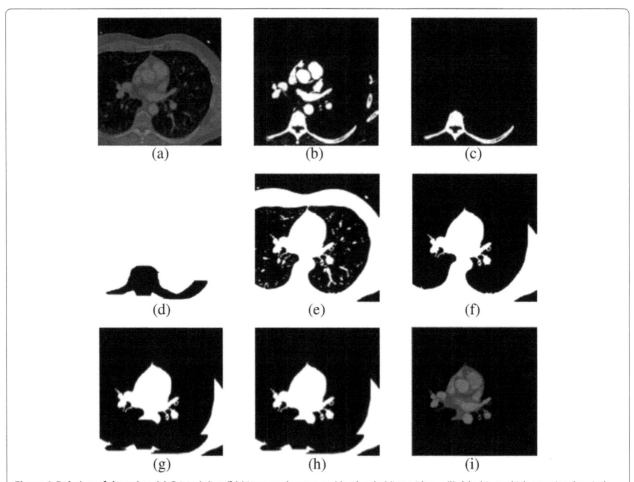

Figure 9 Deletion of the spine. (a) Original slice, **(b)** binary mask computed by thresholding with $\mu_{sup}(k)$, **(c)** object which contains the pixels belonging to the spine, **(d)** binary mask computed as the negative of the morphological dilation, **(e)** binary mask computed by thresholding with $\mu(k)$, **(f)** ROI before the deletion of the spine, **(g)** application of mask **(d)** to the ROI, **(h)** restoration of the aorta, and **(i)** masked slice.

a post-processing of the binary mask is required. First, objects with a size lower than the minimum area a_{min} (chosen as $a_{min} \leq min\{N,M\}$, which has the value of 500 pixels for all CT scans considered in this paper) are removed; the size of the objects can be easily determined after a labeling and pixel counting procedure. Next, objects with a size similar to that of the structures of interest but which do not represent cardiac tissues are also removed. For doing so, we exploit the fact that these undesirable objects are local, i.e., they only appear in a narrow range of slices in the z axis. For the kth image, the algorithm computes the common area between the $2 \times r + 1$ binary masks from $k - r$ to $k + r$, r being the axial range (a value of 5% the number of slices P performs well in all experiments); these masks are the ones obtained through the application of the threshold $\mu(k)$. Unless the computed common area is greater than 30% of its actual area (i.e., 30% of the number of pixels with a value of 1 in the kth slice), an object is removed from the mask. Lastly, a morphological closing by

reconstruction is carried out in order to fill the tiny holes that may appear in the final mask. Figure 10c,d,e,f displays the result of this post-processing stage.

2.3 Left heart segmentation

As already commented in Section 1, the analysis of the LV is of great importance, since this structure supplies the oxygenated blood to distant tissues through the aorta. This subsection illustrates how the left heart (i.e., left ventricle and left atrium) and the aorta can be extracted from the outcome of the methodology presented in subsections 2.1 and 2.2. After the pre-processing and segmentation stages, the resulting images show a quasi-bimodal histogram (i.e., a histogram which consists in two main clusters of gray levels, corresponding to oxygenated and non-oxygenated blood), as shown in Figure 11c. This feature allows us to precisely segment the left heart by means of the algorithm *Isodata* [33], which provides an optimal result with a low

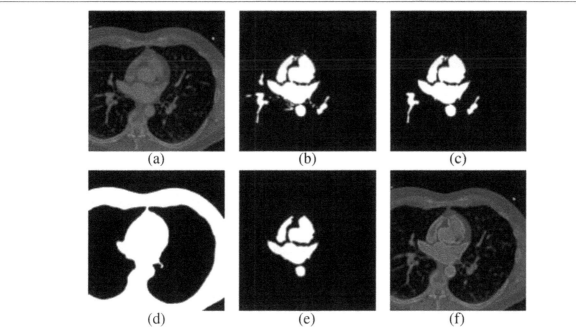

Figure 10 Computation of the final mask. (a) Original slice, (b) binary mask computed by thresholding with μ_{global}, (c) objects with a size higher than a_{min}, (d) common area of binary masks in the considered axial range, (e) final (i.e., post-processed) binary mask, and (f) segmented slice.

computational cost if the two clusters of gray levels are nearly Gaussian distributions (an assumption which is true for virtually all CT scans). The particularization of the *Isodata* algorithm to our scenario is summarized in the following pseudo-code:

1. DO compute the initial threshold t_1 as the mean gray level of the segmented slice
2. DO compute μ_1 and μ_2 as the mean gray level of each of the two classes obtained after thresholding the segmented slice with the threshold t_1

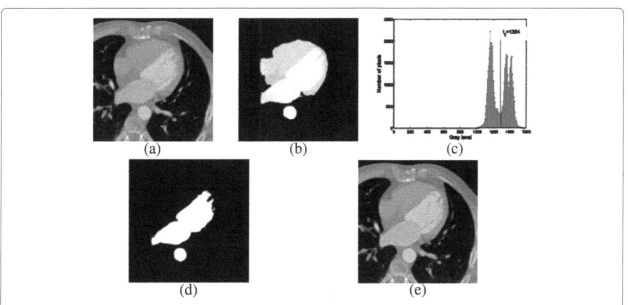

Figure 11 Left heart segmentation. (a) Original slice, (b) original slice masked with the final mask, (c) histogram of the masked image (threshold t_2 is shown), (d) binary mask computed by thresholding with t_2, and (e) segmented slice.

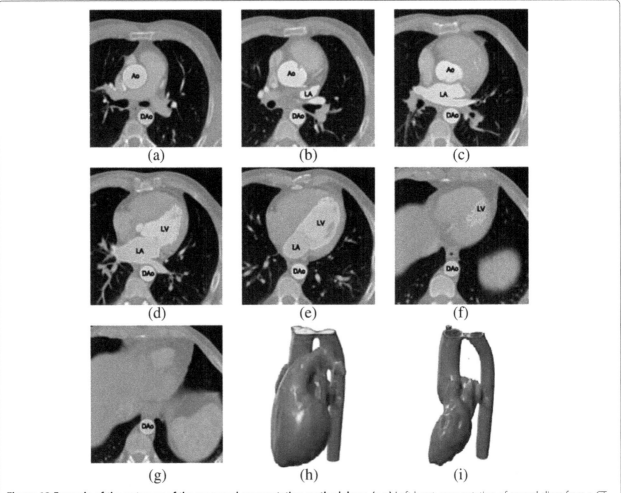

Figure 12 Example of the outcome of the proposed segmentation methodology. (a-g) Left heart segmentation of several slices from a CT scan, **(h)** 3D reconstruction of the whole heart, and **(i)** 3D reconstruction of the left heart.

3. DO compute the new threshold t_2 as the mean value of μ_1 and μ_2: $t_2 = (\mu_1 + \mu_2)/2$
4. IF t_1 and t_2 differ less than 1%
   THEN go to 5
   ELSE $t_1 = t_2$, go to 2
5. RETURN t_2

Once the left heart is separated from the right heart, the resulting mask has to be post-processed as explained in Subsection 2.2.4 (i.e., small objects are removed, contours are smoothed, and holes are filled). The outcome of this procedure is shown in Figure 11.

3 Results
Following the methodology described above, the segmentation algorithm introduced in this paper was applied to 32 clinical exams from randomly selected adult patients (source: Hospital Universitario Virgen de la Arrixaca - Murcia, Spain). The datasets were acquired during multiple breath holds as a stack of 2D + time grayscale axial slices,

using two different CT scanners (Siemens Sensation 64 and Toshiba Aquilion). The imaging protocols are heterogeneous with diverse capture ranges and resolutions. A volume may contain 75 to 190 slices, while the size of each slice is the same with 512×512 pixels. The resolution inside a slice is isotropic and varies from 0.488 to 0.781 mm for different volumes (therefore, the FOV varies from 250×250 mm to 400×400 mm). The slice thickness (i.e., the distance between neighboring slices) is larger than the in-slice resolution and varies from 0.75 to 3 mm for different volumes. All the data is in DICOM 3.0 format. The experiments were carried out on a PC with Intel Core 2 Duo (2×2.4 GHz), 4 GByte of RAM, and the computations were performed under MATLAB 7.6 (R2008a). The mean running time for fully segmenting the cardiac structures varies from 23.1 s ($512 \times 512 \times 75$ voxels) to 110.9 s ($512 \times 512 \times 190$ voxels). The mean running time for segmenting only the left heart varies from 5.6 s ($512 \times 512 \times 75$ voxels) to 25.1 s ($512 \times 512 \times 190$ voxels). It should be noted that all these times could be significantly improved through an optimized implementation of the algorithms in C/C++.

The resulting contours were visually inspected by experienced cardiologists from Hospital Universitario Virgen de la Arrixaca (in the following, HUVA). According to their evaluation, our automatic approach generated acceptable results to clinicians. Noticeable errors were not found. Figure 12 presents some segmentation outputs from our method. More precisely, the outcome of the segmentation of the left heart is shown: left atrium (LA), left ventricle (LV), aorta (Ao), and descending aorta (DAo). Three-dimensional reconstructions of the full heart and the left heart, obtained from the corresponding segmentation (as explained in sections 2.2 and 2.3, respectively), are also displayed.

A quantitative validation was also performed. In this sense, a typically used performance metric is the *correlation ratio* (please refer to [34] for its mathematical definition), which is equivalent to a measure of mass overlapping between the segmentation results and the ground truth. In our case, the ground truth consists in a collection of contours manually delineated by an expert from HUVA. The mean correlation ratio (CR) was 94.42%, where a value of 100% means a perfect match. This value descends down to 87.64% if we consider the whole CT scan, i.e., if we include the slices with too much liver (such as e.g., Figure 12f, in which the expert did not delineate the cardiac structure labeled as LV, but only the descending aorta). The maximum computed CR value was 99.81%, and the minimum value was 46.95% (the latter corresponding to a slice in which the liver was present). Thus, the correlation ratio reveals a good agreement between the automatic and the manual segmentations. Another similarity measure which is broadly used when dealing with contours of segmented objects is the maximal surface distance (refer to [35] for a mathematical definition). The mean value of this measure was 2.36 mm (with a minimum of 1.11 mm and a maximum of 6.12 mm), where 0 mm would mean a perfect match of the compared contours.

Finally, an assessment of the left heart's volume-time curves was carried out. The temporal variation of the volume of the left heart (left atrium and left ventricle) was obtained for both the output of our method and the manually delineated ground truth. As can be appreciated in the example shown in Figure 13, the estimated volumes were very close to the ground truth with a mean error of 1.22% and a standard deviation of 0.68%. It should be noted that in all cases, the ground truth volumes were greater of equal than the computed volumes due to the fact that the output of our method was tightly adjusted to the boundary of the cardiac structures, while the contours delineated by the expert followed more loosely their overall shape.

4 Conclusions

We have developed a comprehensive image-driven segmentation methodology to segment the cardiac structures (or only the left heart) from CT scans by using a processing pipeline of multi-thresholding, image cleaning, mathematical morphology, and image filtering techniques. The algorithm we propose is simple; hence, it is easy to implement and validate. All the contours are delineated automatically, without any initialization or user interaction. Testing

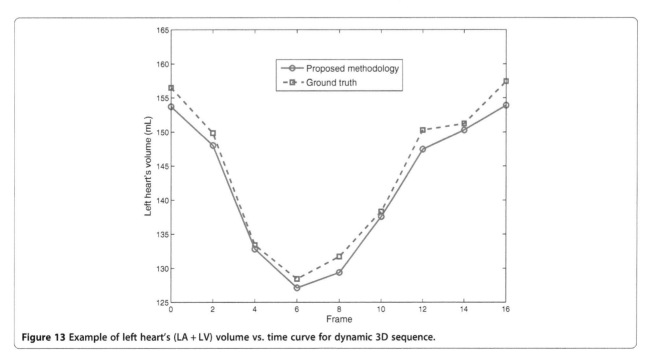

Figure 13 Example of left heart's (LA + LV) volume vs. time curve for dynamic 3D sequence.

results on the data randomly selected from clinical exams demonstrated that our approach can be computed significantly faster than other automated techniques (especially if compared with model-based approaches). This makes it feasible to conveniently calculate online the left heart's volume for all the imaged cardiac phases (not only end-diastolic and end-systolic), which in turn enables the computation of additional quantitative clinical parameters such as peak ejection rate and filling rate. Moreover, this allows for the automatic identification of the imaged time points of the end-diastole and end-systole (which correspond to the maximum and minimum left heart's volume among all time points).

The complete cardiac segmentation methodology performed well on the validation set of 32 clinical datasets acquired on two different CT scanners from two manufacturers. Its accuracy is comparable to other approaches recently published. Additionally, visual inspection by experts showed that the proposed algorithm is overall robust and succeeds in segmenting the heart up to minor local corrections.

A limitation of our method is that it only provides a segmentation of the left heart's blood pool volume (i.e., endocardium). While this is sufficient for computing most of the common clinical quantitative parameters for cardiac function, a segmentation of the left heart's epicardium would provide additional clinical information.

Further directions of our research include the porting of the presented methodology to other modalities, such as cardiac cine magnetic resonance imaging (cMRI).

Competing interests

The authors declare that they have no competing interests.

Acknowledgements

This work is partially supported by the Spanish Ministerio de Ciencia e Innovación, under grant number TEC2009-12675.

References

1. WHO, Cardiovascular diseases (CVDs), *Fact sheet number 317*. Updated March 2013. http://www.who.int/mediacentre/factsheets/fs317/en/index.html
2. MA Zuluaga, MJ Cardoso, M Modat, S Ourselin, Multi-atlas propagation whole heart segmentation from MRI and CTA using a local normalised correlation coefficient criterion. Lect. Notes Comput. Sci **7945**, 174–181 (2013)
3. S Josevin Prem, MS Ulaganathan, G Kharmega Sundararaj, Segmentation of the heart and great vessels in CT images using Curvelet Transform and Multi Structure Elements Morphology. Int. J Eng. Innov. Tech **1**(3), 122–128 (2013)
4. P Shoenhagen, SS Halliburton, AE Stillman, RD White, CT of the heart: Principles, advances and clinical uses. Cleveland. Clinic. J. Med. **72**(2), 127–138 (2005)
5. D Kang, J Woo, PJ Slomka, D Dey, G Germano, C-C Jay Kuo, Heart chambers and whole heart segmentation techniques: review. J. Electronic. Imaging. **21**(1), 1–16 (2012)
6. S Schroeder, S Achenbach, F Bengel, Cardiac computed tomography: indications, applications, limitations, and training requirements. Eur. Heart J. **29**, 531–556 (2008)
7. J von Berg, C Lorenz, Multi-surface cardiac modeling, segmentation, and tracking, in *Proc. FIMH*. Lect. Notes Comput. Sci **3504**, 1–11 (2005)
8. J Peters, O Ecabert, C Lorenz, J von Berg, MJ Walker, TB Ivanc, M Vembar, ME Olszewski, J Weese, Segmentation of the heart and major vascular structures in cardiovascular CT images. In. Proc. SPIE. vol. **6914**, 1–12 (2008)
9. Y Zheng, A Barbu, B Georgescu, M Scheuering, D Comaniciu, Four-chamber heart modeling and automatic segmentation for 3-D cardiac CT volumes using marginal space learning and steerable features. IEEE Trans. Med. Imaging **27**(11), 1668–1681 (2008)
10. CS Coscoso, WJ Niessen, T Netsch, EPA Vonken, G Lund, A Stork, MA Viergever, Automatic image-driven segmentation of the ventricles in cardiac cine MRI. J. Magn. Reson. Imaging **28**, 366–374 (2008)
11. S Huang, J Liu, LC Lee, SK Venkatesh, LLS Teo, C Au, WL Nowinski, An image-based comprehensive approach for automatic segmentation of left ventricle from cardiac short axis cine MRI images. J. Dig. Imaging. **2010**, 1–11 (2010)
12. AB Redwood, JJ Richard, A Robb, Semiautomatic segmentation of the heart from CT images based on intensity and morphological features. In Proc SPIE vol. **5747**, 1373–1719 (2005)
13. JP Morin, C Desrosiers, L Duong, Image segmentation using random-walks on the histogram. In. Proc. SPIE. vol. **8314**, 1–8 (2012)
14. M Lorenzo-Valdes, GI Sanchez-Ortiz, AG Elkington, RH Mohiaddin, D Rueckert, Segmentation of 4D cardiac MR images using a probabilistic atlas and the EM algorithm. Med. Image Anal. **8**, 255–265 (2004)
15. I Isgum, Multi-Atlas-based segmentation with local decision fusion – Application to cardiac and aortic segmentation in CT scans. IEEE Trans. Med. Imaging **28**(7), 1000–1010 (2009)
16. MR Rezaee, PMJ van der Zwet, BPE Lelieveldt, RJ van der Geest, JHC Reiber, A multiresolution image segmentation technique based on pyramidal segmentation and fuzzy clustering. IEEE Trans Image Processing **9**, 1238–1248 (2000)
17. K Park, A Montillo, D Metaxas, L Axel, Volumetric heart modeling and analysis. Commun. ACM **48**(2), 43–48 (2005)
18. O Ecabert, J Peters, MJ Walker, TB Ivanc, C Lorenz, J von Berg, J Lessick, M Vembar, J Weese, Segmentation of the heart and great vessels in CT images using a model-based adaptation framework. Med. Image Anal. **15**, 863–876 (2011)
19. O Ecabert, J Peters, H Schramm, C Lorenz, J von Berg, MJ Walker, M Vembar, ME Olszewski, K Subramanyan, G Lavi, J Weese, Automatic model-based segmentation of the heart in CT images. IEEE Trans. Med. Imaging **27**(9), 1189–1201 (2008)
20. R Sammouda, RM Jomaa, H Mathkour, *Heart region extraction and segmentation from chest CT images using Hopfield Artificial Neural Networks* (International Conference on Information Technology and e-Services (ICITeS), 2012), pp. 1–6
21. A Andreopoulos, JK Tsotsos, Efficient and generalizable statistical models of shape and appearance for analysis of cardiac MRI. Med. Image Anal. **12**(3), 335–357 (2008)
22. SC Mitchell, JG Bosch, BPF Lelieveldt, RJ van Geest, JHC Reiber, M Sonka, 3-D active appearance models: Segmentation of cardiac MR and ultrasound images. IEEE Trans. Med. Imaging **21**(9), 1167–1178 (2002)
23. AP Reeves, AM Biancardi, DF Yankelevitz, MD Cham, CI Henschke, Heart region segmentation from low-dose CT scans: an anatomy based approach. In Proc SPIE vol. **8314**, 1–9 (2012)
24. N Paragios, A level set approach for shape-driven segmentation and tracking of the left ventricle. IEEE Trans. Med. Imaging **22**(6), 773–776 (2003)
25. M Lynch, O Ghita, PF Whelan, Segmentation of the left ventricle of the heart in 3-D + t MRI data using an optimized nonrigid temporal model. IEEE Trans. Med. Imaging **27**, 195–203 (2008)
26. DT Gering, Automatic segmentation of cardiac MRI. Lect. Notes Comput. Sci **2878**, 524–532 (2003)
27. MP Jolly, Automatic segmentation of the left ventricle in cardiac MR and CT images. Int. J. Comput. Vision. **70**, 151–163 (2006)
28. J Lotjonen, S Kivisto, J Koikkalainen, D Smutek, K Lauerma, Statistical shape model of the atria, ventricles and epicardium from short- and long-axis MR images. Med. Image Anal. **8**, 371–386 (2004)
29. A Rao, R Chandrashekara, GI Sanchez-Ortiz, Spatial transformation of motion and deformation fields using nonrigid registration. IEEE Trans. Med. Imaging **23**, 1065–1076 (2004)
30. D Levin, U Aladi, G Germano, P Slomka, Techniques for efficient, real-time, 3D visualization of multi-modality cardiac data using consumer graphics hardware. Comput. Med. Imaging Graph. **29**, 463–475 (2005)

31. RJ van Greuns, T Baks, EH Gronenschild, Automatic quantitative left ventricular analysis of cine MR images by using three-dimensional information for contour detection. Radiology **240**, 215–221 (2006)

32. G Hautvast, S Lobregt, M Breeuwer, F Gerritsen, Automatic contour propagation in cine cardiac magnetic resonance images. IEEE Trans. Med. Imaging **25**, 1472–1482 (2006)

33. TW Ridler, S Calvard, Picture thresholding using an iterative selection method. IEEE Trans Systems. Man and Cybernetics **8**, 630–632 (1978)

34. A Roche, G Mandalain, X Pennec, N Ayache, The correlation ratio as a new similarity measure for multimodal image registration, medical image computing and computer-assisted intervention. Proc MICCAI 1998 and LNCS **1496**, 1115–1124 (1998)

35. S Perkins, *Identification and reconstruction of bullets from multiple X-rays* (Department of Computer Science, Faculty of Science, University of Cape Town, Dissertation for the M.S. Degree, 2004)

14

Three-dimensional face recognition under expression variation

Xueqiao Wang[*], Qiuqi Ruan, Yi Jin and Gaoyun An

Abstract

In this paper, we introduce a fully automatic framework for 3D face recognition under expression variation. For 3D data preprocessing, an improved nose detection method is presented. The small pose is corrected at the same time. A new facial expression processing method which is based on sparse representation is proposed subsequently. As a result, this framework enhances the recognition rate because facial expression is the biggest obstacle for 3D face recognition. Then, the facial representation, which is based on the dual-tree complex wavelet transform (DT-CWT), is extracted from depth images. It contains the facial information and six subregions' information. Recognition is achieved by linear discriminant analysis (LDA) and nearest neighbor classifier. We have performed different experiments on the Face Recognition Grand Challenge database and Bosphorus database. It achieves the verification rate of 98.86% on the all vs. all experiment at 0.1% false acceptance rate (FAR) in the Face Recognition Grand Challenge (FRGC) and 95.03% verification rate on nearly frontal faces with expression changes and occlusions in the Bosphorus database.

Keywords: Dual-tree complex wavelet transform; 3D face recognition; Sparse representation; Linear discriminant analysis

1 Introduction

3D face recognition is a continuously developing subject with many challenging issues [1-3]. These years, many new 3D face recognition methods which were demonstrated on the Face Recognition Grand Challenge (FRGC) v2 data have got good performances.

Regional matching scheme was firstly proposed by Faltemier et al. [4]. In their paper, the whole 3D face images were divided into 28 patches. The fusion results from independently matched regions could achieve good performance. Wang et al. [5] extracted the Gabor, LBP, and Haar features from the depth image, and then the most discriminative local feature was selected optimally by boosting and trained as weak classifiers for assembling three collective strong classifiers. Mian et al. [6] extracted the spherical face representation (SFR) of the 3D facial data and the scale invariant feature transform (SIFT) descriptor of the 2D data to train a rejection classifier. The remaining faces were verified using a region-based matching approach which was robust to facial expression. Berretti et al. [7] proposed an approach that took into

account the graph form to reflect geometrical information for 3D facial surface, and the relevant information among the neighboring points could be encoded into a compact representation. 3D weighted walkthrough (3DWW) descriptors were proposed to demonstrate the mutual spatial displacement among pairwise arcs of points of the corresponding stripes. Zhang et al. [8] found a novel resolution invariant local feature for 3D face recognition. Six different scale invariant similarity measures were fused at the score level, which increased the robustness against expression variation.

The accuracy of 3D face recognition could be significantly degraded by large facial expression variations. Alyuz et al. [9] proposed an expression resistant 3D face recognition method based on the regional registration. In recent years, many methods dealt with facial expression before recognition. Kakadiaris et al. [10] utilized the elastically adapted deformable model firstly, and then they mapped the 3D geometry information onto a 2D regular grid, thus combining the descriptiveness of the 3D data with the computational efficiency of the 2D data. A multistage fully automatic alignment algorithm and the advanced wavelet analysis were used for recognition. Drira et al. [11] represented facial surfaces by radial curves emanating from the nose tips and used elastic shape

---
[*] Correspondence: silvia.wxq@gmail.com
Beijing Key Laboratory of Advanced Information Science and Network Technology, Institution of Information Science, Beijing Jiaotong University, Beijing 100044, China

analysis of these curves to develop a Riemannian framework for analyzing shapes of full facial surfaces. Their method used the nose tips which are already provided. Mohammadzade et al. [12] presented a new iterative method which can deal with 3D faces with opened mouth. They performed experiments to prove that the combination of the normal vectors and the point coordinates can improve the recognition performance. A verification rate of 99.6% at a false acceptance rate (FAR) of 0.1% has been achieved using the proposed method for the all versus all experiment. Amberg et al. [13] described an expression invariant method for face recognition by fitting an identity/expression separated 3D Morphable Model to shape data. The expression model greatly improved recognition. Their method operated at approximately 40 to 90 s per query.

Our method is an automatic method for 3D face recognition. The framework of our method is presented in Figure 1. For data preprocessing, an improved nose detection method is proposed. At the same time, the small pose of the face can be corrected. Then, the face region (face without hair and ears) is gotten using a sphere centered at the nose tip. After finding the face region, the facial expression is removed using a new method which is based on sparse representation. Finally, the depth image is constructed. In the training section, we use all the 943 faces in FRGC v1 for training. First of all, we extract the four-level magnitude subimages of each training faces using DT-CWT. Subsequently, we vectorize the six magnitude subimages into a large vector which dimension is 384 and utilize the linear discriminant analysis (LDA) [14] to learn the subspace of the training faces and then record the transformation matrix. Secondly, the six subregions' four-level magnitude subimages are extracted using DT-CWT, and they are vectorized into a large vector which dimension is 2,304. After that, we utilize the linear discriminant analysis [14] to learn the transformation matrix too. Finally, we get all the gallery faces' two features using DT-CWT and their transformation matrix, respectively, to establish two LDA subspaces. In the testing section, we obtain all the probe faces' two features by using DT-CWT and their two transformation matrices, respectively. Cosine distance is used to establish two similarity matrices. In the end of the method, two similarity matrices are fused, and the nearest neighbor classifier is used to finish the recognition process.

The main contributions of this work can be summarized as follows:

- The first contribution is an improved nose detection method which can correct the small pose of the face iteratively. The proposed nose detection algorithm is

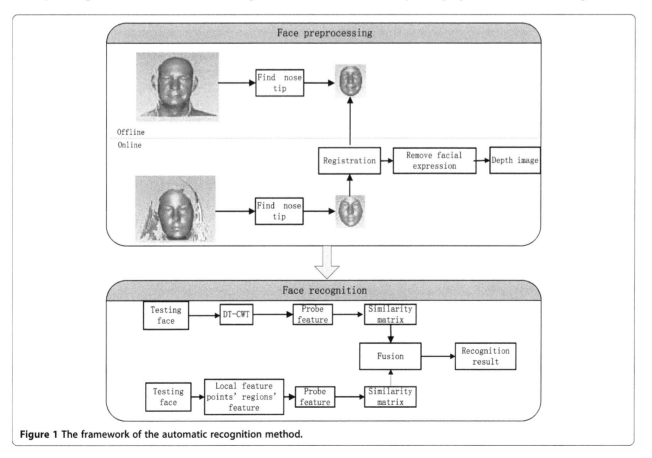

Figure 1 The framework of the automatic recognition method.

simple, and the success rate is 99.95% in the FRGC database.

- The second one is that we propose a new 3D facial expression processing method which is based on sparse representation. Li et al. [15] utilized sparse representation into 3D face recognition, but they applied it in the recognition section. In this paper, sparse representation is used for facial expression processing. The objective of the sparse representation is to relate a probe with the minimum number of gallery dataset. Considering that the first task of our expression processing work is to find the minimum number of expressional components out of the dictionary (because people only make one expression for one time), the objective of sparse representation is naturally better suited for finding the expressional deformation from the dataset. This method is a learning method that can abstract the testing face's neutral component from a dictionary of neutral and expressional spaces, and it only costs 14.91 s for removing one facial expression (The type of our CPU is Intel (R) Core (TM) i3-2120, and the RAM is 2 GB.). The proposed method is more simple and only cost less time.

The paper is organized as follows: In Section 2, the data preprocessing methods are proposed. The improved nose tip detection method is presented in this section. Then, the 3D facial expression processing method is presented in Section 3. In Section 4, the framework of our 3D face recognition method is given. Experimental results are given in Section 5, and the conclusions are drawn in Section 6.

2 3D data preprocessing

Firstly, a 3×3 Gaussian filter is used to remove spikes and noise, and then the range data are subsampled at a 1:4 ratio.

Some 3D faces in the FRGC database contains information of the ears, while some faces' ears are hidden by the hair. For the purpose of consistency, we only use the face region into recognition. Now, we introduce the face region extracting method.

2.1 Nose detection
The nose is the center of a 3D face, so nose detection is important for facial region extraction. The block diagram of the proposed procedure for nose detection is presented in Figure 2.

In this paper, the first step of nose tip detection is finding the central stripe. Details are presented in our earlier work [16].

We use the face with ID 02463d453 in FRGC v1 as the standard face and manually find its nose tip on its stripe. Subsequently, we find other persons' nose tip using an automatic iterative algorithm. Let us suppose that A is the central stripe of the face with ID 02463d453, and B is the central stripe of the face whose nose tip needs to be found. The method is as follows:

(1) Align stripe A to stripe B using the ICP [17] method and record the transformation matrix M_2.
(2) Use M_2 to find point p which is the first person's transformed nose tip.
(3) Crop a sphere (radius =37 mm) centered at point p. The highest point in the sphere is found as the nose tip of B. The step is shown in our previous work [16].
(4) Crop a sphere (radius =90 mm) centered at the nose tip and align to the standard face. Calculate the transformed nose tip $p1$.
(5) Crop a sphere (radius =25 mm) centered at point $p1$. The highest point in the sphere is found as the new nose tip $p2$.
(6) If $||p2 - p1|| < 2$ mm, $p2$ is the nose tip, else, back to step (4).

2.2 Face region
Once the nose tip is successfully found, the region in the last step of nose detection is used as the face region. All the faces with excessive head rotation, hair artifact, and big expressions were successfully segmented by the proposed nose detection algorithm. Some examples are presented in Figure 2.

3 3D facial expression processing method based on sparse representation
Facial expression is one of the biggest obstacle of 3D face recognition because 3D face has less information and some information on the face can be changed easily by facial expression. In this section, we introduce a new expression processing method for removing facial expression which is based on sparse representation. We expect that our method could establish correspondence between an open mouth and estimated neutral component.

3.1 Brief introduction of sparse representation
In this paper, we use L1-regularized least squares regression [6,18] to estimate the coefficients of our model. L1-regularized is known to produce sparse coefficients and can be robust to irrelevant features. In general, the problem can be formulated as:

$$\hat{a} = \text{argmin}\left\{ ||y - Ax||_2^2 + \gamma ||x||_1 \right\} \qquad (1)$$

where y is the test sample, x is the sparse representation on dictionary A, and γ is a scalar constant (we use $\gamma = 5,000$ in this paper). The feature-sign search method [6] is adopted to solve Equation 1.

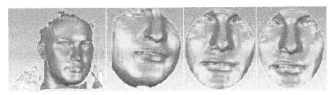

(A) Example of the face with excessive head rotation. After three times nose verification, the pose of the face is corrected.

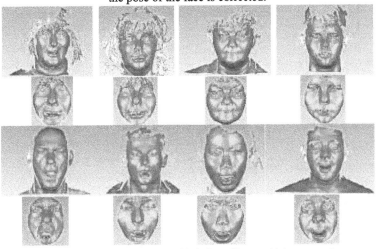

(B) Examples of the faces with hair artifact and big expression.

Figure 2 All such faces were successfully segmented by the proposed nose detection algorithm.

3.2 Facial expression processing method

First of all, we use a triangle-based linear interpolation method to fit a surface $Z = f(X, Y)$ (the size of it is 128×128). Meanwhile, we use a triangle-based linear interpolation to fit a surface too (the size of it is 384×384), and then we establish the depth image using the surface for the feature extraction in Section 4.

We consider face ($F_{face} = Z$) as the sum of a reference face ($F_{reference}$), a neutral component ($\Delta F_{Neutral}$), and an expressional component ($\Delta F_{Expression}$). In this paper, we use the face with ID F0001_NE00 of BU-3DFE dataset as reference.

$$F_{face} = F_{reference} + \Delta F_{Neutral} + \Delta F_{Expression} \quad (2)$$

The goal of this section is getting $F_{Neutral}$:

$$F_{Neutral} = F_{reference} + \Delta F_{Neutral} \quad (3)$$

In this paper, we use sparse representation to evaluate the testing face's $\Delta F_{Neutral}$ and $\Delta F_{Expression}$ from a neutral space and an expressional space, respectively, because we want to find the minimum number of expressional components out of the dictionary and a linear combination of $\Delta F_{Neutral}$ using a neutral space. First of all, the dictionary $A = [A_1, A_2]$ is needed to be established, where A_1 is a neutral space and A_2 is an expressional space.

The results of 275 neutral faces (each person's first face of FRGC v1) subtracting the reference face, respectively, and then vectorizing into 275 large vectors are used to be the neutral space $A_1 = [A_1^1, A_1^2, ..., A_1^{275}]$, where

$$A_1^i = F_{neutral}^i - F_{reference} = \begin{pmatrix} \Delta z_1^1 \\ \Delta z_1^2 \\ \vdots \\ \Delta z_1^n \end{pmatrix}.$$ Then, the results of 460 different expressional faces (the first 10 men's 23 expressional faces from BU-3DFE dataset and the first 10 women's 23 expressional faces from BU-3DFE dataset) subtracting their corresponding neutral face, respectively, and vectorizing into 460 large vectors are applied to be the expressional space $A_2 = [A_2^1, A_2^2, ..., A_2^{460}]$, where

$$A_2^i = F_{expression}^i - F_{neutral} = \begin{pmatrix} \Delta z_2^1 \\ \Delta z_2^2 \\ \vdots \\ \Delta z_2^n \end{pmatrix}.$$

The reference face and the first persons' expressional faces are shown in Figure 3.

In the testing section, the reference face is subtracted from the testing face and the result's sparse representation of the dictionary A is abstracted by Equation 1 $\hat{x} = \arg$

$$\min\left\{\left\|y - [A_1, A_2]\begin{bmatrix}x_1\\x_2\end{bmatrix}\right\|_2^2 + \gamma\left\|\begin{matrix}x_1\\x_2\end{matrix}\right\|_1\right\}, \text{ where}$$

$$y = F_{test} - F_{reference} = \begin{pmatrix}\Delta z_{test}^1\\\Delta z_{test}^2\\\vdots\\\Delta z_{test}^n\end{pmatrix}. \text{ Because neutral}$$

components of neutral faces are highly correlated, this method can find the familiar neutral components of the testing face. After this, we reconstruct the testing face's neutral component using A_1 and sparse vector $\hat{x}_1$:

$$\Delta\hat{F}_{Neutral} = A_1\hat{x}_1 \tag{4}$$

So, $\hat{F}_{Neutral}$ is equal to the sum of $F_{reference}$ and $A_1\hat{x}_1$:

$$\begin{aligned}\hat{F}_{Neutral} &= F_{reference} + \Delta\hat{F}_{Neutral}\\&= F_{reference} + A_1\hat{x}_1\end{aligned} \tag{5}$$

But $\hat{F}_{Neutral}$ is approximate, so each point in $\hat{F}_{Neutral}$ may not exist exactly on F_{face}. In this paper, we use an iterative method to find the neutral face. The method is presented in Figure 4.

The results of expression processing of ten different people are presented in the second line of Figure 5. Error maps are showed in the third line. From the maps, we could find that our method can maintain the rigid parts of the faces. Note that not only can our method remove facial expression, but also it can maintain neutral faces. So in the recognition section, we do not have to

recognize whether the probe face is expressional. Some neutral faces are presented in Figure 6.

Finally, the expression-removed depth images are constructed using F_{Neutral}. The size of the depth image is 128×128.

4 3D face recognition using dual-tree complex wavelet feature

After removing the facial expression, the 3D faces become very similar. Extracting discriminating feature from each face is very important. In this paper, we utilize the dual-tree complex wavelet transform [19,20] to extract expression-removed faces' feature (the size of the face image is 128×128), and six subregions' feature (the six regions are extracted from the face image which size is 384×384 and the size of each region is 128×128). Six feature points are shown in Figure 7A. We used an easy way to find these points. Firstly, we manually defined the six points of a standard face. Then, for each gallery and probe faces, six subregions of size 9×9 which centroids are the same as the standard face are found. Finally, the shape index value [21] refines the six feature points. The local maxima refine landmarks for point 2 and point 5, while the local minima refine landmarks for points 1, 3, 4, and 6. Thus, the six subregions of size 128×128 which centroids are the six refined feature points are defined.

In the training section, we use all the 943 faces in FRGC 1.0 for training. First of all, we extract the four-level magnitude subimages of each training face. Subsequently, we vectorize the six magnitude subimages into a large vector (the dimension is 384), and then we utilize LDA [2] to learn the discriminant subspace and record the

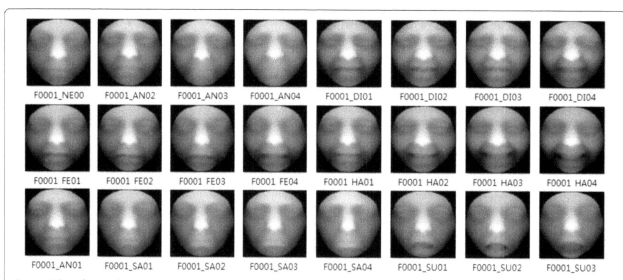

Figure 3 The reference face and expression faces. The first face is the reference face, while the others are the 23 expressional faces which are used to establish expressional space.

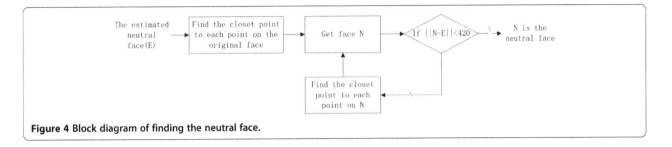

Figure 4 Block diagram of finding the neutral face.

transformation matrix. Secondly, we extract the six subregions' four-level magnitude subimages using DT-CWT and vectorize them into a large vector (the dimension is 2,304) and utilize LDA to learn the subspace too. Finally, we get all the gallery faces' two features using DT-CWT and their transformation matrix, respectively.

In the testing section, we get all the probe faces' two features by using DT-CWT and the two transformation matrices, respectively. Cosine distance is used to establish similarity matrix S_1 and S_2. After this, we normalize them using function (9).

$$S'_{rc} = \frac{S_{rc} - \min(S_r)}{\max(S_r) - \min(S_r)} \qquad (6)$$

In the function, S_{rc} represent an element of similarity matrix S_1 and S_2 (at row r and column c), S_r is the elements of S_1 and S_2 at row r, and S'_{rc} denotes the similarity normalized S_{rc}. Then, the final similarity matrix is established by a simple sum rule $S = S_1 + S_2$. Recognition is achieved by the nearest neighbor classifier.

5 Results and analysis

We perform our experiments on the Bosphorus database [22] and the FRGC [23] 3D face database.

The Bosphorus database consists of 105 subjects in various poses, expressions, and occlusion conditions. Eighteen subjects have beard/moustache and short facial hair is available for 15 subjects. The majority of the subjects are aged between 25 and 35 years. There are 60 men and 45 women in total, and most of the subjects are Caucasian. Also, 27 professional actors/actresses are incorporated in the database. Up to 54 face scans are available per subject, but 34 of these subjects have 31 scans. Thus, the number of total face scans is 4,652.

FRGC v1 contained 943 3D faces, while FRGC v2 contained 4,007 3D faces of 466 persons. The images were acquired with a Minolta Vivid 910. The Minolta 910 scanner uses triangulation with a laser stripe projector to build a 3D model of the face. The 3D faces are available in the form of four matrices, each of size 640 × 480. The data consists of frontal views. Some of the subject has facial hair, but none of them is wearing glasses. The 2D faces are corresponding to their respective 3D face. In FRGC v2, 57% are male and 43% are female. The database was collected during 2003 to 2004. In order to evaluate the robustness of our method against expression variations, we classified 1,648 faces with expression as the non-neutral dataset (411 persons), while 2,359 neutral faces as the neutral dataset (422 persons). The number of the neutral dataset and the non-neutral dataset is not equal because some people in FRGC v2 contained only one face. We use 'N' which represents for neutral, 'E' which indicates for non-neutral, and 'A' which stands for all in the following of the paper.

5.1 Experiments on Bosphorus database

Firstly, to evaluate the performance of the nose tip detection method, we test our method on the Bosphorus database. The results of data preprocessing of the first

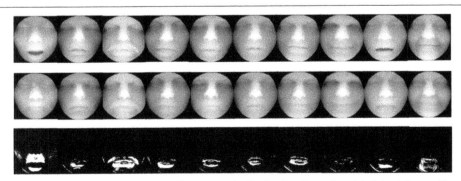

Figure 5 The results of expression processing of ten different people. The first line shows the original depth images. The second line is the expression processing results. The last line is the binary process results of the error maps.

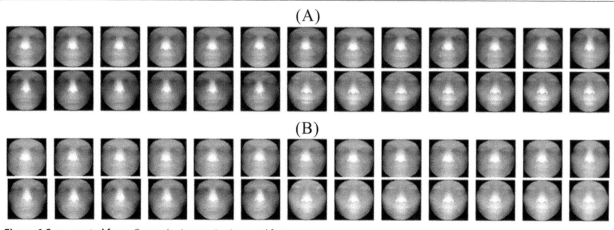

Figure 6 Some neutral faces. Our method can maintain neutral faces.

person are presented in Figure 8. From the figure, we can find that our method can deal with expressional face and posed face which angle is less than 30°, but it cannot find the nose tip of the big angled face (±45° and ±90°), because most part of the face is missing.

To further confirm the effectiveness of the proposed expression processing approach, we perform experiments on nearly frontal faces (those poses are less than 30°) with expression changes and occlusions. We compare the original faces and the expression-removed faces using leave-one-out method. We extract the DT-CWT feature and then use LDA to finish recognition. FRGC v1 is used for training LDA subspace. Receiver operating characteristic (ROC) curves of the experiment were presented in Figure 9. From the figure, we can find that the facial expression-removed faces performed better than the original faces.

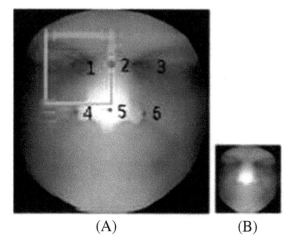

Figure 7 Two depth images with different sizes which are used in the method. (A) Size of 384 × 384. **(B)** Size of 128 × 128.

5.2 Experiments on FRGC
5.2.1 Comparison with original mouths
Dealing with open mouth has been a serious topic in 3D face recognition, and a number of researchers have been working on it. We expect that our method in correctly establishing correspondence between an open mouth and estimated neutral component can greatly improve 3D face recognition.

As a first set of experiments, we test our algorithm on the mouth area of FRGC v2. As the experimental protocol, we constructed the gallery set containing the first neutral face for each subject and the remaining ones made up of the probe set. We compare the expression-removed mouths with the original mouths using the PCA method. The recognition rate of using the original mouths is 52.95%, while the recognition rate of using the expression-removed mouths is 69.5%. We could find that the expression-removed mouths contain more identity information than the original mouths.

5.2.2 Comparison with original faces
Then, for the purpose of evaluating the performance of the expression processing method, we compare the expression-removed faces with the original faces using the Gabor feature [24] and DT-CWT feature of the whole depth image. We finished four experiments which contained the neutral vs. neutral experiment, neutral vs. non-neutral experiment, all vs. all experiment, and ROCIII experiment. In the all vs. all experiment, every image of FRGC v2 is matched with all remaining others. It resulted 16,052,042 combinations. Similarly, in the neutral vs. neutral experiment, every image of the neutral database is matched with all remaining others and it resulted 5,562,522 combinations. In the neutral vs. non-neutral experiment, the gallery images come from the neutral dataset and the probe entries come from the expression dataset. In the ROCIII experiment, the gallery

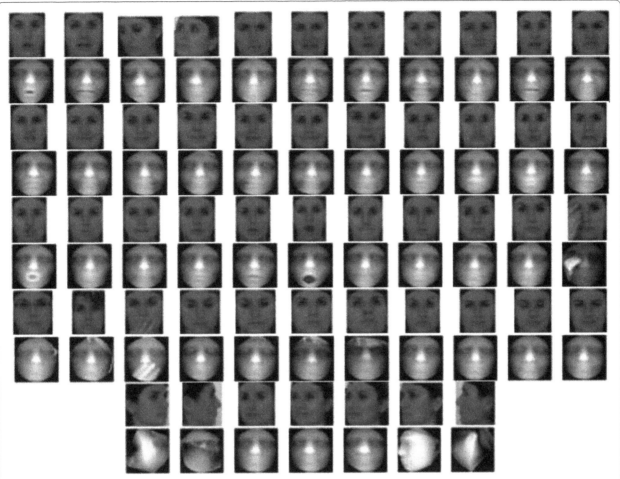

Figure 8 The results of data preprocessing of the first person in the Bosphorus database.

images come from the Fall 2003 semester, while the probe entries come from the Spring 2004 semester.

From Table 1, we can see that the facial expression-removed faces performed better than the original faces. From the N vs. E experiment, we can find that the expression-removed faces are more useful for face recognition. Using the facial expression-removed faces achieved 11.7% higher recognition rate and 12.29% higher verification rate at 0.001 FAR than using the original faces. Meanwhile, we can find that the DT-CWT

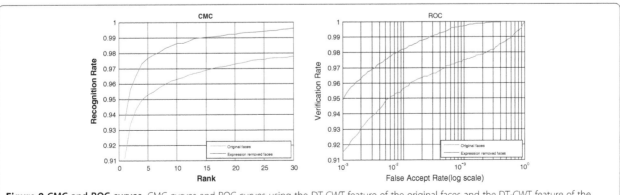

Figure 9 CMC and ROC curves. CMC curves and ROC curves using the DT-CWT feature of the original faces and the DT-CWT feature of the expression-removed faces.

Table 1 Facial expression-removed faces compared with original faces using Gabor feature and DT-CWT feature of whole depth image

Experiments	Feature	Rank one recognition rate		Verification rate at 0.001 FAR	
		Original faces	Facial expression-removed faces	Original faces	Facial expression-removed faces
N vs. N	Gabor	94.57%	95%	96.72%	97.31%
	DT-CWT	98.39%	98.46%	99.09%	99.22%
N vs. E	Gabor	59.92%	67.23%	63.03%	69.88%
	DT-CWT	78.8%	90.5%	81.25%	93.54%
A vs. A	Gabor	83.73%	86.56%	86.79%	90.15%
	DT-CWT	91.9%	95.78%	94.28%	98.03%
ROCIII	Gabor	-	-	81.27%	86.61%
	DT-CWT	-	-	89.68%	95.09%

feature is more effective than the Gabor feature for 3D face recognition.

5.2.3 ROC and CMC of our method

In this section, we employed two different scenarios for the experiments: identification and verification. Four experiments were performed as those in Section 5.1.

CMC curves of the four experiments were presented in Figure 10, while ROC curves of the four experiments were presented in Figure 11. The performance of the feature extracted from the whole face using DT-CWT and LDA, the feature extracted from six subregions using DT-CWT and LDA, and the fusion of the two are shown in each figure. As is seen, combining the DT-CWT

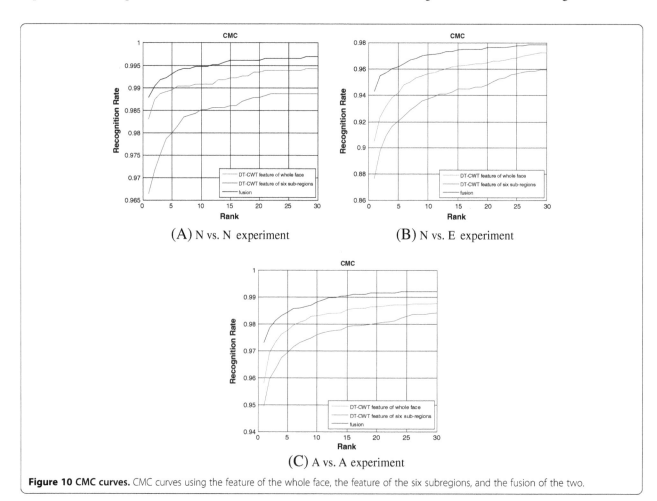

(A) N vs. N experiment
(B) N vs. E experiment
(C) A vs. A experiment

Figure 10 CMC curves. CMC curves using the feature of the whole face, the feature of the six subregions, and the fusion of the two.

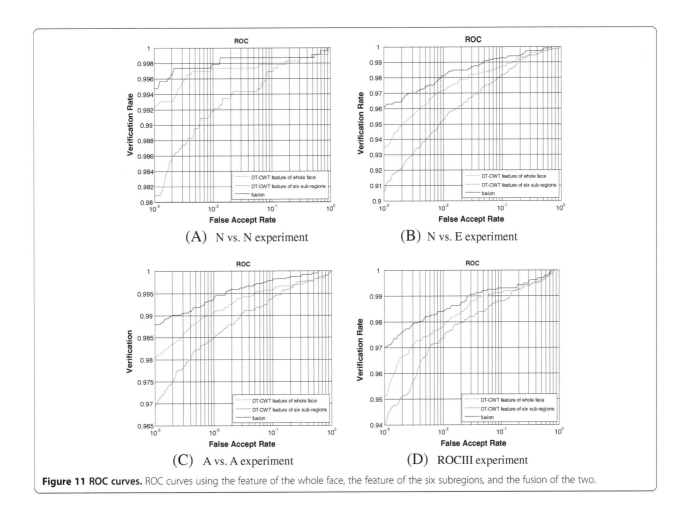

Figure 11 ROC curves. ROC curves using the feature of the whole face, the feature of the six subregions, and the fusion of the two.

feature and the six subregions' feature can improve the recognition performance even further.

5.2.4 Comparisons with other methods

Here, we compared our method with that of the state-of-the-art methods using the fusion results. Table 2 shows the verification results for state-of-the-art methods on the FRGC database as reported in the literature.

Also, the verification rate of our method is shown in Table 2. The performances of A vs. A and ROCIII experiments were slightly lower but still closed to the best.

6 Conclusions

We presented an automatic method for 3D face recognition. We used an improved detection method to correct the pose of the face. We showed that the proposed method could correct posed face which angle is less than 30°.

We also proposed a 3D facial expression processing method, which was based on sparse representation. It could abstract the neutral component from a dictionary which is the combination of neutral and expressional

spaces and enhance the recognition rate. Our method could deal opened mouth and expression of grin. We showed that the estimated neutral faces which are extracted from the expression faces are familiar with that extracted from their corresponding neutral face.

Table 2 Verification rate comparison with the state-of-the-art methods at 0.001 FAR

	N vs. N	N vs. E	A vs. A	ROCIII
Mian [25]	99.4%	-	86.6%	-
Maurer [26]	97.8%	-	87%	-
Cook [27]	-	-	92.31%	92.01%
Faltemier [4]	-	-	93.2%	94.8%
Alyuz [9]	-	-	-	85.64%
Zhang [8]	98.3%	89.5%	-	-
Wang [5]	-	-	98.13%	98.04%
Berretti [7]	97.7%	-	81.2%	-
Kakadiaris [10]	-	-	-	97%
Drira [11]	-	-	93.96%	97%
Mohammadzade [12]	-	-	99.6%	99.2%
Our method (training set: FRGC v1)	99.53%	96.25%	98.86%	97.05%

Then, the facial representation which contained the whole facial feature and the six subregions' feature extracted by DT-CWT were gotten. Holistic and local feature could represent a 3D face more effective for the recognition. Finally, LDA was used to enhance the accuracy of the recognition.

Competing interests
The authors declare that they have no competing interests.

Acknowledgements
This work was supported partly by the National Natural Science Foundation of China (61172128), the National Key Basic Research Program of China (2012CB316304), the New Century Excellent Talents in University (NCET-12-0768), the Fundamental Research Funds for the Central Universities (2013JBM020, 2013JBZ003), the Program for Innovative Research Team in the University of Ministry of Education of China (IRT201206), the Beijing Higher Education Young Elite Teacher Project (YETP0544), the National Natural Science Foundation of China (61403024), and the Research Fund for the Doctoral Program of Higher Education of China (20120009110008, 20120009120009).

References
1. C Zhong, Z Sun, T Tan, Robust 3D face recognition using learned visual codebook, in *Proceedings of IEEE Conference on Pattern Recognition* (Minneapolis, 2007), pp. 17–22
2. C Zhong, Z Sun, T Tan, Learning efficient codes for 3D face recognition, in *Proceedings of 15th IEEE International Conference on Image Processing* (San Diego, 2008), pp. 1928–1931. 12–15 Oct
3. KI Chang, KW Bowyer, PJ Flynn, An evaluation of multi-modal 2D +3D face biometrics. IEEE Trans. Pattern Anal. Mach. Intell. **27**(4), 619–624 (2005)
4. TC Faltmier, KW Bowyer, PL Flynn, A region ensemble for 3-D face recognition. IEEE Trans. Inf. Forensics Secur. **3**(1), 62–73 (2008)
5. Y Wang, J Liu, X Tang, Robust 3D face recognition by local shape difference boosting. IEEE Trans. Pattern Anal. Mach. Intell. **32**(10), 1858–1870 (2010)
6. H Lee, A Battle, R Raina, AY Ng, Efficient sparse coding algorithms. Adv. Neural. Inf. Proc. Syst. **19**, 801 (2007)
7. S Berretti, AD Bimbo, P Pala, 3D face recognition using iso-geodesic stripes. IEEE Trans. Pattern Anal. Mach. Intell. **32**(12), 2162–2177 (2010)
8. G Zhang, Y Wang, Robust 3D face recognition based in resolution invariant features. Pattern Recognit. Lett. **32**(7), 1009–1019 (2011)
9. N Alyuz, B Gökberk, L Akarun, Regional registration for expression resistant 3-D face recognition. IEEE Trans. Inf. Forensics Secur. **5**(3), 425–440 (2010)
10. A Kakadiaris, G Passalis, G Toderici, MN Murtuza, Y Lu, N Karampatziakis, T Theoharis, Three-dimensional face recognition in the presence of facial expressions: an annotated deformable model approach. IEEE Trans. Pattern Anal. Mach. Intell. **29**(4), 640–649 (2007)
11. H Drira, BB Amor, A Srivastava, M Daoudi, R Slama, 3D face recognition under expressions. Occlusions Pose Variat. **35**(9), 2270–2283 (2013)
12. H Mohammadzade, D Hatzinakos, Iterative closest normal point for 3D face recognition. IEEE Trans. Pattern Anal. Mach. Intell. **35**(2), 381–397 (2013)
13. B Amberg, R Knothe, T Vetter, Expression invariant 3D face recognition with a Morphable Model, in *International Conference on Automatic Face & Gesture Recognition* (Amsterdam, 2008), pp. 1–6. 17–19 Sept
14. PN Belhumeur, JP Hespanha, DJ Kriegman, Eigenfaces vs. fisherface: recognition using class special linear projection. IEEE Trans. Pattern Anal. Mach. Intell. **19**(7), 711–720 (1997)
15. X Li, T Jia, H Zhang, Expression-insensitive 3D face recognition using sparse representation, in *Proceedings of IEEE Computer Society Conference on Computer Vision and Pattern Recognition* (Miami, 2009), pp. 2575–2582. 20–25 June
16. X Wang, Q Ruan, Y Jin, G An, Expression robust three-dimensional face recognition based on Gaussian filter and dual-tree complex wavelet transform. J. Intell. Fuzzy Syst. **26**, 193–201 (2014)
17. PJ Besl, ND McKay, A method for registration of 3-D shapes. IEEE Trans. Pattern Anal. Mach. Intell. **14**(2), 239–256 (1992)
18. D Donoho, For most large underdetermined systems of linear equations the minimal I1-norm solution is also the sparsest solution. Commun. Pure Appl. Math. **59**(6), 797–829 (2006)
19. IW Selesnick, RG Baraniuk, NG Kingsbury, The dual-tree complex wavelet transform. IEEE Signal Proc. Mag. **22**(6), 123–151 (2005)
20. C Liu, D Dai, Face recognition using dual-tree complex wavelet features. IEEE Trans. Image Process. **18**(11), 2593–2599 (2009)
21. JJ Koenderink, AJ van Doorn, Surface shape and curvature scales. Image Vision Comput. **10**(8), 557–565 (1992)
22. A Savran, N Alyüz, H Dibeklioğlu, O Çeliktutan, B Gökberk, B Sankur, L Akarun, Bosphorus Database for 3D face analysis, in *Workshop on Biometrics and Identity Management*, 2008, pp. 47–56
23. PJ Phillips, P Flynn, T Scruggs, KW Bowyer, J Chang, K Hoffman, J Marques, J Min, W Worek, Overview of the Face Recognition Grand Challenge, in *Proceedings of IEEE Computer Society Conference on Computer Vision and Pattern Recognition*, vol. 1 (San Diego, 2005), pp. 947–954. 20–25 June
24. JP Jones, LA Palmer, An evaluation of the two-dimensional Gabor filter model of simple receptive fields in cat striate cortex. J. Neurophysiol. **27**, 1233–1258 (1987)
25. AS Mian, M Bennamoun, R Owens, An efficient multimodal 2D-3D hybrid approach to automatic face recognition. IEEE Trans. Pattern Anal. Mach. Intell. **29**(11), 1927–1943 (2007)
26. T Maurer, D Guigonis, I Maslov, B Pesenti, A Tsaregorodtsev, D West, G Medioni, Performance of Geometrix ActiveID TM 3D face recognition engine on the FRGC data, in *Proceedings of the 2005 IEEE Computer Society Conference on Computer Vision and Pattern Recognition (CVPR'05)* (San Diego, 2005), p. 154. 20–25 June
27. J Cook, M Cox, V Chandran, S Sridharan, Robust 3D face recognition from expression categorisation, ICB 2007. LNCS **4642**, 271–280 (2007)

Permissions

All chapters in this book were first published in EURASIP-JIVP, by Springer; hereby published with permission under the Creative Commons Attribution License or equivalent. Every chapter published in this book has been scrutinized by our experts. Their significance has been extensively debated. The topics covered herein carry significant findings which will fuel the growth of the discipline. They may even be implemented as practical applications or may be referred to as a beginning point for another development.

The contributors of this book come from diverse backgrounds, making this book a truly international effort. This book will bring forth new frontiers with its revolutionizing research information and detailed analysis of the nascent developments around the world.

We would like to thank all the contributing authors for lending their expertise to make the book truly unique. They have played a crucial role in the development of this book. Without their invaluable contributions this book wouldn't have been possible. They have made vital efforts to compile up to date information on the varied aspects of this subject to make this book a valuable addition to the collection of many professionals and students.

This book was conceptualized with the vision of imparting up-to-date information and advanced data in this field. To ensure the same, a matchless editorial board was set up. Every individual on the board went through rigorous rounds of assessment to prove their worth. After which they invested a large part of their time researching and compiling the most relevant data for our readers.

The editorial board has been involved in producing this book since its inception. They have spent rigorous hours researching and exploring the diverse topics which have resulted in the successful publishing of this book. They have passed on their knowledge of decades through this book. To expedite this challenging task, the publisher supported the team at every step. A small team of assistant editors was also appointed to further simplify the editing procedure and attain best results for the readers.

Apart from the editorial board, the designing team has also invested a significant amount of their time in understanding the subject and creating the most relevant covers. They scrutinized every image to scout for the most suitable representation of the subject and create an appropriate cover for the book.

The publishing team has been an ardent support to the editorial, designing and production team. Their endless efforts to recruit the best for this project, has resulted in the accomplishment of this book. They are a veteran in the field of academics and their pool of knowledge is as vast as their experience in printing. Their expertise and guidance has proved useful at every step. Their uncompromising quality standards have made this book an exceptional effort. Their encouragement from time to time has been an inspiration for everyone.

The publisher and the editorial board hope that this book will prove to be a valuable piece of knowledge for researchers, students, practitioners and scholars across the globe.

List of Contributors

Lina Jin
Department of Signal Processing, Tampere University of Technology, Korkeakoulunkatu 10, Tampere 33720, Finland

Atanas Boev
Department of Signal Processing, Tampere University of Technology, Korkeakoulunkatu 10, Tampere 33720, Finland

Karen Egiazarian
Department of Signal Processing, Tampere University of Technology, Korkeakoulunkatu 10, Tampere 33720, Finland

Atanas Gotchev
Department of Signal Processing, Tampere University of Technology, Korkeakoulunkatu 10, Tampere 33720, Finland

Said Amirul Anwar
School of Electrical and Electronic Engineering, Universiti Sains Malaysia, Engineering Campus, Penang 14300, Malaysia

Mohd Zaid Abdullah
School of Electrical and Electronic Engineering, Universiti Sains Malaysia, Engineering Campus, Penang 14300, Malaysia

Chandan Singh
Department of Computer Science, Punjabi University, Patiala 147002, India

Neerja Mittal
Central Scientific Instruments Organisation, Sector 30-C, Chandigarh 160030, India

Ekta Walia
Department of Computer Science, South Asian University, Akbar Bhawan, Chanakyapuri, Delhi 110021, India

Mohandass Divya
Department of CSE, SKR Engineering College, Chennai, India

Jude Janet
Department of CSE, SVCE, Andhra Pradesh, India

Ramadass Suguna
Department of CSE, SKR Engineering College, Chennai, India

Mohammed Kadiri
Laboratory of Telecommunications and Digital Signal Processing, Department of Electronics, Faculty of Technology, Djillali Liabes University, Sidi Bel Abbes 22000, Algeria
Department of Material Science, Faculty of Sciences and Technology, University of Mascara, Mascara 29000, Algeria

Mohamed Djebbouri
Laboratory of Telecommunications and Digital Signal Processing, Department of Electronics, Faculty of Technology, Djillali Liabes University, Sidi Bel Abbes 22000, Algeria

Philippe Carré
XLIM-SIC Laboratory, Department of Signal, Image, and Communications, XLIM Institute, CNRS UMR 6172, UFR Sciences-SP2MI, University of Poitiers, Futuroscope Chasseneuil 86073 Poitiers CEDEX9, France

Alex Pereira
Instituto Tecnológico de Aeronáutica (ITA), Praça Mal. Eduardo Gomes, 50, São José dos Campos, BR, CEP 12.228-900

Osamu Saotome
Instituto Tecnológico de Aeronáutica (ITA), Praça Mal. Eduardo Gomes, 50, São José dos Campos, BR, CEP 12.228-900

Daniel Sampaio
Universidade Estadual Paulista, Av. Ariberto Pereira da Cunha, 333, Guaratinguetá, BR, CEP 12.516-410

Jaehyun An
Department of Electrical and Computer Engineering, INMC, Seoul National University, Seoul, Korea

Seong Jong Ha
Samsung SDS, Seoul, Korea

Nam Ik Cho
Department of Electrical and Computer Engineering, INMC, Seoul National University, Seoul, Korea

Bekir Dizdaroğlu
Department of Computer Engineering, Karadeniz Technical University, Trabzon 61080, Turkey
Cognitive Systems Laboratory, Northeastern University, Boston, MA 02115, USA

Esra Ataer-Cansizoglu
Cognitive Systems Laboratory, Northeastern University, Boston, MA 02115, USA

Jayashree Kalpathy-Cramer
Martinos Imaging Center, Massachusetts General Hospital, Boston, MA 02129, USA

Katie Keck4, Michael F Chiang
Department of Ophthalmology, Oregon Health & Science University, Portland, OR 97239-3098, USA
Department of Medical Informatics, Oregon Health & Science University, Portland, OR 97239-3098, USA

Deniz Erdogmus
Cognitive Systems Laboratory, Northeastern University, Boston, MA 02115, USA

Md Saiful Islam
Department of Electrical and Computer Engineering, University of Ulsan, Bldg. #7, Room #318, 93 Daehak-ro, Nam-gu, Ulsan 680-749, South Korea

Uipil Chong
Department of Electrical and Computer Engineering, University of Ulsan, Bldg. #7, Room #318, 93 Daehak-ro, Nam-gu, Ulsan 680-749, South Korea

Taras Iakymchuk
GPDS, ETSE, University of Valencia, Av. Universitad, 46100 Burjassot, Valencia, Spain

Alfredo Rosado-Muñoz
GPDS, ETSE, University of Valencia, Av. Universitad, 46100 Burjassot, Valencia, Spain

Juan F Guerrero-Martínez
GPDS, ETSE, University of Valencia, Av. Universitad, 46100 Burjassot, Valencia, Spain

Manuel Bataller-Mompeán
GPDS, ETSE, University of Valencia, Av. Universitad, 46100 Burjassot, Valencia, Spain

Jose V Francés-Víllora
GPDS, ETSE, University of Valencia, Av. Universitad, 46100 Burjassot, Valencia, Spain

Moumen T El-Melegy
Electrical Engineering Department, Assiut University, Assiut 71516, Egypt

Hashim M Mokhtar
Computer and Information Systems Department, Sadat Academy, Assiut 71111, Egypt

Zoran P Đord̄evic´
Horizon Systems - workshop for HW/SW development, Pirot, Serbia, Knjaza Milosa 2 ulaz 2 stan 27, 18300 Pirot, Serbias

Stevica G Graovac
School of Electrical Engineering, University of Belgrade, Bulevar kralja Aleksandra 73, 11120 Belgrade, Serbia

Srd̄an T Mitrovic´
University of Defence in Belgrade, Military Academy, Pavla Jurisica Sturma 33, 11000 Belgrade, Serbia

Jorge Larrey-Ruiz
Departamento de Tecnologías de la Información y las Comunicaciones, Universidad Politécnica de Cartagena, 30202 Cartagena, Murcia, Spain

Juan Morales-Sánchez
Departamento de Tecnologías de la Información y las Comunicaciones, Universidad Politécnica de Cartagena, 30202 Cartagena, Murcia, Spain

María C Bastida-Jumilla
Departamento de Tecnologías de la Información y las Comunicaciones, Universidad Politécnica de Cartagena, 30202 Cartagena, Murcia, Spain

Rosa M Menchón-Lara
Departamento de Tecnologías de la Información y las Comunicaciones, Universidad Politécnica de Cartagena, 30202 Cartagena, Murcia, Spain

Rafael Verdú-Monedero
Departamento de Tecnologías de la Información y las Comunicaciones, Universidad Politécnica de Cartagena, 30202 Cartagena, Murcia, Spain

José L Sancho-Gómez
Departamento de Tecnologías de la Información y las Comunicaciones, Universidad Politécnica de Cartagena, 30202 Cartagena, Murcia, Spain

Xueqiao Wang
Beijing Key Laboratory of Advanced Information Science and Network Technology, Institution of Information Science, Beijing Jiaotong University, Beijing 100044, China

Qiuqi Ruan
Beijing Key Laboratory of Advanced Information Science and Network Technology, Institution of Information Science, Beijing Jiaotong University, Beijing 100044, China

Yi Jin
Beijing Key Laboratory of Advanced Information Science and Network Technology, Institution of Information Science, Beijing Jiaotong University, Beijing 100044, China

An Gaoyun
Beijing Key Laboratory of Advanced Information Science and Network Technology, Institution of Information Science, Beijing Jiaotong University, Beijing 100044, China